Balanced Scorecard Evolution

The Wiley Corporate F&A series provides information, tools, and insights to corporate professionals responsible for issues affecting the profitability of their company, from accounting and finance to internal controls and performance management.

Founded in 1807, John Wiley & Sons is the oldest independent publishing company in the United States. With offices in North America, Europe, Asia, and Australia, Wiley is globally committed to developing and marketing print and electronic products and services for our customers' professional and personal knowledge and understanding.

Balanced Scorecard Evolution

Evolution

A Dynamic Approach to Strategy Execution

PAUL R. NIVEN

WILEY

Library of Congress Cataloging-in-Publication Data:

Niven, Paul R.
  Balanced scorecard evolution : a dynamic approach to strategy execution/Paul R. Niven.
    pages cm.—(Wiley corporate F&A series)
  Includes index.
    ISBN 978-1-118-72631-0 (hardback); ISBN 978-1-118-93900-0 (ebk); ISBN 978-1-118-93901-7 (ebk)
    1. Organizational effectiveness.   2. Strategic planning.   3. Organizational change.   I. Title.
  HD58.9.N579 2014
  658.4′012—dc23

                                                                 2014012280

Printed in the United States of America
10 9 8 7 6 5 4 3 2 1

Contents

Preface

S HORTLY BEFORE WRITING THESE WORDS, I looked up at the bookshelves lining my office and took in the artful panorama of colors, designs, and intriguing titles. My gaze soon fixed upon the row dedicated to the Balanced Scorecard and strategy execution, and as I reflected on the many titles, it wasn't long before I realized that anyone picking up this new book would quickly arrive at two questions:

1. Why does the world need another Balanced Scorecard book?
2. How is this one different?

 ## LOOKING BACK AND LOOKING AHEAD

To answer those questions let's take a brief tour of the Balanced Scorecard's history. The tool began, humbly enough, as a system for organizations to improve their ability to measure effectively. For centuries the primary measurement of business had been financial. The Balanced Scorecard, while acknowledging the importance of financial yardsticks, represented a breakthrough by supplementing financial metrics with the drivers of future financial success in three distinct, yet related, perspectives of performance: customer, internal process, and learning and growth. The Balanced Scorecard also requires that performance measures used by an organization be derived from its unique strategy. Only then could strategy execution be tracked with rigor and discipline. This first-generation Balanced Scorecard, devoted almost exclusively to improved measurement, was immensely successful and popular, helping organizations around the globe better assess the execution of strategy through a balanced set of measures spanning the Scorecard's four perspectives.

Despite the model's success, a number of early adopters struggled with identifying the best measures to gauge the execution of strategy and often lamented a lack of context during the selection process. To overcome these challenges and assist in identifying better indicators, some Scorecard pioneers began prefacing the discussion of measures with the broader question of "What must we do well?" in each perspective. The answer to that was known as an objective. For example, a customer perspective objective could be "Provide differentiated solutions." As time went on, organizations began paying additional attention to objectives and many created graphical representations featuring the objectives as they flowed through the four perspectives. These documents became known as strategy maps, and proved to be a breakthrough evolution for the Scorecard system. Once the objectives were in place on the strategy map they clearly articulated and communicated the organization's strategy, creating an enhanced context for the measurement challenge and making it simpler to isolate metrics. For our earlier example of "Provide differentiated solutions," the accompanying measures might then be "Time spent with customers" and "Win rate on new projects."

The evolution continued through the next several years with the advent of strategic themes, enhanced software systems, and linkages from the Scorecard to vital management processes such as risk management and corporate governance. Additionally, as the Scorecard has grown, so too have the management systems at its boundaries. A number of so-called gurus have created elaborate management frameworks, of which the Balanced Scorecard is but one component. These systems often feature complex diagrams mapping organizational processes and typically suggest that in order to be successful, an organization must engage in each of the sophisticated steps offered.

We now return to the first question presented at the beginning of this preface. One of the chief reasons I decided to write this book, and why the world really *does* need another Balanced Scorecard tome, is because, as the new management frameworks have proliferated, they have frequently crowded out, and even overshadowed, the Balanced Scorecard itself. These complex conceptual structures promise many benefits that practitioners are eager to reap. However, most organizations possess limited resources and thus spread those available means thinly across the entire spectrum of activities, often failing to devote the effort necessary to create a robust Balanced Scorecard that will serve as the foundation of their efforts. The unfortunate product of this diffuse effort is a Scorecard that is unable to fulfill its responsibility as a vital tool in the execution of strategy.

The modern toolkit for strategy execution is vastly overstuffed, making it difficult for organizations to determine which of the many processes, tools, or interventions to pursue in order to execute their strategy. It can quickly become overwhelming and prove to be a major drain of resources, resulting in a cursory attempt to check off all of the boxes, which undoubtedly leads to suboptimal results. I don't wish to appear a Luddite, rejecting the natural progress of tools with which I've been associated for close to 20 years. I simply recognize, and have seen many times, that without a robust Balanced Scorecard at the core, these sophisticated systems are prone to failure, which inevitably leads to frustration, and ultimately inhibits the indispensable organizational capability of the twenty-first century: strategy execution.

The nature of competition is changing for virtually all organizations today, the methods for creating and implementing strategy are evolving, and the velocity of change is increasing. What has not changed, and what the Balanced Scorecard is still uniquely suited to deliver upon, is the necessity to effectively execute strategy and know, very simply, whether you're winning or losing. To do that, the Scorecard must be cleverly constructed and skillfully utilized. This book, based on two decades of practical experience, intense research, and unremitting passion, was written to ensure both of those conditions of success are an inevitable outcome of your reading investment.

 ## HOW IS THIS BOOK DIFFERENT?

Most critics agree that a film or novel that goes deep—delving fully into the emotional theme of the work, or the protagonist's unique and compelling journey—is more fulfilling and satisfying than an artistic endeavor that goes wide, broadly skimming the emotional or storytelling surface. A number of books on the subjects of Balanced Scorecard and strategy execution suffer from the latter trait. Their authors attempt to cover every aspect of the model, often without the knowledge or experience to do so effectively. This does the reader a great disservice, as a glossy veneer of knowledge is potentially more harmful than no knowledge at all. In this book I've chosen to focus exclusively on what leading research, real-life experience, and thousands of client implementations around the world have demonstrated to be the *most essential* aspects of successfully developing and utilizing a Balanced Scorecard.

Some pundits will argue that what is most important is not the Balanced Scorecard itself, but the strategic conversations it brings forth throughout the boardrooms and corridors of the organization. There is no doubt that having the right conversations with the right people is vital to success, and in this book I'll discuss that topic at length. However, before you can have the stimulating conversations that lead to strategic learning and new heights of success, you must have a fundamentally sound Balanced Scorecard from which you can generate the appropriate questions and discussions. This book presents you with the crucial balance of the Scorecard system as both a noun—encompassing the objectives, measures, targets, and initiatives that form its core—and a verb, using the data produced to conduct more focused and strategic discussions throughout the organization, driving unparalleled results.

In addition to my hands-on work with the Balanced Scorecard, this book draws on the latest research in change management and emerging neuroscience (how brain functioning impacts work and life). Successful implementation of the Scorecard system requires the adept utilization of change techniques, and throughout the text you'll find anecdotes and case studies demonstrating how the application of key change principles will enhance your implementation's effectiveness. Complementing the tenets of change management are insights from leading researchers in neuroscience who are applying their findings to the workplace. In this book, more than my previous texts, you'll also find increased emphasis on how to design, create, and facilitate the workshops that lead to the most robust Balanced Scorecards. Those sections, and many others, benefit greatly from the latest findings in neuroscience.

 ## WHO WILL BENEFIT FROM THIS BOOK?

This book is aimed primarily at three audiences: those developing a Balanced Scorecard for the first time, those who have developed a Scorecard but are not getting the results they need, and those creating or struggling with any type of corporate performance management system.

For those new to the Balanced Scorecard system, the text will provide you with the absolute essentials you must master if you hope to achieve the results that only a Balanced Scorecard can produce. After nearly two decades of experience with the system, I've witnessed and utilized every tip and technique that can increase the odds of success, while developing strategies to eliminate the many pitfalls that can await those undertaking this endeavor. My experience and research have been distilled into vital landmarks to ensure yours is a successful Balanced Scorecard journey.

Current Balanced Scorecard users will also profit greatly from detailed study of the book's contents. Over the years I've met people who, upon learning a bit about my work, will say something to the effect of, "Oh we tried the Balanced Scorecard but it didn't work." This statement never ceases to pique my curiosity and thus I begin asking some basic questions about their experience.

It's not long before we simultaneously discover that their poor results were not due to some inherent shortcoming of the Scorecard itself, but, inevitably, of a failure along the implementation path. If you either have a Balanced Scorecard in place at your organization but are not using it faithfully, or had one that you've abandoned for any number of reasons, you possess a tremendously valuable asset being sadly neglected. It's like having a Ferrari sitting idle and collecting dust in your garage. Fortunately, the Balanced Scorecard system can be easily restored. Most organizations struggle with the same issues: lack of executive sponsorship, no guiding rationale for the Balanced Scorecard (which is often viewed by change-weary employees as a threat), the failure to assign responsibility for managing the Scorecard program to a person or group, poor meetings that barely scratch the surface of the Scorecard's strategic learning potential, disregarding the importance of change-management techniques, and of course poorly designed objectives, dysfunctional measures, inappropriate targets, and unrealistic initiatives. These and many other elements of Scorecard scaffolding are covered extensively throughout the book.

Finally, if you have this book in your hand or are reading the preface online and think it doesn't apply to you because you employ some other form of performance management system, think again. Much of the knowledge shared in these pages is based on change management and neuroscience principles that will enhance the success of any type of performance system, regardless of the moniker.

 ## HOW THE BOOK IS ORGANIZED

Balanced Scorecard Evolution contains a dynamic mix of new and previously published material. The book introduces a multitude of new topics based on my global consulting practice, research, and the latest findings in change management and neuroscience. You'll also find important information from my previous books that is necessary to provide a complete account of any Balanced Scorecard implementation.

The text is composed of nine chapters designed to provide extensive insights on both creating and using the system. In the opening chapter, we'll explore the origins of the Scorecard and learn exactly what the system is, and is not. There are many misconceptions about the Balanced Scorecard, and this opening chapter will clarify the errors and ensure you have a solid understanding of this dynamic framework. Chapter 2 provides an exhaustive array of information on what you must do before creating your Balanced Scorecard system. Among the foundational elements covered are: Why and how you must answer the "Why the Balanced Scorecard?" question; where to build the first Scorecard; and how to secure executive sponsorship, create an office of strategy management to run the program, develop a detailed implementation roadmap, and build a communication plan. The raw materials of every Balanced Scorecard—mission, vision, and strategy—are the subject of Chapter 3. Among many important topics, you'll learn how to create a powerful Balanced Scorecard even without the benefit of a guiding strategy in place. Balanced Scorecard deliverables of objectives, measures, targets, and strategic initiatives are customarily created in workshop settings. Chapter 4 provides extensive tips, tools, and techniques for staging both effective and engaging workshops that lead to robust Scorecard products.

In Chapter 5 we transition to the core aspects of the Scorecard model itself, then delve deeply into strategy maps—powerful communication tools that articulate and describe strategy, bringing it to life for your entire workforce and beyond. I'll share how to create effective and truly strategic objectives, and provide extensive examples from my client roster and beyond. At the heart of the Balanced Scorecard are performance measures. In Chapter 6 we'll utilize the latest research and practice to ensure the measures created accurately capture the essence of strategic objectives and can be used to reliably gauge strategy execution. Chapter 6 also provides extensive information on performance targets, and the strategic initiatives you'll assemble to drive Scorecard success.

To deliver its vast potential, the Scorecard must be actively called upon in strategy execution review meetings to ignite passionate conversations that spark strategic insights. In Chapter 7 you'll discover how to plan for and facilitate meetings so good, people will actually want to attend! Modern organizations rely on the unique talents of every employee to power results, and in Chapter 8 I'll outline how cascading—creating Balanced Scorecards at lower levels of the organization—can unleash the immense power of alignment in your organization. The book's final chapter provides a comprehensive summary of the many change management tools and techniques outlined throughout the text, along with a number of handy checklists you can draw upon throughout the process.

I hope you enjoy and benefit from this journey we're about to share.

Paul R. Niven
San Diego, California
April 2014

Acknowledgments

WHEN PEOPLE ASK ME WHAT I enjoy about the consulting profession, I answer without hesitation, *"The fun and convenient air travel."* Well, of course that's not really what I say. What I do love about my job is the fact that every time the phone rings with a prospective client, it could be anyone from any industry, in any part of the world, reaching out from the other end of the line. Since launching The Senalosa Group, I've had the pleasure of working with a broad array of organizations, including: prestigious companies in the Fortune 100 here in the United States, small nonprofits in the developing world, and government organizations on several continents. All have been kind enough to tell me (and later show me via Scorecard results) that I helped them in some way, and I'm gratified by that. But, as I quickly point out to them, it is I who should be expressing gratitude—for the opportunity to work with dedicated professionals who are as eager as I to expand the boundaries of Balanced Scorecard knowledge. Outlined below are some of the many people I've had the honor to work with and learn from; individuals whose lessons and insights extensively shaped this book.

From NOW Foods, my thanks to Beth Pecenka, Al Powers, El Richard, Jim Emme, Michael Lelah, Dan Richard, Don Wilbur, and Randy Kjell. Their commitment to excellence and integrity is truly inspiring. At Breg (right here in San Diego County) I'd like to thank CEO Brad Lee for his enthusiasm and drive. Working with the following individuals from Goodwill of Orange County (California) was one of the highlights of my consulting career. How I enjoyed our stimulating workshops! Many thanks to: Kim Seebach, Joan Dornbach, Dan Rogers, Corrine Allen, Phillip Runnels, Randy Taylor, Don Voska, Frank Talarico, and Noel Crabtree. At the Compliance and Enforcement department of the New Jersey Department of Environmental Protection, I'm deeply indebted to Knute Jensen, Maria Franco-Spera, Wolf Skacel, and William Davis for their sincere dedication to the ideals of the Balanced Scorecard. From AWAL IT Services, many thanks to Tariq M. Alghamdi for his hard work and commitment. Much gratitude to Nicole Suydam of the Second Harvest Food Bank in Irvine,

California for creating such an inspiring environment. One of the most fun and passionate groups I've worked with over the past several years is the Scorecard team at Panasonic ECO Solutions North America. Thanks so much to Jim Doyle, Keith Hanak, Michael Rocha, Anthony Viola, Anthony Turiello, Larry Toscano, Darren Benike, Richard Ballard, Dan Kramer, Dan Silver, Mercedes Lindao, Jim Dunphy, Beth Allbright and Lourdes Rodriguez. I've been very fortunate to assist the dedicated and hardworking team at Kids Central in Ocala, Florida, and offer thanks to John Cooper, John Aitken, David Destefano, and Barbara Myshrall. Finally, many thanks to the following individuals from Cristal: Dr. Fadi Trabzuni, Dr. Edward Kossakowski, Dr. Malcolm Goodman, Dr. Steve Augustine, Dr. Robert McIntyre, Brian Pickett, Rene Jongen, Richard Gillette, Kerri Knepley, and the many others who participated in our stimulating workshops. It was a true pleasure to work with such an inquisitive, spirited, and committed group of people, all steadfastly dedicated to the principles of the Balanced Scorecard.

In addition to the clients noted above, I have benefited tremendously from my friendship and collaborations with the following people. Strategy execution author and consultant Sandy Richardson has been a great friend and supporter, and I thank her for many spirited conversations on Performance Management and beyond. Readers of my past books will notice an enormous upgrade in the quality of exhibits appearing in this text. That is due entirely to the creativity of Kim Schanz from Eyegate Design here in San Diego. Thanks very much for your patience, Kim, as I continued to add exhibit after exhibit to your inbox. To Boubacar Diallo of Plan International in West Africa, I salute you for your commitment to sharing Balanced Scorecard principles. Boubacar traveled all the way from Africa to Southern California to study Scorecard implementation practices with me. I'm happy to report a friendship bloomed during that visit. Maryam Hussain of Avanza Solutions has been an ardent supporter and kind enough to share my work to many readers in the Middle East region through the journal *Techronicle*. I've been very fortunate to enjoy a long and satisfying partnership with the software firm Corporater. Many thanks to Tor Inge Vasshus, Eric Peterson, and Madhavan Gopalarathnam for your help and support. Speaking of partners, it's been my great pleasure to work with Wael Zein and Fadi Makki of Addima and Bassam Samman of CMCS in promoting Balanced Scorecard use throughout the Middle East and Africa. Chris Richard of Emera (formerly of Balanced Scorecard Hall of Fame utility New Brunswick Power) was a terrific client to work with, and has become an even better friend. Chris and I have had many long conversations about the Balanced Scorecard and his insights contributed greatly to this book. Finally, and most importantly, I thank my wife Lois for her inexhaustible reserve of love and support.

CHAPTER ONE

What Exactly Is a Balanced Scorecard?

ORIGINS, AND A BRIEF HISTORY, OF THE BALANCED SCORECARD

Although its conceptual roots run deep, through work conducted by management thinkers and practitioners from Peter Drucker to Abraham Maslow, including French accounting scholars who developed a similar approach in the 1930s, the Balanced Scorecard as we know it today was invented by two men, Robert Kaplan and David Norton.

The world was introduced to the concept in a 1992 *Harvard Business Review* article, "The Balanced Scorecard—Measures that Drive Performance."[1] That article was based on a research project conducted by Norton's consulting firm, which studied performance measurement in companies whose value creation was highly dependent on intangible assets.[2] As strident advocates for the power of measurement to drive focus and accountability, Kaplan and Norton were convinced that if organizations were to derive the maximum value from their investments in intangible assets, those same intangibles had to be integrated into their measurement systems. At the time, virtually all organizations were measuring financial results, and many were also collecting data on generic customer metrics, such as satisfaction and market share, along with measures of quality and efficiency. With the inclusion of measures tracking intangible assets such as employee skills and engagement, it appeared that management could now confidently cover their measurement bases.

A significant problem existed, however. Many companies that collected data from these diverse areas failed to link the measures together in a meaningful and coherent pattern, instead choosing to select an ad hoc group that simply represented different aspects of the firm's operations. Despite their efforts, most received few benefits. In fact, some early adopters of quality metrics, for example, actually saw their share prices fall dramatically. Kaplan and Norton provided two immediate and profound enhancements. First, they codified the collection of metrics, calling it a Balanced Scorecard and provided a succinct taxonomy that ensured consistency in application. Rather than simply collecting measures that spanned a firm's operations, Kaplan and Norton created the four-perspective framework of:

1. Financial
2. Customer
3. Internal processes
4. Learning and growth

Organizations now possessed a vocabulary for balanced measurement that was previously absent. The measures chosen to populate each perspective were not selected at random but, in Kaplan and Norton's second major contribution, directly translated from the organization's strategy, which endowed them with context for discussion, analysis, and learning. Now, instead of relying on generic financial and nonfinancial indicators, companies could analyze their unique strategic path and create performance measures that would clearly indicate whether or not they were in fact executing their chosen strategy. This seemingly simple, and in hindsight obvious, pronouncement was the breakthrough that was to set the Balanced Scorecard on an astonishing trajectory of acceptance and success. Executives the world over had lamented the difficulty of executing strategy but, with the Balanced Scorecard, Kaplan and Norton put strategy at the center of the firm's orbit by embedding it directly into the measurement process.

Not all was perfect in Balanced Scorecard land, however. Some early adopters struggled with the selection of appropriate performance measures, and received scant benefits from their investment in the Scorecard system. Key to their frustration was finding context for the selection of measures that would gauge strategy execution, and this quickly led to another milestone innovation on the Balanced Scorecard's path—the introduction of strategic objectives. Organizations began prefacing their discussion of measures with that of objectives, concise statements of what they had to do well in each of the four perspectives to execute successfully. So, rather than beginning the process by asking, "What measures are best for us?" they started by asking what they needed to do well in each perspective, and strategy maps were born.

Fast-forward 20 years, several books from Kaplan and Norton, myself, and others, and tens of thousands of successful implementations later, and we find that the Balanced Scorecard is one of the world's most popular management frameworks.[3]

The model's ascendance has not been confined to private sector firms, as both government and nonprofit organizations have steadily migrated to the Balanced Scorecard in order to improve focus, more effectively allocate scarce resources, and, of course, execute strategy. So widely accepted and effective has the Scorecard been that the *Harvard Business Review* hailed it as one of the 75 most influential ideas of the twentieth century. Amid all this acclaim, however, challenges inevitably arise, and the Balanced Scorecard faces an interesting one. In reaching such delirious heights of success it has become synonymous with measurement in the minds of many, regardless of how much (or little) knowledge they actually possess regarding the framework itself. Therefore, many misconceptions, often dangerous and irresponsible, exist and can sometimes derail success. Beginning with the next section of this chapter, and continuing throughout the book, we'll thoughtfully explore the terrain that is the Balanced Scorecard, tackling the misconceptions, exposing the myths, and, most importantly, ensuring you possess the know-how necessary to build an authentic Balanced Scorecard that can transform your business.

 ## BALANCED SCORECARD PERSPECTIVES

You may be wondering why the section following the origins of the Scorecard is not, "What is a Balanced Scorecard?" Before I outline the model it's important to understand the four distinct, yet related, perspectives of performance that bring it to life—Financial, Customer, Internal Process, and Learning and Growth—as they form the scaffolding upon which the entire Balanced Scorecard is constructed.

The etymology of the word perspective is from the Latin *perspectus*: "to look through" or "see clearly," which is precisely what we aim to do with a Balanced Scorecard—examine the strategy, making it clearer through the lens of different viewpoints, and therefore more amenable to execution. Any strategy, to be effective, must contain descriptions of financial aspirations, markets served, processes to be conquered, and the people who will steadily and skillfully guide the ship to success. Thus, when assessing our progress it makes little sense to focus on just one aspect of the strategy when in fact, as Leonardo da Vinci reminds us, "Everything is connected to everything else."[4] To compose an accurate picture of strategy execution it must be painted in the full palette of perspectives that comprise it. Therefore when developing a Balanced Scorecard we use the following four:

1. Financial
2. Customer
3. Internal processes
4. Learning and growth

When building a Balanced Scorecard, or later when it is up and running, you may slip and casually remark on the four quadrants or four areas, or even the four buckets. As colloquial and seemingly inconsequential as this slip of the tongue appears, I believe it has serious ramifications. Take, for example, the word quadrant: the Oxford dictionary begins its definition by describing it as a quarter of a circle's circumference. The word reflects the number four, and in that sense it is almost limiting to the flexible approach inherent in the Scorecard—you may wish to have five perspectives or only three. The Balanced Scorecard views performance from many points of view and I encourage you to be disciplined in your use of this term. Now let's take a brief tour of those four perspectives, beginning with customer.

Customer Perspective

The customer perspective of the Balanced Scorecard must answer three questions:

1. Who are our target customers?
2. What do they expect or demand of us as an organization?
3. What is our value proposition in serving them?

Sounds simple enough, but each of these questions offers many challenges to organizations. Most organizations will state that they do in fact have a target customer audience, yet their actions reveal an all-things-to-all-customers strategy. As strategy guru Michael Porter has taught, this lack of focus will prevent an organization from differentiating itself from competitors.

Determining customer expectations or demands is often the least problematic of the three questions. Most organizations today, regardless of size or location, have many channels to view customer interactions and gather feedback. Chief among them are social media (Facebook, Twitter, and so on), which often provide customers a place to scream , especially when companies fall short of expectations.

Clearly articulating the firm's value proposition is perhaps the most challenging, and vital, of the three tasks in this perspective. Virtually all organizations will choose one of three disciplines, as articulated by Treacy and Wiersema in their book *The Discipline of Market Leaders*:[5]

1. **Operational Excellence:** Organizations pursuing operational excellence focus on low price, convenience, and often no frills. Walmart provides a great representation of an operationally excellent company.
2. **Product Leadership:** Product leaders push the envelope of their firm's products. Constantly innovating, they strive to simply offer the best product in the market. Apple is an example of a product leader in the field of electronics.
3. **Customer Intimacy:** Doing whatever it takes to provide solutions for customer needs helps define the customer-intimate company. They don't seek one-time transactions but instead focus on long-term relationship building through their deep knowledge of customer needs. In the retail industry Nordstrom epitomizes the customer-intimate organization.

I've cited the work of Treacy and Wiersema; however, these ideas have been with us for many years, and have been advocated under different labels by a number of scholars and practitioners. For example, the idea of low cost has been explained as: cost leadership (Porter), operational excellence (Treacy and Wiersema), exploitation (March), and defender (Miles and Snow). Differentiation goes by many names as well: product differentiation (Porter), product leadership/customer intimacy (Treacy and Wiersema), exploration (March), and prospector/analyzer (Miles and Snow). Regardless of the labels applied, the value-proposition concept represents the essence of strategic choice, and, as such, must be clearly represented in your Balanced Scorecard.

Internal Process Perspective

In the internal process perspective of the Scorecard we identify the key processes at which the firm must excel in order to continue adding value for customers, and ultimately shareholders. Each of the customer disciplines outlined above will entail the efficient operation of specific internal processes in order to serve customers and fulfill a chosen value proposition. For example, a product-leading company like Apple may focus on processes that include research and innovation, while an operationally excellent company such as Walmart emphasizes supply chain operations. Finally, Nordstrom's customer-intimacy discipline will dictate a focus on processes such as customer knowledge and retention.

The primary challenge with this perspective is to limit the number of processes included to just the truly strategic that drive the chosen value proposition, fulfill customer demands, and ultimately stoke the economic engine. When prompted, even small companies could list dozens of processes necessary to operate effectively. However, upon close inspection and using strategy as the prism, it should become clear that while necessary, most of the processes are not vital to the execution of the chosen strategy, and therefore do not belong on the Balanced Scorecard, which, we must constantly remember, is a tool for executing strategy.

Learning and Growth Perspective

If you want to achieve ambitious results for internal processes, customers, and ultimately shareholders, where are these gains found? The learning and growth perspective of the Balanced Scorecard supplies the enablers—almost exclusively intangible in nature—of the other three perspectives. In essence, this perspective represents the foundation upon which this entire house of a Balanced Scorecard is built.

The learning and growth perspective is typically populated with three areas of capital: human, information, and organizational.[6] No strategy, regardless of its seemingly unimpeachable brilliance, can be executed without people, and thus our first order of business in this perspective is to ensure our organization possesses the human capital, skills, competencies, and talents necessary for effective execution. In addition to people, all companies today, regardless of size, rely upon robust information technology systems for everything from transactional data processing to strategic decision-making support. We must ensure our investments in information technology are consistent with, and support, our unique strategy. Finally, it is imperative in the modern corporate world to ensure our organizations are capable of growth and change, which are absolute imperatives to enduring success. Under the umbrella of organizational capital we examine crucial components of success such as culture, teamwork, and knowledge sharing. These quintessentially intangible dimensions of performance must be transformed into tangible value should we hope to reap the rewards promised in our strategic plans.

Many organizations I've worked with struggle with the learning and growth perspective. It is normally the last perspective to be developed, and perhaps the teams are intellectually drained from their earlier efforts, or they simply consider this perspective soft stuff best delegated to the human resources group. No matter how valid the rationale seems, this perspective cannot be overlooked in the development process. As mentioned earlier, the learning and growth perspective provides the enablers for the rest of the Scorecard. Think of it as consisting of the roots of a tree that will ultimately lead through the trunk of internal processes to the branches of customer results, and finally to the leaves of financial returns.

Financial Perspective

Financial yardsticks are a critical component of the Balanced Scorecard, especially so in the for-profit world. This perspective tells us whether our strategy execution efforts—detailed extensively in the other perspectives—are leading to improved bottom-line results. We could focus all of our energy and capabilities on improving customer satisfaction, quality, on-time delivery, employee-skills development, or any number of things, but without an indication of their effect on the organization's financial returns they are of limited value. Think of the financial perspective as representing the end in mind of your strategic story; everything contained elsewhere in the Scorecard should be driving enhanced financial results.

We'll return to the four perspectives throughout the remainder of the book, most notably during the discussion of strategy map objectives and performance measures. Speaking of which, now is the time to see how those terms fit into the broader system that is the Balanced Scorecard (see Exhibit 1.1).

WHAT IS A BALANCED SCORECARD?

My trusty Merriam-Webster Collegiate Dictionary defines the word *system*: "A regularly interacting or interdependent group of items forming a unified whole." That is a wonderful way to think of the Balanced Scorecard, because it's not one single thing, but a number of elements that combine to create a powerful unified whole. The Balanced Scorecard system, which is designed to

EXHIBIT 1.1   Balanced Scorecard Perspectives

Source: Adapted from material created by Robert S. Kaplan and David P. Norton.

help any organization effectively execute their strategy, is comprised of four unifying elements:

1. Objectives
2. Measures
3. Targets
4. Strategic initiatives

Objectives are housed on a dynamic communication device known as a strategy map, while measures, targets, and initiatives reside on the Balanced Scorecard. Let's look at each to discover how they combine to create a system whose whole is immensely greater than the sum of its parts.

Objectives and Strategy Maps

Objectives are concise statements of what the organization must do well in each of the four perspectives of financial, customer, internal process, and learning and growth in order to execute its unique strategy. Many early adopters of the Balanced Scorecard used it primarily as a measurement system, translating their strategy into measures that populated each of the four perspectives of the system. However, some of these pioneers struggled with identifying the best measures to track strategic success. To assist in selecting better indicators they began prefacing the discussion of measures with "What they must do well" in each perspective. The answer to "What must we do well?" was known as an objective. For example, a customer-perspective objective could be "Provide differentiated solutions." Objectives always begin with verbs and are intended to bridge strategy and measures.

As time went on organizations began to pay increasing attention to objectives, realizing it was imperative to understand what must be done well to execute the strategy in order to create context for robust performance measures. Experimentation flourished and many companies began creating graphical representations of the objectives spanning the four perspectives. These diagrams became known as strategy maps and have proven to be a revolutionary advance in the field of strategy communication and execution. Today we can define a strategy map as: "A one-page graphical representation of what the organization must do well (in each of the four perspectives) in order to successfully execute their strategy." The strategy map, which is first and foremost a communication tool, translates your strategy into the vital objectives necessary to execute the plan. Whereas your strategic plan may be 50 to 100 pages or more (sadly, I've seen them with much more), the strategy map must be confined to one page in order to fulfill its chief responsibility of clearly communicating and articulating the strategy to employees and, if so desired, external stakeholders. Strategy maps almost always combine words (the objectives noting what we must do well) with images that are culturally resonant for the organization. This creative combination engages employees by bringing strategy, a subject considered by most to be dry and academic, to life by translating it into concrete actions and compelling images. The word *map* fits the document perfectly because, as we all know, a map guides us on a journey, providing the landmarks we must navigate to travel from our current location to our desired destination. In this context the current location is the un-executed strategy and the desired destination is the successful execution of that plan. We'll return to strategy maps in Chapter 5, where you'll discover how to create vibrant documents that translate your strategy with dazzling clarity and simplicity. An example strategy map is shown in Exhibit 1.2.

Performance Measures and Targets

A key principle to keep in mind as you learn about, and work with, the Balanced Scorecard is that of translation. Every component of the Scorecard is translated from the organization's strategy, because that is the system's raison d'etre—strategy execution. We begin by translating the strategy into objectives

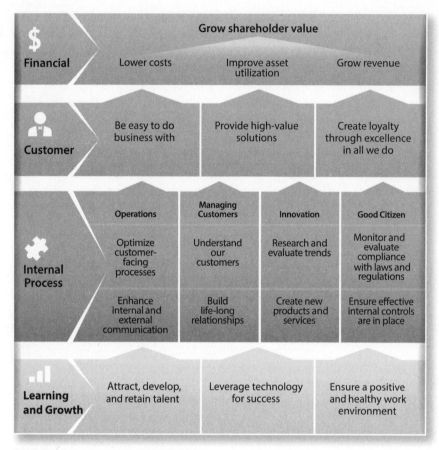

EXHIBIT 1.2 Example Strategy Map

on our strategy map, which communicates what we must do well in order to succeed. Strategy maps are outstanding devices for signaling to everyone in the organization what must be performed flawlessly in order to execute, but at the end of the day we need to know if we have in fact moved the needle on the objectives and progressed towards the execution of our strategy. Enter the performance measures: quantifiable standards used to evaluate and communicate performance against expected results. Those expected results take the form of targets that accompany each measure.

Do you remember that old song, *Love and Marriage?* Feel free to sing along: "Love and marriage, love and marriage, they go together like a horse and carriage . . . you can't have one without the other." It's the same with these two vital links in the chain of strategic success—strategy maps and measures; one just won't do without the other. You may create the most inspirational and visually resplendent strategy map ever conceived in a corporate conference room, but without the accountability and focus afforded by accompanying performance measures, its value is specious at best. The map points to what you must do well, but unless you know whether you're actually doing well, whether you're winning or losing, it's just the product of yet another corporate exercise. On the flip side, while performance measures act as potent monitoring devices, without the benefit of a clear and compelling strategy map much of their contextual value is lost (this was the problem many early Scorecard adopters faced). We'll return to the vital concepts of measures and targets in Chapter 6.

Strategic Initiatives

To quickly recap, a fundamental aspiration of every organization, whether public, private, or nonprofit, is the execution of strategy to drive breakthrough performance. The Balanced Scorecard was conceived to ensure that strategy is translated into action through the interplay of objectives, measures, targets, and strategic initiatives. The objectives appear on a strategy map and are further translated into performance measures, which, in combination with targets, are used to gauge the achievement of those same objectives.

The last piece of the puzzle in using the Balanced Scorecard to execute your strategy is the development and prioritization of strategic initiatives that will help you achieve your targets. Strategic initiatives (often simply referred to as initiatives in the Scorecard vernacular) are the specific projects, activities, or programs you'll embark upon in order meet or exceed your performance targets. A strategic initiative could be anything from launching a career development program for employees to rolling out new financial software to creating an environmental plan. They are, of course, strategy specific, and the portfolio of strategic initiatives you assemble will depend entirely on the unique strategic path you pursue. You may ask, "I notice the examples you use all begin with verbs. Objectives are strategy specific and also start with verbs, so what's the difference between an objective and a strategic initiative?" The primary distinction between objectives and strategic initiatives is that the former are meant to be ongoing, while the latter have a clear beginning and end point. They are projects of a short-term (typically) duration that have been designed to assist an organization in correcting a performance deficit.

To illustrate the use of strategic initiatives, let's say you decide to pursue a customer-intimacy strategy and thus include the objective "Delight our customers" on the customer perspective of your strategy map. One of the accompanying measures you select may be customer loyalty. The reasoning is simple: if you are in fact delighting your customers, you would expect more of them to remain loyal to you. You establish a target and, with sky-high expectations, begin collecting data. After a couple of months the numbers are sobering; customer loyalty is flat and resting at a level far below the rate you anticipated. To close the gap in performance you may decide to establish a customer rewards program as a means to enhancing loyalty. The specific strategic initiative would be the "Development of a customer rewards program," and would entail the allocation of resources, the creation of a detailed plan including key milestones, and an analysis highlighting the anticipated results. While the objective "Delight our customers" will most likely remain on your strategy map until you decide to make a strategic course change, the development of the loyalty program will have a defined beginning and end.

We'll dive much deeper into the world of strategic initiatives in Chapter 6.

This section began by noting the Balanced Scorecard constitutes a system: "A regularly interacting or interdependent group of items forming a unified whole." I'll talk more about terminology later in the chapter, but for now it's important to recognize that when you hear the term Balanced Scorecard, it is a collective noun that encompasses objectives on a strategy map, and measures, targets, and strategic initiatives on a Scorecard. What all the elements of the Scorecard system have in common, what unites and unifies them, is the fact that all are derived from the organization's strategy.

The system that is the Balanced Scorecard serves three primary purposes (see Exhibit 1.3):

1. **Communication:** strategy maps are designed to translate the organization's strategy into action via objectives stitched together through the four perspectives. Just as a map helps guide you through unfamiliar territory by highlighting landmarks on your journey, strategy maps communicate the organization's chosen direction in a simple and powerful manner, allowing all employees, and other stakeholders, to quickly grasp the organization's story of success.
2. **Measurement:** The Scorecard was originally created to alleviate three measurement challenges plaguing modern companies: how to competently gauge the role of intangible assets, balance financial and nonfinancial indicators, and ultimately execute strategy. While strategy maps

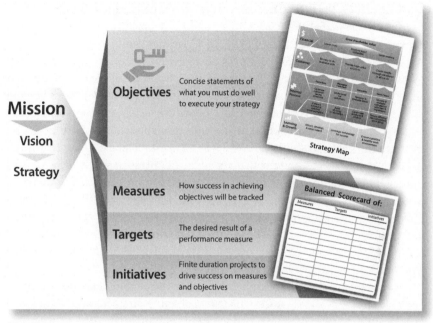

EXHIBIT 1.3   The Balanced Scorecard System

communicate the strategic destination, Scorecard measures (and associated targets) monitor the course, ensuring we stay on track.

3. **Strategic Management:** In this capacity, the Balanced Scorecard can be used as the centerpiece of a broader management system, which links it to such crucial management processes as: budgeting (strategic resource allocation), compensation, board governance, and risk management. In the preface I wrote, "As these new management frameworks have proliferated, they have frequently crowded out, and overshadowed the Balanced Scorecard. These complex conceptual structures promise many benefits that practitioners are of course eager to reap. However, most organizations possess limited resources and thus spread those available means thinly across the entire spectrum of activities, failing to devote the effort necessary to create a robust Balanced Scorecard. The unfortunate product of this diffuse effort is a Scorecard that is unable to fulfill its responsibility as a vital tool in the execution of strategy." In this book I focus on ensuring you build a Balanced Scorecard that will serve as a ready foundation should you choose to instill a broader management framework with it as the instrumental hub.

TELLING THE STORY OF YOUR STRATEGY THROUGH CAUSE AND EFFECT

We know the Balanced Scorecard is designed to execute strategy through translation into objectives, measures, targets, and strategic initiatives, but what is a strategy? That's an enormous and evolving question, well beyond the scope of this book; however, at its core we know strategy represents a hypothesis developed by its creators. Organizations carefully examine their operating environments, consider their unique place in that competitive arena, and look for areas of defensible advantage that form the core of their strategy. Hence the strategy is a hypothesis—a best guess and set of assumptions as to the appropriate course of action given their knowledge of information concerning the environment, resident competencies, competitive positions, and so on. What is needed is a method to document and test the assumptions inherent in the strategy, and the Balanced Scorecard does just that.

By translating the strategy through objectives appearing on the strategy map and measures chosen for the Scorecard, the Balanced Scorecard provides the necessary means to document and test strategic assumptions. Ideally, the objectives and measures chosen should link together in a chain of cause and effect relationships from the performance drivers in the learning and growth perspective all the way through to improved financial performance as reflected in the financial perspective. We are attempting to document the strategy through measurement, making the relationships between the measures explicit so they may be monitored, managed, and validated.

Here is a typical example of cause and effect: Your organization is pursuing a growth strategy. Your objective is "Grow revenue," and therefore you measure revenue growth in the financial perspective of the Scorecard. You hypothesize that loyal customers providing repeat business will result in greater revenues, so you measure customer loyalty in the customer perspective. How will you achieve superior levels of customer loyalty? Now you ask yourself: At what internal processes must the organization excel in order to drive customer loyalty and ultimately increased revenue? You believe customer loyalty is driven by your ability to continuously innovate and bring new products to the market, and therefore decide to measure new product development cycle times in the internal process perspective. Finally, you're challenged to determine how you will improve cycle times. Investing in employee training on new product initiatives may eventually lower development cycle time and is thus measured under the learning and growth perspective of the Balanced Scorecard. This linkage of measures throughout the Balanced Scorecard is constructed with a series of if-then statements: if we increase training, then cycle times will lower. If cycle times lower, then loyalty will increase. If loyalty increases, then revenue will increase. When considering the linkage between measures, we should also attempt to document the timing and extent of the correlations. For example, do we expect customer loyalty to double in the first year as a result of our focus on lowering new product development cycle times? Explicitly stating the assumptions in our measurement architecture makes the Balanced Scorecard a formidable tool for strategic learning (see Exhibit 1.4).

Cause and Effect Linkages in Practice

There is little doubt that weaving cause and effect linkages through your strategy map and Scorecard will yield dividends in the form of enhanced strategic insight. However, perhaps surprisingly, relatively few organizations implement this practice with rigor. In one revealing study of performance measurement practices published in 2003, the authors discovered that of 157 companies surveyed, only 23 percent consistently built and verified causal models.[7] This despite the fact that return on assets were 2.95 percent higher and return on equity 5.14 percent higher in those organizations using causal models.

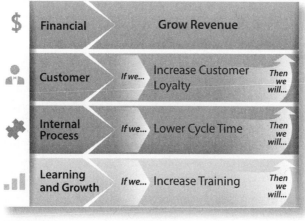

EXHIBIT 1.4 Cause and Effect

As noted, the study referenced above was published in 2003, so in the intervening 10 years, have more organizations availed themselves of the benefits of cause and effect modeling? Columbia Business School finance professor Michael Mauboussin says the answer is no, and has proposed a method for increasing the percentages who do.[8] He argues that two basic questions must be answered before deciding upon which measures to monitor:

1. What is your overarching objective? In business, quite frequently, it's the desire to increase shareholder value.
2. What factors or activities will help you achieve your objective?

With those simple questions answered you're now on the hunt for measures that reliably demonstrate cause and effect, and Mauboussin offers a four-step program for doing so. Step one is clear enough: define your governing objective, which for most profit-seeking enterprises will be the maximization of shareholder value. In step two you develop a theory of cause and effect to assess presumed drivers of that objective. Let's use a bank as an example. They may assume that customer satisfaction drives the use of bank services, and the more services used, the greater the economic value derived by the bank. The bank now measures the correlation between customer satisfaction, usage, and value to determine if the theory of cause and effect is correct. Step three entails the identification of activities that employees can engage in to help achieve the governing objective. Finally, in step four the organization regularly evaluates the statistics to ensure the presumed drivers of value are in fact contributing as theorized.

In my opinion, it is step two that causes most organizations to eschew cause and effect modeling, and therefore fail to benefit from the insights and value it promises. In that step the organization chooses measures and statistically examines correlations. Of course it takes time (and effort) to perform correlation analyses, and many organizations are more interested in using the Scorecard from day one to determine whether they are winning or losing instead of to execute their strategy. It's certainly not controversial to suggest we live in an instant gratification world, and performance measurement is not immune to this phenomenon. Modeling cause and effect linkages exacts the most precious resource companies have: time. Having said that, the growth of analytics software (and the associated knowledge of employees specializing in this field), is making these modeling efforts less demanding, and as a result I expect more organizations will take advantage of the power of cause and effect linkages within their Balanced Scorecards.

Always Strive to Tell Your Strategic Story

Robert McKee is a man who knows a thing or two about telling a story. While you may not recognize his name I'm certain you'll know some of the works produced by his students: *Forrest Gump, The Color Purple, Toy Story,* and *Erin Brokovich,* just to name a few. McKee is arguably the world's greatest screen-writing coach, and the 18 Academy Awards, 109 Emmys, and 19 Writers Guild Awards won by his protégés are very solid testimony to that assertion. McKee understands the necessity of introducing the art of storytelling in a business context. As he puts it, "A big part of a CEO's job is to motivate people to reach certain goals. To do that he or she must engage their emotions, and the key to their hearts is a story . . . if you can harness imagination and the principles of a well-told story, then you get people rising to their feet amid thunderous applause instead of yawning and ignoring you."[9]

The objectives and measures appearing on your strategy map and Scorecard should tell your strategic story. All of the elements you need to create a compelling and dramatic story are present: customers, processes, people, and finances. Your job is to creatively link the objectives and measures in a manner that both tells a spellbinding story and allows you to garner additional insights about your business. While statistically based cause and effect modeling can be a valuable tool in maximizing the benefits of the Balanced Scorecard, it's not absolutely necessary to derive results from the system. You simply need the creativity and acumen to craft a story that works on two levels: entertainment and business logic.

Consider for a moment two possible scenarios for presenting corporate strategy to your employee base. In the first case, your CEO goes to the front of the room, directs the audience's attention to a series of PowerPoint slides and dutifully walks them through a series of charts with exacting precision and detail. My eyes are rolling back in my head as I write that. Contrast that with your CEO telling the story of your company; the strategic destination of financial success, the customer outcomes that will fuel that success, the key processes driving results for customers, and the enabling infrastructure of people, technology, and culture setting the foundation for it all. The linkages among the perspectives bring the story to life, demonstrating that your business is not a patchwork of disparate elements but actually a powerful and cohesive system that, if working seamlessly, is geared for success. Over the years, I've been present at many corporate gatherings during which I can literally see the "Aha" moments as employees, often for the first time, have the curtain pulled back on the mystery that is strategy, and leave the room filled with the liberating knowledge of where the company is going, and how they fit into that direction.

Cause and effect modeling takes many forms, with some organizations drawing links between practically every objective and measure appearing on their strategy map and Scorecard. I call these graphical nightmares *spaghetti diagrams* because they are virtually indecipherable, and thus of no value in communicating and executing strategy. At the other end of the spectrum are maps and Scorecards with virtually no cause and effect relationships whatsoever. For those of you thinking you'll probably come down in the middle on this debate and create fairly simple cause and effect models, emphasizing the relationships among the perspectives, take heart. Simple modeling certainly does not preclude you from enjoying great success with the Balanced Scorecard. Many leading Scorecard adopters exhibit very limited cause and effect among objectives and measures while still garnering tremendous focus, alignment, and improved resource-allocation decisions from their work. The key linkages you should articulate on the Map and in the Scorecard are between the internal process and customer perspectives. In many ways the objectives appearing in the learning and growth perspective are considered the enablers of everything you're attempting to achieve and thus may not warrant one-to-one connections with other sections of the map. However, the link between processes and customers is key, as it is here we signal two major transitions: from internal (employees, climate, processes) to external (customers); and from intangible (skills and knowledge, and so on) to tangible (customer outcomes and financial rewards). Customer outcomes signal the *what* of strategic execution, and internal processes supply the *how*. Every organization should make an effort to explicitly document this equation, articulating how they expect to transform their unique capabilities and infrastructure into revenue-producing results.

 ## KEY BALANCED SCORECARD QUESTIONS AND ANSWERS

We'll conclude the chapter with some fundamental questions surrounding the Balanced Scorecard, all of which are vital to your understanding and use of the system.

What Is the Difference between a Balanced Scorecard and a Dashboard?

As you begin to socialize the Scorecard concept among your team and throughout your organization, it is very likely that at least a few people will say something like, "Oh, so we're building a dashboard." Any tacit agreement to this fundamental misunderstanding will immediately begin to derail your implementation because, although the Balanced Scorecard and dashboards have some elements in common, at their core they serve distinctly different purposes.

The Balanced Scorecard facilitates strategy execution through the translation of strategy into a carefully chosen set of objectives on a strategy map, and then performance measures, targets, and strategic initiatives on a Scorecard. Strategy execution and strategic decision making are aided using the insights gleaned from the Balanced Scorecard. A dashboard on the other hand, focuses on tactical decision making by monitoring the vital *operational* signs of a business that yield immediate understanding into a critical process. While both systems use measures to track progress (often called key performance indicators when used with a dashboard), they are substantially different, as the Scorecard focuses on achieving longer-term strategic goals, while dashboards monitor operations in real time. The following table illustrates key differences between a Balanced Scorecard and a dashboard.

Element	Balanced Scorecard	Dashboard
Purpose	Strategy execution.	Operational efficiency and effectiveness.
Expertise Required	Knowledge of strategy to develop appropriate objectives and measures; ability to interpret trends from the data to glean strategic insights.	Comprehension of esoteric operational processes to drive operational improvement.
Number of measures	Small number, limited to those that serve as translations of the organization's strategy.	Large number, analyzing a process from multiple points of view.
Timing	Long-term: While measure frequencies vary, most companies review Scorecard results monthly to assess progress on strategy execution.	Short-term: Depending on the indicator, dashboards can provide up-to-the-minute information on essential operational processes, and thus may be reviewed in real time in order to make necessary interventions.

Depending on the organizational context and goals, dashboards can fulfill a useful function. However, they are not designed for, or solely capable of, producing the knowledge necessary to drive strategy execution.

Does Balance Mean an Equal Number of Objectives and Measures in Each Perspective of the Balanced Scorecard?

No. There is a misconception that when constructing a Balanced Scorecard you must populate the perspectives with an equal number of objectives and measures, thereby honoring the principle of balance. In practice, the number of objectives and measures appearing in each perspective will depend on your unique strategy and what is necessary for you to execute it at this particular juncture in your history. Having seen thousands of strategy maps and Balanced Scorecards over the past 20 years, I know that while there are no concrete rules prescribing actual figures, it is common to see a roughly similar number of objectives and measures in the financial, customer, and learning and growth perspectives, while the largest number will reside in the internal process perspective. This results from the fact that even small organizations must choose among dozens of potential processes in order to isolate those that contribute directly to the company's chosen value proposition and strategy. Creating the appropriate value chain of processes frequently leads to several strategically vital objectives and measures.

Balance in the Balanced Scorecard reflects three things:

1. A balance between financial and nonfinancial objectives and measures.
2. A balance between leading (predictive; performance drivers) and lagging (end of period) measures.
3. A balance between short-term and long-term success. While some metrics will produce impact immediately, others (innovation and learning, for example) will require a longer period to bear strategic fruit.

As for how technically balanced a Balanced Scorecard should be, it must be modified to meet the unique needs of each organization. Keep in mind that at its core, the Scorecard is a tool for executing strategy, and organizations will pursue different strategies to secure market dominance and financial success. The Scorecard should reflect their strategic priorities. Consider consulting firms. They rely heavily on intangible assets such as the knowledge of their consultants, the ability to share that knowledge, and the opportunity to build on it in future engagements. Therefore, we would expect to see a heavily populated learning and growth perspective. However, the other perspectives of performance are still vital. In the consulting company case, we would expect investments made in people and enabling technology in the learning and growth perspective to drive results in their internal process perspective—perhaps the ability to generate new solutions for clients and do so faster and more efficiently, thereby reducing costs. This in turn should improve outcomes in the customer perspective—client satisfaction being an obvious metric. Finally, everything touched on above should eventually manifest itself in improved financial returns to demonstrate the strategy is, in fact, effective.

What Version or Generation of the Balanced Scorecard Does This Book Cover?

One of the many reasons the Balanced Scorecard is relied upon by thousands of organizations is the fact that it has evolved substantially since its formation in the early 1990s. It was the combined efforts of practitioners, researchers, consultants, and academics alike that propelled the Scorecard's ascendance from humble beginnings as an improved measurement system to the centerpiece of modern strategic management systems. While Scorecard creators Kaplan and Norton have not applied a naming or numbering protocol to the successive versions of the Scorecard, each boasting new functionality, others have filled that void with their own lexicon. Again, no standard naming system exists to chronicle the history of the Balanced Scorecard, but the following classifications have been widely shared in research papers and on the Internet:[10]

First generation: Utilized almost exclusively to capture and analyze financial and nonfinancial measures across the four perspectives.

Second generation: This iteration saw the inclusion of strategic objectives, which created context for the selection of measures, leading ultimately to the invention of strategy maps. Enhanced cause and effect modeling also appeared during this generation.

Third generation: The chief enhancement touted by proponents of third-generation Balanced Scorecards is that of the destination statement:

> A description, ideally including quantitative detail, of what the organization (or part of organization managed by the Balanced Scorecard users) is likely to look like at an agreed future date. Typically the destination statement is subdivided into descriptive categories that serve a similar purpose (but may have different labels) to the "perspectives" in first- and second-generation Balanced Scorecards.[11]

The destination statement serves to clarify and align the management team around a common definition of strategic success, which facilitates the creation of the Balanced Scorecard. I have no quarrel with the concept of destination statements, except to note they really aren't an evolution, because they sound virtually identical to what I described as a vision statement in my earliest book on this subject. In 2002 I wrote: "A vision statement provides a word picture of what the organization intends to become—which may be 5, 10, or 15 years in the future. This statement should not be abstract—it should contain as concrete a picture of the desired state as possible and also provide the basis for formulating strategies and objectives."[12]

The parade of versions marches on and by the time you read these words even more generations may be offered by enthusiastic writers and practitioners. All innovation is positive, and all fresh thinking expands the frontier of knowledge outward, which is admirable and productive. However, my experience in this field tells me that many organizations still struggle with the core elements necessary to derive utility from the Balanced Scorecard: selecting strategic objectives, designing robust measures, and, most importantly, using the Balanced Scorecard to learn more about and execute strategy. My focus in these pages is not on advocating for a specific version of the methodology or promoting an arcane name. Rather, my commitment is to provide you with the tools and techniques you'll need to construct a future-ready Balanced Scorecard.

Does the Balanced Scorecard Change?

It may appear odd to be addressing this now, considering you've yet to construct your Scorecard system, but experience tells me that the question is probably on your mind. During Scorecard training sessions and early in implementations, the question of how rigid or permanent a Scorecard should be is always a popular topic, as some people fear that once they commit to a certain element of performance they're obligated to keep the objective and measure as long as the Scorecard is in existence. That is definitely not the case.

The Balanced Scorecard is designed to be a dynamic tool, flexible and capable of change as conditions warrant. Over time you can expect a number of changes to take place within the realm of your map and measures. In the most extreme case you may abandon a strategy you've pursued, based on Scorecard results that prove much of your hypothesis was invalid. In that case you would likely develop a new strategy for your organization and select updated objectives and measures that act as direct translations of the new strategy.

Recently I've been speaking with a company that adopted the Balanced Scorecard more than 10 years ago, and have been using it faithfully ever since. The organization turned to the tool in an effort to assist them in executing a new customer-driven strategy, one that required substantial changes to their processes, investments in new technologies, and, of course, updated skill sets in their employee base. Like thousands of other organizations they found the Scorecard to be invaluable for successfully unlocking the value of their strategy; as noted above, they've been devoted advocates since that time.

Fast-forward 10 years and the world is a different place, replete with changes that have impacted companies around the globe, including this one. Somewhere along the line their customer-focused strategy gave way to a new commitment to cost leadership, an economic reality in a market that was moving quickly towards commoditization. What they neglected to do was substantially change the Scorecard's core elements to be consistent with their new direction. So, while they've remained committed to the Scorecard, its benefits have waned over the past few years, and managers are openly voicing their doubts about the tool's ongoing efficacy.

This is a company that clearly needs to unfreeze. The Scorecard they instituted years ago is no longer a proper representation of the organization's strategy, and there is little wonder that managers, hungry for every strategic advantage good information provides, have lost faith in the tool. To continue benefiting from the framework, they'll have to carefully reconsider how it fits with their new strategy and how its core elements must be updated in order to reflect current realities. This, of course, may be painful because it will undoubtedly mean selecting new objectives, measures, targets, and initiatives, and in an even more painful step, possibly unhinging mature links between the Scorecard and vital organizational processes such as budgeting, compensation, and employee reviews. However, if the Scorecard is to continue producing benefits, this has to be done.

Of course, you don't need to wait 10 years to update your Scorecard, and may in fact be forced to make changes due to circumstances beyond your control. That was the case for another client of mine, a public sector organization in New Jersey. They had just adopted the Balanced Scorecard and were about to begin using it when Hurricane Sandy battered the state in October 2012. In the aftermath priorities shifted and many of the objectives and measures they had chosen, while important in normal operating circumstances, were no longer appropriate in such an emergency situation. As they put it, "We had to turn out the lights on a number of our measures." Once the worst was over, Governor Christie challenged his teams to have even the most damaged areas open for business by Memorial Day, just a few months later. After discussing the situation, I advised my client to ask: What are the key challenges you're facing right now in light of the governor's goal, and what Scorecard objectives and measures will you enlist to meet the challenge? Based on that, I recommended they shrink their strategy map and Scorecard to the vital few objectives and measures necessary to guide them through those extraordinarily challenging times.

It shouldn't take a natural disaster, however, to cause a thoughtful review of your Balanced Scorecard. Your Scorecard elements should be reviewed at least annually in conjunction with your planning events (strategic planning, business planning, budgeting, and so on). Objectives and measures should be evaluated to ensure they are still valid in light of current and anticipated business conditions, and are able to remain as key chapters in your strategic story.

Many organizations tend to make subtle changes to objectives and measures as they gain experience with the Balanced Scorecard system. With measures, the method of calculation may change to better capture the true essence of the event under investigation, or the measure's description may be enhanced to improve employee understanding of its operational and strategic significance. You may also change the frequency with which you collect performance data. For example, you may have attempted to track employee satisfaction monthly, but the logistics of gathering the data simply proved too challenging. In that case you wouldn't forsake this important indicator, you would simply change the reporting period to something more amenable to measurement. Changing your performance measures is yet another way to tap into the collective knowledge of your organization. Be sure to advertise the fact that you're about to consider measure changes for the coming fiscal year, and give the entire employee base the opportunity to provide feedback regarding beneficial adjustments.

The caveat regarding such changes is this: Don't alter your objectives or measures simply because you don't like the current crop, or the results aren't what you expected. The Balanced Scorecard is about learning. Learning about your strategy, learning about the assumptions you've made to win in your marketplace, and learning about the value proposition you've put forth. Sometimes you won't necessarily enjoy what your results are telling you, but don't simply treat these alterations from plan as defects, instead use them to question and learn about your business.

How Important Is Terminology in a Balanced Scorecard Implementation?

Very! In his 1832 book *On War*, Carl von Clausewitz declared, "The first task of any theory is to clarify terms and concepts that are confused. . . . Only after agreement has been reached regarding terms and concepts can we hope to consider the issues easily and clearly, and expect others to share the same viewpoint . . ."[13] Reaching agreement on terms and concepts is not as easy as it sounds, especially when you consider there are over 14,000 meanings for the 500 most common words in the English language. And of course anyone who has endured a corporate wordsmithing exercise can attest to how quickly it can devolve into a *Dilbert*-esque tableau, leading to frustration and cynicism.

Confusing our words can lead to the transmission of mixed signals to employees and result in less-than-desirable outcomes for the organization. Thus it's imperative we use consistent definitions for key Balanced Scorecard terms and concepts. You probably won't be surprised to learn that I recommend you use the definitions below as you communicate and implement the Scorecard. However, in the end it really doesn't matter what you call the concepts— remember Shakespeare's admonition: "What's in a name? That which we call a rose by any other name would smell as sweet." The key is using your chosen terms with unwavering consistency throughout the organization to ensure there is true consensus on the point, and the term is communicated clearly to all stakeholders. Everyone must be speaking the same language if you expect the Balanced Scorecard, or any change initiative, to be understood, accepted, and able to produce results.

Key Balanced Scorecard Terms and Concepts

Balanced Scorecard—An integrated system for describing and translating strategy through the use of linked performance objectives, measures, targets, and strategic initiatives in four, balanced perspectives— customer, internal process, financial, and learning and growth. The Balanced Scorecard acts as a measurement system, strategic management system, and communication tool.

Initiatives—Strategic initiatives (often simply referred to as initiatives in the Scorecard vernacular) are the specific projects, activities, or programs you'll embark upon in order meet or exceed your performance targets.

Lagging Indicator—Performance measures that represent the consequences of actions previously taken are referred to as lag indicators. They frequently focus on results at the end of a time period and characterize historical performance. Employee satisfaction may be considered a lag indicator. A good Balanced Scorecard must contain a mix of lag and lead indicators.

Leading Indicator—These measures are considered the drivers of lagging indicators. There is an assumed relationship between the two, which suggests that improved performance in a leading indicator will drive better performance in the lagging indicator. For example, lowering absenteeism (a leading indicator) is hypothesized to drive improvements in employee satisfaction (a lagging indicator).

Measure—A standard used to evaluate and communicate performance against expected results. Measures are normally quantitative in nature capturing numbers, dollars, percentages, and so on. Reporting and monitoring measures helps an organization gauge progress toward effective implementation of strategy.

Mission Statement—A mission statement defines the core purpose of the organization—why it exists. The mission examines the raison d'être for the organization and reflects employees' motivations for engaging in the organization's work. Effective missions are inspiring, long term in nature, and easily understood and communicated.

Objective—Objectives are concise statements of what the organization must do well in each of the four perspectives of financial, customer, internal process, and learning and growth in order to execute its unique strategy. Objectives begin with verbs such as increase, reduce, improve achieve, and so on. Strategy maps are comprised entirely of objectives.

Perspective—In Balanced Scorecard vernacular, perspective refers to a category of performance objectives or measures. Most organizations choose the standard four perspectives (financial, customer, internal process, and learning and growth), however, the Balanced Scorecard represents a dynamic framework, and additional perspectives may be added as necessary to adequately translate and describe an organization's strategy.

Strategic Management System—Describes the use of the Balanced Scorecard in aligning an organization's short-term actions with strategy. Often accomplished by cascading the Balanced Scorecard to all levels of the organization, aligning budgets and business plans to strategy, and using the Scorecard as a feedback and learning mechanism.

Strategic Resource Allocation—The process of aligning budgets with strategy by using the Balanced Scorecard to make resource allocation decisions. Using this method, budgets are based on the initiatives necessary to achieve Balanced Scorecard targets.

Strategy—Represents the broad priorities adopted by an organization in recognition of its operating environment and in pursuit of its mission. Situated at the center of the Balanced Scorecard system, all performance objectives and measures should align with the organization's strategy.

Strategy remains one of the most widely discussed and debated topics in the world of modern organizations.

Strategy Map—A one-page, graphical representation of what must be done well in order to execute strategy. Strategy maps are composed of performance objectives spanning the four perspectives and linking together to tell the organization's strategic story.

Target—Represents the desired result of a performance measure. Targets provide organizations with feedback regarding performance, and imbue the results derived from measurement with meaning.

Value Proposition—Describes how an organization will differentiate itself to customers, and what particular set of values it will deliver. To develop a customer value proposition many organizations will choose one of three disciplines articulated by Treacy and Wiersema in *The Discipline of Market Leaders*: operational excellence, product leadership, or customer intimacy.

Vision—"A vision statement provides a word picture of what the organization intends to become—which may be 5, 10, or 15 years in the future. This statement should not be abstract—it should contain as concrete a picture of the desired state as possible and also provide the basis for formulating strategies and objectives."

 NOTES

1. Robert S. Kaplan and David P. Norton, "The Balanced Scorecard—Measures that Drive Performance," *Harvard Business Review* (January–February 1992): 71–79.
2. Nolan Norton Institute, "Measuring Performance in the Organization of the Future: A Research Study" (1991).
3. See, for example, Bain Management Tools 2011, www.bain.com/images/bain_management_tools_2011.pdf.
4. Michael J. Gelb, *How to Think Like Leonardo da Vinci* (New York: Random House, 2004).
5. Michael Treacy and Fred Wiersema, *The Discipline of Market Leaders* (Reading, MA: Perseus Books, 1995).
6. Robert S. Kaplan and David P. Norton, *Strategy Maps: Converting Intangible Assets Into Tangible Outcomes* (Boston: Harvard Business School Press, 2004).
7. Christopher D. Ittner and David F. Larcker, "Coming Up Short on Nonfinancial Performance Measurement," *Harvard Business Review* (November 2003): 88–95.

8. Michael J. Mauboussin, "The True Measures of Success," *Harvard Business Review* (October 2012): 46–56.

9. Robert McKee, "Storytelling That Moves People," *Harvard Business Review* (June 2003): 51–55.

10. See, for example, Gavin Lawrie and Ian Cobbold, "Development of the 3rd Generation Balanced Scorecard." Accessed at http://2gc.eu/files/resources/2GC-WP-Dev3rdGenBSC-090311.pdf.

11. Ibid., 12.

12. Paul R. Niven, *Balanced Scorecard Step by Step: Maximizing Performance and Maintaining Results* (New York: John Wiley & Sons, 2002), 83.

13. Carl von Clasewitz, Michael Eliot Howard (Translator), Peter Paret (Translator). *On War* (Princeton: Princeton University Press, Reprint Edition, 2008).

CHAPTER TWO

2

Just Like the Boy Scouts: Be Prepared

 ## FIRST THINGS FIRST: WHY ARE YOU DEVELOPING A BALANCED SCORECARD?

I can still remember that morning a few summers back. Before the alarm had a chance to shake me from my slumber I jumped out of bed with a great sense of anticipation, stemming from the fact that I was to begin a Scorecard engagement with a new public-sector client that day. After a hearty breakfast of grapefruit and toast (my grandfather's favorite), I opened my front door and took a couple of steps towards my car when it hit me—something you rarely feel in Southern California—humidity. Not the stifling, barely-drag-one-foot-in-front-of-the-other kind of humidity you get in a Florida summer, but a warm and damp enough sensation for me to audibly utter: "Hmmm, strange." But my morning was to get even stranger.

When I arrived at the client's location the standard pleasantries were exchanged, after which I was ushered into a large conference room where I was plunked down at the head of the u-shaped table and introduced to the suspicious crowd as their Balanced Scorecard consultant. As my host enthusiastically outlined my background I thought to myself: "Two minutes into this and we're off the page already." I was sure he was going to reach a crescendo that would go something like, "Now join me in welcoming Paul as he tells us all about the Balanced Scorecard," but just as the humidity had jolted me earlier that morning his next move caught me off guard as well. He did introduce me, but to my pleasant surprise, then kept the floor himself for the next 15 minutes as he regaled the crowd with pledge after pledge of his commitment to the Balanced Scorecard: "The Balanced Scorecard is the most important initiative we'll be pursuing this year." "I'm putting the full weight of my office behind this." "I expect you to give Paul your full cooperation as he assists us in this critical endeavor." I could barely contain myself because, as we'll learn in the next section on executive sponsorship, this sort of promotion for the Scorecard is pure gold and he was in full oratorical sail with no provocation from me. The only concern I had was coming from that little voice within me, the one that has seen its share of good and bad Scorecard implementations, and it was the fact that while his cheerleading skills were second to none he never really did come right out and say why the Balanced Scorecard was so important to the organization.

Two months into the engagement and things were sputtering like the engine of my first car. As hard as we tried to engage people they just didn't seem inclined to get on board with us. Finally, after every logical textbook intervention was considered I simply began directly asking people why they were hesitant to participate. After some gentle prodding the truth emerged. In the absence of a *why* from their leader the grapevine quickly took over the communication challenge and plugged in *for layoffs* as the reason behind the Balanced Scorecard. That notion spread like wildfire and soon nobody wanted to play ball when stepping up to the plate might just hasten the end of your employment. It took us weeks of communication and education to get the real impetus for the Scorecard out on the table and grudgingly accepted by a still largely incredulous rank and file. It turns out the executive who discovered the Balanced Scorecard felt it was the perfect tool to create alignment around the organization's new customer-intimacy strategy but his failure to clearly state that in terms that everyone could rally around ultimately cost him the hearts, if not the minds, of most of his employees.

 ## ANSWERING THE QUESTION: WHY THE BALANCED SCORECARD AND WHY NOW?

We live in a world that has been characterized as one of excess access.[1] These days everything seems to be at the tip of our fingers, and it seems everyone out there wants to keep pushing more our way—products, information, entertainment, you name it. Who among us doesn't feel a little overwhelmed, overworked, and overstressed these days? At home and at the office our senses are constantly being bombarded with attention-demanding stimuli. With time, attention, and energy constituting our most precious of resources, we must be absolutely certain that those things we do allow into our cognitive air space truly warrant our attention. The first and most critical hurdle any new initiative, including the Balanced Scorecard, will face in your organization is: "Why exactly are we doing this?" If you can't supply a simple and compelling answer to that question, how can you justifiably expect your employees to shove aside a Mount Everest-sized pile of competing demands and priorities to focus on the Balanced Scorecard?

As with any other business tool you employ, the Balanced Scorecard must solve a pressing business issue or problem that everyone understands and the importance of which is universally acknowledged. Be forewarned, fashionable clichés—"We're going from good to great" or "We're going to be a cutting-edge company"—won't cut it with a workforce that has more than likely seen their share of such vague platitudes come and go.[2] To have the Scorecard gain acceptance it must be seen as a firehose clearly capable of dousing the flames of challenge at your doorstep. So perhaps the most fundamental question you can ask yourself is, "Do we really need a Balanced Scorecard?" Exhibit 2.1 provides an assessment guide you can use to determine whether or not the Balanced Scorecard is right for you.

Asking why we are doing something, attempting to unearth the true purpose, should become second nature to us in every facet of our lives. Regardless of the pursuit, it's critical to peel away the layer of possibilities and tackle the fundamental question of why something is important to us at this moment. Only then can we sincerely determine whether our full commitment of action is merited. Roger Smith, the former CEO of General Motors learned that lesson the hard way. Here is a quote from Smith as he reflected in retrospect on his turnaround plans for the automotive giant:

> If I had the opportunity to do everything over again, I would make exactly the same decision that I made . . . to rebuild GM, inside out and from the bottom up, to turn it into a 21st-century corporation, one that would continue to be a global leader. But I sure wish I'd done a better job of communicating with GM people. I'd do that differently a second time around and make sure they understood and shared my vision for the company. Then they would have known why I was tearing the place up, taking out whole divisions, changing our whole production structure. If people understand the why, they'll work at it.

To complete the exercise read each statement and determine how much you agree with what is stated. The more you agree, the higher the score you assign. For example, if you fully agree, assign a score of 5 points.

1 2 3 4 5	1. Our organization has invested in Total Quality Management (TQM) and other improvement initiatives but we have not seen a corresponding increase in financial or customer results.
1 2 3 4 5	2. If we did not produce our current Performance Reports for a month nobody would notice.
1 2 3 4 5	3. We create significant value from intangible assets such as employee knowledge and innovation, customer relationships, and a strong culture.
1 2 3 4 5	4. We have a strategy (or have had strategies in the past) but have a hard time successfully implementing it.
1 2 3 4 5	5. We rarely review our performance measures and make suggestions for new and innovative indicators.
1 2 3 4 5	6. Our senior management team spends the majority of their time together discussing variances from plan and other operational issues.
1 2 3 4 5	7. Budgeting at our organization is very political and based largely on historical trends.
1 2 3 4 5	8. Our employees do not have a solid understanding of our mission, vision, and strategy.
1 2 3 4 5	9. Our employees do not know how their day to day actions contribute to the organization's success.
1 2 3 4 5	10. Nobody owns the performance measurement process at our organization.
1 2 3 4 5	11. We have numerous initiatives taking place at our organization, and it's possible that not all are truly strategic in nature.
1 2 3 4 5	12. There is little accountability in our organization for the things we agree as a group to do.
1 2 3 4 5	13. People tend to stay within their "silos" and as a result we have little collaboration among departments.
1 2 3 4 5	14. Our employees have difficulty accessing the critical information they need to serve customers.
1 2 3 4 5	15. Priorities at our organization are often dictated by current necessity or "fire-fighting."
1 2 3 4 5	16. The environment in which we operate is changing and in order to succeed we too must change.
1 2 3 4 5	17. We face increased pressure from stakeholders to demonstrate results.
1 2 3 4 5	18. We do not have clearly defined performance targets for both financial and non-financial indicators.
1 2 3 4 5	19. We cannot clearly articulate our strategy in a one-page document or "map."
1 2 3 4 5	20. We sometimes make decisions that are beneficial in the short term but may harm long-term value creation.

Scoring Key

20–30:	If your score fell in this range you most likely have a strong performance measurement discipline in place. The program has been cascaded throughout your organization to ensure all employees are contributing to your success, and is linked to key management processes.
31–60:	You may have a performance measurement system in place but are not experiencing the benefits you anticipated or need to succeed. Using the Balanced Scorecard as a Strategic Management System would be of benefit to you.
61–100:	Scores in this range suggest difficulty in successfully executing your strategy, and meeting the needs of your customers and other stakeholders. A Balanced Scorecard system is strongly recommended to help you focus on the implementation of strategy and align your organization with overall goals.

EXHIBIT 2.1   Assessing the Need for a Balanced Scorecard

Like I say, I never got all this across. There we were, charging up the hill right on schedule, and I looked behind me and saw that many people were still at the bottom, trying to decide whether to come along. I'm talking about hourly workers, middle management, even some top managers. It seemed like a lot of them had gotten off the train.[3]

POSSIBLE REASONS FOR LAUNCHING A BALANCED SCORECARD

Assuming you've used Exhibit 2.1 to assess your need for the Balanced Scorecard, chances are at least one of the reasons for that decision is reflected in Exhibit 2.2. Exhibit 2.2 outlines a number of possible explanations for launching a Balanced Scorecard effort. All of the possible rationales presented in the exhibit are sound, but some take on increased urgency in today's business environment.

Let's begin with "Drive awareness of corporate goals," since awareness of goals is an obvious prerequisite of execution. In one study, researchers discovered that 15 percent of employees could not identify even one of the top three goals identified by their leaders as keys to success. The remaining 85 percent named what they felt was the primary goal, but it frequently bore little resemblance to what their executives had presented. The study went on to suggest that the further you are from the top of the organization, the lower the clarity and awareness of corporate aspirations.[4] Perhaps not surprisingly, given the low level of goal awareness, even those who did espouse recognition of the primary corporate goal reported low levels of commitment relating to its achievement. About half of respondents said they were passionate about the goal, meaning almost half of all employees were simply going about their daily work with little drive or engagement.

While the statistics cited above are sobering, we shouldn't immediately place the blame on employees, as my experience suggests that senior management often does a poor job communicating strategy and overall goals, or use inappropriate mechanisms in their attempt to spread the message. The Balanced Scorecard is ideally suited to overcome these deficits, primarily through the strategy map which, when constructed properly, clearly communicates (using simple, jargon-free language) where the organization is headed.

EXHIBIT 2.2   Rationale for the Balanced Scorecard

"Creating accountability" is another high-potential reason for launching a Balanced Scorecard program. While there is little doubt today's employees are working harder than ever, often with fewer resources at their disposal, we're not witnessing a commensurate increase in accountability to meet corporate goals. The study discussed above also found that an astonishing 81 percent of those surveyed were not held accountable for progress on their organization's goals, and 87 percent had no clear idea of what they should be doing to achieve the goal. Once again, cue the Balanced Scorecard. Objectives on the strategy map will only come to fruition if targets are achieved, and that can only take place if people are held accountable to deliver those results. Accountability is a hallmark of the Scorecard system.

Although accountability is a necessary element of success, you cannot use fear to motivate accelerated performance. In their zeal to deliver breakthrough results, some leaders may introduce accountability and other dimensions of the Scorecard in a negative fashion, attempting to scare their employees into compliance with the new way of doing things. This will never work because fear, although it may temporarily drive people out of complacency, will in the long run prohibit necessary new action and behaviors from taking root. In a situation fraught with peril most people will logically default to self-preservation, in effect declaring, "Who cares about the organization and its goals, I need to take care of myself!" Your responsibility in introducing the Balanced Scorecard is to find the delicate balance between creating a sense of urgency to promote change without instilling debilitating fear. That sweet spot exists for all us. Back in 1908, scientists Robert Yerkes and John Dodson discovered what they termed the Inverted-U model of human performance, which dictated that performance was poor at low levels of stress, hit the sweet spot at reasonable levels of stress, and diminished under high stress conditions.[5] A reasonable level of stress will be organization dependent, but, in general, when implementing the Scorecard the goal should be to clearly outline why the change is necessary and how the status quo is unacceptable, while also creating positive forward motion toward a desired future state.

SEND YOURSELF A POSTCARD FROM THE FUTURE

Answering the question "Why the Balanced Scorecard?" is imperative to gain support for the program, but beyond some guiding rationales, you should motivate your team by creating a vivid picture that shows exactly what success will look like when you've completed the journey. Regarding the Balanced Scorecard, it could be a multitude of things; for example, perhaps you suffer from poor management meetings, dreaded by your team because they drain time and energy while accomplishing nothing of strategic significance. Contrast that with a finish-line image of the Balanced Scorecard that features bold images of productive and efficient management meetings during which lively and passionate exchanges lead to true strategic insights, better decisions, and ultimately improved results. This can happen, by the way. The CEO of one early Balanced Scorecard hall-of-fame company said that once the Scorecard was in place and used to guide management meetings, he could have sold tickets to them!

The power of this approach lies in balancing rational analysis with emotional impact. To reach your destination you need more than staid business prose that does little but engender skepticism and, often, mistrust. What's required is an emotional appeal that will hit people at a visceral level. In the example above, everyone can relate to time-sucking meetings that yield no benefits, and they can also get excited on an emotional level about taking part in discussions that are truly professional and stimulating.

So you have your *why* taken care of, and recognize the importance of balancing rationality and emotional impact in your messaging. What's next?

 ## START WITH A PROVOCATIVE ACTION

All of the potential reasons for launching Scorecard programs shared in Exhibit 2.2 are perfectly logical and make sense, but frequently when selling the need for change (and the Balanced Scorecard does represent a change initiative) we must move beyond rational arguments consisting of facts and figures to dramatic demonstrations of why change is demanded that engage our emotional sides. There is an old saying in screenwriting, "Show, don't tell," which admonishes writers to let the actions of characters reveal their true nature and feelings rather than having them spoon fed to the audience through dialog, which is far less satisfying and not nearly as dramatic. Often, when launching a Balanced Scorecard it's also more effective to show rather than tell.

Here is an informative and entertaining story that recounts how one company used the show-don't-tell principle to great advantage in selling the necessity of a change. It's called "Gloves on the Boardroom Table." One manager was sure the company was wasting a lot of money in their purchasing processes, so much so he felt it was possible to drive down purchasing costs by a billion dollars over the next five years. Problem was, nobody in senior management saw the problem and, therefore, nothing was happening. The enterprising manager took things into his own hands. He had a summer student research how much they paid for the different kinds of gloves used in their factories and how many different gloves they bought. He chose gloves because they were simple, and something all the plants used. Shortly thereafter the student reported that the company purchased 424 different kinds of gloves! Worse yet, every factory negotiated separate purchase agreements so the same glove might cost $5 at one plant and $17 at another. The student was able to collect a sample of every one of the 424 gloves. She tagged each one with the price and factory it was used in. They gathered all the gloves, put them on a boardroom table and invited the division presidents to visit. What they saw was a large, expensive table, normally clean or with a few papers, now stacked high with gloves. Each of the executives stared at this display for a minute. Then each said something like, "We buy all these different kinds of gloves?" Well, as a matter of fact, yes we do. "Really?" Yes, really. Then they walked around the table. Most were looking for the gloves that their factories were using. They could see the prices. They looked at two gloves that seemed exactly alike, yet one was marked $3.22 and the other $10.55. The normally verbose executives were at a loss. The glove exhibit quickly gained notoriety and soon a road show was under way, during which the gloves visited every division and dozens of plants. Enhancing the already dramatic effect, competitor information was added showing how much extra the company was spending. The mandate for change was clear and soon executives were leading the we-must-act-now chorus.[6]

One client of mine was so inspired by this story they decided to modify it to demonstrate the need for a Balanced Scorecard. In a simple online survey they asked executives how many performance reports they thought the company issued each month, and which reports were of greatest value to them. My contact at the company, we'll call her Kathy, knew the organization was producing in excess of a dozen reports every month, many of which had been around for years and were of dubious value, but had become sacred for no real reason. In a nod to the "Gloves on the Boardroom Table" story, Kathy then assembled all of the reports for just one month and spread them on a conference room table. Also on the table were individual placards with executive guesses to the number of reports produced and names of the most valuable reports. The executive team was invited into the room and were immediately shocked the by reams of paper on the table. When it came to knowing how many reports were actually produced each month, not a single executive came close to accurately gauging the correct number, with most proposing two or three. Also revealing were the placards noting which reports the executives identified as valuable, because most of those were blank. In other words, a majority of the executive team found the current reports virtually useless for their most critical tasks of strategic learning and decision making. Kathy used the demonstration to lead a discussion of the Balanced Scorecard, focusing on how the company could use Scorecard results as the one source to ignite strategic discussions during executive-team meetings. The case for change was clear, and the Scorecard was adopted.

Here are a couple of additional examples that showcase people and organizations who recognize actions trump words every time when it comes to igniting a spark of change: A Danish organization, tired of watching customers defect because of frustrating and outdated policies and procedures, vowed to re-engineer the customer experience. Rather than begin the effort with a dry discussion of what was to be done, executives gathered the many volumes of current policies and procedures, stacked them up, and to the delight of assembled employees, threw a torch on the pile. The signal that things were about to change was clear. One more example: A Cedars-Sinai doctor was frustrated that hand-washing levels of other doctors at the hospital remained stuck at 80 percent, despite the fact that everyone knew frequent hand washing was critical in reducing patient infections. Weary of spouting statistics and exhorting his colleagues to wash up more frequently, he took the creative step of having a sample group press their hands in a mold and then analyze what they contained. It turns out the doctors' hands were covered in bacteria. The same doctors who would later be examining a patient were unknowingly harboring an army of germs. Not surprisingly, when this revolting truth was revealed, hygiene rose to 100 percent, where it remained.

There's a place for speeches, posters, and slogan-emblazoned coffee mugs when setting on the path to change, but to really kickstart your Balanced Scorecard effort, and win your share of people's ever-dwindling attention, you need to shelve the rhetoric and start with an emotion-inducing, provocative action. All of the organizations chronicled above recognized, and benefited from, the wisdom in that old saying: Actions speak louder than words.

 ## OVERCOMING SKEPTICISM

Even if you're armed with a rock-solid rationale for pursuing the Balanced Scorecard, you can almost certainly expect some skepticism to creep in from your team. This is to be expected. After all, today's employees are inundated with change—new business models, entire new strategies, sophisticated technology platforms, cultural interventions—the list goes on and on. Organizations are forever on the hunt for the magic bullet that will transform their operations, and who can blame them? By all accounts, competition is greater than it's ever been and every organization needs an edge to remain relevant in a global business theater. Problems arise, however, when companies grasp at each new promising methodology or program, attempting to force it to fit their organization even if it clearly doesn't match their strategy or culture. Chasing these programs du jour creates fertile ground for cynicism to take root. Although the Balanced Scorecard is, at its core, a common sense idea, just the fact that it's new to your organization will be enough for a vocal minority to cry, "Here we go again!"

There are different types and intensities of skepticism, thus requiring precise and organization-specific interventions; however, one general method of overcoming it is to engage in what experts term *shrinking the change*. Here's a great example of how and why this works: A car wash ran a promotion using loyalty cards. One set of customers were given cards and told they'd receive a stamp for each wash. Once they had accumulated eight stamps they would receive a free wash. Another set of customers were told they'd need to collect 10 stamps, but were given a head start in the form of two stamps on their cards. In both cases the goal is the same: accumulate eight stamps to receive a free car wash, however, the psychology is significantly different. In one case you're starting from nothing, while in the other you're already 20 percent of the way there. A few months later the results came in and they were revealing: only 19 percent of the eight-stamp customers had received a free wash versus 34 percent of those with a head start. It's clear that we're more motivated to be part of the way through a long journey than to be just starting a short one.[7] Your challenge in launching the Balanced Scorecard is in finding and sharing your two stamps with employees to demonstrate that you're already moving toward success. For instance, chances are you already collect performance data in multiple areas, so why not use that fact to share how the Scorecard is an improvement on your current methods by telling a complete strategic story? It's also a virtual guarantee that you're conducting monthly or quarterly meetings to assess progress. Use that as a free stamp, by informing your team that the Scorecard will provide a sharper lens for those meetings making them more efficient and productive.

BENEFITS OF A GUIDING RATIONALE

For the Scorecard to succeed, it cannot be viewed as a one-time event. Determining your objectives in developing the Balanced Scorecard will go a long way in securing the evolution of the tool in your organization. Once you've made the decision to go forward, your first obligation is to clearly explain why that choice has been made, and what benefits you expect as a result. The more specific the better—outline in vivid detail the challenges you face from competitors, changing customer tendencies, supplier pressures, stakeholder demands, and so on. Demonstrate to your team why change is not simply an option, but an imperative if you're to stay in the game and sustain your success.

When you have a well-understood, agreed upon, and widely communicated rationale for implementation, you possess a valuable tool to expand the role of the Balanced Scorecard. Management and employees alike will view the development of objectives and measures in a Balanced Scorecard framework as the first of many stops on the road to a new and powerful management system for the organization. The consensus achieved from an overarching rationale for the Balanced Scorecard greatly assists your communication efforts as you focus and educate all employees on the goals of the implementation. Finally, every implementation loses momentum at one time or another; the practical realities of modern business and its multitude of attendant priorities make that a virtual certainty. The true test is whether you can emerge from these periods of corporate lethargy with renewed vigor and enthusiasm for the task at hand. A guiding rationale for your Balanced Scorecard can serve as your rallying cry, bringing the entire organization together under the banner of why you made this decision in the first place.

 ## WHERE DO WE BUILD THE BALANCED SCORECARD?

Scorecard architects Kaplan and Norton have described the Balanced Scorecard as simple but not simplistic. This is the first of probably several times I will call upon that reference as we develop your Balanced Scorecard. While the concept itself is relatively straightforward—balancing financial and non-financial objectives and measures to drive strategy—the execution of those tasks will involve many difficult deliberations on a wide variety of topics. We just described one such issue when we examined the rationale for developing a Balanced Scorecard. In this section we'll explore another important subject requiring careful consideration, the choice of an appropriate unit in which to develop your first Balanced Scorecard.

Sensing possible resistance and attempting to limit downside risk will lead some organizations to begin their Balanced Scorecard effort at the business unit or department level, piloting the program in an attempt to generate quick wins and enthusiasm for a broader rollout. The goal inherent in this choice is that pilot groups will profit from their investment in the Balanced Scorecard through strategic insights gleaned from innovative performance measures. With results in hand, they'll be quick to recommend the program be spread throughout the organization.

Despite the possible challenges, including resistance and logistical constraints, most organizations believe starting at the top represents the most logical choice, and frequently this is in fact the case. A corporate-level Balanced Scorecard provides the means of communicating strategic objectives and measures across the entire organization. The focus and attention derived from these high-level metrics can serve to bring together disparate elements of the organization toward a common goal of implementing the strategy. The objectives and measures on the corporate strategy map and Scorecard then become raw materials for cascaded Scorecards at all levels of the firm, producing a series of aligned systems, which allow all organizational participants to demonstrate how their day-to-day actions contribute to long-term goals.

CRITERIA FOR CHOOSING AN APPROPRIATE ORGANIZATIONAL UNIT

If, for whatever reason, a Balanced Scorecard at the highest level is not possible for your organization at this time, yet you'd still like to enjoy the benefits it confers, you'll need to make a decision as to where you should begin. Several elements contribute to the selection of an appropriate organizational unit for your first Balanced Scorecard, and they are displayed in Exhibit 2.3.

Let's consider each of these seven criteria in turn and then discuss a method for using them to make this important decision.

1. **Strategy:** A vital criterion in making your selection is whether the unit under consideration possesses any form of a strategic plan. After all, the Balanced Scorecard is a methodology designed to assist you in translating your strategy into objectives and measures that will allow you to gauge

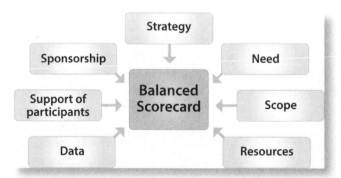

EXHIBIT 2.3 Seven Criteria for Choosing Where to Begin Your Balanced Scorecard

your effectiveness in delivering on that strategy. Without a strategic stake in the ground you may end up with an ad hoc collection of financial and nonfinancial objectives and measures that do not link together to tell the story of your strategy. Having said that, notice I used the words "any form of a strategic plan" above. A freshly minted document produced by high-paid external consultants is not a necessary input, whereas a clear understanding of markets served and value propositions offered is crucial. Recently I worked with a large international company that decided piloting the Balanced Scorecard at two business units was the preferred method to begin. Neither of these units had formal strategic plans in place, but one had a transformation plan, akin to a strategy, while the other had produced a strategic change agenda highlighting the stark differences between where they stood today and where they wished to be in the future—very similar to a strategy. Both produced robust Balanced Scorecard systems.

2. **Sponsorship**: In the next section of this chapter we'll take a close look at the necessity of executive sponsorship for your Balanced Scorecard effort. For the purposes of this discussion, suffice it to say that if your leader is not aligned with the goals and objectives of the Balanced Scorecard and does not believe in the merits of the tool, your efforts will be severely compromised. An executive sponsor must provide leadership for the program in both words and deeds.

3. **Need for a Balanced Scorecard:** The importance of a guiding rationale for the Balanced Scorecard program was discussed earlier in the chapter. Based on that review, does the unit you're considering have an overarching impetus for their implementation? Is there a clear need for revamping their performance management system?

4. **Support of participants:** In my experience, bright spots of performance management exist in every organization. These are the groups, typically led by enthusiastic and vocal supporters of tools like the Balanced Scorecard, that are currently using performance management in some form and are anxious to showcase their value to the broader organizational audience. Groups like this are pure gold! I've been fortunate to come across many in my years of consulting, like this one: A sheriff's deputy in a large California county had the foresight to recognize the potential of the Balanced Scorecard and wouldn't stop until he proved it to the entire organization. From the first day the process was introduced, he made it clear that his team wanted to develop a Scorecard because they were convinced of the benefits it could deliver in times of shrinking budgets. At every ensuing meeting of county leaders he extolled the virtues of the program and his

enthusiasm proved infectious. Soon other executives were clamoring to get on board and take advantage of this powerful tool. Look for the bright spots in your company when selecting a candidate for the Balanced Scorecard. Not all members of these groups will demonstrate such a willingness to participate, however. Managers and supervisors will often remain silent or demonstrate muted enthusiasm, which workers quickly interpret as a questionable show of support for the program.[8] When choosing your organizational unit for the Balanced Scorecard, make an honest evaluation of the management team and supervisors you'll be relying on for participation and support.

5. **Organizational Scope:** The unit you choose should operate a set of activities across the typical value chain of an organization. In other words they should have a strategy, defined customers, specific processes, operations, and administration. Selecting a unit with a narrow, functional focus will produce a Scorecard with narrow, functionally focused metrics.

6. **Data:** This criterion encompasses two elements. First, does this unit support a culture of measurement (i.e., would they be amenable to managing by a balanced set of performance measures)? While every group within a modern organization should rely on performance measures, for your first attempt you may wish to choose a unit with a history of measurement use. Second, will the unit be able to supply data for the chosen performance measures? This may be difficult to assess initially since some of the measures on your Balanced Scorecard may be as yet unidentified data sources. However, if the unit has difficulty gathering data for current performance measures, they may be reluctant or unable to source the data you'll require for your Balanced Scorecard.

7. **Resources:** You can't build this new management system on your own. The best Balanced Scorecards are produced from a team of individuals committed to a common goal of excellence. Ensure the unit you choose is willing and able to supply ample resources for the implementation. If your experience is like many that I've had, you'll find people's time is something they vigorously defend, and rightly so.

Exhibit 2.4 provides a simple worksheet you can use to determine the right organizational unit for your initial Balanced Scorecard effort. In this example, Business Unit *A* is being considered for a Scorecard implementation. Plotted along the left-hand side of the table are the seven criteria I discussed above. In the next column, I assigned a score out of 10 for this unit against each of the criteria. The third column represents weights for each of the seven dimensions

Balanced Scorecard Implementation
Organizational Unit Assessment Business Unit _A_

Criteria	Score (Out of 10)	Weight	Total Points	Rationale
Strategy	10	30%	3	This unit has recently completed a new strategic plan for the next five years.
Sponsorship	9	30%	2.7	New unit president has successfully utilized the Balanced Scorecard with two other organizations before joining us.
Need	5	15%	0.75	Results for this group have been excellent, and they may not see the need for this tool to sustain future efforts.
Support of Participants	7	10%	0.7	Young, energetic management group willing to experiment with new approaches.
Scope	8	5%	0.4	This unit produces, markets, and sells a distinct group of products.
Data	4	5%	0.2	Despite their success, they have not utilized sophisticated performance measurement systems in the past.
Resources	4	5%	0.2	Unit is understaffed and will have difficulty finding resources for this project.
Total		100%	7.95	

Overall Assessment: This unit scores a very high 7.95 out of 10 and is an excellent candidate for the Balanced Scorecard. The data and resource issues, while not insignificant, are mitigated by the strong leadership of the unit president and the creation of a new strategic plan. Early education initiatives within this unit could focus on the value of the Scorecard as a means of sustaining results for the long term. This may reduce skepticism surrounding the implementation based on the past success of the unit.

EXHIBIT 2.4   Sample Worksheet for Choosing Your Organizational Unit

based on my judgment and experience. You may feel more comfortable assigning equal weights to each of the seven items, but clearly some areas, such as sponsorship and strategy, are imperative to success and should be weighted accordingly. The fourth column contains the score for the unit within each criterion. Under strategy they were assigned a score of 10, which when multiplied by the weight for that category yields 3 total points. In the final column I've provided a rationale for the scores assigned based on an assessment of the unit in the context of that specific criteria. It's important to document your decision-making process in order to validate it with others responsible for choosing the Balanced Scorecard organizational unit. Finally, a total score is calculated and an overall assessment provided. The overall assessment provides worksheet participants with the opportunity to discuss potential strengths and weaknesses of the unit, mitigate significant risks, and offer opinions on the viability of this group for the Balanced Scorecard project.

 ## EXECUTIVE SPONSORSHIP: A CRITICAL ELEMENT OF ANY BALANCED SCORECARD PROGRAM

One of my favorite aspects of delivering talks on the Balanced Scorecard is the question and answer period, when the audience grills me with queries large and small on everything Balanced Scorecard, and occasionally beyond. There is a standard slate of questions that I hear repeatedly:

> "How big an organization do you have to be to derive benefits from the Balanced Scorecard?"
> "How long does it take to implement?"
> "What are some of the key success factors in implementing the Balanced Scorecard?"

To use a sports metaphor, I consider these and other similar questions to be soft balls tossed right over the heart of the plate just waiting for me to knock them out of the park with a solid answer. I say that because a body of experience has accumulated over the past two decades, which allows me to competently and confidently reply to such questions. However, at some point in virtually every session someone will throw me a curveball, a question that makes my knees buckle like a badly fooled batter, as I search for the best response. That question is simply, "How do I get a reluctant or disinterested executive to pay attention to, or sponsor, the Balanced Scorecard?" The questioner realizes, as does everyone else in the room, that without executive sponsorship the Balanced Scorecard, or any change initiative for that matter, is ultimately doomed to failure.

Scorecard architects Kaplan and Norton believe senior management commitment is necessary for a number of reasons:[9]

- **Understanding of strategy:** Since it was most likely conceived by their superiors, most middle managers lack an in-depth knowledge of the organization's strategy. Only the senior management team is able to effectively articulate an ongoing strategy. Additionally, research has determined, not surprisingly, that employees want to learn about the strategy directly from the executive team, with no middlemen. Ideally, the communication features unvarnished communication and reciprocal exchanges, during which employees have the opportunity to voice concerns and ensure their voice is heard.[10]

- **Decision rights:** Strategy involves trade-offs between alternative courses of action, determining which opportunities to pursue and, more importantly, which not to pursue. Middle management does not possess the decision-making power to determine strategic priorities such as customer value propositions and related operating processes, which are critical to the development of any Balanced Scorecard.
- **Commitment**: While knowledge of the enterprise's strategy is necessary, the emotional commitment of executives to the Scorecard program is the true differentiating feature of successful programs.

Kaplan and Norton aren't alone in issuing dire warnings about the necessity of executive sponsorship. Writing in their provocatively-titled book *Confronting Reality*, authors Charan and Bossidy state:

> The usual reason for the failure of an initiative is that it was launched halfheartedly, or was beyond the ability of the organization to master. Here's what tends to happen: the leaders announce a bold new program and then walk away from it, leaving the job to others. With no clear impetus from the top, the program will wander and drift. An initiative, after all, is add-on work, and people already have full plates. Few of them can take it seriously if the boss doesn't. Eventually the effort bogs down and dies . . . Real results do not come from making bold announcements about how the organization will change. They come from thoughtful, committed leaders who understand the details of an initiative, anticipate its consequences for the organization, make sure their people can achieve, it, put their personal weight behind it, and communicate its urgency to everyone.[11]

It's clear that sponsorship is paramount to launching and sustaining a Balanced Scorecard initiative, but how do we secure it?

Securing Executive Sponsorship

Although every organization is unique and has their own set of challenges, one common thread uniting all is the declaration: "We're busier than we've ever been!" Downsizing, rightsizing, early retirement, operational efficiency, lean manufacturing, and a host of other productivity boosters have conspired to not only enhance our output, but to do so in many cases with considerably fewer resources. So we're run off our feet and, with a million things screaming for our attention, more than ever we look to our executives for guidance. What are they watching? What gets their attention? As the old saying goes, if it's interesting to my boss, it's fascinating to me. Employees simply aren't going to commit to the Balanced Scorecard without a passionate, committed, and informed executive leading the charge. So how do you install the Balanced Scorecard on their already overcrowded radar screens?

The answer is science. No test tubes, white coats, or sterile labs off the New Jersey Turnpike, mind you. In fact, to those of you possibly intimidated by the very notion of science in a book devoted to the Balanced Scorecard, consider the words of English biologist Thomas Henry Huxley, who suggested, "Science is, I believe, nothing but trained and organized common sense."[12] In this section we'll be relying on the trained and organized common sense of Mr. Robert Cialdini, author of the wonderful book *Influence: The Psychology of Persuasion*.[13] Cialdini and his team of researchers have been studying the science of persuasion for more than 30 years and have developed a set of straightforward principles you can use when engaging a recalcitrant executive in a discussion of why the Balanced Scorecard is right for your organization. Described next are the principles of persuasion as developed by Professor Cialdini. I'll briefly outline each, provide an example of the principle in action from real life, and then discuss how you can mold it to work in your efforts to secure executive sponsorship.[14]

Liking

People tend to like those who like, and are similar to, themselves. Thus, in order to influence others we must uncover real similarities and offer genuine praise. An article in the *Journal of Personality* discovered that participants stood closer to one another after learning they shared political beliefs and social values. I'm sure we've all experienced the liking phenomenon in our own lives. Before engaging with clients in a workshop setting, I always try and meet as many of the participants as possible. Inevitably I'll share something with at least one, perhaps we have a hobby in common, or we root for the same football team, it could be anything. It's amazing how often those people will tend to be more responsive and active during the subsequent session. It's simply because we've established a connection.

In applying this principle to executive sponsorship I suggest you focus on the similarity principle and link the Scorecard to something about which the executive feels passionate. Any executive is more inclined to lend vocal and active support to an initiative appealing to a core belief or value; thus it is incumbent upon you to find that linchpin and discuss how the Balanced Scorecard can transform it from rhetoric to reality. For example, perhaps she is acutely aware of the power of intangible assets such as culture and customer relationships in transforming your business. Discuss the proven ability of the Balanced Scorecard to translate intangibles into real business value. If quality is their first love, demonstrate the idea of cause and effect, outlining the fact that quality is a result of unique organizational elements such as training and culture, and quality drives customer satisfaction and ultimately financial rewards, all key dimensions of the Scorecard framework.

You might also choose to emphasize another angle of the liking equation— employees may like, or certainly respect, the CEO more if he chooses to embrace the Scorecard methodology. Research has demonstrated that when the CEO makes it a priority to balance the concerns of customers, employees, and the community, while also taking environmental impact into account (sounds a lot like a Balanced Scorecard approach), employees perceive him or her as visionary and participatory.[15]

Social Proof

We follow the lead of similar others, so whenever possible use peer power to create influence. In his book Cialdini cites a group of researchers who went door to door in Columbia, South Carolina soliciting donations for a charity campaign and displaying a list of neighborhood residents who had already donated to the cause. They found that the longer the donor list was, the more likely those solicited would be to donate as well. It's important to note his admonition of similar others, when exercising this dimension of persuasion. Influence is reduced when the social proof relies on strangers. This is perhaps the easiest of the persuasion levers to pull for those of us soliciting executive sponsorship. The business literature is literally crammed with examples of organizations generating breakthrough results from the Balanced Scorecard. With just a modicum of research on the Web you'll doubtless uncover organizations, or in Cialdini's words similar others, that have harnessed the power of the Scorecard to tremendous advantage. Share these stories with your executive and watch their antennae go up.

Authority

People defer to experts in all situations. In fact, according to one study, a single expert opinion news story in the *New York Times* is associated with a 2 percent shift in public opinion nationwide. Airing the expert's view on television can sway public opinion as much as 4 percent.

This is a technique upon which I, and virtually all consultants, rely heavily. Click on my Web site at www.senalosa.com and one of the first things you'll see are pictures of my book jackets. They're not there because I like the artwork—although I do. The books are a direct message to visitors that I am an expert in this field and they are very safe in my hands. The use of expertise to influence executives is certainly not lost on my clients. I'll often receive calls from prospective clients telling me that although the CEO understands and believes in the Scorecard, "They need to hear it from an expert." You too can utilize this mechanism. Hire a consultant perhaps, or simply look for recommendations on the Balanced Scorecard from renowned management experts. Many have advocated the Scorecard as a critical tool in the arsenal of the modern organization.

Scarcity

We naturally want more of what we have less of, so when attempting to influence others it's vital to highlight unique benefits and exclusive information. Consider the Bose organization, purveyors of high-end audio systems. When launching their Wave radio a number of years ago the company focused their advertising on what was new about the product: new styling, new elegance, new sophistication, and of course new and improved sound quality. The campaign flopped. One simple but fundamental change was made to the campaign and it resulted in a 45 percent increase in sales. What was that change? The slogan became, "Hear what you've been missing." By focusing on loss or scarcity, Bose tapped into a universal human phenomenon to want more of what we have less of.[16]

One of the first statistics I use to get an audience's attention, one meant to elicit a startled response, is this: Only 10 percent of organizations effectively execute their strategies. That means nine out of ten fail to do so. And even for those that do manage to execute, research has demonstrated that they generate just 63 percent of the financial gains anticipated.[17] Talk about scarcity! These nuggets are sure to make the hair on the back of the neck stand up as executives realize that the mere formation of a strategy, even a seemingly brilliant plan, is in no way a guarantee of success.

The Balanced Scorecard can parachute to the rescue here. It's a proven tool for executing strategy used by tens of thousands of organizations around the globe. By dangling this scarcity nugget you should at the very least get the attention of your senior executive, and thus you should be ready with an ample supply of literature and case studies to swing the influence pendulum in your favor.

Reciprocity

Give what you hope to receive and people will tend to repay in kind. Charity organizations are the classic beneficiaries of this time-tested principle. For example, consider the Disabled American Veterans Organization. Using just a well-crafted fundraising letter, for many years they generated a very respectable 18 percent response rate. When they begin stuffing their envelopes with personalized address labels, a very modest gift, the response rate nearly doubled to 35 percent.

Gift giving can prove to be a crude application of this principle, however, and not one most of us can rely on in a tangible way. I doubt, for example, you'll bounce into your CEO's office with a new Rolex hoping he or she will reciprocate by sponsoring the Balanced Scorecard. But what you can give are results in the form of a pilot Scorecard implementation. As the preceding section advised, look for an area in your organization where you can launch the Scorecard without fanfare and the inquisitive glare of the senior leadership. Chances are once that pilot demonstrates success, your CEO will stand up and take notice. And no wonder, you're generously supplying the greatest gift of all—alignment and success.

Consistency

People align with their clear commitments, thus it's imperative to make them active, public, and voluntary. First let's distinguish between the three types of commitment outlined in the previous sentence. Active commitments represent those either spoken out loud or written down. Much research has demonstrated that when commitments are active they are considerably more likely to direct someone's future conduct. As the word implies, public commitments are those made in front of others. Cialdini cites a classic 1955 experiment in which students were asked to estimate the lengths of lines on a screen. Some were asked to write down their estimates, sign them, and turn them over to the researcher. Others were asked to write them down on an erasable slate, then erase the slate immediately. A third group was instructed to keep their decisions to themselves. The researchers then presented all three groups with evidence that their initial choices may have been wrong. By a wide margin the group most reluctant to shift from their original choices was those who had signed and handed them to the researcher. This experiment highlights how much most people wish to appear consistent to others. Finally, in order to prove effective commitments must be voluntary. As the poet Samuel Butler warned more than 300 years ago, "He that complies against his will is of his own opinion still."

Every single executive I've spoken with during Scorecard engagements has told me they fully support the implementation. Every single one. What many of them have failed to do, however, is make that commitment public. It's nice to tell me, but the audience that really needs the message is their employees, who want to hear their boss shout from the rooftop: "I'm behind this and here's why!" My first exposure to the Balanced Scorecard was with a utility back in the very early 1990s. As part of our overall Scorecard communication plan, we had our CEO issue a letter to employees in which he discussed exactly why we were embarking on the Scorecard journey, what employees could expect to see, and what resources were available. On the bottom of the inspiring note appeared his signature. I've always felt that act—signing the letter—was his public commitment to our implementation. And he never wavered. So, for those of you battling for CEO sponsorship, ensure their commitment is voluntary, public, and actively provided.

 ## SPONSORSHIP ADVICE FOR EXECUTIVES

If you are a senior executive sponsoring the Balanced Scorecard program within your organization, how do you know you're walking the talk? Try this test: When you feel that you are talking up a change initiative at least three times more than you need to, your managers will feel that you are backing the transformation.[18] It takes that much, probably more, to get the message across to a change-weary, constantly bombarded-from-all-sides employee base that is looking to you to set the course your ship is going to sail.

One simple acronym for executives to keep in mind when attempting to exhibit sponsorship for the Balanced Scorecard is SCARF, which stands for status, certainty, autonomy, relatedness, and fairness.[19] Let's look at how you can apply each. Earlier in this section I noted the desire of employees to have strategy communicated directly from executives. In doing so, however, you must remember that status differences may impact the effectiveness of your communication. Rather than issuing edicts such as "We're launching the Balanced Scorecard—either get on board or get out," which reek of hubris, use humility to share your own vulnerability by directly acknowledging the challenges you face, and letting it be known you can't solve them on your own. Only through the concerted efforts of the entire workforce, committed to using the Balanced Scorecard, will you prevail. *Certainty* is enhanced by frequently referencing your vision for a more prosperous future, powered in part by the insights gleaned from the Balanced Scorecard. Including members of your team in the creation of the Scorecard and, once it's complete, having employees from all levels discuss and debate it will greatly increase *autonomy* throughout the implementation. Great leaders work hard to be authentic and real in their interactions with their teams, creating a sense of *relatedness*. Once again, revealing some humility and acknowledging you can't develop the Scorecard on your own will be a great asset in your implementation. Finally, it's imperative you keep your promises throughout the process, ensuring a sense of *fairness* is in play. If, for example, you vowed to eliminate all nonessential monthly reports and replace them with the Balanced Scorecard, you'd better stand by that to earn the continued trust of your team.

Every opportunity to reinforce the importance of the exercise must be utilized. One of my favorite examples of this stems from a common lament I hear during Balanced Scorecard workshops: the woe is me "What time is this session going to end? I have real work to do" complaint often lobbed from a disengaged participant. I was once in a strategy mapping workshop with a large telecom company when a vice president tossed just such a verbal grenade into the late afternoon air. I was poised to answer his query in my most restrained manner when I was rescued by the CEO himself, who said to the unsuspecting culprit: "What could possibly be more important than what we are doing right here and now? We're shaping the tool that we'll use to execute our strategy over the next three years, and frankly if you don't understand the importance of this exercise then maybe you don't belong at this table." The silence that followed was, as they say, deafening. In the intervening moments before he went on to further articulate his feelings, everyone sitting around that table had to dig deep within themselves and critically evaluate their commitment, knowing full well the views of their boss. Not surprisingly as the implementation unfolded it was among the most successful I've ever had the privilege to engage in, and I pin that not on my consulting acumen but on that single incident which clearly demonstrated the passion this executive held for the Balanced Scorecard.

YOUR BALANCED SCORECARD TEAM

Teams have become a very popular concept in today's organizational world, and for good reason. Enterprises around the globe are realizing that in an economy dominated largely by intangible assets, it's collaboration among employees spanning the entire organization that drives results. The Balanced Scorecard is very well suited to a team approach. No one person in your organization possesses the singular knowledge required to build a strategy map and Balanced Scorecard that tells your strategic story. The best Maps and Scorecards represent the collective know-how and experience of people from across the enterprise. In the following sections, we'll consider the key aspects of your Balanced Scorecard team, look at the roles and responsibilities of team members, and conclude with an examination of who should run your Balanced Scorecard program on an ongoing basis.

Choosing the Team

In an ideal world your organization's full executive team would take complete responsibility for developing the Balanced Scorecard, investing the time and energy necessary to produce a product to guide the entire organization. If you're fortunate enough to enjoy this situation, I offer you congratulations—your Scorecard effort has a great head start. However, I'm guessing a more likely scenario is one in which you have the support of one or maybe two executives (perhaps you are a senior executive yourself) but you require other members of your organization to step up and assist in the effort of crafting your Balanced Scorecard. Don't despair; you can develop an effective Balanced Scorecard without your entire executive team working exclusively on the implementation.

If you don't have the luxury of the entire executive group constituting your team, the next best thing is, of course, as senior a group as possible. In the past I've had clients who ignore this suggestion, believing the biggest hurdle to clear in successfully implementing the Balanced Scorecard is the buy in and support of front-line staff, and quite frequently this is a very pragmatic point of view. To leap the obstacle and generate staff-level support they surmise that appointing a team comprised of lower-level employees will indicate their confidence in the group to deliver a sound product and simultaneously silence critics who suggest only the organizational elite have any say so in important matters. Philosophically I am all for this approach, but practically I have, unfortunately, seen it backfire, leaving once promising implementations in tatters.

There are several problems with delegating the development of your Balanced Scorecard to a low-level staff team: first of all, many people at this end of the hierarchy simply don't possess the deep knowledge of strategy and competition necessary to forge an effective Scorecard. I am not suggesting front-line associates are not critical to the company's success. In fact the opposite is often true; for example, one study noted the strategic importance of cashiers to a retailer's fortunes.[20] What I am suggesting is front-line associates are not typically steeped in the strategy at a deep enough level to meaningfully contribute to a Scorecard's development. From this lack of in-depth strategic acumen another debilitating cousin often stems: indecision. How do they know the decisions they are making, in this case vital considerations impacting the future health of the company, are the right ones? Finally, we need to face the fact that many associates comprising the lower rungs of the corporate ladder don't desire *any* change to rock the comfy status quo they've been enjoying for who knows how long. As author William Bridges puts it, "Simply to turn the power over to people who don't want a change to happen is to invite catastrophe."[21]

To prove beneficial your Balanced Scorecard must ultimately be owned by the senior leadership of your organization, and it is therefore vital to ensure your Scorecard development team is comprised of senior-level people possessing the knowledge, credibility, and decision-making rights to build a tool that will be accepted, and more importantly, utilized by the ruling body.

How Many People Should Be on Your Balanced Scorecard Team?

We have a love affair with the concept of bigger is better in the modern world—cars with bigger engines, big-box retail stores that span city blocks, and, of course, big serving sizes at our favorite restaurants, which are contributing rapidly to our big waists. We could debate the merits of bigger being better for days, maybe while sucking down a 32-ounce Coke at Costco before we load our SUV with the 44 packages of paper towels we just bought, but let's isolate the discussion to the notion of Balanced Scorecard team size.

In another of my books I quoted a study that suggested a majority of Balanced Scorecard implementations utilized teams consisting of 10 or more people.[22] While I didn't endorse that number back then, I didn't reject it either. Let me be very clear in this new book, based on my experience having facilitated thousands of workshops, that 10 people on a team is too many if you expect to have meaningful discussions that actually result in decisions being made. Come to think of it, if you hope to have productive meetings in general,

10 people are far too large a crowd. Think about it. Start with one person, that's one calendar to manage. Add a second and the task of finding a mutually convenient time to meet has doubled in complexity. A third person makes it three times as difficult, but when you get to about the fifth person the challenge expands exponentially. By the time you've reached the tenth person it could actually be simpler to convene the leaders of the G8 nations. I worked with a large nonprofit client a few years back that insisted on having a hefty team to develop their Balanced Scorecard. I knew simply scheduling meetings would be a challenge with this not-so-intimate group of 12, but when I learned almost half the group was on the east coast and half were stationed on the west coast I knew we were headed for trouble. Sure enough, the development of the strategy map and measures took almost twice as long as we had originally estimated because of the difficulties of balancing calendars.

Thus far my primary criticism of large groups has centered on the challenges of actually convening meetings. However, a much more pressing problem, one with far reaching implications for the success of your Scorecard program, is the deliverable produced by bigger groups. In this case, bigger definitely doesn't result in better outcomes. When building a Balanced Scorecard you'll depend on passionate debate and careful analysis of your unique situation to lead you to reasoned conclusions surrounding the choice of objectives and measures. The larger the group the more opinions you'll invite into the fray, and that's definitely a positive; unfortunately it's common for a few loud voices to dominate the proceedings, drown out the thoughtful arguments of others, and truncate productive discussions. Achieving consensus is almost impossible for mammoth groups, and ultimately nobody is truly satisfied with what is developed. One phrase I've heard many times over the years, and have come to dread is "I can live with that . . . let's just move on." A frustrated participant who feels he has been railroaded into accepting the inclusion of an objective or measure that doesn't accurately reflect the strategy typically delivers this line. Whenever I hear it, I know we need to roll up our sleeves once again, until we arrive at a conclusion that all participants are willing to passionately support.

The U.S. Navy SEALs, who know a thing or two about complex missions, suggest that six is the ideal number of participants on any high-intensity team.[23] I can't say with certainty that six is the exact right number for your Scorecard team, however, I do like the five to seven notion very much. This size, while still presenting logistical challenges, is a relatively small number that allows for the cognitive space to emerge where meaningful discussions occur. A group of this size can find its own identity, and members can take the necessary time in their discussions to truly understand the point of views of their colleagues without feeling the necessity to get something out before losing the floor to a host of other people craving the momentary spotlight.

If you're not comfortable designating a certain number, use this approach. Base the team size on the precept of representing all the areas of your organization that you expect to be using the Scorecard. If, for example, you're creating a high-level Balanced Scorecard you should strive for representation from each of your departments or groups. Should you have more than five or six departments, you may require a larger Balanced Scorecard team than I normally advise. If your Scorecard effort is beginning at the department level, then key representatives within the unit should have a presence on the team. Remember our earlier admonition—no one person has all the knowledge of strategy, stakeholder needs, and competencies to build an effective Scorecard. The knowledge you need to build an effective Balanced Scorecard resides in the minds of your colleagues spanning the entire organization.

What Skill Sets Should Team Members Possess?

Although primarily tasked with strategy execution, in fulfilling that promise the Balanced Scorecard possesses all the characteristics of a change project, and must be managed accordingly. While theories on change abound, most experts agree that the right team is crucial to driving change. Outlined below are key characteristics you must be cognizant of as you select the team that will lead your Scorecard implementation.[24]

- **Environmental knowledge:** All team members must understand the trends and issues that shape the company's competitive environment. Objectives and measures are forged through an understanding of your position in the overall marketplace, and thus external market knowledge is vital.
- **In-house credibility:** Your team will serve as ambassadors for the Scorecard program and other employees will draw their inspiration, or conversely, ambivalence for the program from the core team. Ideally, you'll choose people who are well regarded throughout the company, have many connections among various layers of the hierarchy, and are seen as credible change agents.
- **Cultural knowledge:** Let's use "The way we do things around here" as a working definition of the word *culture*. The Scorecard team must have an astute awareness of the firm's unique culture and how it may impact the adoption of a change program like the Scorecard. Sniffing out internal

barriers to action and smoothing the path for people to join in the change will be key accountabilities for all team members.

▪ **Position power and managerial skill:** Those constituting the team must be adept in the core project management skills of planning and organizing, while also possessing enough position power to make things happen when momentum is slowing.

▪ **Leadership:** As noted above, all employees will look to the team as ambassadors of the Scorecard, and thus each member must be able to craft a compelling and confident vision of the future with the Balanced Scorecard.

The skills above apply to individuals, but one overall dimension the team should enjoy is diversity—of viewpoints, functions, age, gender, and racial profile. Diverse team composition will spark passionate debates that ultimately yield improved outcomes, benefiting from the assortment of thought. If you put together a homogeneous group, you can expect the same tired groupthink and little in the way of strategic insights. Potentially more damaging is the fact that homogeneous groups, once drawn together, tend to form conclusions more extreme than any would conceive on their own. To prove this point, Harvard Law School professor Cass Sunstein and some colleagues conducted an experiment in which they divided liberals and conservatives into like-minded groups and had them deliberate on socially controversial issues like same-sex marriages and affirmative action. In most cases, the group settled on a more extreme view than that expressed by most individuals in interviews conducted prior to the discussions. The views of the individuals became more homogeneous after they spent time with their groups.[25] In the case of the Balanced Scorecard this lack of diversity could lead to mistaken assumptions that are amplified into objectives that prove to be wildly off the mark in terms of strategic relevance.

Team Member Roles and Responsibilities

Many academics and consultants suggest a Balanced Scorecard should be the exclusive domain of the executive team. In other words, for the Scorecard to prove successful, your senior leaders must solely craft it. There are exceptions to every rule, and I have witnessed successful Scorecard implementations led by teams comprised of mid-level staffers. However, their path to success was about as smooth as landing a Cessna in a snowstorm. To prove beneficial, your Balanced Scorecard must ultimately be owned by the senior leadership of your organization, and it is therefore vital to ensure, whenever possible, your Scorecard development team is comprised of senior-level people possessing the knowledge, credibility, and decision-making rights to build a tool that will be accepted and, more importantly, utilized by the ruling body. Let's look at the typical roles and responsibilities that should be present on your Balanced Scorecard team.

Executive Sponsor

In *The Heart of Change*, authors Dan Cohen and John Kotter observe, "Many change initiatives flounder because they're headed up by people who lack the time or the clout to accomplish what's necessary."[26] The Balanced Scorecard can easily suffer this fate without a strong executive sponsor skillfully orchestrating the process. Using the knowledge they've accumulated, the sponsor will provide invaluable insights into mission and strategy. He or she will also be relied upon to maintain constant communication with key stakeholder groups, such as Boards of Directors. As the senior member of the Balanced Scorecard team, the sponsor should also ensure the team receives the human and financial resources necessary for a successful implementation.

Perhaps most important, the sponsor must prove to be a tireless advocate and enthusiastic ambassador of the Balanced Scorecard. As we previously discussed, people watch what the boss watches and will carefully evaluate both the words and actions of your executive sponsor. To accomplish all of this and still have time for a day job, the sponsor must possess ample credibility within the organization. "Credibility derives from organizational achievements, trust, and the visible support of other top executives. Every time he's been asked to perform, he has always delivered."[27] The executive sponsor is not expected to provide full-time support to the Scorecard effort. However, attendance at Scorecard meetings and an open-door policy for the Scorecard team should be considered mandatory.

Balanced Scorecard Champion or Team Leader

Balanced Scorecard co-developer David Norton believes many Scorecard success stories share a common trait. Virtually every senior executive sponsor had a partner, "a change agent who played the lead role in introducing the Balanced Scorecard."[28] I would call this change agent the Balanced Scorecard champion, and suggest this role is perhaps the most vital ingredient of Scorecard success. If the executive sponsor paves the way for success, it's the champion who ensures the smooth flow of traffic on the Scorecard freeway. This individual will guide the Scorecard process both philosophically (providing thought leadership and best practices) and logistically (scheduling meetings, ensuring tasks are completed, etc.).

The role is a challenging one and demands a skilled communicator and facilitator. While the champion is fully expected to contribute to Scorecard development, he or she also has the often-challenging tasks of team building and conflict resolution. As with the executive sponsor, the champion should enjoy widespread credibility throughout the organization. However, the source of credibility does not necessarily need to emanate from a long history within the organization. Some very skilled champions are recruited from outside the ranks of current employees based on their Scorecard knowledge and expertise. This confers credibility of another sort—expert credibility, which is often in short supply at the outset of a Scorecard implementation. One very successful Scorecard client recruited a person from outside their industry to run the Balanced Scorecard program. This individual's track record of Scorecard success and their deep reservoir of tools and techniques helped the organization reap swift benefits from their implementation. Should you decide you'd prefer to have a current employee assume the role of Scorecard champion, don't be afraid to choose someone who will need to stretch into the role. Over the years I've witnessed tremendously successful Balanced Scorecard champions who were not members of the senior executive team. Some in fact were two or three levels removed from that lofty status. However, they more than compensated for any lack of hierarchical power with organizational knowledge, exceptional communication skills, and the enviable ability to liaise easily and comfortably with all levels of the organization.

The Balanced Scorecard champion should transition into the leadership of your Office of Strategy Management, which will be examined shortly. While the role is permanent, you can expect some variations in the key tasks over time. At various times the champion will act as missionary, consultant, point person to fight resistance, and chief of staff or general manger.[29]

Balanced Scorecard Team Members

Your executive sponsor and Balanced Scorecard champion will provide background, context for the Scorecard implementation, and subject-matter expertise. The job of the Scorecard team members is to translate that material into a working strategy map and Scorecard that effectively tells the story of your strategy. You'll rely on your team members to bring specialized knowledge of their functional areas and, if they are not senior leadership team members themselves, to liaise closely with their own senior leaders. Building support and momentum is a never-ending task of any Scorecard implementation. Team members must constantly communicate with their leaders—building support, sniffing out any possible resistance, and providing feedback to the larger Scorecard team. They should also identify resources within the organization that will prove valuable as the Scorecard development continues—for example, noting who controls key performance data.

During the implementation phase of the initiative expect your team members to devote approximately 25 percent of their time to this effort, although this number will vary depending on the intensity of your effort (number of meetings, pre-work requirements, etc.). Any potential team member who can offer only 5 to 10 percent of their time must be viewed with caution. While they may carry valuable knowledge of their particular area, this must be weighed against the very negative lack of participation in the effort.

The Balanced Scorecard represents a major departure in performance management for many organizations. Strategy, not financial controls, dictates the firm's direction, and the Scorecard creates a powerful new language for employee change. However, like any transformation this one has its share of roadblocks. The inclusion of an organizational change expert on the Scorecard team can mitigate many of the change-related issues that arise during the implementation. Any major change initiative will bring to the surface a number of concerns from those affected. For example, how will this change affect my routines and processes? What does the organization expect from me as a result of this change? Is this change even necessary? Your organizational change expert can work with your team and projected users of the Balanced Scorecard to investigate the root causes of any concerns and design solutions to reduce, and hopefully eliminate, any potentially serious threats to the Scorecard's success. The role is very important but not required as a full-time resource to the team. Draw the change expert in at regular intervals to review progress and issues. I urge you to pay close attention to this topic during your own implementation. You may feel it's soft stuff, but it's not the technology or the methodology that can cause these initiatives to fail, it's the people, every time! Exhibit 2.5 summarizes the roles and responsibilities of your Balanced Scorecard team.

Training Your Team

I don't know if it's a sudden thirst for knowledge or a classic midlife crisis, but recently I've become very interested in cars. Not just a typical urge characterized by the purchase of a sleek new sports car, but instead I've cultivated a desire to

Role	Responsibilities
Executive Sponsor	• Assumes ownership for the Balanced Scorecard implementation • Provides background information to the team on strategy and methodology • Maintains communication with senior management • Commits resources (both human and financial) to the team • Provides support and enthusiasm for the Balanced Scorecard throughout the organization
Balanced Scorecard Champion	• Coordinates meetings; plans, tracks, and reports team results to all audiences • Provides thought leadership on the Balanced Scorecard methodology to the team • Ensures all relevant background material is available to the team • Provides feedback to the executive sponsor and senior management • Facilitates the development of an effective team through coaching and support
Team Members	• Provide expert knowledge of business unit or functional operations • Inform and influence their respective senior executives • Act as Balanced Scorecard ambassadors within their unit or department • Act in the best interests of the business as a whole
Organizational Change Expert	• Increase awareness of organizational change issues • Investigate change-related issues affecting the Balanced Scorecard implementation • Work with the team to produce solutions mitigating change related risks

EXHIBIT 2.5 Balanced Scorecard Team Roles and Responsibilities

---

learn how cars work. Why do the brakes take us from 60 to 0 in a few seconds? How exactly is power delivered from the engine to the four wheels? These and many other questions appeared seemingly from nowhere and I was suddenly gripped with a desire to answer them.

To assist in my quest, I bought an inexpensive project car, one I felt I could learn with, and then enlisted the aid of a good friend who is a car junkie, the kind of guy who frequently wears a T-shirt that says, "Will Talk Cars With Anyone." We decided on our first project, and in anticipation of our work I read portions of a how-to book, watched a few videos online, and convinced myself I was well prepared. The appointed day arrived and we assembled in the garage, popped the car's hood, and my friend handed me a wrench. I eagerly bent over the engine, paused, and was suddenly overtaken by the sinking feeling that I didn't have a clue what to do.

After reflecting on this sorry incident I realized the same thing could occur with organizations implementing the Balanced Scorecard. They get excited about the prospects of developing a Scorecard, are tantalized by the many promised benefits, and decide the time is right to dive in. A team is formed and some of the more enthusiastic participants read parts of a book on the Scorecard, peruse articles on the Internet, and may even join an online forum or two, exchanging opinions with other devotees. With that training completed, they feel they're ready to take on the Balanced Scorecard challenge. They bring their team together for the initial Scorecard workshop, and then, when it comes time to create the tool, they're just like me looking over the bewildering labyrinth of hoses, pumps, and blocks in my engine compartment. Instead of a wrench in their hand, they've got a scented marker and are standing in front of an empty flip chart wondering just exactly what they're supposed to do next.

It doesn't matter whether it's car repair, implementing the Balanced Scorecard, or becoming adept at origami—interest, reading, and hope only get you so far. Granted, all three are necessary, but they're definitely not sufficient. When pursuing any meaningful endeavor, we must first study the craft and master its fundamentals. Again, it's no different than my desire to understand the inner workings of my car—I thought the cursory scan of a book, some YouTube videos, and a sincere desire would transform me into a mechanic. Not so. It takes time and an ongoing commitment to the task at hand. In my case, I needed to roll up my sleeves and spend a lot more time getting my hands dirty if I expected to really unlock the secrets of how my car works.

For the majority of employees within your organization, the team you assemble will be the embodiment of the Balanced Scorecard. If the members don't appear as knowledgeable and credible sources of information you can be certain that skepticism for the initiative will increase. Some team members may come to the implementation with a background in performance management and Balanced Scorecard concepts, while others may be experiencing their first exposure to these topics. Either way, to ensure a level playing field for the entire team, you have to invest heavily in up-front training. I'm a strong believer in the power of training to improve business results, and I'm not alone. I'm a strong believer in the power of training to improve business results. Well-trained and dedicated employees are a major sustainable source of competitive strength.

Start your education efforts by preparing and distributing a comprehensive primer on the subjects of performance management and the Balanced Scorecard. These topics are quite mature, and a rich and abundant supply of literature is available. There are literally hundreds of articles and white papers to choose from, so narrow your search by including any documents that specifically reference your industry or implementation focus (corporate wide versus business unit, for example). A number of good quality books have been published on the Balanced Scorecard, and you should consider providing at least one to each of your team members. Your team will also benefit from attending one of the many excellent conferences on performance management and the Balanced Scorecard. Again, you have the opportunity to tailor your training with your implementation by choosing an event focused on your industry type or implementation plan. They provide a very valuable exchange of ideas, challenges, and solutions.

Forgive the pitch, but I suggest a consultant or other expert in the Balanced Scorecard field conduct your initial training session. The last thing your fledgling initiative needs at this critical juncture is someone stammering at the front of the room grasping painfully to provide answers to commonly asked questions. A knowledgeable guide in this area will typically structure a training agenda that includes the following elements: background on performance management, drivers of this topic in the modern organizational world, Balanced Scorecard fundamentals including strategy maps and performance measures, success stories, and hands-on exercises to apply the learning. Let's spend a moment on that last component of the agenda: hands-on exercises to apply the learning. At the conclusion of my Scorecard education sessions I challenge the participants to create a strategy map for a fictitious organization. What matters is not getting the right answer but demonstrating the ability to think critically about what objectives are best suited to tell the story of the case company's strategy. It's not uncommon when introducing the task to have some attendees suggest they'd be better suited using their own company for the exercise, thereby simultaneously enhancing their knowledge while creating an actual strategy map for their firm. In my experience this is not a good idea because the focus of the participants, who are mostly Scorecard neophytes at this point, is diverted from applying what they've learned to solve a specific problem related to their company's operations.

Continuing with the theme of learning by doing, I would suggest your team develop a strategy map and set of Balanced Scorecard measures specifically for the implementation. The purpose of this exercise is two-fold. First a pragmatic reason: The strategy map will act as a powerful communication tool to the implementation's stakeholders, and performance measures serve to keep the team focused on the critical tasks at hand. Your team will require yardsticks to gauge their implementation progress, and the Balanced Scorecard provides a powerful means for accomplishing this task. Second, developing the objectives and measures for their Scorecard gives team members a unique opportunity to engage in the mental gymnastics required to create an effective Scorecard. Who are our customers? What are their requirements? At what processes must we excel? What competencies do we require? These are all questions your team

Develop a Balanced Scorecard Meeting All Stakeholder Expectations

Strategy Map	Measures
Customer C3—Maintain Customer Satisfaction C1—Increase BSC Knowledge C2—Reduce Revisions	C3—Executive satisfaction with Balanced Scorecard C2—Number of revisions per Scorecard draft C1—Percentage of surveyed employees aware of the Balanced Scorecard implementation
Internal Process I1—Share Knowledge I2—Achieve Milestones	I2—Percentage of planned tasks completed on time I1—Number of BSC presentations given (all audiences)
Learning and Growth E2—Increase Skills E3—Access to Tools E1—Ensure Team Involvement	E3—Percentage of identified resources available to the team (technology, BSC literature, etc.) E2—Percentage of team members attending advanced BSC training events E1—Percentage of team meetings with 100 percent attendance
Financial F1—Fiscal Stability	F3—Variance to initiative budget

EXHIBIT 2.6   A Sample Balanced Scorecard for Your Implementation Team

will be posing to others in your organization very soon, so isn't it perfectly appropriate that they go through the process themselves? Exhibit 2.6 shows a sample team strategy map and set of Balanced Scorecard measures. Notice that the financial perspective represents a constraint (i.e., budget dollars for the initiative) rather than an overall goal as it would in most profit-seeking enterprises. This is a good demonstration to the team of the Balanced Scorecard's flexibility.

A strong Balanced Scorecard team, equipped with knowledge and enthusiasm, is vital to your execution efforts, but once the Scorecard is actually created, you'll need someone or some group to run the program on an ongoing basis. The Balanced Scorecard isn't like an app that you load on to your phone, and—presto—you're good to go. It requires a guiding hand to ensure it becomes ingrained in the fabric of your organization. That guiding hand takes the form of an Office of Strategy Management, which you'll learn about in the next section. Of the team members we've discussed thus far, typically only the Balanced Scorecard champion will be part of this new office.

 ## MANAGING THE BALANCED SCORECARD ON AN ONGOING BASIS: THE OFFICE OF STRATEGY MANAGEMENT

As the practice of commerce has evolved, particularly over the past 150 years or so, organizations have made several internal adaptations to meet the formidable challenges they faced. Financial considerations have always been central to organizations, but as the stewardship function has grown exponentially, we've seen the advent of the chief financial officer (CFO) to track the complex web of debits and credits while complying with ever-changing statutes and regulations. Similarly, as technology has transformed the way in which we work and live, chief information officers (CIOs) have become critical contributors at the strategy table of virtually all organizations. Cast your glance anywhere in the modern organization and you'll discover similar instances of specialization emerging: chief knowledge officers, chief talent officers, chief marketing officers, and so on.

Most companies of a certain size will employ many of the functional specialists outlined above and, in addition, will house a group known as strategic planning. While the specific duties of a strategic planning function can vary tremendously, given the enormous number of definitions spanning the strategy spectrum, as a common thread most will concentrate on scanning the environment, seeking new information, and using their findings to help inform the organization's response to the changes it faces. The focus is on strategy formation. Strategy execution, however, is left to the entire organization; the responsibility for making the strategy happen, seeing it transformed into living, breathing reality each day is diffused among everyone occupying a cubicle, office, or suite within the firm. This is not surprising because strategy execution is everyone's job and requires cross-functional collaboration to occur. But as we all know, simply willing the silos to disperse and have people come together in a spirit of strategic harmony doesn't happen through slogans or speeches; the process must be managed precisely and with as much rigor as every other specialty for organizations to achieve any benefit from their strategic planning efforts.

A new discipline has emerged within organizations seeking to bridge this strategy formation and execution chasm: the Office of Strategy Management

(OSM). Originally introduced by Scorecard creators Kaplan and Norton through their observation of highly successful Balanced Scorecard companies, this novel approach applies the age-old wisdom of specialization to the challenge of executing strategy by resting in one group the dual responsibilities of facilitating the development of strategy and shepherding its execution, primarily through the Balanced Scorecard system.[30]

The Office of Strategy Management is the moniker pinned to the function by Kaplan and Norton, but in practice I've seen many descriptions, including: Office of Performance Excellence, Performance Management Office, or Office of Transformation. As we discussed when reviewing terminology in Chapter 1, words do matter, and you should attempt to create a name for the function that resonates with your unique culture. More important than the name, however, is putting this office in place. Simply put, this may be the single most important enabler of Balanced Scorecard success—having someone run the program once the initial building blocks are in place. Without it, you can almost certainly count on organizational sclerosis to appear in the form of urgent priorities, pressing problems, and the thousand and one other things that have to get done instead of actively managing strategy. The ironic thing is, of course, that all of the fires we fight day in and day out keep us busy and feeling productive, but for the most part they do nothing to move us forward along the path of execution. Strategy execution, like every function noted above (finance, HR, IT, etc.), must be a standalone discipline with resources allotted and accountability clear. I've given this advice to every client I've ever worked with and I can say unequivocally that those who heeded it have profited more from their Scorecard investment than those who have not—and I'm not talking about slight improvements, but rather orders of magnitude.

Let's take a closer look at this function and explore how you may use it within your organization. As you will discover, the OSM could be considered an umbrella agency for many of the Balanced Scorecard tasks discussed throughout this book.

FUNCTIONS OF THE OFFICE OF STRATEGY MANAGEMENT

Successful execution of strategy requires each person in the organization, from every discipline, to combine their efforts in a unified push towards a common cause. Coordinating that effort is the domain of the OSM. While in the past, diffusion of efforts frequently transpired with no single group orchestrating the strategy execution process, the OSM takes responsibility for the complex and coordinated effort required to execute the organization's strategy. Collaboration and integration aren't left to chance, but are carefully managed under the auspices of the OSM. Let's examine some of the office's core functions.

- **Change Management:** At its very core, strategy is about doing something different, choosing a different set of activities and processes than your rivals, and executing them flawlessly. Therefore, the notions of strategy and change are inextricably linked, since strategy introduces novelty in the form of a new organizational direction. As we all know, change is a difficult concept to operationalize for most organizations. As Machiavelli reminds in his classic work *The Prince*, "It ought to be remembered that there is nothing more difficult to take in hand, more perilous to conduct, or more uncertain in its success, than to take the lead in the introduction of a new order of things."[31] As perilous as the task may be, it must be accomplished should organizations hope to reap the rewards of differentiating strategies. Therefore, among the first responsibilities of the OSM is change management. OSM staffers must outline the rationale for the change, discuss how it will be implemented, clarify expectations, and, most vitally, clearly establish what benefits await employees willing to accept the change.
- **Strategy Formation and Planning:** The OSM doesn't have responsibility for crafting the organization's strategy; that vital task is better left to leaders from across the organization's functions. However, the office facilitates the process through a number of potential responsibilities, including: gathering relevant strategy inputs such as environmental information, conducting scenario planning, facilitating strategic dialog and debate, and orchestrating the strategy timetable. To effectively execute this responsibility it is critical that the OSM work closely with the senior-executive team.
- **Balanced Scorecard Coordination:** An obvious role of the OSM is custodian of the organization's Balanced Scorecard process and its attendant responsibilities. Members of the OSM team must demonstrate their strategic acumen as they work closely with the executive team to develop the organization's Balanced Scorecard. After the Scorecard is created, much of the OSM's work is still to be done: Scorecard training throughout the enterprise, facilitation of Scorecard result meetings, guardianship of the information systems used to display and disseminate results, and cascading the Scorecard to lower levels of the organization, to name but a few.

- **Strategic Communication:** Unfortunately, gold stars for communication are not in the immediate future for the vast majority of companies. When it comes to sharing information the rule of thumb for many organizations appears to be: too little, too late, and top down. In the era of scientific management at the turn of the twentieth century this oversight could be readily ignored; employees of that epoch generally required little in the form of communication to perform their laborious and repetitive tasks. The knowledge economy of the twenty-first century, however, demands more from our leaders. Should they expect to win both the hearts and minds of their staff they must engage in virtually constant communication of the building blocks of success: mission, vision, strategy, and the necessity of change. Working with other constituents across the organization (such as corporate communications), the OSM should coordinate communication activities centering on strategy. A key tenet of this work is the use of many and varied communication devices, including town hall meetings, presentations, and e-learning opportunities, all segmented by audience.

- **Alignment:** Inconsistency is a ticking time bomb in many organizations, just waiting to explode and destroy any hope of success. Frequently the inconsistencies, while philosophically simple, are profound in their damaging effects. For example: constantly espousing the value of team work but rewarding individual performance, or touting the critical nature of innovation but refusing to provide budget dollars for experimentation. Credibility is potentially the most valuable currency possessed by leaders, and when they say one thing and do another it is substantially eroded, leaving employees scratching their heads as to why they should expend one ounce of precious energy when they know priorities are as stable as leaves blowing in the wind. The OSM must ensure that all critical organizational processes are in alignment with the strategy, thereby eliminating the possibility of inconsistencies. One of the most vital links is that between strategy and performance management, including personal-development planning and compensation. Human capital is the real driver of the knowledge economy and every organization must ensure this most-scarce resource is aligned with their strategy.

- **Initiative Management:** For many organizations, a high payback on their OSM investment is received when they actively manage the initiative process. Most truly strategic initiatives are cross-functional in nature, frequently requiring collaboration among business units, information technology, and other entities, and thus must be managed in a cross-functional manner. One telecommunications company client recognized the value of this approach. In the past, their strategic initiatives were created from a bottom-up build, culminating in a broad list of initiatives spanning the company's units. The Balanced Scorecard ushered in a new day in the development and reporting of strategic initiatives, featuring the creation of a cross-functional planning council. With the Balanced Scorecard in place, this cross-functional group facilitated a two-day session during which business unit Scorecards and accompanying initiatives were presented with the aim of determining strategic alignment, discovering organizational synergies, and calculating resource requirements. The council sessions proved to be a highly effective forum for discussing initiatives, and have taken permanent root in the company in the form of monthly conference calls during which critical initiatives are reviewed. Owners submit updates on their initiatives in advance of the call, and a fixed amount of time is allocated for a review of milestones, budgets, and so on. Based on the discussion, strategic initiative updates are prepared for the executive team who will discuss them further during their meetings.

- **Governance Coordination:** We've undoubtedly entered a new era of corporate governance in the wake of the many scandals that have plagued the business world for the past several years. To fulfill their significant, and now highly regulated, responsibilities, boards of directors (and other external stakeholders) require information that goes beyond high-level graphs and abstractions and provides a penetrating view inside the organization's strategy and value-creating mechanisms. Going a step further, management professor and governance catalyst Edward Lawler has suggested boards need a Balanced Scorecard to illuminate corporate performance: "Boards need indicators of how customers and employees feel they are being treated . . . how the company operates . . . about the culture of the organization."[32] The OSM has the opportunity to break new organizational ground in this regard by working with the board and other external stakeholders to proactively determine their information needs and meet them in a timely and efficient fashion.

- **Risk Management:** In addition to the many examples of corporate malfeasance over the past several years, the world has also witnessed a number of high-profile calamities (the BP oil spill, global financial meltdown, and Fukushima nuclear disaster) that clearly highlighted a lack of thorough risk assessment and planning. As a result of these dismal events, risk management has taken on greater prominence, and the OSM, with its connection to both strategy and execution, is a logical candidate to facilitate the process of risk identification, mitigation, and management.

▪ **Performance Review Administration:** Strategy must constantly be monitored and tested in real time to determine its efficacy, and the strategy execution review meeting is the setting for this learning laboratory. The OSM coordinates the overall performance and strategy review process by determining the timetable, developing the agenda, facilitating the discussion, and ensuring follow-up actions are documented and completed.

Initial Considerations in Establishing a Strategic Management Office

There exists in the field of social psychology a phenomenon referred to as diffusion of responsibility, which often manifests itself in scenes of personal tragedy; for example, we've all heard of people suffering from heart attacks on bustling city streets only to be ignored as they cry out for help. That's diffusion of responsibility in action—we all assume that someone else will jump in and lend a hand. In less dramatic fashion, this phenomenon is played out in the halls of organizations each and every day as various functions work independently of one another, often suboptimizing overall results. The OSM can help you overcome this deficiency by acting as connective tissue that binds together the many processes with a stake in the strategy. But where to begin? Two initial, critical considerations are staffing and areas of emphasis. Let's examine each briefly.

In order to fulfill its vital role the OSM must have a seat at the executive table, or at the very least report to a senior executive within the organization. The office will be called upon to work across organizational boundaries and, if necessary, must have the ability to play the position power card to bring disparate organizational audiences together. As for the size of the OSM, the number of staff typically varies depending on the size of the organization and the responsibilities assigned to the office.

Creating and managing an office of strategy management where none existed in the past is a significant undertaking, and is best considered from an evolutionary frame of mind. It will prove virtually impossible (given logistical challenges for one) to simultaneously master each of the functions noted in the section above. Therefore, organizations must determine their greatest pain points and strategically administer aid in the form of OSM interventions. For example, communications may have been nonexistent in your organization in the past, and therefore among the first-year imperatives of the OSM may be the creation and administration of a strategic communication plan. Of course, in order to make strategy execution a core competency, each of the functions must be attended to; as with all things it is ultimately a matter of balance.

YOUR BALANCED SCORECARD DEVELOPMENT PLAN

From time to time my phone rings with a request to help turn around a troubled Balanced Scorecard implementation. As you know, challenges in executing change initiatives can stem from any number of sources, but in one large non-profit that contacted me the culprit was a distinct lack of planning. This agency was as unprepared from a planning standpoint as it was enthusiastic about the Scorecard. Unfortunately, the interest and exuberance they felt for the tool failed to compensate for their lack of organization. Virtually every meeting was slowed to a merciless crawl to discuss process questions. Team members and other stakeholders were naturally curious about the next steps in the process, but the leaders of the Scorecard implementation had barely thought through the current meeting, let alone the entire implementation journey. This lack of planning significantly slowed what could otherwise have been a very swift and successful implementation.

As with any major initiative you'll require a carefully crafted development plan to guide the work of your Balanced Scorecard team. Every organization is different when it comes to planning and executing significant change efforts. Some feel a highly detailed plan that encompasses thousands of lines in Microsoft Project is the only way to capture all the necessary elements of the work. I recall arriving at the offices of one new client, barely completing introductions to the Scorecard team, and having a phonebook-sized plan thrust upon my lap. Others use less formal means, outlining only the most critical tasks and tracking them on MS Excel or Word documents. This section will outline the key steps to develop your Balanced Scorecard based on experience and research. When creating your own plan, develop one that will be accepted by your team and sponsor based on the prevailing culture of your organization. The important thing is to include all the necessary elements of the implementation. Whether you display them as big chunks or decompose them into a thousand steps is up to you.

The Planning Phase

Before you begin the work of building a Balanced Scorecard you must lay the groundwork for the implementation ahead. This chapter was written to help you do just that. To summarize, the planning phase includes the following steps:

- Step 1—Develop a guiding rationale for your Balanced Scorecard.
- Step 2—Determine the appropriate organizational unit.

- Step 3—Secure executive sponsorship.
- Step 4—Form and train your Balanced Scorecard team.
- Step 5—Formulate your implementation plan.
- Step 6—Develop a communication strategy and plan for your Balanced Scorecard implementation.

Clients sometimes tease us consultants because we tend to answer many questions with, "It depends." But this response is often necessary since much of the work we perform is a function of many variables often beyond our control. So it is with the caveat of "it depends" that I suggest timing for this and all phases of the implementation plan. If you have a full-time Balanced Scorecard champion leading the events outlined above you should be able to accomplish them within four to six weeks. I urge you to take the necessary time to successfully complete these actions. Nothing is stopping you from developing a Balanced Scorecard without a communication plan or clear objectives for the implementation, but rest assured your efforts will be severely compromised without these stakes in the ground. When we discuss the learning and growth perspective of the Scorecard, I'll describe it as the enabler of the other three perspectives. The planning phase of the initiative is similar in that it enables the development work to follow by clearly articulating what you plan to achieve, with whom, why, and how.

The Development Phase

Consider the steps presented below as a framework for your development of the Balanced Scorecard. As noted in the opening to this section, every organization is unique and will want to emphasize different aspects of the Scorecard process. One of the many benefits of the Scorecard, one that has greatly contributed to its longevity and unabated growth, is its flexibility to adapt to the constraints of every organization. Take advantage of that flexibility when constructing your plan.

You will note that a number of executive workshops are built in throughout the process. The importance of executive consensus throughout the development phase cannot be overemphasized, hence the inclusion of these checkpoints. However, it may prove virtually impossible to convene your senior-management team this frequently. If group meetings are not possible, ensure your team members are consistently reporting to their home executives with team progress, and gathering feedback from the executive that can be used to guide the future direction of the team's work.

Step One—Gather and distribute background material. The Balanced Scorecard is a tool that describes strategy. In order to fulfill this promise your team must have ample access to background material on the organization's mission, vision, strategy, competitive position, value chain, and employee core competencies. Use internal resources such as your strategy, human resources, finance, and marketing groups to assist you with this effort. If you're publicly traded, many resources are at your disposal to garner information on past performance. Press releases, stories in the business media, analyst reports, and so on all provide valuable information.

Step Two—Provide Balanced Scorecard education. At this point in the process you have steeped your team in the fundamentals of the Balanced Scorecard but the tool still represents a great black hole to many employees, including perhaps even the senior-management team. Plug this gap early and effectively with a comprehensive Scorecard training session designed to outline the challenges leading you to select the Scorecard, fundamental principles of the model, success stories, and how you plan to guide the implementation. Invite as many people as you can comfortably fit into a venue for this first training session—this is no time to practice education snobbery; you need to garner the commitment and support of every employee, explaining to them what the Balanced Scorecard is all about.

Step Three—Develop or confirm the mission, vision, and strategy. Based on the information gathered in step one you should be able to generate a consensus of where your organization rests in terms of these critical items. If you do not have one or all of these Scorecard raw materials you may have to work with your executive team to develop them. While all are important, it is critical to have a quantified vision that you can later decompose through the achievement of Balanced Scorecard targets. Chapter 3 provides a detailed review of each of these elements of an effective Scorecard.

Step Four—Conduct executive interviews. I've previously stressed the importance of executive involvement in the Scorecard process, and thus it should come as no surprise that involving the entire executive team in the process at an early juncture is an absolute must. During this interview with senior management the team will gather feedback on the organization's competitive position, key success factors for the future, and possible Scorecard objectives and measures.

Step Five—Develop your strategy map. Armed with a solid working knowledge of the Balanced Scorecard's core principles, having reviewed copious amounts of background materials, and possessing years of combined industry knowledge and experience, your team is well prepared to construct the organization's strategy map of performance objectives. The one-page graphical representation of your strategy will describe and powerfully communicate to everyone in the company what is absolutely critical to your success in each of the four Balanced Scorecard perspectives. We'll immerse ourselves deeply in the development of strategy maps during Chapter 5.

Step Five (a)—Executive workshop. Gain senior management consensus on the strategy map developed by the team. Capture and incorporate any recommendations from the executive group.

Step Five (b)—Gather employee feedback. Ultimately, you expect your Balanced Scorecard to provide information that allows all employees to determine how their day-to-day actions link to the organization's strategic plan. Therefore, you need to poll your managers and employees to ensure they feel you've captured in the strategy map the critical elements of value to your whole organization.

Step Six—Develop performance measures. Returning to the ancestral homeland of the Balanced Scorecard, which was created many years ago as a measurement system, your team will translate each of the objectives on the strategy map into metrics you can track to provide insight into the execution of your strategy and establish accountability throughout the company. Chapter 6 is devoted to the topic of performance measures.

Step Six (a)—Executive workshop. The process begins to become real when actual hard-hitting metrics are laid on the table for executive review. It is vital that all members of the executive team commit themselves to the measures brought forward.

Step Six (b)—Gather employee feedback. This represents an optional step. While you desire employee feedback at every turn of the Scorecard wheel, ultimately senior management must own the highest-level performance measures, and therefore you would expect their stickiness factor to be off the charts. Consider using this opportunity to explain to your staff precisely why the particular measures you plan to use were chosen.

Step Seven—Establish Targets and Prioritize Initiatives. Without a target for each of your measures, you'll have no way of knowing whether improvement efforts are yielding acceptable results. The data from your metrics provides you with only half the picture. A target gives meaning to measure results by affording a point of comparison. However, setting targets may be among the most challenging aspects of your entire implementation. Many organizations have little actual practice or techniques for the establishment of meaningful performance targets. Additionally, you'll require a small portfolio of strategic initiatives designed to bring the targets to fruition. Chapter 6 explores these topics in greater depth, providing advice on setting targets and methods to prioritize competing initiatives.

Step Eight—Gather data for your first Balanced Scorecard report. Dare to be bold and proclaim that within 60 days of developing your performance measures you will be conducting your first management meeting with the Balanced Scorecard at the helm. To do this will, of course, require gathering the data necessary to supply that initial report. You may be thinking, "We'll never have all the data!" and you are probably correct, since most new Scorecard adopters will be missing at least a portion of the data for performance metrics as they ramp up their reporting efforts. However, don't let that stop you from the many significant benefits that can accrue from discussing the measures you do have: focus, alignment, and improved resource-allocation decisions to name but a few.

Step Nine—Hold your first Balanced Scorecard meeting. There is an old joke about a man named Gus who was so deeply in debt that he goes to church each day and prays to win the lottery. "Dear Lord," he pleads, "Please let me win the lottery to get out of debt and I'll be a good servant for the rest of my life." A week goes by and no lottery win. Gus goes back to church, "Please Lord, please let me win the lottery and I'll be a good and faithful servant." He leaves feeling confident the money is about to flow in, but another lottery draw comes and goes with no win. So back to church Gus stomps, pleading once again, "Lord, I've said my prayers, why haven't you let me win the lottery?" With that there is a rollicking clap of thunder, the Lord appears before Gus and says, "Gus, meet me halfway . . . buy a ticket." Some Scorecard implementing organizations remind me of Gus. They make the same mistake by talking a great game about the alignment and focus they are going to derive from the tool but failing to achieve it because they simply refuse to place the Scorecard at the center of their management meeting and reporting agenda, which is the only means by which they'll achieve their desired result. Repeat after me: To execute strategy, we must discuss strategy. Getting to your first Balanced Scorecard report should be the number-one priority in the initial stages of your implementation.

Step Ten—Develop the ongoing Balanced Scorecard implementation plan. The steps outlined above will get you from point zero to the development of a Balanced Scorecard that is primarily a communication and measurement tool. Once the system is established you will likely decide to link it to key management processes within the firm. Those linkages should be charted in detail, with both timing and specific steps necessary clearly documented.

Getting from Step One in the planning phase to Step Ten in the development phase can take anywhere from 3 to 12 months—I've seen both. The amount of time your organization expends on the implementation will *depend* (there is that word again!) on a number of factors: commitment of the executive team, allocation of resources to the project, the size and complexity of the organization, and organizational readiness for a change of this magnitude. Exhibit 2.7 displays a possible timeline for both the planning and development phases, with special emphasis on the word *possible.* As discussed above, your timing will be impacted by several factors and may not follow the linear approach suggested in the exhibit.

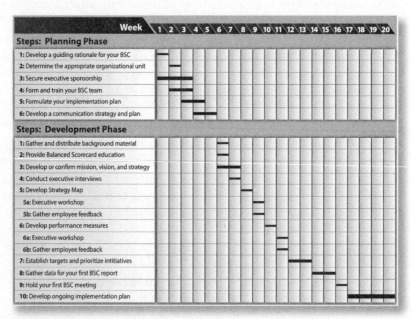

EXHIBIT 2.7   Balanced Scorecard Implementation Timeline

You may be wondering, "Is there a *preferred* amount of time for developing the Balanced Scorecard?" As I noted above, you have to bend to your unique circumstances when building the system, and be flexible based upon what is happening in your world. Having said that, I do advocate for creating the Scorecard as swiftly as you can in order to generate a much-needed driver in any organization: momentum. This story I came across recently illustrates this point nicely: A ceramics teacher announced on the opening day of class that he was dividing the participants into two groups. All of those on the left side of the room would be graded solely on the *quantity* of work they produced, while those on the right would be graded solely on its *quality*. His procedure was simple: on the final day of class he would bring in a scale and weigh the work of the quantity group. Fifty pounds of pots rated an *A*, forty pounds a *B*, and so on. Those being graded on quality, however, needed to produce only one pot—albeit a perfect one—to get an *A*. Come grading time a curious fact emerged: the works of highest quality were all produced by the group being graded for quantity. It seems that while the quantity group was busily churning out piles of work and learning from their mistakes, the quality group had sat theorizing about perfection, and in the end had little more to show for their efforts than grandiose theories and a pile of dead clay.[33] Your Scorecard initiative can suffer the same fate of paralysis by analysis if you search endlessly for the perfect objectives and measures, rather than create a Scorecard that represents your strategic hypothesis and move quickly to test assumptions and learn about the strategy.

 ## BE FAST, BUT BE THOUGHTFUL IN YOUR APPROACH

It's well documented that organizations struggle with change. In one of many studies on the topic, Michael Beer and Nitin Nohria of Harvard Business School estimate failure rates as high as 70 percent.[34] Of course you don't need a couple of Harvard professors to tell you what you've most likely experienced many times during your working life. So what, or who, is to blame for the high flameout rate of change? Many experts point the finger at the organization's employees, who we often assume are weary from past efforts, and generally skeptical of anything that comes down from the executive floor. A typical lament I hear from executives is, "If only our employees would come around, accept the change and understand how it benefits the company, everything would work out." But is it really the rank and file who are responsible for the glut of change failures plaguing organizations in every corner of the world?

A recent conversation with a client implementing the Balanced Scorecard in a large public-sector organization has me rethinking this basic assumption.

When discussing what I considered to be best practice change principles with this client, I provided tip after tip about how to win over those on the front lines, including using varied communication mediums, getting everyone involved, defining the WIIFM (what's in it for me) message, and many other nuggets gained from more than 20 years in the field. He nodded his head throughout, but when I finished he offered something I think all of us tend to overlook in change management initiatives—the unintentional sabotage of well-intentioned leaders.

People ascend to leadership for many reasons: knowledge of the organization and its markets, the ability to craft a compelling vision, and often through the ability to deftly negotiate office politics. Smart and savvy executives, those who have been around the organizational block more than a few times, not only possess the intellectual skills necessary to lead, but experience has taught them how to run through the organizational minefield relatively unscathed. It is those leaders who may unintentionally sabotage change efforts, including the Balanced Scorecard.

When an organization introduces a new program, it's not uncommon for these seasoned leaders to dive in headfirst, forge ahead at light speed, and expect everyone below to follow suit. They value speed as paramount, look for quick wins, but see a structured-implementation approach as potentially limiting. If problems do arise in the chain of command above them they can maneuver through the organizational obstacle course thanks to experience, knowledge, and power.

In the case of a Balanced Scorecard initiative, this need for speed can manifest itself in a leader's efforts to have just a few individuals craft a strategy map for the entire organization, do so in one short meeting, and have the document ready for organizational use the following day. But when velocity of development is the top priority for a Scorecard effort, the product that emerges tends to miss the mark in several ways: its contents don't reflect the careful thought, debate, and dialog necessary to create a truly strategic document, it can be overly simplistic or unduly complex, and perhaps most importantly it won't generate the buy-in of those responsible for executing the objectives.

As I shared in the preceding section, there is little doubt that creating momentum is vital to any change effort, but most initiatives (Balanced Scorecard included) require a certain amount of seasoning and review before being able to serve as a key tool in decision making. Additionally, the Scorecard, again as with all change programs, requires a steady and structured approach if you hope to achieve optimal benefits from its use. Employees throughout the organization must be able to clearly grasp how the Scorecard fits into the larger context of the organization's journey; how it helps transform strategy into reality, and guides day-to-day actions they'll take.

What is most important for results-driven leaders to recognize is that structure not only serves a valuable purpose in guiding the implementation, but also acts as a soothing balm for employees not quite prepared to journey into the unknown represented by the initiative. As with all things, a balanced approach is required when implementing the Scorecard system, one that recognizes both the imperative to get things done quickly and the importance of a well thought-out roadmap for success.

DEVELOPING A COMMUNICATION PLAN TO SUPPORT YOUR BALANCED SCORECARD INITIATIVE

Communication: A Vital Link to Success

How do you feel about the communication that takes place within your company? What's your opinion of the effort that's expended on communication? Any better? Most organizations feel they do a decent job of the latter, exerting effort on communication, but aren't pleased with the overall results. Neither, apparently, are employees. In a Harris Interactive poll of 23,000 workers, only 17 percent felt their organization fostered open communication that is respectful of differing opinions and that results in new and better ideas.[35]

Needless to say this is an enormous problem since new and better ideas are the currency of today's organizational success, and as noted above their development is a direct product of effective communication. Speaking on the essential role of communication, Peter Drucker once said that the most important thing an organization can do is "to build itself around information and communication instead of around hierarchy."[36]

Before we go any further, I have to relate to you this story that is very indicative of the state of sorry communication that exists in many organizations. Standing in line for a flight I overheard two people behind me talking about recent job experiences. It didn't take long for them to note some pretty significant weaknesses with previous employers. Of course the usual suspects were bandied about: pay, benefits, and working conditions, but for one of them it was the people running the ship that caused him to make the leap to greener pastures. As he put it, "They didn't know what they were doing. . . . there was no leadership, literally. They called themselves 'Leadegement,' leadership and management. Any time you have to make up a word you know how *Dilbert*-esque the situation is!" As a consultant for the past 15 years or so, and a long-time corporate employee before that, I thought I'd heard it all, but "Leadegement!" Never before, and I hope never again! I'm sure this leadership/management team had their hearts in the right place when they concocted this unique moniker, but to their employees it was probably seen as just the latest in a long series of smoke-and-mirror attempts to keep them utterly confused.

Why Communication Is Critical to Your Balanced Scorecard

Quick quiz: The system that is the Balanced Scorecard serves what three primary purposes? I'm sure you recall—without referring back to Chapter 1—they are:

1. Communication
2. Measurement
3. Strategic management

All of these represent significant changes in how the organization gauges its success. Hence, the Balanced Scorecard, more than anything else, represents a change initiative. And we all know change is tough, really tough, especially when you're introducing something that is potentially threatening. For those affected by the change, it can be unsettling, frightening, confusing, and painful. In other words, something to be avoided at all costs. Change efforts struggle for many reasons, but fundamentally the vast majority of organizations struggle with change because of their inability to answer these five questions on the part of those undergoing the change.

1. What do you want me to do?
2. What's in it for me?
3. How will this change affect me?
4. What will you do to help me make the change?
5. How am I doing?

Communication planning holds the key to unlocking many of the answers. A well-conceived and well-delivered communication strategy and plan gives you the opportunity to proactively shape your message, ultimately making change if not pleasant, at least palatable. This is the chance to sell your message of change, improvement, and success to all your stakeholders. Jack Welch, the former CEO of General Electric, is someone who knows a thing or two about what it takes to make change happen within organizations. He suggests—no, bellows—"I learned that for any big idea you had to sell, sell, and sell to move the needle at all."[37]

A Guiding Rationale for Your Communication Plan

By now you should be getting the impression that I take the idea of determining the reasons for doing something pretty seriously: a guiding rationale for your Balanced Scorecard program, for your training sessions, and now for your communication plan. Whatever you're doing, the first step should always be a careful and critical exploration of why you're engaging in the activity in the first place. What is the purpose, and what are your over-riding objectives? This is especially critical for communication planning, since this process centers on the delivery of key messages and information that can literally make or break the success of your implementation.

The guiding objectives you select for your communication plan should, of course, represent your unique situation. The list below contains a number of objectives commonly cited by organizations when they develop communication strategies and plans.

■ Build awareness of the Balanced Scorecard at all levels of the organization.
■ Provide education on key Balanced Scorecard concepts to all audiences.
■ Generate the engagement and commitment of key stakeholders in the implementation.
■ Encourage participation in the process.
■ Generate enthusiasm for the Balanced Scorecard.
■ Ensure team results are disseminated rapidly and effectively.

    At Nova Scotia Power, a Canadian electrical utility, the Balanced Scorecard team used this vision to guide their communication efforts: "To present the concepts of the Balanced Scorecard to the key constituents involved in both sponsoring and providing input to the implementation, and to provide all involved with regular updates regarding the team's progress during the implementation."[38] This simple statement provided the basis for all future communication efforts during the rollout. Another client stated their guiding communication principles this way: The objective of this plan is to develop a communications and education program for:

■ Users—Those who use the balanced scorecard as a management tool.

- Developers—Those in the process of developing a Balanced Scorecard based on their operating company's scorecard and the scorecard one level above them.
- Employees—Those employees not actively involved in developing or measuring against a balanced scorecard.

Setting objectives for the communication plan will often lead you to the establishment of a theme or metaphor you can use to creatively trademark your overall Balanced Scorecard implementation. Some people like slogans and themes, others think they're hokey and convey little if any value. Whatever your opinion, there is little doubt that themes are colorful, and often memorable. And stickiness is a huge weapon in the arsenal of communication. One client termed their Balanced Scorecard LENS, an acronym for learning, execution, navigation, and strategy. A humanitarian organization I consulted with seized the opportunity to take advantage of the ubiquity of GPS devices in our lives, branding their implementation GPS: global poverty strategy.

Branding your implementation is one of the simplest and most effective things you can do to generate quick interest in, and support for, the Balanced Scorecard. A clever name can capture the essence of your implementation, why you're investing in the Scorecard, and what you hope to achieve. Finally, picking a name for the implementation can simply be a lot of fun and a pleasant diversion from the intellectual sweat necessary to actually construct the system. That was the case with a recent client. After a long day spent selecting strategic objectives to populate the strategy map we closed up our binders and headed out to a local restaurant for dinner. Much of the subsequent evening was spent brainstorming names for the Balanced Scorecard. There was wine involved, and yes, the names did become more creative as the night wore on. In the end they agreed on a name that was the perfect fit, but equally as important the team bonded over the importance of the implementation. Whatever moniker you choose should reflect your organization, your culture, and your aspirations.

Key Elements of a Communication Plan

One simple and effective method of designing your communication plan is to take advantage of the W5 approach—who, what, when, where, and why. Each is discussed below in the context of communication planning.

Who: The Target Audiences

The size of your organization and scope of your implementation will help you define the specific audiences for your communication plan. In general, you should consider each of the following groups: senior leaders, management (those with direct reports), all employees, the Balanced Scorecard core team, a steering committee (if you use one), and boards of directors. Each group is a key recipient of communication, but pay special attention to management, as they are sometimes overlooked. Strategy execution expert Jeroen De Flander, in his colorfully titled book *Strategy Execution Heroes*, suggests, "Managers are the most important players in the execution contest. In fact, strategy remains a paper exercise without managers taking the right actions and fulfilling their roles."[39] He emphasizes the necessity of managers understanding strategy execution, acknowledging its importance, seeing it as key to their role, and knowing how to maximize their efforts in execution. Since the Balanced Scorecard is designed primarily to execute strategy, it's vital you provide clear, unfiltered communication to managers (and all other groups noted above).

Who: The Communicator

Once you've determined your target audiences you can match them with appropriate message providers. Each group will have different needs, and require specific messaging. A board of directors, for example, would likely receive more formal communications consisting of presentation material and oral updates, typically delivered by senior leaders. In contrast, a newsletter written for the employee body may connote a more casual attitude and be written by a member of the implementation team.

Purpose/Message (What/Why)

Describes the information content defined in the plan. All communication plans will contain key messages that must accompany information deliveries. Your Balanced Scorecard initiative may have a number of key messages, including: how the Scorecard aligns with strategy implementation, the role of the Balanced Scorecard in relation to other change initiatives, or the new management philosophy represented by the Scorecard. Other content defined in the communication plan may include timelines, development status, issues, and education. Since the roles and responsibilities of your audience groups vary, the information messages should be tailored toward the target's role. Of course, before you begin providing communication on the Balanced Scorecard you should share as much as you can about its foundational raw material: strategy. As celebrated strategy guru Michael Porter says: "Strategy is useless if it's a secret."[40] He suggests that good leaders should also be strategy professors, in the sense that they're sharing the message at every possible opportunity.

In what is my favorite piece of practical advice from Porter on sharing strategy, he recommends leaders sit in on their direct reports' meetings to ensure the message they're conveying is consistent with the leader's original conception.

When: The Frequency of Communication

All effective communication shares one common trait: targeting specific needs. The frequency of your communication will vary depending on the needs of your target audiences. For example, you'll want to keep your senior leaders well informed on a frequent basis. Your core team also requires up-to-date information. On the other hand, you could meet the information needs of a board of directors with less frequent communiqués. Having said all that, I should remind you of what one leading change expert has said about communication. "Without credible communication, and a lot of it, employees' hearts and minds are never captured."[41] Those are the words of change guru John Kotter, who also places tremendous faith in the power of repetition. Kotter knows that audiences have to hear the message repeatedly in order to be aware of it, understand it, and begin acting upon it. Heed this advice and, if anything, err on the side of too much, rather than too little, communication.

Where and How: Communication Vehicles

Ah, now the fun part—the communication vehicles! Have you ever opened a greeting card and been assaulted with a song or other musical accompaniment? A friend once told me the computer power offered in that card's tiny chip would have matched the output of the world's greatest computers of just 50 years ago. Urban myth? In any event, the point is we've made tremendous technological advances in the past few decades. Today, with even the humblest of office software packages you possess a plethora of graphical and communication options. Add to the mix some good old-fashioned creativity and imagination and you're off to the communication races.

Despite the technological leaps I've just touted, face-to-face communication remains the most reliable form of interchange. Getting out and speaking directly to your target audiences is your best chance of truly influencing attitudes and stacking the deck of change in your favor. But, if you're going to get on your Scorecard soapbox, you've got to be prepared to answer the tough questions you're sure to get from a sometimes skeptical and typically apprehensive audience. Honesty is, naturally, the best policy, and you should answer all queries to the best of your current ability. It's also very helpful to develop your key messages, thereby ensuring the responses you're broadcasting are consistent across time and audience groups. Dennis Madsen, former CEO of outdoor gear store REI, understands the power of effective face-to-face communication. He notes:

> I spend most of my time staying in front of employees, engaging them in dialogues. The executive team and I do quarterly "town hall meetings" with groups of 200 employees at a time, where forty minutes of the hour is devoted to questions and answers. Employees won't always tell you what's on their minds if they're forced to raise their hand in a public forum. So we leave three-by-five inch index cards and pencils taped to every chair in the auditorium. Employees can write their questions, the cards are collected and brought up, and we answer them on the spot.[42]

Leaving the index cards for shy employees is a simple gesture, but it connotes a strong commitment to ensuring every employee's voice is heard.

Two increasingly popular communication vehicles are the Internet and the organizational intranet. Both are reliable, relatively inexpensive, and easy to use. Most of my clients will now build an internal Web site to provide education, share resource materials, and keep everyone informed on progress. Not all organizations will possess the technical or financial resources necessary to develop a sophisticated intranet, but, fortunately, alternative communication vehicles abound; it's simply a matter of finding what works best for your audiences, given cultural preferences, demographics, and so on. Consider any or all of the following as possibilities: group presentations, implementation plans, newsletters, workshops, brown-bag lunches, video presentations, message kits, e-mails, news bulletins, raffles and contests, demonstrations, road shows, town-hall meetings, Facebook posts, Twitter feeds, maybe even instant messages. Just think, you could IM your BFF about your BSC. Health care provider Kaiser Permanente accompanies every change effort with a change package.[43] A set of detailed, clearly written guidebooks fully describe the change, the reasoning behind its creation, the process by which it was developed (with nods to staffers who participate), the benefits it's meant to produce for patients and staff alike, user testimonials gathered during pilot implementations, and the metrics that will be used to evaluate its performance over time. Different versions of the package target business leaders, project managers, and frontline staff members.

Evaluating the Effectiveness of Your Communication Efforts

When it comes to evaluating the outcomes of communication plans, "often overlooked" would probably be a charitable grade. "Don't even consider it" is probably more reflective of what actually takes place. But the good news is that even anecdotal evidence can help you gauge the effectiveness of your communication efforts. For example, are groups completing their Scorecard tasks on time? Are you receiving questions about the Scorecard? Have requests been made for Scorecard presentations? At budget time, are teams looking for the guide you've prepared on the subject? These are all indications that your messages are probably reaching a receptive ear.

For those who have the means and the inclination, a formal survey of audiences is recommended. Using survey data, you can assess your efforts on the following criteria:

- **No contact:** Has not heard of the Balanced Scorecard implementation.
- **Awareness:** Has heard about the initiative, but doesn't know what it is.
- **Conceptual understanding:** Understands the Balanced Scorecard and any individual effects.
- **Tactical understanding:** Understands both the personal and organizational effects of the Balanced Scorecard.
- **Acceptance:** Will support the Balanced Scorecard and the changes it promises.

A simplified communication plan is shown in Exhibit 2.8.

Audience	Purposes	Frequency	Delivery Vehicle	Communicator
Executive Team	• Gain commitment • Remove obstacles • Report progress • Prevent surprises	Bi-weekly	Direct contact	Executive Sponsor
Management	• Convey purpose • Explain concepts • Report progress • Gain commitment	Bi-weekly	• E-mail • Mgt. Meetings • Articles	Champion/ Team Members
All Employees	• Convey purpose • Introduce concepts • Eliminate misconceptions • Report progress	Monthly	• E-Mail • Newsletters • Town Hall Meetings	Scorecard Team Members
Project Team	• Track progress • Assign tasks • Review expectations	Weekly	• Team Meeting • Status Memos	Champion

EXHIBIT 2.8 A Simplified Communication Plan for Your Balanced Scorecard Implementation

Final Thoughts on Communication Planning

Writer and aviator Anne Morrow Lindbergh remarked,"Good communication is as stimulating as black coffee and just as hard to sleep after."[44] In today's hectic world we are literally awash in communication. But how much of what passes for communication would meet Lindbergh's standard of good? Your challenge is to cut through the clutter that can surround a new initiative such as the Balanced Scorecard and focus on delivering the right message to the target audience, at the right time, in the appropriate manner so it resonates with your audience.

Let me conclude this section with the story of a leader who understood the power of communication to generate understanding and support for change in a very tumultuous time.[45] When Paul Levy became CEO of Beth Israel Deaconess Medical Center (BIDMC) in 2002, he faced an organization truly on the brink. Formed by the 1996 merger between two hospitals, Beth Israel and Deaconess, each of which had very distinguished reputations, noted global experts, and dedicated staffs, BIDMC's troubles began almost immediately after the union. By the time Levy arrived, the hospital was losing $50 million a year, relations at all levels were strained, and a once proud and devoted team of employees was deeply demoralized by the precipitous fall their once-legendary institutions had suffered. Facing a turnaround challenge of near epic proportions, Levy knew his actions had to be both bold and swift. True to that vision of change, during his very first morning on the job he delivered an all-hands-on-deck e-mail to staff which contained four broad messages: the proud history of the organization, the very real threat of a sale to a for-profit chain if the situation did not improve, the actions staff could expect him to take in the face of this threat, and finally, the open-management style he would adopt, including an abundance of direct and open communication.

Throughout the challenging period of change Levy continued to communicate openly and effectively with all staff, always putting the organization's cards on the table and using simple language that left little possibility of creative interpretation. During one critical juncture, he issued a lengthy e-mail to employees that accompanied the change plan devised by the organization's leaders and a team of consultants. This note, consistent with his day-one missive, began on a positive and uplifting note, emphasizing, among other things, the uncompromising values the institution held dear. The note went on to outline key points of the turnaround plan, including some of the sure to be unpopular measures that would ultimately become necessary. Levy also used the note to directly respond to anticipated concerns the staff would likely harbor, openly acknowledging past missteps leadership had taken. He went on to reiterate his key points at every possible opportunity: meetings with employees, interviews with the press, and public speeches among them. His ceaseless communication efforts convinced all stakeholders of the very real threat they faced, the necessity of change for survival, and helped everyone clearly understand the steps that must be taken.

By any yardstick, Levy's tenure at BIDMC was remarkably successful. The original restructuring plan noted a three-year improvement process, transitioning from a $58 million loss in 2001 to breakeven in 2004. By the conclusion of the 2004 fiscal year, performance was tracking well ahead of plan, with the organization reporting a $37 million gain from operations. Revenues were up, costs down, and morale reached premerger levels. Open, candid, and frequent communication, while not a panacea for all that ails a modern organization, is, as this case illustrates, a powerful tonic in the fight to ensure alignment and execution of strategy.

FINAL ASSESSMENTS TO MAKE BEFORE YOU BEGIN BUILDING A BALANCED SCORECARD

We've covered a lot of terrain in this chapter, and if you've followed its advice you're laying a solid foundation for the development of your Scorecard system. Before we move on, outlined below are some additional assessments to consider in preparing for the work that lies ahead.

If You Already Have a Strategy Map or Balanced Scorecard of Measures, Are You Willing to Change It?

Not every organization that contacts me for consulting assistance is starting their Scorecard initiative from scratch. Some have already created, either with another consultant or through the services of an in-house team, a strategy map, Scorecard of measures, or both. While they possess some of the work products that represent the Balanced Scorecard, they realize they don't have a tool that is functionally suited to serve as a true strategic-management system. Quite often, when they send me what they've produced I'm (how to put this tactfully?) not impressed. The maps are typically convoluted spaghetti diagrams attempting to link every conceivable objective that may or may not be relevant to the company. This is not an appropriate starting place for the Scorecard system and it's my sad duty to inform them of this fact. On several occasions, when presenting my case of why the map they've produced will never produce the results they desire, they protest and cling to what they've manufactured, usually expressing that wish with something like, "Well our executive team built this and they really like it." What's worse, in many cases when they share what they've rendered with employees, they receive a chorus of negative feedback, but even that doesn't sway them.

In the executive sponsorship portion of the chapter I introduced you to the work of Robert Cialdini and his findings on the key drivers of influence. You may recall one was consistency, declaring that people will align with their previous commitments. That's what you're battling here—the very human proclivity to vigorously believe in and advocate for what you've previously created. However, in order to move forward in the Scorecard process you must be willing to unshackle yourself from a previous work product if it doesn't stand up to harsh scrutiny and in the end won't move you any closer to the execution of your strategy. When new and contrasting evidence appears, confirmation that what you've built simply won't cut it and will only serve to frustrate employees craving straight talk and clear communication on the strategy, you must take heed of it. As with most things change related, you'll require the ability to skillfully balance emotion and a passion for what you're doing with rational analysis.

Critically Examine the Existence of Common Change Blockers

Change experts suggest that three sets of behaviors commonly stop the launch of needed change within organizations:

1. Complacency
2. Immobilization
3. Anger and pessimism[46]

Let's unpack each of these. *Complacency* is often driven by hubris based on past success. This will manifest itself in proclamations from people who boast, "We're doing great; why should we change?" To counteract this tendency, it's vital that you carefully consider why you're creating a Scorecard system. With that knowledge you can then recite the challenges that crowd your path, and communicate to a sometimes-dubious audience that if you don't confront the challenges head-on using a well-designed Scorecard, danger awaits.

Fear and panic are frequently underlying causes of *immobilization*, with people doing everything they can to protect themselves while this latest tempest of change blows over. Employees operating in a constant state of fear will never be capable of sustaining the energy and courage necessary to alter your current operating model in favor of a Balanced Scorecard. Therefore, once again, it's incumbent upon leaders to openly acknowledge the challenges faced by the firm, but then convincingly lay out the plans for overcoming those roadblocks, including the Scorecard's role in that transformation.

Anger is frequently displayed in passive-aggressive behavior that conveys to all concerned, "You can't make me change!" I saw this defiant behavior play out in one of my earliest exposures to the Balanced Scorecard. The company was part of a very mature industry and enjoyed a vaunted position within it, having earned steady profits for decades. When the Scorecard was introduced as a means of fortifying the company's position for years to come, many well-tenured employees raised their hackles, dug in and said, "No, thanks" to the change. Several years ago, professor and bestselling business author Jim Collins coined the now well-worn phrase "Get the right people on the bus," which was his way of saying the first job of leadership is to staff the company's ranks with people who are skilled and willing to travel the rocky path to greatness. Those not willing or able to make the journey have to go—it's as simple as that. When launching a Balanced Scorecard you may be faced with this difficult assignment. There may be people whose bitterness and overall attitudes toward needed change are simply too toxic to be tolerated, and for the sake of the organization they may need to go.

How Fast Are Things Changing in Your Environment?

When the topic of change is introduced there is a kneejerk reaction among most people to quickly state that it's occurring at a dizzying pace, faster than ever before. But is that an accurate depiction? Not necessarily. By many economic measures, we're living in less turbulent times than ever before. In the United States, the volatility of gross domestic product (GDP) growth decreased from 3.0 percent in the period 1946 to 1968 to 1.2 percent in the period 1985 to 2006; the volatility of inflation decreased from 3.2 percent to 0.6 percent over the same two periods; and the volatility of corporate profit growth decreased from 16.7 percent to 12.8 percent.[47] Compared with the tidal waves of change during the Great Depression, the economic disturbances of the past 50 years are akin to a summer's day surf. We also speak of disruption with great urgency; technological changes, new business models, and so on, all primed to radically transform the business world. However, they are hardly more destabilizing than the railroad, automobiles, electricity, the telephone, and mass production were during their time.

Your Balanced Scorecard will be translated from your strategy, which in turn will be impacted by the rate of change in your industry. The objectives and measures on your strategy map and Scorecard will be affected by the nature and velocity of change you face. For example, if you're operating in a highly volatile industry characterized by rapid change, you will undoubtedly have a greater number of short-term measures from which you can quickly extract information used to make necessary strategic course corrections. Should you reside in an industry less burdened by the demands of change, your Scorecard will contain a greater mix of both short-term leading indicators and long-term lagging measures.

Do You Have a Strategy?

Executing strategy is far and away the most popular rationale stated when I ask clients why they've decided to pursue the Balanced Scorecard, and it's a powerful impetus, since research suggests just 10 percent of organizations effectively execute their strategies. Frequently, however, a slight problem will emerge as we begin our work together. When I ask the seemingly straightforward question, "Can I see your strategy?" it's not uncommon for the heads of my clients to bow forward ever so slightly as they whisper in barely audible tones, "Well, we really don't have a strategy per se," or "We've got a strategy but it's not written down anywhere." Others will trot out Dead Sea scroll-length documents that contain nothing more than a wish list of everything good and noble they would like to accomplish. Regardless of the forms they take, none of these represent a true strategy. If you find yourself in this situation you have a decision to make—do you stop and create a real strategy that can be used as the clay from which a Balanced Scorecard is molded, or do you use the Balanced Scorecard as a process to both craft a coherent strategy and simultaneously execute it?

If you don't currently have a real strategy in place, a document that cogently outlines your chosen markets, value proposition, key trade-offs, and so on, you can still move forward with the Balanced Scorecard. I call this method reverse engineering the strategy through the priorities inherent in the strategy map and measures, and while you can generate tremendous results from the Scorecard in this manner, keep in mind that the Balanced Scorecard is first and foremost a tool for translating a strategy, and was not designed primarily as a tool for creating strategy. If your strategy canvas is currently blank, you may be better served by focusing on painting that masterpiece before taking it to the world in the form of a Balanced Scorecard. To help you make the decision, I'll talk more about strategy in the next chapter.

NOTES

1. Marcus Buckingham, *The One Thing You Need to Know* (New York: The Free Press, 2005).
2. William Bridges, *Managing Transitions* (Cambridge, MA: Perseus Books, 2003), 63.
3. Jeanie Daniel Duck, *The Change Monster* (New York: Three Rivers Press, 2001), 51.
4. Chris McChesney, Sean Covey, and Jim Huling, *The Four Disciplines of Execution: Achieving Your Wildly Important Goals* (New York: Free Press, 2012), Kindle edition, location 483.
5. David Rock, *Your Brain at Work* (New York: Harper Collins, 2009), Kindle edition, location 1087.
6. Chip Heath and Dan Heath, *Switch: How to Change Things When Change is Hard* (New York: Crown Business, 2010), Kindle edition, location 541.
7. Ibid., location 1846.
8. Janice A. Klein, "Why Supervisors Resist Employee Involvement," *Harvard Business Review*, (September–October 1984).
9. Robert S. Kaplan and David P. Norton, *The Strategy Focused Organization*, (Boston: Harvard Business School Press, 2000).
10. Charles Galunic and Immanuel Hermreck, "How to Help Employees Get Strategy," *Harvard Business Review* (December 2012): 24.
11. Ram Charan and Larry Bossidy, *Confronting Reality: Doing What Matters to Get Things Done* (New York: Crown Business, 2004), 195.
12. Quoted in Fred R. Shapiro, ed., *The Yale Book of Quotations* (New Haven: Yale University Press, 2006).
13. Robert Cialdini, *Influence: The Psychology of Persuasion*, 2nd ed. (New York: Collins, 2006).
14. The real-life examples are drawn from Cialdini's *Influence: The Psychology of Persuasion*.
15. Nathan T. Washburn, "Why Profit Shouldn't be Your Top Goal," *Harvard Business Review* (December 2009): 23.
16. From interview with Robert Cialdini on *The Small Business Advocate*, June 9, 2008, www.smallbusinessadvocate.com/small-business-interviews/robert-cialdini-5890.
17. Michael C. Mankins and Richard Steele, "Turning Great Strategy Into Great Performance," *Harvard Business Review* (July–August 2005): 65–72.
18. Harold L. Sirkin, Perry Keenan, and Alan Jackson, "The Hard Side of Change Management" *Harvard Business Review* (October 2005): 108–118.
19. David Rock, *Your Brain at Work*, (New York: Harper Collins, 2009), Kindle edition, location 3757.

20. Mark A. Huselid, Richard W. Beatty, and Brian E. Becker, "'A Players' or 'A Positions'?: The Strategic Logic of Workforce Management," *Harvard Business Review* (December 2005): 110–117.
21. William Bridges, *Managing Transitions* (Cambridge, MA: Perseus Books, 2003), 19.
22. Best Practices Benchmarking Report, *Developing the Balanced Scorecard* (Chapel Hill, NC: Best Practices, 1999).
23. John Hamm, "The Five Messages Leaders Must Manage," *Harvard Business Review* (May, 2006): 114–123.
24. John P. Kotter and Dan S. Cohen, *The Heart of Change: Real-Life Stories of How People Change Their Organizations* (Boston: Harvard Business School Press, 2012), Kindle edition, location 676.
25. Michael J. Mauboussin, *Think Twice: Harnessing the Power of Counterintuition* (Boston: Harvard Business School Press, 2009), Kindle edition, location 676.
26. Cohen and Kotter, *Heart of Change*.
27. Nick Wreden, "Executive Champions: Vital Links Between Strategy and Implementation," *Harvard Management Update* (September 2002).
28. David P. Norton, "Change Agents: The Silent Heroes of the Balanced Scorecard Movement," *Balanced Scorecard Report* (May–June 2002): 1–4.
29. Ibid.
30. See for example, Robert S. Kaplan and David P. Norton, *The Execution Premium: Linking Strategy to Operations for Competitive Advantage* (Boston: Harvard Business School Press, 2008), 281.
31. Niccolo Machiavelli, *The Prince*, W.K. Marriott, trans. Vol 23, *The Great Books of the Western World* (Chicago: Encyclopedia Britannica, 1952), 9.
32. "Board Governance and Accountability," An interview with Edward E. Lawler III, *Balanced Scorecard Report* (January–February 2003): 12.
33. Josh Kaufman, *The First 20 Hours* (New York: Penguin, 2013), Kindle edition, location 416.
34. Michael Beer and Nitin Nohria, "Cracking the Code of Change," *Harvard Business Review*, (May–June 2000): 133.
35. Stephen R. Covey, *The 8th Habit* (New York: The Free Press, 2004), 3.
36. Peter F. Drucker, *Managing the Non-Profit Organization* (New York: Harper Collins, 1990).
37. Jack Welch and John Byrne, *Jack: Straight From the Gut* (New York: Warner Business Books, 2001).
38. From internal Nova Scotia Power documents shared with the author.
39. Jeroen De Flander, *Strategy Execution Heroes* (Brussels, Belgium: The Performance Factory, 2010), 19.
40. Joan Magretta, *Understanding Michael Porter* (Boston: Harvard Business School Press, 2012), 208.

41. John P. Kotter, *Leading Change* (Boston: Harvard Business School Press, 1996).

42. "Gearing up at REI," *Harvard Business Review* (May 2003): 20.

43. Lew McCreary, "Kaiser Permanente's Innovation on the Front Lines," *Harvard Business Review* (September 2010): 96.

44. Thinkexist.com. Available at http://en.thinkexist.com/quotation/good_communication_is_as_stimulating_as_black/8594.html.

45. David A. Garvin and Michael A. Roberto, "Change Through Persuasion," *Harvard Business Review* (February 2005): 104–112.

46. John P. Kotter and Dan S. Cohen, *The Heart of Change: Real-Life Stories of How People Change Their Organizations* (Boston: Harvard Business School Press, 2012), Kindle edition, location 365. *Note:* In the book they note four sets of behaviors, the fourth being "A very pessimistic attitude that leads to constant hesitation." I feel this is often manifested in one of the other three behaviors and have thus, chosen not to include it.

47. Matthew Stewart, *The Management Myth: Debunking Modern Business Philosophy* (New York: W.W. Norton, 2010), Kindle edition, location 4511.

CHAPTER THREE

Balanced Scorecard Building Blocks: Mission, Vision, and Strategy

 MISSION

In *The Dilbert Principle,* oft-quoted business sage Scott Adams has this to say about mission and vision:

> The first step in developing a vision statement is to lock the managers in a room and have them debate what is meant by a vision statement, and how exactly it differs from a mission statement. These are important questions, because one wrong move and the employees will start doing "vision" things when they should be doing "mission" things and before long it will be impossible to sort it all out.[1]

So, let's heed Scott's advice and sort this whole thing out before confusion reigns. What follows is my thinking on mission, vision, and strategy based on experience and the work of many writers, theoreticians, and practitioners.

What Is a Mission Statement, and Why Is It So Important?

Anyone encountering your company, whether it's a customer, current or potential employee, or strategic partner, will undoubtedly have a number of questions in mind. Who are you as an organization? Why do you exist? It is the mission of your organization that provides the answers to these vital questions.[2]

A mission statement defines the core purpose of the organization, its raison d'être, that is, why it exists. The mission also reflects employees' motivations for engaging in the company's work. In the private sector, which is strongly influenced by shareholder concerns, a mission should provide the rationale for a company's existence beyond generating stockholder wealth. Interestingly, corporate charters of the nineteenth century were regarded as a privilege—and with that privilege came the corporate obligation to serve the public interest. Even in today's Wall Street numbers-driven markets, the mission statement should describe how an organization is indeed serving the public interest and why it matters—the true responsibility of any organization.

In work, as in life, we all strive to make a contribution. Purpose and fulfillment are not achieved from the collection of a paycheck, but rather are derived from contributing to something greater than ourselves, doing something of value. The organization's mission is the collective embodiment of this most basic of human desires. Hewlett-Packard co-founder David Packard held this belief deeply and made it the cornerstone of his management philosophy. This is how he described Hewlett-Packard's mission in a 1960 speech that is as relevant today as it was over a half century ago.

> A group of people get together and exist as an institution that we call a company so they are able to accomplish something collectively that they could not accomplish separately—they make a contribution to society, . . . do something which is of value.[3]

The best of our organizations offer us the opportunity to accomplish something of value, to attain true meaning and fulfillment through work.

Unlike strategies that may be achieved over time, you never really fulfill your mission. It acts as a beacon for your work, constantly pursued but never quite reached. Consider your mission to be the compass by which you guide your organization. And just as a compass can lead you to safety when you're lost in unfamiliar terrain, a powerful mission can serve as your guide in times of organizational uncertainty. Consider the case of Bon Secours Health System.[4] Several years ago this health care provider, which has existed since 1824, was considering the purchase of a group of nursing homes. The deal looked good on paper, but some additional research on the acquisition revealed a troubling source of the potential good fortune. Low pay and inadequate employee benefits were the true driving force of the nursing home company's profits. Bon Secours reconsidered the acquisition in light of its mission statement. In addition to providing a caring environment for patients, the mission also stressed the same treatment for employees. Investing in the nursing homes would clearly have violated this component of Bon Secours' mission, and the deal was rejected.

Effective Mission Statements

Now that we know what they are, let's look at some of the attributes that make for an effective and enduring mission statement.

- **Simple and Clear:** Peter Drucker has said one of the greatest mistakes organizations make is to turn their missions into "hero sandwiches of good intentions."[5] I've read thousands of pithy quotes over the years but this may very well be my all-time favorite. It's short, colorful, and most important, 100 percent accurate. I have yet to share this nugget of sage advice with an audience and not have the entire room nod in unison or chuckle somewhat apologetically, as if to say, "Okay, you got us on that one." As admirable as your intentions may be, they aren't necessarily practical. You can't be all things to all people and still expect to maintain the focus necessary to accomplish specific goals. The mission must mirror your chosen field of endeavor.
- **Inspire Change:** While your mission doesn't change, it should inspire great change within your organization. Since the mission can never be fully realized it should propel your organization forward, stimulating positive change and growth. Consider the mission of Walmart: "We save people money so they can live better."[6] Retailing may look vastly different in 100 years than it does today, but you can wager safely that people will still want to save money.
- **Long Term in Nature:** Mission statements should be written to last 100 years or more. While strategies will surely change during that time period, the mission should remain the bedrock of the organization, serving as the stake in the ground for all future decisions. The mission of biopharma company Bristol-Myers Squibb is: "To discover, develop and deliver innovative medicines that help patients prevail over serious diseases."[7] This would be as appropriate 10 decades from now as it is today.
- **Easy to Understand and Communicate:** Nobody would argue that our modern organizational community is awash in jargon. Buzzwords abound in offices around the world as we invent new and curious words and phrases to describe the world around us. While many people react negatively to buzzwords, others say they simply represent a sign of "words in action and a culture on the move."[8] Regardless of your opinion on the

role of buzzwords in our modern life, they really have no place in a mission statement. The last thing you want to do is turn this exercise into a game of buzzword bingo: leading edge, quality first, proactive, good to great . . . buzzword bingo! Your mission should be written in plain language that is easily understood by all readers. A compelling and memorable mission is one that reaches people on a visceral level, speaks to them, and motivates them to serve the organization's purpose.

Developing Your Mission Statement

"The first question is always, what's the mission? Ask yourself what you'd like to achieve—not day to day, but your overarching goal."[9] This is the advice offered by former New York City Mayor Rudy Giuliani. But how do we answer that question—how do we develop the mission? In the sections that follow I'll provide you with a number of options for creating your own mission statement.

As you'll see, most exercises designed to help you develop a mission center on posing a number of key questions. When creatively combined, your thoughtful answers to these questions will lead to a galvanizing mission statement for your organization.

The 5 Whys

A very effective method for developing your mission is based on a concept known as the 5 Whys developed by Jim Collins and Jerry Porras.[10] Start with a descriptive statement such as, "We make X products or delivery Y services." Then ask, "Why is this important?" five times. A few whys into this exercise and you'll begin to see your true mission emerging. This process works for virtually any product or service organization. A waste management organization could easily move from "We pick up trash" to "We contribute to a stronger environment by creatively solving waste management issues" after just a couple of rounds. A market research organization might transition from "Provide the best market research data" to "Contribute to customers' success by helping them understand their markets." An accounting department might begin their deliberations by suggesting "We keep the books." One or two whys later that stale notion can be transformed to the significantly more meaningful and inspiring mission of "We help all leaders make better, more informed decisions through accurate and timely financial reporting."

You'll discover that with each round of why, your true reason for being as an organization becomes clearer, and the value or contribution you strive to create or make becomes apparent. This process is powerful because it builds on the notion of abstraction. I define abstraction as moving to a different level, leaving characteristics out. We humans are great abstractors; just ask anyone about themselves and chances are the first thing you'll hear is "I'm an attorney" or "I work in high tech." We tend to let these descriptions or abstractions define us, and we perceive the world around us through that particular lens. Why not move down the abstraction ladder a bit and see yourself as a husband or wife, neighbor, movie lover, baseball fan, and so on? Doing so opens up a world of possibility in our lives.

Similarly, most organizations focus intently on the minutiae of their operations, failing to see the bigger issues that underlie their purpose. The 5 Whys force us to abstract to different levels, thereby leaving behind the myriad specific characteristics of our organizational being, and unearthing our true meaning.

From 5 Whys to 6 Questions

Let's move from the 5 Whys to the following six questions. Your responses to these queries will help you frame the fundamentals of your mission:[11]

1. **Who are we?** The answer to this seemingly innocuous question should provide stakeholder opinion on what makes the organization different, and why it will endure. When answering this query it's important to not restrict yourself. Don't focus on what is written on your organization's stationery, instead expound on the central themes that define you.
2. **What basic needs or problems do we exist to meet?** The answer to this question will provide justification for your existence.
3. **How do we recognize, anticipate, and respond to these problems or needs?** Look outside yourself and consider the wider environment when tackling this question. Liaising with other organizations, conducting research, sharing best practice information, all of these activities are geared toward an external orientation that permit the organization to stay in constant touch with developments in the field.
4. **How should we respond to all of our key stakeholders?** Satisfying stakeholder needs is central to the success of all organizations. When contemplating this question, consider all of your stakeholders (employees, customers, shareholders, community groups), their varied needs, and how you propose to respond to these needs.
5. **What is our guiding philosophy and culture?** Once you've developed a mission, vision and strategy will follow. To successfully implement the

strategy, it should be consistent with your guiding philosophy and culture. Therefore, it's important to consider these items now and clearly articulate them in your statement of core purpose—the mission.

6. **What makes us distinctive or unique?** Competition is intensifying throughout our global economy and has a tremendous impact on both individual company and overall industry success. Organizations must determine exactly what elevates them from others willing and able to provide similar services, in order to truly distinguish themselves in the eyes of all stakeholders.

Gast's Laws

The late business professor Walter Gast formulated a series of principles in the 1940s and 1950s that suggested organizational success was more than a function of simply generating profitable returns, but was in fact something deeper. His principles have been adapted and used to help many organizations develop mission statements. Here are the six questions based on Gast's Laws:[12]

1. What "want-satisfying" service do we provide and constantly seek to improve?
2. How do we increase the quality of life for our customers and stakeholders?
3. How do we provide opportunities to productively employ people?
4. How do we create a high-quality work experience for our employees?
5. How do we live up to the obligation to provide just wages?
6. How do we fulfill the obligation of providing a return on the financial and human resources we expend?

A Simpler Approach

Each of the techniques outlined has significant merit and will undoubtedly lead to the creation of an inspiring mission. In keeping with the old 80/20 rule (80 percent of the value with 20 percent of the effort), Exhibit 3.1 provides a simple template that can help you get the mission ball rolling within your organization.

Who Writes the Mission Statement?

An important consideration when writing your mission statement is: Who should be involved in the process? There are different schools of thought on this subject. Some argue the senior leader or other executives should craft the mission, send it out for comments and revisions, and finalize it without any meetings or committee involvement. Others believe the mission statement,

---

We exist to *(primary purpose, need served, or problem solved)*

_____

_____

_____

For *(primary clients or customer)*

_____

_____

_____

In order to *(core services offered)*

_____

_____

_____

So that *(long-term outcomes determining success)*

_____

_____

_____

EXHIBIT 3.1   A Simplified Mission Statement Template

---

with its inherent focus on capturing the hearts and minds of all employees, cannot possibly be drafted without employee participation.

I'll provide my recommendation in just a moment, but first, let me share what you definitely don't want to do: Commission a large committee to write the mission statement. The perils of this approach were humorously outlined by blogger David Silverman who used some very familiar text as an example of what can go dreadfully wrong: the United States Constitution.[13] It begins:

> We the People of the United States, in Order to form a more perfect Union, establish Justice, insure domestic Tranquility, provide for the common defence, promote the general Welfare, and secure the Blessings of Liberty to ourselves and our Posterity, do ordain and establish this Constitution for the United States of America.

Silverman imagined what might happen to that august text if it had been submitted to a committee for review and editing. Here's what you might expect to see:

> *We the People* [Does this include all citizens? What about people who are traveling?] *of the United States* [Later on you say "United States of

America." Is this a different "United States" here?], *in Order to form a more perfect Union* [You can't be more perfect. Do you mean "better"? If so, you need to define better or it could open us up to litigation if a citizen is expecting more sunny days, for example, and we are in no position to provide that. Also, what's this term "union". Do you mean government? Terms are important, please stick to a set of words we can be sure everyone will understand.]

The edits go on, but you get the point. Next we have the nearly final version that incorporates all of the reviewers' comments:

We the People currently located in and either a citizen of through birth or an approved naturalization ceremony of the United States of America (hereafter "U.S."), in order to form a ~~more perfect~~ better ~~Union~~ government, defined as a government superior to the prior in terms of quality of government actions related to those projects and programs developed and implemented by the government and measured, as necessary, on a basis as determined by the government; ~~establish~~ promote, as required, the practice of legal justice; ~~insure~~ facilitate, where appropriate, domestic matters that are documented (see Appendix) as pertaining to the actions of the government, provide, where possible, for the common defense; ~~promote the general welfare~~ and ~~secure~~ select, where available, the blessings of liberty, which are not to be construed as actual blessings, but a symbolic sense of liberty that can be, when requested, documented by the government and made available to ourselves and our posterity, at a cost to be determined by the government and at a time and place of the government's choosing; do ~~ordain and establish~~ this Constitution for the ~~United States of America~~ U.S.

Writing by committee is a recipe for stiff, jargon-filled prose that not only fails to inspire but also may invite swift and vehement contempt. So, where does this leave us with writing our mission statement (and the vision which comes next)? In this debate of one person writing the document versus a group, I fall somewhere in the middle, advocating for a very small (two or three people) group.

Mission statements require the broad and high-level thinking of senior executives to consider the many possibilities available to the organization. Charismatic leaders often possess the enviable ability of crystallizing the organization's place and future goals in compelling terms to be shared with all employees. And let's not forget that contemplating purpose is a primary responsibility of every senior executive, especially the CEO. Harvard strategy professor Cynthia Montgomery believes that when it comes to planning, senior executives must reach beyond external analyses, market data, and competitor profiles to ask a fundamental question that underlies all of that activity: What will this firm be, and why will it matter?[14] That is the essence of mission. Don't deny yourself the opportunity of gleaning your executives' wisdom and foresight.

We live in an era during which collaboration and involvement of all organizational participants are cherished traits, and rightly so. Therefore, while a small and very senior group should craft the mission, you should also involve as many people as possible in reviewing the draft statement. Let employees at every level of the organization have the opportunity to kick the tires of this most-important document. Reviewing is not tantamount to rewriting, however. This is your chance to defend what you've written, reinforce your rationale, while also incorporating salient changes you feel improve the document, not those that are included simply to sound a conciliatory tone.

If You Already Have a Mission

Chances are, whether you know it or now, your company probably already has a mission statement. Perhaps it's proudly adorning office walls throughout your organization, or sadly gathering dust on a shelf, or tucked out of sight in a desk drawer somewhere. If yours falls into the latter category that is, you haven't seen, or heard much about your mission for a while—that's probably a good sign that it's time to reexamine it.

Start by evaluating your mission in the context of the attributes presented earlier in the chapter. Does your statement contain all of these attributes? Here are some additional questions to ask if you're uncertain about the efficacy of your current mission:[15]

- **Is the mission up to date?** Does it reflect what the organization actually does, and is all about?
- **Is the mission relevant to all stakeholders?** Does a compelling reason for your existence present itself from a review of your mission?
- **Who is being served?** Should you rewrite the mission to more accurately reflect your current customer base?

Exhibit 3.2 contains sample mission statements from a diverse group of organizations.

Google: To organize the world's information and make it universally accessible and useful.

Merck: To discover, develop and provide innovative products and services that save and improve lives around the world.

Verizon: To enable people and businesses to communicate with each other.

Walmart: We save people money so they can live better.

Amazon: To be Earth's most customer-centric company, where customers can find and discover anything they might want to buy online, and endeavors to offer its customers the lowest possible prices.

Starbucks: To inspire and nurture the human spirit—one person, one cup and one neighborhood at a time.

Hyatt: To provide authentic hospitality by making a difference in the lives of the people we touch every day.

Sony: To experience the joy of advancing and applying technology for the benefit of the public.

Facebook: To give people the power to share and make the world more open and connected.

EXHIBIT 3.2 Sample Mission Statements

Why Mission Is Critical to the Balanced Scorecard

The Balanced Scorecard was not designed to act as an isolated management tool; rather, it is part of an integrated approach to examining your organization and provides you with a means to evaluate your overall success. Above all, the Scorecard is a tool designed to offer faithful translation. What does it translate? The Scorecard decodes mission, vision, and strategy into performance objectives and measures in each of the four Scorecard perspectives. Translating this DNA of the organization with the Balanced Scorecard ensures all employees are aligned with, and working toward, the mission. This represents one of the great benefits of the Scorecard system.

The mission is where you begin your translating efforts. A well-developed Balanced Scorecard ensures the objectives appearing on the strategy map and the measures you track on the Scorecard are consistent with your ultimate aspirations, and it guides the actions of employees in making the right choices.

When developing objectives on the strategy map and performance measures you must critically examine them in the context of the mission you've written for the organization to be certain they are consistent with that purpose. Would a measure of "market share of the richest 1 percent of Americans" make sense in light of Walmart's mission? Probably not—in fact it would reflect a fundamental shift in purpose. While Walmart welcomes all shoppers, and I'm sure many price-conscious wealthy people shop there, they rely on a strategy of low prices to attract those who aren't "rich."

The Balanced Scorecard is *descriptive*, not *prescriptive*, in other words there are no hard-and-fast rules. So you could build and implement a Balanced Scorecard without a mission statement for your organization. However, consider for a moment the tremendous value and alignment you create when developing a Scorecard that truly translates your mission. Now you have a tool that can act as your compass, and guide the actions of your entire employee team. If you do have a mission, make certain the Balanced Scorecard you develop is true to the core essence reflected in the document. If you don't have a mission statement, I would strongly encourage you to develop one and see for yourself the focus and alignment you create when translating your mission into a Balanced Scorecard framework.

 VISION

The Role of Vision through History

Human history has been marked by momentous events that have forever changed the way we think, act, and live. Let's assume for a moment that time travel is possible, and you suddenly have the chance to take a front-row seat at any of these history-altering occasions. Which would you choose? Lincoln's Gettysburg address perhaps? Or maybe the downing of the Berlin Wall? I could literally list hundreds. If I had the opportunity, there are two legendary addresses I would love to have heard in person. The first is Martin Luther King Jr.'s "I Have a Dream" speech delivered on the steps of the Lincoln Memorial on August 28, 1963. Here is a small portion of that stirring oratory:

> I have a dream that one day this nation will rise up and live out the true meaning of its creed: We hold these truths to be self-evident: that all men are created equal.

In my opinion, it's virtually impossible to read these words, conceived with clarity and delivered with passion and eloquence, and not feel compelled toward action.

My second window-on-history choice would be President John F. Kennedy's impassioned plea to have the United States commit to sending a man to the moon, delivered to the U.S. Congress on May 25, 1961. Here is a small portion the president's remarks:

> Now it is time to take longer strides—time for a great new American enterprise—time for this nation to take a clearly leading role in space achievement, which in many ways may hold the key to our future on Earth.
>
> I believe that this nation should commit itself to achieving the goal, before this decade is out, of landing a man on the Moon and returning him safely to the Earth.[16]

With these words President Kennedy inspired a generation of citizens and won their commitment to a seemingly impossible task. You may not have to shoulder the responsibility of inspiring millions, but you do have a duty as leaders to help yourself and your employees find meaning in their work and be compelled toward great things.

What Is a Vision Statement?

Thus far we've discussed the importance of a powerful mission to determine your core purpose as an organization. Based on the mission, we now require a statement that defines where we want to go in the future. The vision statement does just that, signifying the critical transition from the unwavering mission to the spirited and dynamic world of strategy.

A vision statement provides a word picture of what the organization intends ultimately to become—which may be 5, 10, or 15 years in the future. This statement should not be abstract—it should contain as concrete a picture of the desired state as possible, and also provide the basis for formulating strategies and objectives. A powerful vision provides everyone in the organization with a shared mental framework that helps give form to the often-abstract future that lies before us. Vision always follows mission (purpose). A vision without a mission is simply wishful thinking, not linked to anything enduring. Typical elements in a vision statement include the desired scope of business activities, how the corporation will be viewed by its stakeholders (customers, employees, suppliers, regulators, etc.), areas of leadership or distinctive competence, and strongly held values.

Effective Vision Statements

Everything discussed in this chapter is critical to your organization and Balanced Scorecard implementation. However, the vision may represent the most critical component since it acts as a conduit between your reason for being as reflected in the mission and the strategy you'll put into place to reach your desired future state. Without a clear and compelling vision to guide the actions of all employees you may wind up with a workforce lacking direction and thus unable to profit from any strategy you create, no matter how well conceived. Let's look at some characteristics of effective vision statements:

■ **Quantified and Time-Bound:** An organization's mission describes its reason for being; its core purpose. Typically these statements are composed of inspirational prose, but do not include numerical aspirations or timing of any kind. The vision, however, must include both in order to be effective. Visions are concrete representations of the future, and as such they must provide specific details about the envisioned future state of the company. Although it will depend on the unique circumstances of each organization, many choose to wrap their vision in long-term financial goals of seemingly audacious revenue or profit targets. Others may include daring goals related to the number of customers served or geographies entered. Without numbers it will be impossible to measure progress towards the vision in the Balanced Scorecard. Additionally, the goals expressed in the vision statement serve as raw materials to assess the gap between current and desired performance. Closing that gap will be the purview of the objectives, measures, and targets populating the Balanced Scorecard. Similarly, the vision statement should include a time element so that subsequent measures and targets in the Scorecard can be designed to close the performance gap over the prescribed period dictated by the vision.

- **Concise:** The very best vision statements are those that grab your attention and immediately draw you in without boring you from pages of mundane rhetoric. Often the simplest visions are the most powerful and compelling. When Muhtar Kent assumed the CEO position at Coca-Cola in 2008 he was asked about his top priority moving forward. Without hesitation he replied, "Establishing a vision . . . a shared picture of success. We call it 20/20 vision and it calls for us to double the business in 10 years. It's not for the fainthearted but it's clearly doable."[17] His vision is both succinct and powerful. Notice, also, that his vision is both quantified and time-bound.

- **Appeals to all stakeholders:** A vision statement that focuses on one group to the detriment of others will not win lasting support in the hearts and minds of all constituencies. The vision must appeal to everyone who has a stake in the success of the enterprise: employees, shareholders, customers, and communities, to name but a few.

- **Consistent with mission:** Your vision is a further translation of your mission (why you exist). If the mission suggests solving problems for customers and one of your core values is constant innovation we would then expect to see a reference to innovation in your vision statement. In the vision you're painting a word picture of the desired future state that will lead to the achievement of your mission, so ensure the two are aligned.

- **Verifiable:** Using the latest business jargon and buzzwords can render your vision statement nebulous to even the most trained eye. Who within your organization will be able to determine exactly when you became world class, leading edge, or top quality? Write your vision statement so that you'll know when you've achieved it. Notice again Muhtar Kent's specificity of doubling the business in 10 years. While the mission won't change, we would expect the vision to change, since it is written for a finite period of time.

- **Feasible:** The vision shouldn't be the collective dreams of senior management, but must be grounded solidly in reality. To ensure this is the case you must possess a clear understanding of your business, its markets, competitors, and emerging trends.

- **Inspirational:** Your vision represents a word picture of the desired future state of the organization. Don't miss the opportunity to inspire your team to make the emotional commitment necessary to reach this destination. The vision statement should not only guide, but also arouse the collective passion of all employees. To be inspirational, the vision must first be understandable to every conceivable audience from the boardroom to the shop floor. Throw away the thesaurus for this exercise and focus instead on your deep knowledge of the business to compose a meaningful statement for all involved.

Developing Your Vision Statement

A rich body of literature exists on the subject of creating a powerful vision statement. As you might expect, given this abundant supply of material, there are many possible ways to craft the document. In this section I provide you with a few alternatives. Consider using one of the following or combining those elements of each that appeal to you.

The Interview Method

As you might have guessed, executive interviews are the key component of this technique for developing your vision. Each of the senior executives of your organization is interviewed separately to gather their feedback on the future direction of the organization. I would suggest using an outside consultant or facilitator to run the interviews. A seasoned consultant will have been through many interviews of this nature and have the ability to put the executive at ease, ensuring the necessary information flows freely in an environment of trust and objectivity. The interview should last about an hour and include both general and specific (industry and organization) questions, as well as a mix of past, present, and future-oriented queries. Typical questions may include:

- Where and why have we been successful in the past?
- Where have we failed in the past?
- What makes us unique as an organization?
- Why should we be proud of our organization?
- What trends, innovations, and dynamics are currently changing our marketplace?
- What do our customers expect from us? Our shareholders? Our employees?
- What are our greatest attributes and competencies as an organization?
- Where do you see our organization in 3 years? 5 years? 10 years?
- How will our organization have changed during that time period?
- How do we sustain our success?

The results of the interviews are summarized by the interviewer and presented to the CEO. At this point the CEO will have the opportunity to draft the vision based on the collective knowledge gathered from the senior team. Once the draft is completed the entire team convenes and debates the CEO's vision, ensuring it captures the essential elements they discussed during their interviews. You would not expect to have the first draft be accepted by everyone, and that's the idea—involve the whole team in the creation process. However, by mandating the CEO with the initial responsibility for declaring the vision, you ensure his or her commitment to the vision and have a working draft from which to begin the refinement process. Once the team has hammered out the vision statement it should be reviewed and accepted by as many levels in the organization as logistically possible, and with today's technology that should include just about everyone.

Back to the Future Visioning

This exercise can be administered either individually or with a group. In describing the method I'll assume a group session. Distribute several 3 × 5 index cards to each of the participants. To begin the session, ask the group to imagine they awake the next morning 5, 10, or 15 years in the future (your choice of time increment). In order to record their impressions of the future they've each been given a disposable camera to capture important images and changes they hoped might take place within their organization. At the end of each day's adventure they must create a caption for the pictures they've taken during the day. Instruct the group to use the index cards you distributed to record their captions. By the end of the trip they've catalogued the future in detail. Give the participants about 15 minutes to imagine their trip to the future and encourage them to visually capture as much as possible in their minds' eye. Ask the group: "What has happened with your organization, are you successful?" "What markets are you serving?" "What core competencies are separating you from your competitors?" "What goals have you achieved?" Record the captions from the index cards on a flip chart or laptop computer and use them as the raw materials for the initial draft of a vision statement. I enjoy this approach to vision-statement development because it challenges the participants to engage all of their senses in the process, not simply their cognitive abilities.

"Borrowed Heroes"[18]

I opened this section with a short review of passionate addresses by Dr. Martin Luther King Jr., and former President John F. Kennedy. Of course, these erudite and articulate men aren't the only ones known to stir a crowd with their oratorical genius and powerful visions. You may have your own heroes from the worlds of politics, science, sports, spirituality, or entertainment. In this next exercise you'll create a dialog for your vision by drawing on the words of those who have inspired you.

Here's how it works: First have the group listen to, or read, a stirring and inspirational speech from your borrowed hero. It could be Martin Luther King Jr.'s "I Have a Dream" speech, President Kennedy's "Landing a Man on the Moon" address or any other you choose. Next discuss the fact that you've just heard this leader at a specific point in time. Notice that he or she did not address the current state of affairs, but instead tapped the aspirations of all by painting a vivid word picture of future events. What was so inspiring and why?

Use the discussion to develop a vision for your organization. Imagine that *Forbes* or *Fast Company* is writing a story about your organization 5, 10, or 15 years from now. You've achieved your vision, and the reporter asks how you accomplished the impressive feat. Discuss and record what you've accomplished, how the world is better off, whom you've served, and how you did it. This open and creative discussion should lead you to the elements of a powerful vision for your organization.

Once you've developed your vision you'll be amazed at the power it provides, and this is the case regardless of the industry in which you work. Michael Kaiser is president of the Kennedy Center for the Performing Arts in Washington, D.C. As you'll read, the power of vision is every bit as vital at this renowned performing arts center as it is at a manufacturing plant or high-tech laboratory. Mr. Kaiser explains:

> I think what leaders have to do is to provide a vision for the future. And what has been remarkable to me . . . is the power of a vision. If you can present (that vision) to people, either to people inside the organization who have been damaged or people outside the organization who have lost faith in what the organization can do, the power is remarkable.[19]

VISION STATEMENTS AND THE BALANCED SCORECARD

As noted earlier in the chapter, a well-constructed vision statement, one that effectively portrays the company's desired future state, must be both quantified and time bound. The quantification dimension is often stated in terms of enhanced revenue, profit, customers, markets served, and so on. Timing is at the discretion of the organization, but is typically mid- to long-term in nature (often 5 to 10 years or more). With the quantified and time-bound vision created, an organization possesses the ability to deduce the gap between current and desired performance. Objectives, measures, targets, and initiatives in the

Balanced Scorecard will all subsequently be designed to close that performance gap, and hence vision is critical to the maximum utilization of the Balanced Scorecard.

The Balanced Scorecard will provide a new, laser-like focus to your business, and as such the potential problems represented by a misguided vision are significant. We've all heard terms like "what gets measured gets done," "measure what matters," and many others. The Scorecard is essentially a device that translates vision into reality through the articulation of vision (and strategy). A well-developed Balanced Scorecard can be expected to stimulate behavioral changes within your organization. The question is: Are they the sort of changes you want? Be certain the vision you've created for your organization is one that truly epitomizes your mission, because the Scorecard will give you the means for traveling first class to that envisioned future.

A Rose by Any Other Name

I'm sure you're familiar with the oft-cited Shakespeare quote from *Romeo and Juliet*: "A rose by any other name would smell as sweet," which suggests, in essence, that the word is not the thing; what matters in the end is not the descriptor we use, but in this case the tantalizing aroma of the rose itself. So it is with vision statements. In Chapter 1 I introduced the concept of destination statements:

> A description, ideally including quantitative detail, of what the organization (or part of organization managed by the Balanced Scorecard users) is likely to look like at an agreed future date. Typically the destination statement is subdivided into descriptive categories that serve a similar purpose (but may have different labels) to the "perspectives" in first- and second-generation Balanced Scorecards. The destination statement serves to clarify and align the management team around a common definition of strategic success, which facilitates the creation of the Balanced Scorecard.

As I noted then, destination statements are quite similar to vision statements, assuming the latter is quantified, as all should be. As with the scent of a rose, it matters little what terminology you use, so long as you begin with some form of quantified statement of what you would like the organization to achieve in the future. By providing necessary context, that vision or destination will greatly simplify the task of creating relevant objectives for your strategy map, and appropriate measures on the Balanced Scorecard.

 **STRATEGY**

Since its inception, the phrase Balanced Scorecard has been inextricably linked with the word strategy. Indeed, the subtitle of Kaplan and Norton's seminal book, *The Balanced Scorecard*[20] is fittingly presented as "Translating Strategy Into Action." From the very beginning, it has been taken as an unquestioned fact that the Balanced Scorecard is designed to translate (into objectives, measures, and initiatives) and ultimately execute an organization's strategy. Thus, for every organization choosing to implement the Balanced Scorecard there is an unspoken assumption that a strategy does in fact exist, and is in a sufficient state of readiness to serve as the critical raw material for the Balanced Scorecard system.

Like all assumptions, this one must be carefully and critically unpacked before we can accept it as fact. Unfortunately, in my experience, the assumption that a strategy exists is often not accurate, and many organizations I've encountered don't possess a true strategy. As noted in Chapter 2, when I begin working with a new client, one of my first questions is, "May I see your strategic plan?" A logical query, since the Scorecard we'll be creating together will be translated from that document. Over the years the reactions I've received to that simple and straightforward question have frequently surprised me. There is the subtle rolling of the eyes that suggests, "You've got to be kidding," to the somewhat defensive, "Well, we don't really have a strategy written down, but it's out there," to the most troubling response of all, "Strategy? That's why we're developing a Balanced Scorecard." I say most troubling because, as noted above, the Balanced Scorecard was originally conceived as a methodology for strategy execution, not strategy formation. Speaking with other consultants and practitioners in the Scorecard field, I realize that mine is not an isolated experience. There is a dearth of actual strategy in place at many organizations, especially small- and medium-sized companies. Why do so many organizations talk a good game where strategy is concerned, but fail to produce a robust plan that will differentiate them from their competition? Let's explore some of the pressing problems with both strategy and the strategic-planning process that plague many organizations.

Problems with Strategy and Strategic Planning

Perhaps one of the reasons so few companies develop compelling strategies is the state of strategy itself. In one survey, conducted by global consulting firm McKinsey, only 45 percent of 800 surveyed executives were satisfied with the strategic-planning process at their companies, and a mere 23 percent indicated that major strategic decisions were made within the borders of the process. Here are some of the pressing challenges plaguing strategy and the strategic-planning process.

Flawed and Numerous Definitions of Strategy

Before you can design the strategy that will elevate you above your competition, you must begin by determining exactly what you consider a strategy, since the definition of the term will of course impact what you create. So, here's a simple exercise: Ask five people in your organization to define the term strategy for you. I've done this, and the lack of consistency in replies never fails to astonish me. Even senior teams that appear to be very much aligned in their thinking will ascribe vastly different meanings to the term strategy. For some the word represents inspirational goals, such as "Become customer-centric," while for others a strategy is more akin to the specific tactics pursued by the firm in service of core objectives, such as growth or profitability. Some others take strategy to convey the very long-term aspirations of the company, for example, "Expand to 20 new markets in 10 years," which in my parlance is closer to vision than strategy. The definition you use will directly impact what is produced from your planning efforts, and thus it's vital you have a consistent definition of the term throughout your organization.

My working definition for strategy, honed from practical experience, research, and years of field application, is: The broad priorities adopted by an organization in recognition of its operating environment and in pursuit of its mission. Broad priorities relate to the most important choices an organization must make in framing their strategy, including target customers and geographies; product and service offerings; and perhaps most importantly, the chosen value proposition. In no way am I suggesting this is the most precise or correct definition of the word strategy. While my clients have used it as a guide to developing plans that feature important trade-offs and clear choices, enabling them to make more effective decisions on a day-to-day basis, the phrasing and elements may not be right for you. What's most important here is settling upon a consistent definition of the term, one that is shared from the C-suite to the front lines, so that what you create reflects the shared understanding of your entire organization. As mentioned in Chapter 1, confusing our words can lead to transmission of mixed signals to employees and result in less-than-desirable outcomes for the organization.

A Lack of Strategic Choice

Strategy is primarily concerned with making choices, determining what to do and, perhaps more importantly, what not to do when facing a universe of potential options to pursue. Turning your back on potentially lucrative ideas is a challenging but necessary condition of effective strategic planning. Steve Jobs recognized this when he declared, "People think focus means saying yes to the thing you've got to focus on. . . . But that's not what it means at all. It means saying no to the hundred other good ideas." [21]

Unfortunately many organizations either neglect to consider this or perhaps (my cynical side here) simply choose to ignore it because it's too difficult an assignment, and therefore wind up creating the classic hero sandwich of good intentions introduced in Chapter 2. In other words, the plan is a gallant recitation of every good and noble thing the organization dreams of accomplishing: "We will do this, and that, and this and that. . . ." The matter of choice, of prioritizing among competing alternatives, which is inherent in the proper crafting of a strategy, is sadly missing from these documents. Of course, as we all know, a strategic plan is worth little more than the paper on which it's printed. What's really vital is executing the plan, and that task is rendered virtually impossible to those attempting to take a bite out of the hero sandwich of good intentions. There are simply too many options, too many roads to travel, and thus, stymied by indecision, organizations simply trod the comfortable path of the old and familiar, frustrating employees starving for direction as they face decisions on the front lines of the business.

Fluff Masquerading as Strategy

Related to the above are those organizations producing strategies better suited to a game of buzzword bingo than to providing a clear and direct response to their environment. For example, "Our strategy is to provide leading-edge, world-class products by capitalizing on synergistic opportunities that will catapult us from good to great." My eyes are glazing over just reading that sentence. How can employees possibly be expected to act on such a sugary-sweet concoction of popular jargon? The short answer: They can't. What exactly is leading edge? How do we know we're world class? And when can we precisely determine we've crossed the chasm and passed from good to great?

Author Richard Rumelt paints such strategies with the derogatory label, fluff. He asserts, "Fluff is a superficial restatement of the obvious combined with a generous sprinkling of buzzwords. Fluff masquerades as expertise, thought, and analysis."[22] To support his claim he shares a quote from a major bank's internal strategy document. It reads: "Our fundamental strategy is one of customer-centric intermediation." He goes on to skewer this strategy by correctly noting that intermediation simply means the company accepts deposits and then lends them to others; in other words, it's a bank. The term customer-centric might be taken to suggest the bank competes on superior service or better terms, but a reading of their internal policies reveals no such distinction. Thus, customer-centric in this context is pure fluff. So in summary, remove the fluffy coating and you're left with the superficial and redundant statement "Our bank's fundamental strategy is being a bank."

Your first step in considering the challenge of strategy is a straightforward evaluation of where you stand in relation to the issues noted above. If you have multiple definitions of the word strategy, if your plan avoids real and consequential choices, or if the document consists of nothing more than vacuous statements, then you don't possess a true strategy. If that's the case, can you build a Balanced Scorecard? We'll examine that question in the next section.

Co-Creating a Strategy and Balanced Scorecard

If your strategy diagnosis reveals that you're suffering from any or all of the issues above, then before embarking on the creation of a Balanced Scorecard you're faced with a choice: Do we stop and create a strategy? Or, do we forge ahead and use the principles of the Balanced Scorecard to simultaneously co-create a strategy and Scorecard?

Option one, minting a fresh new strategy, is beyond the scope of this book, as hundreds (at a minimum) of texts have been written on the many and varied schools of strategy formation. In fact, I've written one myself, *Roadmaps and Revelations: Finding the Road to Business Success on Route 101.*[23]

It's a management fable chronicling one company's challenge in drafting an authentic strategic plan. The book uses a fictional narrative, but I'm sure you'd recognize many of the challenges faced by the characters. To help them solve their problem, the text provides four fundamental questions that must be answered when devising a strategic plan. In the appendix of this chapter, you'll find an introduction to the model, and an overview of the four questions.

Your second option is co-creating a strategy and Balanced Scorecard—developing both simultaneously. Should you choose to pursue this path, you won't develop two separate documents—a strategic plan and a Balanced

Scorecard. Rather, in answering specific questions related to each of the four Scorecard perspectives, your implicit strategy will emerge and be translated by the objectives, measures, and strategic initiatives present in the Balanced Scorecard.

Purists may blanch at the thought of creating a Balanced Scorecard without first penning a strategic plan but, realistically, despite the widespread acceptance and popularity of strategic planning, the fact is that most organizations struggle with this most basic corporate assignment. Recall from our discussion above that less than half of all organizations are satisfied with the process. Additionally, the nature of traditional strategy is under assault and we're witnessing a transformation in how companies approach the very idea of planning. For one, strategic time horizons are shrinking rapidly. In today's hypercompetitive, global economy it's virtually impossible for companies to gaze into a crystal ball and accurately envision what might take place years forward. This leads to the second major rethinking of strategy: Increased flexibility and agility are now the order of the day.

During our most recent recession companies began to realize that shifting course on the fly was far more valuable than tediously drawing out plans that would most likely not withstand the test of actual use in the field. In one survey of 377 global executives, more than two-thirds said that the ability to adapt is becoming a much more important factor in competitive advantage in their industry.[24] In another study of 350 executives from around the world, conducted by the Economist Intelligence Unit, 90 percent stated that organizational agility was critical to success in today's business environment. These leaders characterized agility as rapid decision making and execution.[25] As a final nod to the ever-increasing role of agility, here are the words of Harvard guru John Kotter on the subject:

> Companies used to reconsider their strategies only rarely. Today any company that isn't rethinking its direction at least every few years—as well as constantly adjusting to changing contexts—and then quickly making significant operational changes is putting itself at risk. . . . Strategy should be viewed as a dynamic force that constantly seeks opportunities, identifies initiatives that will capitalize on them, and completes those initiatives swiftly and efficiently.[26]

To strengthen the agility muscle, companies must engage in perpetual seeking mode—observing activity in their constantly shifting operating environment; challenging assumptions, asking questions, orienting to what is actually taking place in the market, and attempting to gather as much real-time knowledge as possible in order to apply flexible solutions to current demands. Many of the questions that must be answered are raised organically during the development of a Balanced Scorecard, and thus, this transformation of strategic planning, from a long-range, number-crunching exercise to a dynamic assessment of current reality, enhances the Scorecard's value as both a strategy insight and execution framework. Let's look briefly at each of the Scorecard's four perspectives to examine how the worlds of strategy formation and execution intersect in this dynamic and evolving methodology.

Customer Perspective—What Customers, What Products or Services, What Value Proposition?

It has been widely heralded in the business press and by scholars of much renown that we have clearly crossed the threshold into the age of the customer. With the rise of the Internet, the advent of smartphones and other ubiquitous digital assistants, the balance of power in virtually all commercial transactions has shifted from supplier to consumer. Understanding and reacting to the ever-changing landscape of customer behavior is the province of the customer perspective. Here companies must determine, after canvassing the current environment, what group constitutes their target market, what products and services they'll offer them, and what value proposition (why the customer should buy from them) they'll provide. Based on their responses, appropriate objectives, measures, and strategic initiatives will be chosen to populate this dimension of the Balanced Scorecard.

Internal Process Perspective—the Value Chain

Uber-strategy expert Michael Porter describes a company's value chain as "the discrete activities performed to design, sell, deliver, and support products and services."[27] This sounds simple enough, but it encompasses an enormous number of activities and subactivities elegantly designed to deliver on the company's particular area(s) of advantage.

When creating a Balanced Scorecard it's crucial for companies to critically examine their value chain in light of new information washing ashore from their analysis of the operating environment. This is where flexibility is most demanded and ultimately rewarded—in fully exploiting a value chain aligned around a value proposition poised to capitalize on market strength. The greatest rewards are reserved for companies able to discover and swiftly capitalize on unique differentiators in their value chain that allow them to deliver a distinctive value proposition to customers. In Chapter 5, the value chain's role in creating internal-process objectives will be examined in greater detail.

Learning and Growth Perspective—the Enablers

Virtually every strategic plan, assuming it was created with rigor, will include the items discussed above—customers, markets, value proposition, and value chain. Enabling those processes and customer deliverables are intangible assets that must be aligned with the desired outcomes. The right people, equipped with the necessary skills and technology, and operating in an environment conducive to growth and change (the hallmarks of agility) are represented in this perspective of the Balanced Scorecard.

Financial—Bottom Line

The principal reason organizations dedicate so much time and energy to engineering strategic plans is to reap financial rewards in the form of growth, profitability, improved asset utilization (or all of the above) by sustaining a competitive advantage over their rivals. This perspective represents the end in mind of our strategic story, and in populating it companies will outline their expectations of successful execution in dollars and cents.

 ## STRATEGIC THEMES

Another method of integrating strategy and the Balanced Scorecard is through the use of strategic themes. These action-oriented statements serve as broad components of a strategy, and are comprised of linked objectives flowing through the four perspectives of the Balanced Scorecard. Possible examples of strategic themes include: "Excel in operational excellence," "Be customer-focused," and "Innovate constantly." Most organizations will first determine their themes and then translate them into a series of linked objectives weaving through the four perspectives.

Themes do represent a viable shortcut to the process of strategy formation, and may be used in the creation of a Balanced Scorecard, but they are not without issues. My chief concern is the fact that most organizations default to a standard set of themes, and as a result fail to demonstrate any strategic choice that would differentiate them from their competitors, thus forfeiting the value of both strategy and the Balanced Scorecard. Let me explain this a bit further.

Since virtually every position on the strategy canvas represents some combination of customer intimacy, innovation, and operational excellence, these became the default themes utilized by most organizations (my examples above represent each), and the objectives that are derived lack originality or strategic relevance. As a result, many theme-based maps resemble one another, and you have a difficult time truly deciphering any strategic choice. I've seen maps that could be for McDonald's, Nordstrom, General Motors, or even my company, The Senalosa Group. By ticking the boxes of each general theme (operational excellence, customer intimacy, innovation) the maps become generic, thereby defeating the entire purpose of the exercise. For themes to be effective they must represent the differentiating strategic elements of the firm—the particular mix of targeted customers, value proposition, value chain, intangibles, and price point that set you apart from your competition.

Regardless of the Method—Hard Work Is Required

Whether you choose to build strategic themes, or use the questions that must be raised when creating a Balanced Scorecard, you can co-create a strategy and a Balanced Scorecard. By advocating this position, I'm not suggesting these processes represent a simple shortcut. Crafting a strategy or building a Balanced Scorecard are complex and intellectually challenging tasks that must be approached with rigor if a successful outcome is to be achieved. So, should you decide to simultaneously create strategy and a Scorecard, you must be prepared to engage in the significant analytical effort that accompany both.

APPENDIX 3A: AN INTRODUCTION TO THE ROADMAP STRATEGY PROCESS

Before writing *Roadmaps and Revelations*, I reviewed hundreds of strategic plans, and scoured the literature from the likes of Michael Porter, Henry Mintzberg, Michael Raynor, W. Chan Kim, Renee Mauborgne, and many others. During the process I constantly asked myself what core elements appeared again and again—what, in fact, represented the DNA of effective strategic planning? There are literally hundreds of approaches to strategic planning, but my investigation yielded a set of questions that appeared in one form or another in virtually all of the materials I discovered. Those core questions came to form the basis of Roadmap Strategy, a process I documented in the book. As you can see, the process draws its name from the book's title.

Roadmap Strategy

The following diagram provides an overview of the process—you'll see the four fundamental strategy questions, and on the outer ring of the diagram you'll find what I call the four lenses, each of which will assist you in answering the fundamental strategy questions. At the center of the diagram is the word strategy, as the four questions and accompanying lenses are designed to drive strategy formulation.

Four Fundamental Questions You Must Answer When Creating a Strategy

Let's review each of the four questions, beginning with the first: What propels us forward?

At this very moment, your organization is being propelled in some direction by a force put in place through years of decisions made about everything: how you allocate your financial resources, whom you hire, how you employ technology. What propels you forward represents, in many ways, your corporate identity. In other words if people were to say, "They are a _____ company" the blank in the sentence will often describe what propels you forward.

Most organizations will typically be propelled by one of six forces:

1. **Products and services:** Companies propelled by products and services may sell to many different customer groups, using a variety of channels,

but their focus is on a core product or service. Consider Coca-Cola. They focus exclusively on nonalcoholic beverages, with hundreds of global brands.

2. **Customers and markets:** Organizations dedicated to customers and markets may provide a number of product or service offerings, but they are all directed at a certain core audience. Johnson & Johnson's diverse wares have one thing in common: they're aimed at the needs of their core markets—doctors, nurses, patients, and mothers.

3. **Capacity or capabilities:** Hotels focus on capacity. They have a certain number of rooms available and their goal is to fill them, simple as that. Airlines operate on the same premise, using available seats. Organizations propelled forward by capabilities possess expert skills in certain areas and will apply that toolkit of skills to any possible product or market.

4. **Technology:** Some organizations have access to a proprietary technology that they leverage to a number of different products and customer groups. Consider DuPont, which discovered nylon in the 1930s. They went on to apply the technology to a varied range of offerings, including fishing line, stockings, and carpet.

5. **Sales and distribution channels:** The operative word with this focus is *how*, not what or who. Organizations that are driven by sales channels will push a diverse array of items through their selected channels. TV shopping networks are a great example. Where else can you buy makeup one hour and DVD players the next?

6. **Raw materials:** If you're an oil company, everything you sell is going to be derived from that that black gold you pumped from the ground. You may have the skills and technology to mold the oil into a number of things, but all will be directly descended from the original raw material.

Some may view the six areas above and claim they can, and must, do all in order to succeed in our hypercompetitive marketplace. I suppose in theory that's possible, but it will prove exceedingly difficult to go beyond simply skimming the surface of what each area has to offer if you attempt to pursue all six at the same time. Doing so will inevitably lead to confusion from an already skeptical employee audience, wondering which path to choose when presented with alternative opportunities. Ultimately, a focus on all is a focus on none, leading to suboptimal results. In order to truly capitalize on this principle you must commit to one driving force for your organization and align your resources, human and financial, around that decision. Determine what propels you forward, and focus on optimizing it.

What Do We Sell?

Regardless of which of the six areas propels you forward as an organization, you must sell something, some mix of products or services, to your customers in order to keep your business alive. The challenge inherent in this question is making the critical determination of which products and services you'll place more emphasis on in the future, and which you'll place less emphasis on.

Take for example, the American cable television channel, The CW. Parent companies Time Warner Inc. and CBS Corporation had high hopes when they launched the new network, but it failed to deliver results and soon there were whispers it would be shut down. Recognizing that a strategic choice had to be made, CW recently returned to its ancestral roots and decided to focus on programs geared towards young women. Dawn Ostroff, former CW Entertainment President addressed the change, when she said, "We really needed to stand out in the marketplace and not be another broadcaster . . . It was important for us to differentiate and create a brand that hopefully will be a real legacy here." CW bet its future on new and current shows such as *Gossip Girl*, the new *90210*, a new *Melrose Place*, and *Vampire Diaries*, all focused on content relevant to young women.

Who Are Our Customers?

When determining whom you'll sell to, you are once again faced with a choice: which customer groups (and geographies) do we place more emphasis on in the future, and which deserve less of our attention? The first step in answering this question is acquiring a clear understanding of your current group of customers by reviewing standard metrics such as: customer satisfaction, loyalty, profitability by customer group, retention, and market share. It's also vital to experience things from your customers' point of view in order to glean insights not visible from within the walls of your corporate headquarters.

The upscale beauty company Estee Lauder, which controls 29 brands including the iconic MAC and Clinique, is examining this question, and making strategic choices as a result. CEO Fabrizio Freda has decreed that reducing the company's dependency on declining U.S. department stores, which accounted for nearly one-third of Estée Lauder's sales, is a top priority. A new geographical focus is in the works as well, as Estee Lauder plans to focus on emerging markets and Asia.

Often, responses to the questions "What do we sell?" and "Who are our customers?" will be revealed in unison, as analysis on one leads to insights on both, ultimately creating answers for both queries. Consider once again The

CW. By making the strategic choice to offer programs geared to young women (What do we sell?) they are simultaneously committing to young women as their core customer group.

How Do We Sell?

This is perhaps the most crucial of the four questions, as it determines value proposition. In other words, how do you add value for customers, or to put it even simpler: why would anyone buy from you? Despite the importance of the question, the choices awaiting you are limited and basic: you can either attempt to offer the lowest total cost of ownership to your customers, or you can put forth a differentiated product or service.

Companies that compete on lowest total cost invest deeply in capabilities, processes, and assets that allow them to standardize their operations, and create a repeatable formula that results in low prices for the consumer. Think of Walmart in the retail world or McDonald's in the fast food industry.

Those who choose to compete based on differentiation will find two potential paths to follow. The first is differentiation based on cultivating deep and rich relationships with customers, so that your focus is not on a single transaction but building something that lasts years, maybe even decades or a lifetime. Nordstrom is a great example. Their customer service is legendary and keeps customers coming back for years.

Competing based on the superior functionality of your products offers the second choice of differentiation. Innovation, cutting-edge design, and the latest technology are all hallmarks of organizations, like Apple, that choose to sell based on product leadership.

As I noted above, if I had to choose one question that is most critical for your team to achieve consensus on, this is it. In many ways it represents the aggregation of your responses to the previous questions, and it will directly impact, in a significant way, every decision and investment you make going forward.

The Four Lenses

So how do you answer these strategy questions? On the outer ring of the Roadmap Strategy diagram you'll find what I call the four lenses. Think of each of these as just that, a lens through which to consider the question you're pondering, or a different perspective to adopt as you deliberate on your alternatives.

As you work through each of the fundamental questions you can turn the dial on the outer ring to a different lens. I like to think of it as clicking the dial on a safe, although when you're rotating a safe's dial there is only one correct combination. With the four lenses, every combination of question and lens is a winner, because each challenges you in a new and enlightening way. Each is summarized below.

1. **Social/Cultural:** In *Roadmaps and Revelations*, a mentor character notes, "You've got to start with the heart." When discussing and debating strategy questions and developing possible responses, consider which potential answer most resonates with your passion as an organization. For example, if you're propelled by a proprietary technology and have a long and proud tradition of technological achievement, one which your employees are justifiably proud of, it may not make sense from a social and cultural standpoint to shift your focus to customers and markets, or any other alternative. The evidence suggesting that such a shift will lead to profound success had better be substantial to over-ride what's in the hearts of your people.

2. **Human:** When debating alternative responses to the strategy questions, it's vital to be ruthlessly realistic about your team's skills and talents. You may wish to sell surfboards because three members of your team are avid surfers, but if your sales associates have never been to the beach you've got very little chance of succeeding. In that case, to make the transition, you'd have to be willing to invest in training, perhaps consultants (surfer-dude consultants?), and new hires to bridge the potential skills gap.

3. **Technological:** Technology has become a critical enabler of virtually every industry, and it must be carefully considered as you answer the four fundamental strategy questions. Will the answer you're contemplating require an investment in new technology? What about the current technology you employ; will it become redundant? And, it's important to realize that the lenses impact one another. New technology may require new skill sets, the human lens. And technology is one of the most threatening things you can introduce, especially to seasoned employees, so you better have a good grasp on your cultural and social lens.

4. **Financial:** Perhaps the most basic of the four lenses, but certainly not to be overlooked. Every decision you make when answering the four questions will most likely entail the allocation of resources, for example: training your people to cover a skills gap (Human lens), investing in new technology (Technological lens), or creating a communications campaign to support your chosen direction (Social/Cultural lens). And on the opposite side of the ledger, each decision must be examined in light of the potential revenue and profit that will result from pursuing that course of action.

A Strategy to Create True Alignment from Top to Bottom

If you were to ask a group of CEOs what they most desire for their company, it's a safe bet that many would defer to the tried and true response of increasing shareholder value, which is understandable since this is a prime obligation of a profit-seeking enterprise. But how do they accomplish that goal? When that question is put forth, a number of inspiring sentiments will be lobbied, including the virtues of creating alignment within their organization from top to bottom, ensuring everyone is rowing in the same direction as it were. I agree that alignment is vital to any organization, be it private, public, or nonprofit, so how do we stack up in terms of actually creating alignment? Not so well, according to one study that found just 23 percent of U.S. workers had a clear understanding of what their company was trying to do and why.

For any person in an organization, from the C-suite to the shipping-room floor, to be aligned with the organization's direction they must first understand specifically where the organization is headed and why they've chosen that course. Our flawed strategic-planning processes, with their blind devotion to numbers and reluctance to make true strategic choices, render that knowledge practically impossible. Roadmap Strategy, on the other hand, focuses on the fundamentals of strategy as outlined above and the result is a simple statement, often just a paragraph in length, that clearly articulates what the organization is about, what it sells, to whom, and how. Armed with this precise information, employees can make more informed decisions relating to scarce resources, and align themselves in a common purpose towards the mission. Sun Tzu reminds us in *The Art of War*, a prerequisite for any student of strategy, "He whose ranks are united in purpose will be victorious."

 NOTES

1. Scott Adams, *The Dilbert Principle* (New York: Harper Business, 1996).
2. Michael Allison and Jude Kaye, *Strategic Planning for Nonprofit Organizations* (New York: John Wiley & Sons, 1997), 56
3. James C. Collins and Jerry I. Porras, "Building Your Company's Vision," *Harvard Business Review* (September–October 1996).
4. Tom Krattenmaker, "Write a Mission Statement That Your Company Is Willing to Live With," *Harvard Management Update* (March 2002).
5. Peter F. Drucker, *Managing the Non-Profit Organization* (New York: Harper Business, 1990), 5.
6. Accessed on November 11, 2013, at http://stock.walmart.com/faqs/.

7. Accessed on November 11, 2013, at www.bms.com/ourcompany/mission/pages/default.aspx.

8. Julia Kirby and Diane L. Coutu, "The Beauty of Buzzwords," *Harvard Business Review* (May 2001).

9. Rudolph W. Giuliani, *Leadership* (New York: Hyperion, 2002).

10. Collins and Porras, "Building Your Company's Vision."

11. John M. Bryson, *Strategic Planning for Public and Nonprofit Organizations* (San Francisco: Jossey-Bass, 1995), 76–78.

12. Krattenmaker, "Write a Mission Statement."

13. David Silverman, "That Written-By-Committee Flavor," *HBR Blog Network* (December 21, 2009).

14. Ken Favaro and Art Kleiner, "The Thought Leader Interview: Cynthia Montgomery," *Strategy + Business* 70 (Spring 2013).

15. Thomas Wolf, *Managing a Nonprofit Organization in the Twenty-First Century* (New York: Fireside, 1999), 347.

16. From: Space.com. "May 25, 1961: JFK's Moon Shot Speech to Congress." Available at http://www.space.com/11772-president-kennedy-historic-speech-moon-space.html.

17. Muhtar Kent, "Shaking Things Up at Coca-Cola," *Harvard Business Review* (October 2011), 94–99.

18. This method is adapted from material developed by Robert Knowling in "Why Vision Matters," *Leader to Leader* 18 (Fall 2000): 38–43.

19. Interview on National Public Radio's *Morning Edition*, March 26, 2001.

20. Robert S. Kaplan and David P. Norton, *The Balanced Scorecard: Translating Strategy Into Action* (Boston: Harvard Business School Press, 1996).

21. Robert Simons, "Stress Test Your Strategy: The 7 Questions to Ask," *Harvard Business Review* (November 2010), 92–100.

22. Richard Rumelt, *Good Strategy, Bad Strategy: The Difference and Why it Matters* (New York: Crown Business, 2011), Kindle edition, location 740.

23. Paul R. Niven, *Roadmaps and Revelations: Finding the Road to Business Success on Route 101* (Hoboken, NJ, John Wiley & Sons, 2009).

24. Chris Zook and James Allen, *Repeatability: Building Enduring Businesses for a World of Constant Change* (Boston, MA: Harvard Business Review Press, 2012), 127.

25. Ed Barrows and Andy Neely, *Managing Performance in Turbulent Times: Analytics and Insight* (Hoboken, NJ: John Wiley & Sons, 2012), Kindle edition, location 453–461.

26. John P. Kotter, "Accelerate," *Harvard Business Review* (November 2012), 44–58.

27. Joan Magretta, *Understanding Michael Porter: The Essential Guide to Strategy and Competition* (Boston: Harvard Business Review Press, 2012).

CHAPTER FOUR

Conduct Effective and Engaging Workshops

L ET'S TRY SOME FREE ASSOCIATION; I'll give you a word and you think of the first things that come to mind in relation to it. Ready? The word is workshop. Okay, what did you come up with? Did any of these words pop into your consciousness: effective, efficient, productive, lively, engaging, spirited, informative, or rewarding? How about: inefficient, boring, time wasting, dispiriting, or failure?

Depending on your personal work experiences and the cultures you've been part of, your workshop hours may have been extremely positive, with the first set of words presented above springing to mind; conversely, you may assign some of the negative words above based on the sorry excuse for workshops you've been subjected to during your working life. For the vast majority of organizations investing in a Balanced Scorecard solution, the construction of the system's core components will take place in a workshop setting, and thus these working sessions are vitally important in determining the quality of the ultimate deliverable. Therefore, to ensure a successful outcome we must do everything we can to ensure the workshops we design engender open, spirited discussions that produce a vibrant and robust Balanced Scorecard.

Over the past 15 years I've facilitated literally thousands of workshops for clients around the globe. I'd be stretching the truth to say that every single one of them went off without a hitch—early in my consulting career, there was a time in Chicago I thought I had a mutiny on my hands—but in the exceedingly vast majority of cases I've been fortunate to enjoy high-quality and engaging sessions that bring the best out of people and lead to the results everyone expects and requires. If you're paying attention and are keen to learn, then it's impossible to amass so many hours engaged in a particular activity and not determine exactly what works and what doesn't. My note pads are crammed with helpful insights I've gleaned from interacting with clients in workshop settings. In addition to practical facilitation experience, I've benefited from a wave of innovative and insightful research on group dynamics, organizational change, and neuroscience that has influenced my thinking and provided me with much additional knowledge on the effective creation and facilitation of group workshops.

My goal in this chapter is to share with you what I consider the most simple, yet powerful tips, tools, and techniques for conducting effective and engaging workshops, the kind that leave people saying, "Wow—that flew by, where did the time go!" rather than standing around the snack table morosely munching away on cookies while thinking, "There's eight hours of my life I won't get back." We'll begin by examining what you must do before your participants, most likely still a bit skeptical at this point, enter the meeting room, and then transition into what must occur during the workshop itself to ensure engaged participants and a successful outcome. One final note, the advice that follows applies for all of your Balanced Scorecard workshops: strategy mapping, measures, strategic initiatives, and any other Scorecard-related sessions you may engineer. Taking that a step further, I'd suggest the guidance below could be used to help you improve any workshop you conduct at your organization.

BEFORE THE WORKSHOP

Plan

During his nearly three decades at the helm of the UCLA men's basketball team, legendary coach John Wooden racked up an unprecedented 10 national championships. He was known to legions of admirers as the Wizard of Westwood, one who clearly elevated basketball strategy to new heights, but beyond his acumen for the game lay another secret to his success: planning. He described his philosophy this way:

> When I coached basketball at UCLA, I believed that if we were going to succeed, we needed to be industrious. One way I accomplished this was with proper planning. I spent two hours with my staff planning each practice. Each drill was calculated to the minute. Every aspect of the session was choreographed, including where the practice balls should be placed. I did not want any time lost by people running over to a misplaced ball bin.[1]

The same attention to detail that served as a hallmark of Coach Wooden's principles for success will serve you well as you prepare for your Balanced Scorecard workshops.

Over the years my clients have run the gamut on the planning spectrum—from those, Coach Wooden–like, who work intensely with me to carefully consider every conceivable detail, to others who completely ignore the planning, delegating all aspects of the event to me. Which do you think produce better outcomes? If you said those who work collaboratively with me, pat yourself on the back. While I diligently study each and every client organization I'm privileged to work with, at the end of the day I'll always be an outsider, and there is no way I can be cognizant of the dynamics that may be in play once the group is huddled around a conference room table hashing out their Balanced Scorecard objectives and measures. So, whether you're creating a Scorecard on your own, or with the assistance of a consultant or other outside facilitator, your first and primary challenge is to think through every aspect of the event using the lens of your unique culture. I recently worked with a large client in the chemical industry who took the planning challenge to heart and deliberated with me for several hours to ensure our initial workshops would be deemed a success by all attending. Before writing this section, I reviewed my notebook from that meeting and the pages dedicated to it numbered close to 20. We scrutinized every possible element we could imagine, resulting in a list that spanned multiple flip-chart pages. Here is a small sampling of what we discussed:

- Which members of the group work well together?
- Conversely, who should never be paired together in small-group settings?
- How should we time agenda items to maximize flow and energy?
- Which hot-button issues need to be addressed, but must be introduced with care?

- What is the most effective facilitation methodology?
- What materials should be used during the workshop (PowerPoint slides, etc.)?
- What is the nature and timing of pre-work?

I would suggest you begin planning by asking yourself how you would describe a successful outcome for the workshop: What does a successful session look like to you? Next, invert the question and challenge yourself to conjure up possible scenarios that would lead to a poor and unproductive session. What went wrong? The negative-oriented question tends to produce more pragmatic and probable experiences, those that require your attention before you convene your team. There are numerous other considerations when planning for your workshops. A number of the more essential items are outlined below.

Determine Where to Hold the Workshop

Deciding where to hold your workshop will very likely hinge on your view of whether, and to what degree, setting matters in endeavors of this sort. If you're convinced you could hold your workshop anywhere—in a bowling alley, the nearest Starbucks, or your own conference room—and generate the same results, then setting is not an issue for your organization. Despite that philosophical inclination, I urge you to read on, however, because I believe setting does matter.

While I don't have any statistical evidence to bolster my case, I believe strategy maps and other Scorecard deliverables created in offsite locations tend to be of a higher-quality than those cranked out in a sterile corporate meeting room. For many people, office meeting rooms carry with them the stigma of long, dry, and useless information exchanges, and wastes of never-to-be-retrieved time. Perhaps the biggest issue with holding workshops at your own location is the vexing challenge of herding harried and distracted participants back into the room after breaks. Over the years I've probably logged the equivalent of several marathons zipping along corporate corridors and ducking into offices searching for wayward workshop attendees. This is meeting management 101, I know, but in my experience it's practiced poorly in most organizations and leads to frustration on the part of those who do honor time commitments, and an overall sense that the workshop must not be that important if some participants must be continually coaxed back into the room, pried from their real work.

Why not tip the workshop balance in your favor by taking your group to a fresh new place, one stripped bare of any preconceived notions or baggage, where creativity and insight can blossom? Although I strongly believe, and research backs this up, getting out in nature promotes better thinking, you don't need to go to a mountain in Tibet—just break up the routine a little, that's all. Over the years I've held sessions in rustic log cabins, restored manors, country inns, corporate retreat centers in breathtakingly beautiful surroundings (my favorite was in Sedona, Arizona) and, of course, many hotel conference rooms.

Decide on the Day

What do you think is the best day of the week to announce a merger? Interestingly, the answer depends on how you want the market to react to the announcement. Penn State accounting professor Amy Sun and a co-author discovered that investor attention varies depending on the day of the week a major corporate event is announced, and the variation in attention can have a dramatic impact on the stock market reaction to the news. It turns out that Friday is probably the worst day for an announcement. Says Sun: "If people were not distracted on Fridays, we would not observe any difference in the trading volume between transactions announced on Fridays and those announced on other weekdays, but we do see a huge difference."[2] Corporate managers either instinctively know this bias exists or are paying attention to the research, because statistics show about 26 percent of announcements are made on Monday. The percentage of announcements gradually declines throughout the week, with a mere 14 percent on Friday.

As we learned above, venue location can have a dramatic impact on the success of your workshop. The same can be said for the day of the week on which you choose to stage your event, and while Mondays are popular for merger announcements, for a number of reasons they are not your best choice for holding an important workshop. First of all, when people open their office doors or walk into their cubicles on a Monday morning they're instantly reminded of everything they need to get done. Once they sit down the phone is likely to start ringing, and when they open their computers the flood of e-mails crashes down, drowning them in a sea of seemingly urgent actions. Any free time someone may be fortunate enough to carve out on a Monday is typically used to plan the rest of the week. So Monday is out, how about Friday—bad for mergers, good for workshops? Nope. Friday is also a poor choice. Most office dwellers, the conscientious ones anyway, will focus on tying up loose ends on Friday, getting everything in order for the following week, ensuring they can leave the building in a stress-free state and enjoy the weekend. That is, if they're not working over the weekend as so many people are these days.

Neither a Monday nor a Friday workshop will be appreciated by those who work at your office, but do you know who will like those days even less? Anyone who has to fly in for the event from some distant locale, and in my experience virtually every workshop is attended by at least one (but usually more) people from out of town who are making a special trip to attend. For those weary travelers the choice of day, regardless of whether the event is scheduled for Monday or Friday, translates to sacrificing time with family and instead venturing to that most dreamy and happiest of places . . . no, not Disneyland—the airport. Many of my clients have international operations, and if the Scorecard workshops are being held in the United States, they will often invite participants from Europe, Asia, the Middle East, and other far-flung regions of the globe. Oh, the haggard, jet-lagged, coffee-guzzling multitudes I've witnessed on Monday mornings. Groggy individuals who are now expected to be at their intellectual and strategic best, despite having spent 12 of the last 24 hours crossing five time zones while crammed into an airplane.

With the bookend days of the workweek out of the equation, we're left with Tuesday, Wednesday, and Thursday. Any of these are far superior to Monday or Friday, but my pick would be Wednesday. The traditional "hump day" is your best choice because its place at the center of the workweek allows participants two full days to clear their desks, alleviating themselves of the most pressing issues before the workshop, and two additional days to get back into the rhythm of their work and tidy things up before the weekend. If you're scheduling multiday workshops (perhaps a vision session followed by strategy mapping), selecting from Tuesday to Thursday is still the best course of action.

Determine Who Will Attend the Workshop

The obvious answer here is your Balanced Scorecard team, which we discussed in Chapter 2. You might recall that, for a number of reasons, I argued passionately to keep the numbers on that team relatively low, reminding you of the Navy SEAL finding that six is the optimal number for any high-intensity team. Under this scenario, these individuals, hopefully senior in nature, would come together and create your strategy map, Scorecard of measures, and other system deliverables. There is, however, another possibility for crafting your Scorecard, one that relies on two teams that I would like to share here. This method, which I'll dub the *counter approach* to Scorecard development, features a very small team, most likely two carefully selected individuals working optionally with an outside consultant, who create drafts of Scorecard products, which are then vetted with the larger formal Balanced Scorecard team. Again, as noted in Chapter 2, your senior team must accept ownership for the Balanced Scorecard, so it would be highly beneficial if one of the two-person team is part of the leadership team within your organization. Failing that, you will be best served by highly thought-of individuals who report directly to members of your senior executive team.

The small team engages in a number of tasks prior to creating the straw man Scorecard products, including: in-depth executive interviews to gauge leadership thinking on key strategic issues, environmental analysis, identification of trends affecting the organization, key challenges the organization faces, and so on. At that point they take the necessary time and engage in the deep thinking required to engineer a strategy map, Scorecard of measures, and portfolio of strategic initiatives that squarely faces the organization's most pressing challenges and provides a sound and reasoned strategic response. Then, in a workshop setting, our small group presents their findings to the larger team who are invited to critically examine, critique, and ultimately strengthen the final product.

The reason I'm offering this second alternative to creating your Balanced Scorecard is the fact that large-group brainstorming, the method most frequently employed by organizations in creating strategy maps and measures, is of dubious value, and may in fact be counter-productive. In her book *Quiet*, author Susan Cain notes:

> Some forty years of research has reached the same startling conclusion. Studies have shown that performance gets worse as group size increases: groups of nine generate fewer and poorer ideas compared to groups of six, which do worse than groups of four. The evidence from science suggests that business people must be insane to use brainstorming groups.[3]

According to psychologists there are several reasons for the failure of group brainstorming. The first is social loafing, which posits that when in a group setting some people will tend to sit back and let others do the heavy intellectual lifting. A second issue is production blocking, the fact that only one person at a time is able to talk or produce an idea, while others are forced to sit in silence, often focused more on their own stream of consciousness flow than the ideas of their vocal colleagues. Finally, we have evaluation apprehension, or more simply, the fear of looking stupid in front of our peers, which precludes some from offering any input, despite how useful it may be to the discussion at hand.

Cain, along with a growing list of business and science writers, suggests that in order to discover creative solutions to pressing problems, people require deep, time-consuming concentration on the task. Only then can they generate novel insights, those that are infrequently produced in a large group setting where creativity on demand is expected and rarely achieved. Of course, a critical flaw with the large group workshop approach, a session that would include your entire team in creating the Balanced Scorecard, is that it doesn't allow for the deep, mindful concentration on the task at hand which, as noted above, is required for breakthroughs. You often witness debate and passionate discussions in these one-day sessions, but they can only go so deep because of the time constraints and lack of pre-thinking done by the participants. As a result compromises are required, and suboptimal choices are made, which, ironically, lessen the support participants will have for something they themselves created.

Using a very small team to produce initial drafts of the Balanced Scorecard may not eliminate the problem of full commitment to what has been created (some people, for various reasons—often political—will never be happy with everything on the Balanced Scorecard), but the preparers should have the necessary knowledge to cogently defend why they chose what they did, so that even if someone doesn't like it, they must respect the thinking behind it. In a half- or full-day workshop with a large group of participants, it's very difficult to engage in such deep thinking.

In past books I have advocated for the large group workshop approach, suggesting that "people will only support what they help create," but in reality that is not always the case. For one, I support many things in my daily life that I didn't help create—laws, informal mores with my family, and so on. Corporate employees support numerous things they didn't create—policies and procedures, compensation structures, communications, and strategy. Especially with the Balanced Scorecard, there is no way we can have every employee involved in its creation, but we're banking on their acceptance for its successful implementation. The key to accessing that commitment is not necessarily involvement, but understanding of the final product and why it's necessary for the organization at this time.

I promised this book would be very practical in its approach, and it is in that spirit that I offer a final reason for considering the small team counter approach to Balanced Scorecard development. As discussed in the day of the week section above, many organizations investing in a Balanced Scorecard will have a large, geographically dispersed workforce, requiring workshop participants to descend upon a central location for the working sessions. Such was the case with a recent client of mine. Although not international in nature, the company did have representatives stationed around the United States, and the team that was convened featured individuals from several locations, converging on a central location to build the Scorecard. While I applauded the heterogeneity of the team, and the diverse viewpoints they brought to the table, actually conducting the sessions became problematic. This group met in person so infrequently that they seized the opportunity of using the Scorecard sessions to book multiple meetings with other head-office staff, socialize with erstwhile colleagues, and catch up on nagging issues such as having the IT group fix laptop problems. When we did actually sit down to build the Scorecard, they spent an inordinate amount of time discussing issues of mutual interest that, while undoubtedly urgent, were not necessarily strategic or germane to the conversation at hand. I'm all for bringing your team together to discuss the issues you face, but that must be done separately from the task of building the Balanced Scorecard. With this particular group the time and effectiveness of our workshops were negatively impacted. This is not an isolated incident, and can happen whenever you bring together a group that only occasionally enjoys the opportunity to meet in person.

Assign Pre-Work

Should you decide to employ the small team approach to Scorecard development, your two intrepid guides will engage in an array of pre-work prior to creating draft versions of the strategy map, performance measures, and strategic initiatives. It won't be necessary to assign this to the individuals as all pre-building tasks—executive interviews, strategic assessments, and so on—will surface organically in their work. If, however, you choose the large group option to design your Scorecard, assigning pre-work is essential for successful workshops.

As discussed above, generating new, innovative solutions and ideas requires a depth of thought and contemplation that is very difficult to achieve given the time constraints of a typical workshop. Therefore, in order to prime the participants and stimulate their thinking on the core elements of the Balanced Scorecard, it's crucial to supply them with provocative questions they must answer prior to the first session. Completion of homework assignments serves dual purposes: Primarily it forces participants to confront the issues they'll be tackling in the workshop and determine their own point of view on the best course of action to pursue. They will be expected to share their perspectives with their colleagues during the working sessions. A second benefit of the homework assignment is conferred upon the facilitators. By transcribing the responses, they hold a repository of participants' thinking on the key issues and, based on those reflections, possess a head start on how they'll steer the upcoming discussions.

As for the specific questions to assign in advance, it will depend upon your unique situation; however, outlined in the chart below are a number of questions I've used to advantage with many clients.

Question	Rationale
Based on the attributes of an effective vision (*Note:* participants are typically supplied with a copy of my book), do you feel your vision paints an effective word picture of your desired future?	The quantified vision represents primary material for Scorecard construction, and with this question you're determining the level of alignment relating to the vision, and also identifying necessary enhancements.
Please summarize the key challenges faced by your organization in the next three years.	With strategic timelines shrinking for most organizations, enumerating key challenges is central to strategic decision making. The challenges identified here will have a direct impact on the selection of objectives, measures, and strategic initiatives.
What do you feel you and your colleagues are most passionate about and why?	This question is designed to assist in the identification of the organization's chosen value proposition—typically customer intimacy, operational excellence, or product leadership. I've discovered that subtly wrapping the question in the guise of passion helps reveal more telling insights.
Strategy represents the means of an organization's movement from a somehow deficient current state to a desired future state. List a number of key attributes that define your as-is state (items requiring a change) and for each, please note a corresponding desired future state.	Like the second question on key challenges, this query should highlight the main areas requiring strategic change within the organization. I'm always curious to see how much overlap there is between the responses to the two questions.
If you are to execute your strategy, what financial objectives must you pursue?	From this point forward, we're transitioning to more pragmatic questions relating to potential strategic objectives. *Note:* Similar questions will be issued at a later phase of the engagement to cover possible performance measures, and strategic initiatives.
What are your customers' expectations or demands of you as an organization?	The voice of the customer should be represented in the customer perspective, and this question seeks to find that voice.

How would you describe the organization's value proposition? Are you customer-intimate, operationally excellent, or an innovative product leader?

Above I asked respondents to discuss what the organization is most passionate about in order to discover the value proposition. Here I'm asking the question directly, looking for consistency of responses. If most recipients provide different answers for the two questions that will necessitate greater emphasis on this component of the strategy mapping workshop.

In order to meet customers' needs and deliver on your value proposition, there are certain internal processes at which you must excel. Please identify and list what you consider your key internal processes.

A very open-ended question that will produce a large number of unique responses. Again, I'm looking for consistency here; key themes or major processes that provide differentiation for the company and drive their value proposition.

Do you believe the organization has the skills required to meet current and anticipated demands?

This is the first of three questions relating to the Learning and Growth perspective. Here I'm interested in whether or not they believe employees possess the skills necessary to drive processes and deliver the value proposition.

Is information technology (IT) leveraged for success within the organization?

Kaplan and Norton term this *information capital*, the alignment between technology and strategy. Since most organizations invest heavily in technology, we must determine whether the tools in place are in fact serving the execution of the chosen strategy.

How would you describe the culture of your organization?

Another very open-ended question, and one that often yields revealing responses. My quest here is to assess whether the organization is living its declared strategy. For example, if they stress cooperation and teamwork in their strategy, perhaps in service of a customer intimacy value proposition, yet most respondents report an information hoarding, power-is-everything culture, I know they have a significant problem, one that may require intervention prior to the creation of the Balanced Scorecard.

To administer the homework questions I recommend using an online tool such as Survey Monkey. Once your list has been typed in the software tool you'll be provided a link, which you'll send to the recipients. Forwarding that link is a great opportunity to not only request their participation in completing the survey questions, but also to lay the groundwork for what is to follow in the workshops. I'm reminded here of an old presentation adage that admonishes us to: Tell them what you're about to tell them, tell them, and then tell them what you told them. Take every opportunity you have at your disposal to inform participants of what will be occurring in the workshops—the work you'll be engaging in, and what is expected of them during their time in the room. You'd be surprised, or then again perhaps you won't be, at how often workshop participants are confused about why they're present and what the goals of the session are. Outlining in Technicolor detail what will take place and what is expected when the group convenes is an example of clearing the path for your participants, making it easier for them to fully engage in the process.[4] This is another change-management technique you must be cognizant of throughout the implementation.

Clearing the path has been demonstrated to work in a multitude of circumstances, including: corporate environments, retail sales, and charitable giving. An example of its dramatic impact on the latter is demonstrated in a study on why college students did or didn't donate food to a canned-food drive. Going into the study, the researchers were aware that some students would be more inclined to give than others. Their goal was to alter the situation so that nongivers would give as well. To determine who was more likely to donate they polled students in a particular dorm, asking them to assess which of their dorm mates (out of a population of roughly 100) were most and least likely to give. Compiling those results gave them a good idea of which students were most and least inclined to donate to the food drive. For simplicity, those with the proclivity to give were called saints, and those less likely to donate were termed jerks. Now it was time to clear the path to transform nongiving students to generous philanthropists. One group of random students received a very basic letter noting that a food drive was taking place the next week and asking them to bring a canned food item to a booth at a well-known location on campus. Other random students, however, received a much more detailed letter, including a map to the exact spot, a request for a can of beans, and a suggestion that they think of a time they might be near the drop-off spot so that it would be convenient for them to make their donation. Once the food drive was over the researchers compiled their results, which were astonishing. Students who had received the basic letter were not very generous, with just 8 percent of the saints donating, and not a single one of the jerks. But students who received the more detailed letter were substantially more inclined to participate in the food drive—42 percent of the saints donated, as did 25 percent of the jerks. By simply clearing the path a bit, the researchers were able to get 25 percent of the worst individuals to donate. Remember that every step along the Balanced Scorecard path is new, different, and considered potentially hazardous by your team, and thus it's incumbent upon you to shape your environment, ensuring there is not a single pothole on your implementation route.

 DURING THE WORKSHOP

The coffee pot is already half empty, most of the breakfast snacks have been eaten, some people are sitting quietly in their chairs pecking out a text message, while others stand and share a laugh with their colleagues. You look down at your watch. 8:30 a.m. Drawing a deep breath, you step to the front of the room and say with pleasant authority, "Okay everyone, it's 8:30; let's get started." The workshop is about to begin, so let's make it count. Outlined next are practical techniques, tools, and tips to ensure your gathering is a successful one.

Getting Started: The Power of Story

What business book would be complete without a quote from the Greek philosopher Plato? I'll slip mine in here—"The beginning is the most important part of the work." I doubt Plato had Balanced Scorecard workshops in mind when he proposed this, but his declaration does resonate, and there can be no doubt that getting off to a good start and building positive momentum is vital to the success of any type of workshop. Beyond the customary recitation of logistical details (restroom locations if you're offsite, break times, etc.) the best way to launch your session is with a story or anecdote that encapsulates why everyone is there and why what you're about to embark upon is so important. The story doesn't necessarily have to be about your own company, although anything emanating from your corporate history will certainly capture the attention of your audience, but it must represent the essence or spirit of the event. Having facilitated workshops for going on two decades, I have a repertoire of stories to draw upon, depending on the type of workshop, industry represented by the company, demographics of the audience, and so on. I can regale them with anecdotes about the great film director Otto Preminger, the French sculptor Auguste Rodin, Russian ruler Catherine the Great, or, more humbly, even myself. While the characters and eras are different, what binds my tales is their message, which always links directly to the topic at hand. Are you curious yet? Here's a humorous story I tell about myself that serves as a good icebreaker while also reinforcing the theme of the session.

On a recent trip, just after I got to my hotel room and closed the door behind me I could hear a buzzing sound in the room. I walked about the room, looking up, looking down, examining walls and furniture along the way but couldn't find the source of the sound that by this time was becoming quite distracting. Projecting ahead several hours, there was no way I was going to be able to stay in the room with that noise. I called the front desk and asked if there was any maintenance going on, thinking perhaps work on the heating or air conditioning systems might be causing a temporary buzz. The desk clerk, friendly but somewhat perplexed, assured me there was no maintenance taking place that could be producing the buzzing sound I described. So I asked if I could come down and change rooms.

As I left my room and walked, with luggage in hand, down the corridor to the elevator I was sure I could still hear the buzzing sound. Even in the elevator it seemed present. Am I losing my mind, I wondered? When the elevator door opened I was relieved to no longer hear the buzz and proceeded to turn in my key card for another one and was soon back on my way. But when I got back in the elevator there it was—the buzz, distant, but definitely present. When I got to my new room, much to my dismay I was greeted by, you guessed it—buzzing! By this point I was frustrated, confused, and a bit stressed out, thinking I'd now have to change hotels and what a hassle that would be. Before taking that step I called down to the front desk once more and again told my sorry tale to the clerk who remained remarkably perky despite my insistence on a phantom sound permeating the hotel. In a last ditch effort to solve the problem she dispatched a hotel engineer to my room to investigate.

A few moments later he arrived, quickly acknowledged the buzzing (good, I'm not crazy) and immediately began his sleuthing—placing his head close to the TV, examining all the vents, looking under the bed. Finally, just when I thought he was going to suggest I do in fact change hotels he circled and cast his gaze intently on my suitcase. "It's coming from in there," he said confidently. "Can't be," I replied. But when I put my head next to my bag it was clear the sound was indeed emanating from within. I opened the bag and found, deep within, an electric beard trimmer buzzing away. It must have been tossed around at some point in the journey causing the on switch to engage. We had a good laugh about it—mine nervous and self-conscious and his slightly mocking—and he left. When I thought about it later I realized my critical error was in assuming the sound was somewhere in the room and couldn't possibly be linked to me. That assumption led me to ignore the evidence and, although not a big deal in the grand scheme of things, inconvenience both myself and members of the hotel staff.

That's the story. How does it link to the Balanced Scorecard? After recounting the tale I ask the audience, "Does this sound familiar to all of you—the idea of accepting things without really challenging them?" Most hands extend skyward immediately. I then go on to explain that making assumptions without challenging them is definitely the case in the world of performance measurement and management. Most of us assume that performance measurement is the primary domain of financial metrics, but to be successful today we must balance financial metrics with the drivers of future financial success. I then say: "Our purpose today is to challenge the assumptions of performance measurement and look at a proven tool that has in many ways revolutionized how organizations track their performance. That tool is the Balanced Scorecard, and I'm here to share its story with all of you."

Many people will kick off their workshops by reviewing the agenda, but that's a mistake. As the pithy old maxim goes, you only have one chance to make a first impression. You need to grab your audience's attention immediately with a story or anecdote that cleverly expresses why you're meeting, captures their imagination, and leaves them with an enduring image you can mutually draw upon throughout the event. There is nothing more powerful than a well-crafted, confidently delivered story to convey meaning.

Tell Them Again and Again . . .

Earlier, in the pre-work section, I suggested you take every opportunity at your disposal to inform participants of what will be occurring in the workshops—the work you'll be engaging in, and what is expected of them during their time in the room. Now is the time to repeat that step, by outlining the agenda you've designed for the session, and emphasizing why this particular group was chosen. Beyond the rote repetition of times and activities, it's important to address how the group may be feeling during certain stages of the event. Sorting out your strategy, creating strategic objectives, measures, and initiatives is messy business and it's very likely that at some junctures in the process people may feel anxious, confused, and at least a bit frustrated. The time to acknowledge that miasma of emotions is now, not when the group is about to either throw up their hands in despair or declare mutiny on you, the facilitator. Let people know it's okay to feel this way, it's a natural part of the process and in some ways healthy, because it indicates some aspect of what's taking place troubles them. Encourage them to voice their feelings throughout the day with the promise that this is a safe environment where all comments are welcomed. I'm making the assumption, of course, that it is a safe environment, and you do welcome comments, concerns, and critiques. If that's not the case you probably have issues that swell considerably beyond the need for a Balanced Scorecard.

Even if you've delivered your opening story with the oratory flair of a Lincoln or Dr. Martin Luther King and have promised safe haven for the full canvas of possible emotional reactions during the workshop, it doesn't guarantee your audience will be giving you their full attention. I'll discuss dealing with distractions a bit later, but right now you need a practical method to ensure the focus is on you. Enter Stephen Covey's principle of third-person teaching, which suggests the best way to learn something is to teach it yourself. In applying that maxim to our present circumstances, before you begin outlining the agenda and discussing the work processes in detail (information that is essential to the participants) inform them that at the conclusion of your overview you'll be calling upon a random person in the group to come up and repeat what you said. Not verbatim, like a parrot, but in a manner that captures the spirit of your intentions. They can only return to their seats once they've shared their understanding of the event thoroughly and secured your approval of the same. Trust me, there is nothing like the threat of an extemporaneous speech to get the blood flowing in the cerebral cortex and capture the full attention of your audience.

Answering the Why Question

Despite stacking the deck with a great opening story and clearly outlining your agenda, the possibility remains that someone in the group will, very early on in the event, slump back in their chair and launch this verbal grenade your way: "Tell me again why we're doing this?" If you've followed the advice found in Chapter 2 on communication planning, education, and so on, then there is really no valid reason for this question to ever surface at this point. Quite frequently this represents good, old-fashioned corporate passive-aggressive resistance, but the possibility of it being a sincere inquiry also exists. Either way you need to handle it effectively, and I believe, dramatically. Respond this way: "Everyone, take out a piece of paper and write down the three (could be more) most important things we need to do in the next 12 to 18 months. You have two minutes." They may very well protest, "We need more time." But you can say, "We should all know exactly what we need to do well, we shouldn't need time to think about it, because it should be top of mind." Wait the two minutes then have people read their answers, which you can capture on a flip chart. My experience tells me there will be little consistency in the responses. If the responses are in fact scattered a mile wide with everything from increasing the bottom line to restructuring the organization, you say: "This is why we're doing this, because as a leadership team we should all know, without hesitation, what the most important objectives of our business are, and the Balanced Scorecard drives that alignment."

On the very off chance that people are aligned on the key objectives, and I'm talking a 99 to 1 long-shot chance, take it to the next level. Congratulate them and say, "Okay, take out another piece of paper and write down the most vital metrics we should be tracking in order to gauge our accountability in achieving those objectives." Again, most evidence suggests you will not receive consistent replies, and can then reiterate the purpose of developing a Balanced Scorecard.

Prime Participants for Success

Social psychologists and other researchers have consistently demonstrated that people's performance can be influenced by the introduction of subtle factors, such as priming. When people are exposed to a certain stimulus—whether a physical object, concept, or stereotype—they are primed to react in a certain way. Stereotypes may or may not be accurate, but they are almost always influential. For example, in one experiment researchers gave Asian–American women a math test. Before one group took the test, the researchers emphasized the fact that they were women, which primed them to recall the stereotype that women aren't good at math. For the second group, they emphasized that they were Asian, which encouraged them to recall the stereotype that Asians are good at math. When the results were tabulated the group that was primed with women performed significantly worse on the test then the group primed with Asian.[5]

Priming can be used with participants in your workshop as well. During your opening remarks, sprinkle your comments with reminders that everyone in the room was selected for their unique perspective or exemplary knowledge. These terms and many others at your disposal will conjure images of insight, knowledge, and creativity, which the participants can draw upon throughout the workshop.

Speaking of priming effects, here is one last semi-facetious tip to ensure a successful workshop, one featuring an abundance of knowledge sharing, collaboration, and absolutely no political backstabbing: Put teddy bears in the room. Yes, you read that correctly, teddy bears. In a study, researchers had people play classic psychology games in which they controlled the amount of money other people earned, and could earn more themselves if they lied. Half the subjects were in a room with children's toys and half in a room with no childhood cues. The results were astonishing: in rooms with toys, cheating dropped almost 20 percent.[6] It turns out that we adults are less likely to cheat and more inclined to pro-social behaviors when reminders of children, like teddy bears and crayons, are present. Researchers suggest that child-related cues may unconsciously activate notions of goodness and drive us to a pure state that we don't want to pollute. So instead of handing out markers along with those flip-chart pages, make sure you have an ample supply of crayons instead.

Facilitating the Session

How you facilitate the session will depend upon which workshop method you're using—the conventional or counter approach. Recall from our earlier discussion that the counter approach to Scorecard development is characterized by a very small team (usually two people, possibly with the assistance of a consultant) developing draft Scorecard products and using a workshop setting to vet, critique, and ultimately improve them thanks to the participation of a larger group. The conventional method entails using a larger group (but still a relatively small number of people) to create the Scorecard in a workshop setting, without the aid of any draft products having been previously developed. While I feel the counter approach is underutilized, it's fair to say there are pros and cons to each alternative, and in the end your decision will be based upon your unique culture and goals for involvement in the implementation. Since a majority of organizations I've encountered continue to rely on the conventional approach, my recommendations below are based on that choice.

A commonplace approach to developing Scorecard products is using group brainstorming. As I noted earlier in the chapter, large group brainstorming suffers from a number of critical flaws that inhibit its effectiveness: social loafing, production blocking, and evaluation apprehension among them. However, if you have a large group in the room, anything that numbers more than six or seven, engaging in some form of brainstorming is unavoidable. To counteract the risks inherent in the approach, I modify it this way: Rather than me standing at a flip chart inviting attendees to voice their suggestions, I begin by splitting the group into two teams. Let's say we have 10 participants who have convened to create the strategy map; I create two teams of five and have them work independently for approximately 30 to 40 minutes, depending on the task at hand. For example, creating objectives for the customer perspective typically requires more time than the financial perspective. At the conclusion of the 40 minutes, each team reports their findings, outlines the rationale for their selections, and answers questions from me and the other team. Once both teams have reported, all possible objectives appear on flipcharts and I facilitate a plenary discussion during which the group settles on the final set of objectives for that perspective. Smaller groups offer many advantages:

- There is less likelihood of social loafing, since in a small group there will be enhanced peer pressure to share your opinions.
- People tend to be less inhibited and fearful of saying the wrong thing in smaller groups.
- A healthy sense of competition is fostered between the teams as they over-hear each other's spirited discussions.
- Commitment to ideas is enhanced, leading to spirited debates and improved outcomes as ideas are critically examined from all sides.

When the teams huddle to create their objectives (again assuming this is a strategy mapping workshop) I roam the room, traveling between the two groups, listening in on their conversations, answering questions, and steering them back when I feel they've veered off course. Of course the facilitator can't be in two places at one time and thus the possibility exists that a group will mean-der off topic or come to conclusions that, while reflecting their shared think-ing, will ultimately not serve their strategy map well. To lower the risk of poor objectives (or measures, or initiatives), I arm each team with simple checklists outlining the characteristics of effective objectives. The humble checklist has been proven effective in medical settings, ensuring that harried doctors avoid potentially life-threatening errors, and it is gaining traction in many other fields, including the corporate arena, where they may be applied with advantage in a wide variety of settings, including Balanced Scorecard workshops.

Perhaps the biggest challenge you will encounter in any Balanced Score-card workshop is coming to consensus as a group on your final set of objectives, measures, or initiatives (whatever the deliverable you're creating in the work-shop). After conducting thousands of workshops with hundreds of clients, I can say unequivocally that achieving complete consensus on every single element of your Scorecard is virtually impossible. Accompanying you in any workshop setting are fellow human beings, each of whom has accumulated a lifetime of unique experiences that shape their singular viewpoint and philosophy. Despite the unrealistic nature of the quest, I've had clients who insist on remaining in the room until everyone agrees with every point that is circled or checked on a barely decipherable flipchart. The underlying intent is honorable—ensuring the team is 100 percent committed to what has been agreed upon by the majority in the room—however, at some point what appears to be commitment may well be fake compliance wrought by fatigue and frustration.

Aiming for complete unanimity is unrealistic and, in the long run, likely not advantageous. While the desire for agreement on the elements of your Scorecard is a natural impulse, you must remember that those elements, be they objectives, measures, or initiatives, should remain malleable in light of ever-changing conditions in your corporate orbit. Dissenting voices will be a valuable aid when environmental factors signal that a change is necessary. Rather than shooting for complete consensus during your workshops, why not consider a Marine dictum that pronounces "When you're 70 percent ready and have 70 percent consensus, act. Don't shoot from the hip, but also don't wait for perfection."[7] Of course, the 70 percent is not a strict metric but represents a metaphor for the necessity to balance deliberation and action. Nothing bogs down a workshop more than protracted discussions, typically featuring intense and non-value-added wordsmithing, that have no end in sight and offer little in the way of additional insights. As with most things Scorecard-related, momentum is paramount to garnering buy-in and support.

Encouraging Full Attention and Dealing with Distractions

Unlike some other writers and facilitators, you will not find me advocating a cell phone ban in Balanced Scorecard workshops. My pledge to you was a book full of practical and realistic guidelines for constructing a future-ready Balanced Scorecard, and it's neither practical nor realistic to expect people, at least those not living under a rock as of last week, to surrender their smartphones upon entering a meeting room. Over the years I've heard all the tricks designed to liberate people from their phones, but just as malicious hackers in search of our credit and debit card numbers always seem to be one step ahead of corporate IT departments, cunning workshop participants are a step ahead and have a ceaseless variety of rationales for why they absolutely must have their phone on during the session. The most common, and difficult for me to protest is: "I'm expecting an important call from a customer." This reminds me of someone declining a dinner party or any other social engagement they're clearly not interested in with the line, "I've got some family issues to deal with." It stops you in your tracks and renders any counterassault pointless. The explanation offered for using laptops is usually coated in a glaze of potential productivity: "I'm going to take notes during the session." Curiously enough, no one has ever e-mailed me their notes after a workshop. Phones, tablets, and laptops have become workshop fixtures as ubiquitous as urns of bitter coffee and disagreements about the room temperature, and I'm not going to suggest you prohibit their use. I am, however, going to alert you to some of the negative impacts these devices can have on individual and group productivity, so that you can make your own decision on whether or not to answer that text just as your team is about to make a final decision on the objectives that best represent your customer value proposition.

The primary impetus for using a phone, laptop, or tablet in any meeting setting is ostensibly to enhance productivity through multitasking. Today's always-on, never-out-of-touch culture demands that even during an important workshop that requires intense focus and concentration, people must maximize the value of every minute and engage in multiple tasks. The desire to push the productivity frontier to its edges is natural and positive, but the fact of the matter is that multitasking simply doesn't work and is in fact dangerously counterproductive. For more than 30 years, hundreds of experiments have documented the deleterious effects of attempting to do two things at once, even if they are relatively simple and trivial tasks. For example, in one study researchers had volunteers press one of two keys on a pad in response to whether a light flashed on the left or right side of a window. One group repeated this task again and again. A second group had to define the color of an object at the same time, choosing from among three colors. These are simple variables: left or right, and only three colors. Yet doing two tasks took twice as long, leading to no time saving. The neurological phenomenon in play here is known as dual-task interference, which denotes our inability to process or engage in two activities simultaneously and effectively. So powerful is this condition that it can render someone's immediate cognitive capacity from that of a Harvard MBA to an eight-year-old.[8]

Constant texting and e-mailing have a seductive appeal, satisfying our innate urge to do more, produce more, and remain in close contact with our ever-expanding networks. For some, it may even seem we're boosting our intelligence by participating in so many varied threads, contributing our insights at a moment's notice. That is far from the truth, however. A University of London study found that constant e-mailing and texting lowers mental capability on an IQ test by an average of 10 points. The impact is similar to missing a night's sleep and for men is about three times more than the effect of smoking cannabis.[9] So if you live in Colorado, where, as of this writing, marijuana is legally available for recreational use, lighting up isn't as damaging as being glued to the perpetual ramble of texts flowing on to your phone screen.

Stanford professor Clifford Nass has studied multitasking extensively and warns that, "The neural circuits devoted to scanning, skimming, and multi-tasking are expanding and strengthening, while those used for reading and thinking deeply, with sustained concentration, are weakening or eroding."[10] He goes on to suggest that perpetual multitaskers may be sacrificing performance on the primary task, labeling them "suckers for irrelevancy." Multi-tasking, in whatever form that takes, impedes our ability to think deeply and creatively, skills that virtually every modern knowledge worker must possess in order to contribute value to the organization.

The primary task that Nass notes above is, in our context, the selection of objectives, measures, and strategic initiatives that will form the basis of our Balanced Scorecard. When a team is engaged in making those important selections, and some group members break away, even for just a few seconds, to respond to a text or e-mail, they're cognitively hindered and unable to fully participate in the decision making because their attention has been diverted and it requires substantial neural resources to shift back to where it was before the interruption. If the topics being discussed are new to you, and chances are at least components of them will be, then the neural circuits you're creating in those conversations are relatively new, and any shift in attention will neces-sitate reactivating billions of still-fresh circuits that are apt to disappear as quickly as a shooting star across the night sky.

Be Present and Listen More

As I write this, the 2014 Winter Olympics are fast approaching and, like many people around the globe, I'm anxiously awaiting the fierce competition among nations. A particular highlight is the opening ceremonies, replete with splen-dor and pageantry, vivid colors, and national pride. I'll probably watch on the NBC network as I did for the games back in 2010. I just hope this time around Bob Costas listens a bit more attentively to his co-host Matt Lauer. The two were providing commentary for the opening ceremonies and as the Canadian team entered the arena amid boisterous cheers from the home crowd (those games were staged in Vancouver), Matt mentioned the team's audacious goal to "own the podium" in Vancouver, and noted that some people in the coun-try considered this public pledge to achieve victory very un-Canadian-like behavior. As a Canadian I was still pondering that, when a few minutes later, as the large Canadian contingent marched on, Bob Costas said the exact same thing. I don't mean he paraphrased Matt, or that he summarized what Matt said. No, he repeated it word for word, verbatim. There was no, "As Matt said a moment ago . . . " or "To reiterate what Matt said . . ." It was clear that Bob wasn't listening to what Matt had said just moments earlier. In his defense, studies suggest we humans tend to listen at about a paltry 25 percent comprehension rate.

I would suggest that we live amidst an epidemic of poor listening, whether at home or at work. Some of the causes for this dearth of listening are biological, while others are uniquely germane to our modern world. One of the innate reasons we have difficulty listening is the fact that we tend to talk at a rate of somewhere between 125 and 175 words per minute, while we listen at a rate of 125 and 250 words a minute, but we're capable of thinking at a staggering 1,000 to 3,000 words per minute.[11] That gulf between thinking and listening opens up a huge opportunity for our brains to become distracted and cease paying any attention to a speaker in our midst. With its constant temptation, the dazzling array of technology we have at our fingertips only exacerbates the problem, and frequently drives us to literal distraction.

This is a battle you can't afford to lose; the stakes are simply too high, especially when you've gathered your best minds to create the Balanced Scorecard that will drive your strategy execution. The best defense, one you must enthusiastically encourage with your participants, is to be truly present during the workshops. When conducting workshops with clients, my top priority and number one goal is to be completely present for them during the session. That means crowding all competing thoughts out of my head while paying strict attention to, and processing, what they're saying. Believe me, it can be a hard-fought battle at times. I may have a tight connection at the airport that night, other client responsibilities to attend to, issues at home that have be dealt with, e-mails and texts piling up, the list is endless. But just before each meeting I tell myself that for the next six hours, eight hours, whatever it is, when I have a competing thought I will accept it, but treat it like a cloud that is simply floating by, soon to be out of my consciousness. It takes practice and a heaping dose of discipline, but over time I've become better and better at the practice, to the point where I now feel when I'm in a meeting my focus is exactly where it should be—on helping my clients, and I can only do that when I'm present for them. A favorite author of mine, Ernest Hemingway, once noted: "I have learned a great deal from listening carefully. Most people never listen."[12] I believe he's right on both counts—truly listening is a pathway to learning, and sadly most people never do fully listen.

FAR Moments

Developing a Balanced Scorecard requires the full cognitive capacity of every participant, and diverting attention for even a moment to respond to a text or deal with a thought that's suddenly elbowed its way into your head can seriously debilitate one's contribution. This can then lead to participants compromising on important decisions, not because they are committed to what is being recommended by others, but because they don't understand all of the ramifications or consequences, owing to their momentary diminished capacity.

Despite the dire statistics on distractions and listening presented above, it's clear that some people will continue to multitask during at least part of your workshops, whether it's checking their phones or at the very least thinking about something else that is going to mentally remove them from the room. To counteract that tendency, and in recognition of the fact that it will be exceedingly difficult for people to be fully present the entire time, I suggest you acknowledge it directly, perhaps even citing some of the statistics and anecdotes recounted here, but note that at certain critical junctures, you are going to declare what I call a full attention required (FAR) moment. Meaning you need everyone to fully commit 100 percent of their brains to processing what is happening at that moment. Finalizing your quantified vision, determining your value proposition, and deciding on the final set of objectives and measures, are all possible examples of times when full attention is required from the entire group. During these moments, which represent a small percentage of the entire workshop duration, request that phones be silenced, laptops shut, and if random thoughts flutter through participants' consciousness, they jot them down to close that loop and return their full attention to the conversation at hand. This process is not granting license for attendees to multitask or daydream at any point, it simply recognizes what is basically human nature and near-universal corporate behavior, especially in the early twenty-first century.

Avoiding Rabbit Holes

This chapter has provided extensive background on, and advice for overcoming, the cognitive form of distractions you may face in your workshops. However, if your distractions manifest themselves in the human variety, most notably someone who clings to an argument like a stray dog with a bone or a participant who insists on leading you down an off-topic path you know will yield nothing but frustration and discontent, consider the Rat card displayed in Exhibit 4.1. Yes, the Rat card. If you sense the conversation spiraling downward, and heading for a black hole, proudly toss your Rat card in the air,

EXHIBIT 4.1   The Rat Card

bringing an immediate halt to the proceedings. A client introduced this technique to me at a Scorecard workshop and it worked like a charm. Even the CEO was wary of the rodent interjection device, prefacing one controversial remark with the words, "At the risk of having a Rat card thrown at me . . ." It lightened the mood and served its purpose admirably—a great combination.

 ## THE ROLE OF EXECUTIVES IN WORKSHOPS

First Things First

It should go without saying (but since I'm writing this I guess it doesn't) that the most important thing an executive can do to ensure the success of a Balanced Scorecard workshop is to understand the Balanced Scorecard. Not just a cursory recognition of the tool, perhaps a passing acquaintance with its four perspectives, and the idea of balanced measures. No, to prove effective in their role as chief custodians and ultimate owners of the Scorecard, senior leaders must possess a strong working knowledge of the system—its makeup, how it is effectively implemented, why it's being called upon at this particular time, and how it will drive strategy execution.

Before writing this section, I spent some time reviewing the client's folder on my computer, quickly scanning the names and recalling the role each senior executive played in the client's implementation. I've been very fortunate to work with many CEOs, executive directors, and other senior leaders who grasped the significance of their role and took it upon themselves to become quick studies in the Balanced Scorecard field. Unfortunately, I've also struggled through the occasional engagement in which the senior executive clearly didn't understand even the most basic tenets of the Balanced Scorecard. One experience springs to mind whenever I recall the worst offenders in this category. It was the senior executive of a large nonprofit client. I could sense his supercilious attitude towards the Balanced Scorecard from our very first meeting, as if it were the most basic concept imaginable, hardly worth his precious time and attention. Of course I shared my concerns with the designated Scorecard champion, lobbied for extra time with the executive in order to subtly expound on the Scorecard, and provided as much reference material as I could, to no avail. During our first workshop to create the strategy map, he sat dumbfounded in his chair throughout, continually ranting, "When do we get to the measures, isn't this all about measures?" Initially, the rest of the team rallied to my aid, explaining that we were crafting objectives, with measures to follow, and the map would provide a powerful communication tool and create the context for measures. He wouldn't hear it. To him the Balanced Scorecard was tantamount to measures and that was that.

It's a well-known phenomenon in the organizational world that everyone watches what the boss watches, and feeds off their energy and interest, or lack thereof, in a particular topic. The neurological basis for this behavior is the presence of mirror neurons, which represent the brain's way of knowing what other people are intending and feeling in any particular instance, and how you should respond. Since people in a work setting are focused on their boss's behaviors, the impact is amplified and the boss's emotions are mirrored in others. That effect is the most deleterious impact of an executive not understanding the Balanced Scorecard and demonstrating their ignorance in a workshop setting—it sets off mirror neurons in others, even those who may strongly believe in the necessity of the Scorecard, and causes them to wonder, "Well if he isn't interested in this, why should I be?" That exact house of cards fell on me in the example noted above (which is why I said the team *initially* came to my aid). After the executive's repeated outbursts one executive after another, even those who in meetings with me demonstrated an understanding of the tool and a commitment to its use, began to question the purpose of the exercise. It wasn't pretty. Eventually we were able to get back on track and complete the strategy map, but the energy had been sucked from the room and the implementation never did gain the traction necessary for proper execution. The lesson here is clear—to successfully implement the Balanced Scorecard, your senior executive must possess a working knowledge of all facets of the system.

You're the CEO for a Reason

Before the first workshop with a client I meet with the organization's CEO or executive director to share with them the purpose of the event, outline my approach, and review their role in helping the group achieve its desired outcomes. As noted above, this is also a last opportunity to ensure that, based on their knowledge of the system, they are fully prepared to participate. Although every individual is different, I've witnessed a remarkable commonality among the responses I receive from CEOs when discussing their role in the meeting. "Don't let me dominate" is their universal refrain, followed quickly by "I need to hear what other people have to say." On certain occasions such a caution is in order, as some leaders will seize the floor and refuse to let go, leaving others to wonder why they were asked to attend in the first place.

In most cases, however, I find the opposite actually occurs—leaders are too quiet in the workshop. They sit back, cast a pensive look at their constant companion, nod a lot, laugh when appropriate, but rarely offer their point of view. The desire to draw out the opinions of their team, seeking a broad spectrum of views, is undoubtedly valuable and to be commended, but ultimately their reticence is as problematic as taking the meeting hostage by controlling the flow of dialog.

As discussed above, it's an inevitable fact of organizational life that we all look to our leaders for cues. Therefore, when in a workshop or meeting, we find an otherwise ebullient CEO sitting back and offering no guidance or personal insights, other attendees can misinterpret that silence as a signal the chief isn't engaged in the process. Once again the mirror neurons produce a leap of logic: If he or she isn't engaged, then the meeting probably isn't that important. This culminates with: If it's not important, why am I here, when there is plenty of work stacked up at my desk right now?

At the end of the day, the CEO is there for a reason—to make the difficult decisions. Taking the counsel of well-informed subordinates and listening to a diverse array of opinions is vital and sure to lead to better decisions and improved buy-in from everyone, but when push comes to shove leaders must illuminate the organization's path forward. This doesn't mean forcing their opinions on the team, but balancing humility and openness with focused action.

I've had the privilege of working with many brilliant senior executives over the years, and my favorites are those who have mastered the delicate balance of seeking input from others but always making a firm commitment based on their own knowledge and beliefs. In meetings these leaders, typically gifted individuals by all accounts, are fully present, ask seemingly simple questions, show their vulnerability, but never fail to lend several insightful comments to the discussion. When it is time for a decision to be made they summarize the key points raised to ensure they are accurately portraying the opinions that had been presented, then proceed to lay out the rationale for their decision. You are free to challenge it, of course; constructive conflict is always welcomed, but when it is time for action they accept responsibility and issue the final word on the subject.

Ultimately, the greatest leaders are able to achieve the challenging balance between humility and a bias for action. Strong, focused action from our leaders is something we're all familiar with, while humility is often relegated to the shadows. I'm going to end this chapter with my absolute favorite story about the power of humility. I hope you enjoy it.

John Masefield was Poet Laureate of the United Kingdom for 37 years, from 1930 until his death in 1967. During this time he wrote countless poems marking royal occasions or noteworthy public events, all of them designed to appear in *The Times* on the day in question. Despite Masefield's prolific contributions to poetry, fiction, and the theater, he remained throughout his life a most humble man. After his death *The Times* revealed that accompanying each manuscript he sent was a self-addressed stamped envelope so that the work might be returned to him if deemed not acceptable.[13]

 NOTES

1. John Wooden and Jay Carty, *Coach Wooden's Pyramid of Success* (Ventura, CA: Regal, 2005), 34.
2. See www.futurity.org/end-of-week-mergers-often-get-missed.

3. Susan Cain, *Quiet: The Power of Introverts in a World That Can't Stop Talking* (New York: Random House, 2012), Kindle edition, location 1673.

4. Chip Heath and Dan Heath, *Switch: How to Change When Change is Hard* (New York: Crown Business, 2010), Kindle edition, location 2630.

5. Sally Linkenauger, "You'll Golf Better If You Think Tiger Has Used Your Clubs," *Harvard Business Review* (July–August 2012): 32–33.

6. Sreedhari Desai, "Adults Behave Better When Teddy Bears Are In the Room," *Harvard Business Review* (September 2011): 30–31.

7. Michael Useem, "Four Lessons in Adaptive Leadership," *Harvard Business Review* (November 2010): 86–90.

8. David Rock, *Your Brain at Work* (New York: Harper Collins, 2009), Kindle edition, location 686.

9. Ibid, location 703.

10. Chris McChesney, Sean Covey, and Jim Huling, *The Four Disciplines of Execution: Achieving Your Wildly Important Goals* (New York: Free Press, 2012), Kindle edition, location 778.

11. The statistics on listening were drawn primarily from the International Listening Association at www.listen.org.

12. The Hemingway quote was found at www.thinkexist.com.

13. John Gross, ed., *The New Oxford Book of Literary Anecdotes* (New York: Oxford, 2006).

CHAPTER FIVE

Building Powerful Strategy Maps That Tell Your Strategic Story

 ## WHAT IS A STRATEGY MAP?

A strategy map is a one-page graphical representation of what an organization must do well (in each of the four perspectives) in order to successfully execute its strategy. Strategy maps are composed of objectives, which represent the concise statements of what the organization must do well in each of the four perspectives of financial, customer, internal process, and learning and growth. While strategic plans may often run dozens of pages, the strategy map must be confined to just one page in order to serve its chief purposes of clarifying and communicating strategy. A strategy map is a graphical representation, which deems that it contain not only a narrative (objectives) but images that bring the words to life and imbue the document with a sense of the organization's unique culture.

Breaking It Down

To enhance our understanding of a strategy map, let's break the phrase down into its component parts. First, we'll examine the word *map*, then we'll take another look at *strategy*. With those pieces in place we'll look at the role of cause and effect in strategy map development.

A map provides a graphical representation of the whole or part of an area. A good map is essential to help us navigate unfamiliar terrain. Speaking of unfamiliar terrain, although I make my home in California, I'm originally from the province of Nova Scotia, Canada. Perhaps some of you have visited my beautiful homeland. For those of you who have not, consider this an invitation. Let's say for a moment you decide to follow my suggestion and plan to visit Nova Scotia during your next vacation. I suggest that if you fly to Nova Scotia, you then drive from Halifax, the provincial capital, to my hometown of Sydney, on Cape Breton Island. I'm certain you'll find the scenery breathtaking. Now look at the two maps I've provided of the province in Exhibit 5.1. With the map on the left, do you think could you find your way from Halifax to Sydney? Without some advance knowledge of the province, the answer is probably no. The picture becomes much clearer with the graphic on the right, because now, in addition to a map of the province, you have landmarks to guide you from place to place, simplifying your navigational challenges significantly. Following the landmarks will lead you to your chosen destination.

Let's now return to the word strategy. Like your fictional visit to Nova Scotia, strategy is a new destination for most organizations, one to which they have never traveled. Although most organizations bandy the word strategy around in virtually every conversation of business significance, most fail to execute their chosen strategy to the degree they desire. Thus, in many ways, strategy is reminiscent of the map on the left side of Exhibit 5.1. It's a picture of where we would like to go, but the landmarks to guide us on our journey are missing. This is where performance objectives come in. The objectives on a strategy map serve as the landmarks on the road to strategy execution.

Telling the Story through Cause and Effect

Translating the strategy through objectives appearing on the strategy map provides the necessary means to document and test strategic assumptions. Ideally, the objectives chosen should link together in a chain of cause and effect relationships from the performance drivers in the learning and growth perspective all the way through to improved financial performance as reflected in the financial perspective. We are attempting to communicate and articulate the strategy through objectives, making the relationships between them explicit so they may be monitored, managed, and validated.

Here is an example of cause-and-effect modeling: Let's assume your organization is pursuing a strategy based on innovation and new products. A financial objective is "Grow revenue," because you ultimately envision enhanced

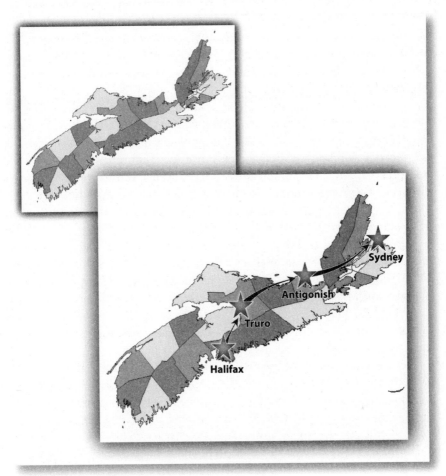

EXHIBIT 5.1   Landmarks Are Critical to Any Map

revenue flowing in from the stream of innovative new products you'll develop and deliver. In the customer perspective, one of a number of objectives may be "Adoption rate of new products," since a critical plank of your strategy's success is customer acceptance, purchase, and use of new products. Within the internal processes perspective, you're examining what you must do well internally to drive customer outcomes. Here you'll focus on the value chain necessary to propel innovation and new product development, a chain that will likely feature an objective such as "Enhance new product cycle time." Finally, housed in the learning and growth perspective are the enabling objectives, the intangibles that will produce real value in the other perspectives of the map. A possible objective here may be "Identify and meet strategic skill needs." If innovation represents a new strategic direction, it's likely you'll need to retool skill sets throughout the organization, an imperative acknowledged with this objective. Working upward our chain of cause and effect looks like this: *If* we ensure our team has the strategic skills we require *then* they will be able to develop new products faster (shrinking the cycle time). *If* we reduce our new product cycle time *then* we'll have more products available for customers to learn about, buy, and use. *If* customers buy more of our new products, *then* we will grow revenue in the financial perspective. When considering the linkage between objectives we should also attempt to document the timing and extent of the correlations. Explicitly stating the assumptions in our map design makes the Balanced Scorecard a formidable tool for strategic learning.

One-to-one relationships, as described earlier, are not a prerequisite to garner value from cause-and-effect modeling. A simpler method that demonstrates higher-level linkages among the perspectives can also prove effective in telling your story. Regardless of the method employed, robust cause-and-effect modeling also presents a wonderful opportunity to educate your employees about the interrelationship among objectives and measures, demonstrating how they work together to deliver your strategic promise. One nonprofit client of mine had such an opportunity recently. Like many nonprofits, this organization, Goodwill of Orange County California (GWOC), has been facing the stark reality of reduced government funding, and realized that to combat this trend it must find additional ways to enhance revenue. Only then will they be able to work towards their noble and pragmatic mission: to help "people who are facing barriers get and keep jobs, which provides purpose, pride and dignity."

GWOC is fortunate to have a thriving retail division, operating more than 20 high-traffic stores throughout Orange County. Capitalizing on this strength, and in recognition of reduced government funding, their map (which is shown in Exhibit 5.2) contains an objective relating to increasing revenue from all areas, with an associated measure tracking the percentage of government funding to total revenue. Upon reviewing the strategy map and measures, some employees voiced their concern towards this combination, noting that less government funding may reduce the number of people the organization serves. This is exactly the sort of strategic question a strategy map (and Balanced Scorecard) should engender, and the GWOC executive wasted little time in turning the opportunity into a teachable moment. Chief Operating Officer Kim Seebach discussed the dynamic with employees and issued this e-mail, signifying the importance of looking at the map and measures in their entirety.

EXHIBIT 5.2   Goodwill of Orange County Strategy Map

Source: Courtesy of Goodwill of Orange County.

Our strategic priorities along with our objectives and measures are all interrelated and need to be viewed as a whole. For example: At the same time that we are focusing on increasing revenue from our highest revenue generators, we are also focused on increasing the number of people served by our retail program through our Mission Integration initiative. By doing so, and if we are disciplined in our expense management, we will decrease our level of dependency on Government contracts while at the same time increasing the number of people served.

The Board of Directors and the Executive Team have recognized for some time that Government funding is not guaranteed and will most likely continue to be reduced. We also recognize that the government contracts in and of themselves do not provide enough funding to provide the high quality supports that Goodwill would like to provide. Goodwill would prefer to be in a financial position to provide more services to clients at the level of quality we want, without Government or Fund Development dollars at all. This is especially important given the significant amount of net revenue we must generate through our own means to sustain high-cost programs such as the Goodwill Fitness Center.

The Scorecard measure provides a benchmark for what we believe at this time is a reasonable level of government & fund development dependency. If our business revenue increases the amount of money represented, the benchmark will also increase and allow for new contract opportunities. If our revenue generation increases as we have planned, we will be able to fund additional services from those revenues. Either way, more people are served.

As you know this is an evolving dialogue, but the goal is to be stronger financially and less dependent overall on government and non-business related dollars.

I could tell you how I felt about Kim's e-mail, but in the spirit of sharing communications, let me simply provide the transcript of my reply to him:

Great response! I love how you discuss the fact that objectives and measures are interrelated. That's exactly how a strategic management tool should be used—not to focus on one area but to demonstrate how these things impact one another, and how decisions made in one area necessarily impact other dimensions of performance.

Always remember that the strategy map is primarily a communication tool, signaling to everyone what the organization must do well in order to execute its chosen strategy, and providing a means for all employees to determine their unique contribution. The map helps to embed the strategy at every level by making it explicit and encouraging strategic learning as we saw above.

 ## WHY YOU NEED A STRATEGY MAP

In their bestselling book *Blue Ocean Strategy*, authors Kim and Mauborgne paint a dismal picture of strategic planning as practiced at most organizations:

The process usually culminates in the preparation of a large document culled from a mishmash of data provided by people from various parts of the organization who often have conflicting agendas and poor communication. In this process, managers spend the majority of strategic thinking time filling in boxes and running numbers instead of thinking outside the box and developing a clear picture of how to break from the competition. . . . Executives are paralyzed by the muddle. Few employees deep down in the company even know what the strategy is.[1]

The entire quote is a flaming indictment of the process, but what stands out most for me is the concluding sentence—"Few employees deep down in the organization even know what the strategy is." Forget corporate malfeasance as it plays out on the front page of the *Wall Street Journal,* with Armani-clad corporate titans being dragged away for insider trading, this— the inability to communicate strategy to those responsible on a day-to-day basis for its execution—is the great corporate crime of our time. Organizations invest countless hours and spend sums that would rival the GDP of small nations on crafting differentiating strategies, yet time after time they fail to embed the strategy in the minds (and cliché as it sounds, the hearts) of their employees.

Strategy maps hold the potential to undo this travesty of poor communication by breathing life into the stale rhetoric that tends to populate most sleep-inducing strategic plans, those with 50 to 100 pages of graphs, charts, and endless paragraphs in 8-point font. Most employees will probably never have the chance to thoroughly examine your strategic plan, but even if they were granted that privilege, given the state of most plans they'd probably take one suspicious glance at the weighty tome, make sure nobody in their vicinity was looking, and then toss the thing into the nearest recycling bin.

Through the creative combination of text and culturally resonant images, the strategy map will transform employee understanding and buy-in of your strategy. I'm not suggesting your employees need pretty pictures with small words, not at all. I'm simply putting forth the notion that, given the noise in most organizational environments, people need something that cuts through the clutter, a tool that dismisses with the usual jargon-filled memos and presents your story in a clear, compelling, and simple fashion. Strategy maps do just that.

 ## THE SPECTRUM OF STRATEGIC PLANS

Taming the wild ambitions of their strategic plan is another reason strategy maps should be required for many organizations. Since launching The Senalosa Group I've read hundreds of strategic plans, and it's safe to say that when penning these documents the vast majority of organizations aren't afraid to shoot for the stars. But why not aim for the heavens? After all, a strategic plan should emphasize your differentiating strengths and demonstrate how you'll conquer your chosen markets. Modesty, a virtue in most aspects of the human condition, probably wouldn't serve you well in this setting, and thus typically isn't the dominant narrative reflected in strategic plans. As a result, the organization sets out, in exhausting detail, every remotely strategic goal imaginable. The problem, of course, is that the typical organization simply doesn't possess the resources (either human or financial) to deliver on the countless lofty goals recited in their plan. Once again, the strategy map can help by identifying the critical few strategic priorities that must be tackled immediately in order to launch the organization towards its desired future and establishing the objectives that will set the trajectory.

While some strategic plans will provide exhaustive lists of every conceivable tactic associated with the stated direction, others offer only high-level guidance on the firm's course of action. For example, I've read many strategic plans that simply enumerate what are termed strategic priorities; broad phrases such as "Build Our brand," "Invest in Our People," or "Focus on Innovation and New Products." All grand and noble ideas, but where do you start? Once again, a strategy map proves its worth in these situations by translating these vague concepts into time-based strategic objectives that form the building blocks of strategy execution. Take innovation, a theme that is ubiquitous in strategy. An organization can't simply flick a switch and be innovative, especially if their history has been dominated by a reliance on one core product or family of products. Making a transition of this nature requires a series of carefully choreographed steps orchestrated over a period of time. New skills will have to be developed or acquired, processes put in place to encourage and facilitate innovation, extensive customer research conducted, and so on. All of these provide the basis for strategy map objectives that will transform the broad directive of innovation into action-oriented steps that create a path to execution.

Author John Gardner suggests, "Most ailing organizations have developed a functional blindness to their own defects. They are not suffering because they cannot resolve their problems but because they cannot see their problems."[2] In a very literal fashion, working in concert with the measures on a Balanced Scorecard, strategy maps bring problems and issues from darkness into light, allowing them to be combated and mitigated. The map acts as an early warning system for the organization's strategy, signaling trouble when indicators suggest a problem with any element that has been designed to propel the organization towards successful execution.

An example strategy map of a fictitious distribution company is shown in Exhibit 5.3. I emphasize the word *example* because no two strategy maps should

EXHIBIT 5.3 Example Strategy Map for a Fictitious Distribution Company

look the same. Each document should faithfully depict the distinctive strategy of the organization it represents, and thus be unique.

 ## DEVELOPING STRATEGY MAP OBJECTIVES

In the sections that follow, I'll supply practical advice for creating the objectives that will compose your strategy map. In the first section you'll find overall tips on the process, while in the second we'll look at each of the four perspectives in detail, with specific guidance for each perspective along with lists of potential objectives to kickstart your efforts.

Creating Effective Objectives

Here are a number of practical tips and techniques to keep top of mind during your strategy-mapping workshop.

Start Objectives with a Verb

It's the most basic and simple piece of advice, yet I'm surprised how often this core tenet is ignored. A strategic objective is a concise statement of what the organization must do well in order to execute its unique strategy. The words "must do well" imply action, and thus it's imperative that every objective begin with a verb to connote the action being pursued and the desired direction of the objective.

The strategy map's primary function is to communicate strategy, and a principle attribute of effective communication is clarity. Therefore, the map should portray your desired direction in crystal-clear fashion, making it obvious to every reader where the organization is focusing its finite reserves of energy and attention. For reasons of simplicity and brevity, some organizations will truncate their objectives. For example, it's not uncommon to find the objective "Customer loyalty" appearing in the customer perspective. That objective is vague and of little value in providing employees with direction on how to act in order to achieve it. Does the company want to maximize loyalty, build loyalty, leverage loyalty? Each of these is quite different and would drive diverse performance measures, strategic initiatives, and actions throughout all levels of the organization. Every word in a strategy map matters, and perhaps the most important are those at the beginning of each objective—the verbs that bring them to life.

Determine What's Holding You Back

London, 1841. American portrait painter John Goffe Rand faced a frustrating challenge plaguing all artists of his day—keeping his oil paints from drying out before he could use them. The best solution available to Rand and his contemporaries was using a pig's bladder sealed with a string. To expose the paint, an artist would prick the bladder with a tack, but of course there was no way to completely seal the plug afterwards, leading to the vexing problem of prematurely dry paint. Additionally, pig bladders were not the best travel companions, frequently bursting open and wasting what was then an expensive commodity. Rand studied the problem extensively and devised a solution—the tin paint tube. Although it was slow to catch on, it soon proved to be exactly what Impressionists required to escape their studios and capture inspiration from the natural world around them. Thanks to Rand's portable invention, for the first time in history it was possible for a painter to produce a work onsite, whether in a café, a garden, or waterfront. The paint tube also revolutionized the use of color, since it was now practical and affordable to produce and carry dazzling new pigments such as chrome yellow and emerald green, allowing the artist to capture the full majesty of any moment. So important was this invention that Renoir declared, "Without colors in tubes there would be no Cezanne, no Monet, and no Impressionism."[3]

Your art history lesson is over; let's get back to strategy maps. The moral of this story is the power of recognizing and overcoming problems to improve your situation, and that applies as much to strategy maps as it does to Impressionist paintings. Strategy implies the movement from your current position to a new and favorable destination in the future, and getting there will inevitably necessitate overcoming critical challenges. When considering possible objectives for the strategy map, ask yourself what problems are holding you back from executing the strategy, and apply the prism of each perspective to your discussion. For example, let's say you've decided to pursue a new strategy focused on creating enduring relationships with customers to build a strong sense of customer intimacy. What's holding you back from executing this new strategy? Perhaps you don't know your customers as well as you should in order to forge strong bonds. "Create profiles for targeted customers" could be an objective within the internal processes perspective. If your sales team has traditionally been focused on selling product attributes rather than providing solutions to customer needs (a key dimension of customer intimacy) you may require retraining, which could drive an objective such as "Match skill sets with strategy" within the learning and growth perspective. Taking an unvarnished look at the problems that separate you from the successful execution of your strategy is a great starting point in the creation of strategy map objectives.

Be Open to Creative Ideas

Everything about the Balanced Scorecard process is embroidered with creativity—devising objectives that are novel to the organization, translating those into innovative and meaningful performance measures, managing with a new strategy-focused philosophy. Thus you may wonder why I'm suggesting you be open to creative ideas when creativity is at the core of this entire exercise.

Writing in the Journal *Psychological Science*, researchers Jennifer S. Mueller, Shimul Melwani, and Jack A. Goncalo state:

> Our (research) results show that regardless of the degree to which people are open-minded, when they feel motivated to reduce uncertainty (either because they have an immediate goal of reducing uncertainty or they feel uncertain generally), they may experience more negative associations with creativity, which results in lower evaluations of a creative idea. Our findings imply a deep irony. Prior

research shows that uncertainty spurs the search for and generation of creative ideas, yet our findings reveal that uncertainty also makes people feel less able to recognize creativity, perhaps when they need it most.[4]

The authors also noted the appearance of the bias in situations during which participants espoused creativity as a desired goal. I believe this bias has major implications for strategy mapping, because the process dwells in a world of uncertainty. Since the execution of strategy requires new modes of thinking and new actions from the organization, when creating objectives you're working in a new and unfamiliar realm, one characterized by an overall sense of uncertainty. In that environment, whether we're cognizant of it or not, the tendency to eschew creative ideas in favor of more conservative options is a definite threat. As a practical matter, when creating your strategy map endeavor, keep this proclivity in mind, and when a colleague offers an objective that at first glance appears considerably off base or wildly impractical, be open to fully exploring it, as the idea may not be as crazy as you think.

Always Remember—This Is Your Strategy Map, not Google's, Amazon's, or Apple's

When I began my university business studies in 1982, all the cool kids in class were toting copies of *In Search of Excellence*, the Peters and Waterman tome destined to become the first true business blockbuster and a must-have on the credenza of every credible executive. I quickly discovered that the mere ability to parrot a few choice passages or tell the simplified tale of one of their exemplary companies awarded one a certain cachet and prestige both in and out of class. Later, when I entered the job market, it was *Built to Last*, then *Re-Engineering the Corporation*. The most recent phenomenon was *Good to Great*. There have been many others as well. Sometime in the early 1990s, I also began a subscription to the *Harvard Business Review*, a relationship I have maintained ever since. Of course, I've read hundreds of other magazines and studies over the years as well.

Reflecting back on all those many pages, what stands out to me most are not the lessons imparted by the gurus of each successive age, but the repetition in the use of certain companies to prove their particular theory of choice. It didn't matter whether it was re-engineering, strategy development, lean manufacturing, acquiring and keeping the best talent, or enterprise performance management. Regardless of the principle in play, the same companies were used again and again. When I was starting out writers were erecting statues in ink for the likes of Atari and Xerox. Later it was Enron (yes, that Enron), Toyota, and Dell; and now the darlings appear to be (among others) Google, Amazon, and Apple. To be perfectly honest, I'm tired of every second article or book I pick up having a title something to the effect of *Run Your (fill in the corporate necessity of the moment) like Google!*

Recall from the discussion of executive sponsorship in Chapter 2 my reference to *Influence: The Science of Persuasion.*[5] In the book author Robert Cialdini identifies social influence (or simply peer pressure) as one of six proven and reliable drivers of persuasion, regardless of the situation. Nowhere is this attribute more in play than in the business press. It's as if business authors wouldn't dream of even proposing their idea without the so-called proof of success at one of the companies in the spotlight at the moment. When I read these stories, now I often find myself thinking, "I wonder if the people at Google or Apple even know they're doing this?" Most of the time they didn't invent the phenomenon in question. The authors have an idea, want to show its efficacy, and feel the best and most persuasive way to do this is to link it with a successful company. That makes sense, but the problem arises when we put these companies on a pedestal for all of their innovative practices, only to see them occasionally tumble in humiliating fashion. And tumble they do. Atari, praised effusively by Peters and Waterman, has been moribund since 1983. Dell has certainly had their share of troubles, as has Toyota, not long ago mired in a quality mess that's seen their highly burnished reputation take a sizeable hit. And of course, don't even get me started on Enron—once hailed "America's Most Innovative Company" a stunning six years in a row by *Fortune*.

Amazon, Google, Apple, and the others stars shining in the business galaxy today are unquestionably successful companies, but it's both dangerous and unfair to emulate them with singular devotion and expect the rewards to suddenly rain down upon you. All of these companies perform a specific combination of activities that act together in a synergistic way to drive the execution of their strategies. If we could all copy everything they do, we would, but it's obviously not that simple. Nor should you want to follow blindly what others do. There is an enormous gap between admiring and learning from a company versus trying to copy its success. It's healthy and productive to learn from others, but you still need to apply a liberal dose of homegrown wisdom and know-how forged in the battles that shaped your unique culture if you hope to achieve success yourself. So, when creating your strategy map, it's certainly healthy to discuss the achievements of today's business darlings and consider some of the objectives they pursue, but those objectives should appear on your strategy map if, and only if, they are directly linked to the successful execution of your unique strategy.

Critically Examine Expert Advice

Not long ago I had the chance to hear a well-known business guru address an audience on a number of topics, including talent management and how to successfully negotiate change. His advice for talent? Hire all the 23-year-olds you can, because they'll ask questions older workers are too hardened to ask. Huh? This flies in the face of most thinking about maximizing human capital and harnessing employee knowledge. And it's ridiculous to suggest that older people don't want to learn. Later, on the subject of change, he suggested that when people criticize the case for change ask them why five times and you'll eventually get to something that's embarrassing to them. I question this as well. Why would you try to humiliate someone to get them to support your change agenda? Surely there are better, more humane and dignified ways.

There is so much advice out there these days, and in order to stay relevant and create attention for themselves in an increasingly crowded market, it seems some so-called experts feel they have to constantly push the envelope of accepted practice. However, in doing so their advice sometimes races past the respectable label of iconoclastic and simply doesn't fit with reality on the ground. When developing your strategy map, you may have participants who are ardent supporters of certain gurus and are quick to share their hero's particular panacea, suggesting the advice be overlaid on your efforts, however crude such an application may prove to be. As with the advice above on exercising prudence when considering the actions of other companies, you must be diligent when exposed to expert advice and ensure their solutions are in fact relevant to your particular situation.

To Simplify, Make the Difficult Choices

If you had one of the top productivity blogs on the Web, do you think it would be wise to suddenly tell your readers they should "Toss productivity advice out the window?"[6] Seems crazy, or at least counterintuitive, but that's exactly what Zen Habits blogger Leo Babauta did in a recent post. For years he doled out advice on getting more done and being more efficient. But now, based on his own experiences, he's recommending doing less in order to simplify life; pushing aside the urgent, and freeing up space and time for what's truly important.

In the post he says, "Simplifying means making choices about what's important, rather than ignoring that question." Simplicity in this context implies reducing what you do to the essentially important items that make a difference in your life. I'm sure the last thing he had on his mind when he wrote that was strategy mapping, but it's perfectly applicable. A well-constructed map should tell the story of the organization's strategy by outlining the vital objectives that will be used in assessing the firm's success in executing that strategy. The objectives shouldn't be plucked randomly from an online list, or chosen during a 30-minute brainstorming session. Instead, they should reflect careful contemplation of what is absolutely necessary to bring the strategy to life.

With some Scorecard users I've witnessed a reluctance to embrace the principle of choosing a smaller number of objectives. Not because it doesn't necessarily resonate with them—every head in the room nods when you suggest keeping things simple, and thus selecting only the critical few objectives—but because in the end, it's just too hard. It's much easier to choose the first objectives that come to mind and cram your strategy map with every conceivable notion, in essence covering all your bases. But of course what is created in those circumstances is not strategic at all. Strategy, and the map that results from it, must reflect carefully reasoned and considered choices, sometimes very difficult ones. Only then can you be certain you've chipped away the urgent, the easy, and the readily available in favor of what truly matters.

When building a strategy map it's extremely tempting to say, "Well, everything is important," and cram the document with dozens of seemingly crucial objectives. But that is not a discerning, and in the end effective, method for creating the communication tool that will light your path from strategic intent to execution. Your challenge is to ignore the seductive simplicity of what's urgent, and focus on the dimensions of execution that are most important.

Although it's unquestionably difficult to isolate your objectives to the critical few of genuine value, in the end the experience is very rewarding. In fact, the exercise of prioritizing anything has value in and of itself. This concept is beautifully depicted in a quote from Michael J. Gelb, who says, "The discipline of ordering . . . the discipline of choosing one over another, ranking one a level higher than another, and then articulating why you chose the way you did requires a depth and clarity of consideration and comparison that inspires richer appreciation and enjoyment."[7] I absolutely love this quote for both its elegance and the lesson it shares. Gelb is right when he suggests that by making choices you'll ultimately enjoy a richer appreciation and enjoyment of your selections thanks to the careful work you did in making the difficult decisions.

DEVELOPING OBJECTIVES FOR EACH OF THE FOUR PERSPECTIVES

In this section of the chapter, we'll examine each of the four perspectives in greater detail. I'll provide background information on each and supply lists of possible objectives you can draw upon when creating your map. Don't feel, however, that you must include in your map every objective and topic covered in the pages that follow. The suggestions are based on my review of hundreds of strategy maps and the common themes that emerge again and again. However, as stressed in the section above, the objectives you choose must be translated directly from your individual strategy.

Developing Objectives for the Financial Perspective

For as long as the profit imperative has been present in commercial enterprises, the focus has been directed at increasing value for shareholders through the creative balance of driving revenue growth and enhancing productivity. Thus when developing objectives for the financial perspective of the strategy map, virtually all profit-seeking enterprises will canvass the themes of revenue growth and productivity, both pursued in an effort to ultimately drive greater value for shareholders.

Revenue growth, which we'll discuss in greater detail below, is customarily accomplished in one of two ways: selling entirely new products and services to the market or deepening relationships with existing customers, thereby enhancing the value offered and generating additional profitability. Some enterprising organizations will attempt to do both. Enhancing productivity is similarly achieved using a two-pronged approach. The first option, one exercised by virtually every client I have ever worked with, is simply reducing current costs, be they personnel or administrative in nature. While this theme can often be recklessly pursued using a hacksaw approach, our second option under the productivity umbrella is improving asset utilization, and to be rendered effectively it requires the precision of a scalpel. For example, utilizing lean techniques provides companies the opportunity to support greater sales with lower levels of inventory.

Although the choice of objectives for the financial perspective appears relatively limited, this portion of the strategy map introduces a tension that must be managed should we hope to ultimately derive economic benefits from the execution of our strategy. The tension comes in the form of finding an appropriate balance between the two seemingly contradictory forces of revenue growth and productivity; just how much do we step on the pedal of growth without breaking the bank in the process? Conversely, if we focus almost exclusively on austerity as our model, do we risk alienating a marketplace hungry for innovative new products? Analyzing results over time will help you determine how to dynamically shift the focus between these two levers, but the point remains that in order to the drive shareholder value that, if yours is a for-profit endeavor, should sit atop your strategy map, you must include both revenue growth and productivity objectives.

A Closer Look at Growth, and Why Balance Is Critical

If you ask executives at any for-profit enterprise to outline their key priorities, you're certain to hear the word growth at or near the top of the list. Increasing revenue has become an unquestioned barometer of corporate success, and organizations the world over are constantly scanning their strategic frontiers, attempting to open new markets, find new customers, and enhance the all-important top line.

But growth is remarkably difficult to achieve, and sustaining it is more elusive yet. Writing in the *Harvard Business Review*, Rita Gunther-McGrath reported that only 8 percent of 4,793 companies in a recent study sample grew their revenues by at least 5 percent year after year.[8] Authors Zook and Allen report similar findings, noting that:

> A decade ago we found that only about 13 percent of companies in the world had achieved on average even a modest rate of profitable growth (5.5 percent in real terms) over the decade while also earning their cost of capital. In the last decade, ending in 2010, the percentage had dropped to only 9 percent—this despite the fact that well over 90 percent of companies aspire to this level of performance in their strategic plans.[9]

In spite of the substantial challenges associated with growth, executives continue to see opportunities all around them. In one study 50 percent cited tremendous opportunity in the North American market, 65 percent in Europe, and more than 85 percent in Asia. A mere 15 percent suggested growth was inhibited by a lack of opportunities. However, almost all respondents were concerned with internal barriers, such as organizational effectiveness, excess complexity, difficulty achieving focus, or a risk-averse culture.

Reading these statistics only bolsters my confidence in placing the Balanced Scorecard at the strategic helm of any organization. Growth cannot magically result from sheer force of effort or wishful thinking, and certainly can't be considered in isolation. It must be cultivated through an execution approach that recognizes the power of balance and interdependency inherent in the Scorecard system. Our path to sustained profitable growth begins in the learning and growth perspective, where every organization must determine whether they have the right talent to spot and exploit growth opportunities. Talent is just one element of the winning equation, however. It is here that we also assess, using engagement surveys and other techniques, whether the firm's culture is aligned with a strategy focused on growth and reflects the risk-taking necessary to achieve that end. In the internal process perspective, we highlight the differentiators of our value chain that propel our unique value proposition to customers. This perspective also provides the opportunity to take a critical look at complexity issues that may plague growth initiatives. Market share and customer loyalty are achieved when processes and people align in a common direction and are reflected in the customer perspective. Finally, the end in mind of our strategic story—the growth we so highly covet—is manifested in the financial perspective. In the pages that follow, you'll learn how to create objectives in the remaining perspectives that will drive your growth and other financial aspirations (see Exhibit 5.4).

What do financial stakeholders expect or demand?

If we are to achieve our vision what will that mean financially— which of the levers to the right do we need to pull?

Possible Financial Objectives

- Increase shareholder value
- Maintain positive cash flow
- Grow net profit
- Minimize costs
- Increase revenue
- Improve project profitability
- Increase revenue from new products
- Achieve targeted gross profit
- Achieve sustainable profitability
- Invest strategically
- Optimize asset management
- Broaden revenue mix

Note: These are generic objectives, and should be refined/altered to suit your strategy execution needs.

EXHIBIT 5.4   Sample Financial Perspective Objectives

Developing Objectives for the Customer Perspective

The customer perspective must provide answers to three questions:

1. Who are our target customers?
2. What do they expect or demand of us as an organization—what needs are we serving?
3. What is our value proposition in serving them?

Those questions will be extensively unpacked in the pages that follow, providing you with insights to be used when developing your own customer objectives.

Who Is the Customer?

Drawing upon his extraordinary business acumen and no-nonsense approach to tackling issues, Peter Drucker provided a template for organizational success followed by countless leaders. One of the mantras he frequently shared was, "The purpose of a business is to create and keep a customer." In order to create and keep a customer, you must first identify the customer you're targeting. Sounds simple enough, but are you able to immediately declare your target customer? If you were to ask your entire senior leadership team the question, would they hold a consensus view on the topic? What about your employees? Is each and every one clear and focused on who you serve? My experience tells me the answers to all of the questions raised above is no. Every executive or manager, if appropriately prodded, will produce an answer, identifying a certain segment or group as the customer of choice for the organization. Frequently, however, their behavior in the marketplace belies their definitive response. Many organizations, uncomfortable with the risk inherent in making pure strategic choices, instead hedge their bets by attempting to serve a diverse number of customers, which in the end often leads to confusion, inefficient use of resources, and mediocre results. Serving customers requires the allocation of extensive resources; thus, attempting to cater to the needs of a broad swath of potential customers stretches resources very thin and typically results in very little attention being paid to any particular group. Strategy, it is frequently declared, is as much about what not to do as what to do, and this advice applies readily to the choice of a customer segment; not every potential customer group will fund your profitable growth or find your offerings valuable.

This first of our three customer questions is literally make or break, because your choice of primary customers will determine, as noted above, how you allocate your resources. Simply put, in order to execute your strategy you'll want to commit all possible resources to your primary customers in order to ultimately exceed their needs and drive your value proposition. Consider the case of McDonald's.[10] The restaurant behemoth feeds over 60 million people a day in more than 33,000 outlets around the globe. Critical to the company's success has been the clear choice of a primary customer and the willingness to change when circumstances dictate. In the 1980s and 1990s, McDonald's considered multisite real estate developers and franchise owners to be its primary customers, to the exclusion of the people who actually ate in their restaurants. This choice, resulting in resources being spent on centralized real estate development, franchising, and procurement, propelled the chain's growth and it opened as many as 1,700 new stores a year. By 2003, however, same store sales were declining as global markets became saturated and customers voiced dissatisfaction at the company's standardized fare. Jim Cantalupo, the CEO at the time recognized the crisis and declared, "The new boss at McDonald's is the consumer." This decision had profound impacts on resource allocation. Since consumer tastes vary widely in the 118 countries McDonald's serves, the company has reallocated resources from centralized corporate functions to regional managers who can customize local menus and décor. In the UK you can have porridge for breakfast at McDonald's; in France your burger may be topped with French cheese. The change in primary customer and the associated reallocation of resources fueled 81 months of consecutive same store sales growth around the world, and led to consistently rising customer satisfaction scores.

Clearly McDonald's chose correctly, and the dividends were handsome. Contrast that with the saga of Home Depot during the tenure of CEO Robert Nardelli. Under his watch the company declared that contractors, not consumers, would be their primary customers. Consistent with this decision, the company laid off thousands of orange-apron-clad customer service employees and used the savings to fund an $8 billion acquisition spree, snapping up 30 wholesale housing supply companies. If you shopped at a Home Depot in the early part of the 2000s, you know the story—customer satisfaction plummeted. In fact, Home Depot's consumer satisfaction scores suffered the biggest drop of any American retailer in history. While shoppers were leaving in droves, the wholesale business was also enduring problems because it wasn't getting the support required to obtain the efficiencies necessary for such a low margin business. In 2007 the new CEO, Frank Blake, refocused the business, announcing that homeowners would once again be the company's primary customers.

As these stories clearly illustrate, choosing the right customer is essential to your success. Your challenge is determining which groups constitute the best market for your particular offerings, in light of your strategy, and focusing your strategy map objectives on that subset of customers.

Serving Customer Needs and Meeting Expectations

All customers hold certain expectations of value, and while some are explicitly stated (and frequently shouted on social media), others are implied based on their behavior and often manifested in the unfortunate form of defection to competitors. When that regrettable outcome does occur it's quite often a result of mistaken assumptions on the part of management as to what customers really value and what needs the company is best suited to meet. To reference Peter Drucker once again, he would chafe at the thought of making general assumptions about what customers value; grand illusions conjured up in the ivory tower of executive suites and painfully divorced from what's really taking place on the ground. Instead he would challenge leaders to look "not in the mirror, but out the window" for trends that are impacting the way people use their products and services, for changing needs, and for larger trends in the world around them. Above all else, Drucker would implore us not to assume, but to go and look.

As Drucker observed, "The view from the Matterhorn cannot be visualized by studying a map of Switzerland." The revered U.S. general George S. Patton was also a staunch advocate of challenging assumptions by examining what was actually taking place on the ground. He believed strongly in having his officers face the realities of the situations they were facing. When they were in combat, at least one officer from each staff section was dispatched to visit the fighting elements every day to observe, not to meddle, and this practice would later enhance understanding of conditions at the front.[11]

In my management fable on strategic planning, *Roadmaps and Revelations,* I tell the story of Bill Bratton, former chief of the New York Transit Police Department. He understood that in order to bring about change in the minds of his team it was vital for them to challenge the deeply held assumptions they had regarding the subway system, derisively known as the electric sewer; and the only way that was possible was to direct them to actually ride the sewer. Seeing, hearing, feeling, and touching what was taking place below ground opened their minds to what was really occurring on their watch and motivated them to move toward bold change. Bratton didn't rely on reports of what was taking place in the subterranean tunnels of New York. He knew the truth could only be discovered if he and his people heeded Drucker's wisdom to go and look. The lesson is clear: in order to understand our customer's needs and meet (or hopefully exceed) their expectations, we must first see for ourselves what is actually occurring on the street with real customers making real decisions. The only way to get concrete feedback is to go and see for yourself what is happening on the front lines of your business.

Once you've gone and looked to find out exactly how customers are using your products or services, and what needs you must meet, you may consider engaging in a *painstorming* process.[12] Bring your team together and, based on your observations in the field, make a list of customers' greatest pain points for which you are uniquely suited to provide relief. The results of your painstorming efforts will most likely lead directly to valuable customer perspective objectives for your strategy map. Think back to our friend John Goffe Rand, whom you learned about earlier in the chapter—he observed what was taking place, both in his own endeavors and with fellow artists. Then, in his own version of nineteenth-century painstorming, he set about to solve the problem.

What Is Our Value Proposition?

This final question demands that you clearly articulate a chosen value proposition. In other words, why do people decide, despite a galaxy of competition, to buy from you?

Recall from our introduction to the Balanced Scorecard that virtually all organizations will choose one of three disciplines, as articulated by Treacy and Wiersema in their book *The Discipline of Market Leaders*:[13]

1. **Operational Excellence:** Organizations pursuing an operational excellence discipline focus on low price, convenience, and often no frills. Walmart provides a great representation of an operationally excellent company.
2. **Product Leadership:** Product leaders push the envelope of their firm's products. Constantly innovating they strive to offer simply the best product in the market. Apple is an example of a product leader in the field of electronics.
3. **Customer Intimacy:** Doing whatever it takes to provide solutions for unique customer needs defines the customer-intimate company. They don't seek one-time transactions but instead focus on long-term relationship building through their deep knowledge of customer needs. In the retail industry, Nordstrom epitomizes the customer-intimate organization.

In the paragraphs that follow I'll outline each of these value propositions using the taxonomy of Treacy and Wiersema. However, if you'd like to learn more about these topics, do remember that Treacy and Wiersema are just two in a long line of writers, scholars, and practitioners advancing similar concepts.

OPERATIONAL EXCELLENCE The operationally excellent organization can be summed up in one word: formula. These companies make hard choices to stay ahead of the competition: "Less product variety, the courage not to please every customer, forging the whole company, not just manufacturing and distribution, into a single focused instrument."[14] It's evident even from that short quote that operationally excellent organizations have considered the first two questions we examined. They have the courage not to please every customer and choose to offer less product variety, which will serve the needs of only a subset of the overall public.

Companies that excel operationally focus on all those things we as consumers don't see; what's behind the curtain and out of our view, but vital to offering a combination of quality, price, and ease of purchase that competitors can't match. As noted above, the word formula is apt, since these companies attempt to deliver consistent experiences with little variation from encounter to encounter, so customers know what to expect every time they make a purchase. Walmart is probably the most highly recognized example of an operationally excellent company. Their logistical prowess—the engine that drives their ability to offer consistently low prices—is legendary, and whether you love them or hate them (and there are plenty of people on both sides of that fence) you can't argue that they are outstanding exemplars of their chosen value proposition.

PRODUCT LEADERSHIP Product leaders aren't content with a new and improved strategy. Instead they focus on pushing their products into the realm of the unknown, the untried, and the highly desirable. You often pay more for these breakthrough products, but in the minds of most consumers the unmatched functionality offered more than compensates for the higher price point. Does this description sound like any iconic company you know? I'm sure you started thinking Apple about halfway through the first sentence of this paragraph. They are, after all, the very paragon of product leadership and innovation, unleashing a steady stream of blockbuster products (and services) from the iPod to the iPhone to the iPad, all of which captivated consumers and ushered in a new golden age of mobile communication and entertainment. Several years ago, Steve Jobs dramatically upheld Apple's commitment to product leadership when he was asked by a reporter if the company planned to produce a netbook, the low-priced (typically around $300 to $400), low-functionality laptops that had become popular at the time. Jobs, in typically imperious fashion sneered that Apple would produce a netbook when they could create something for less than $500 that wasn't a piece of junk. His remarks and the company's history reflect the fact that Apple has no interest in the shallow end of the functionality and price pool, a position more amenable to operationally excellent companies. A recent quote from current chief executive Tim Cook proves Apple's unwavering commitment to product leadership has not diminished since Jobs' untimely passing. As demand accelerates for low-cost smartphones, particularly in emerging markets, Cook was asked if Apple planned to target that growing market. His simple, yet telling reply: "Our objective has always been to make the best, not the most."[15]

Customer Intimacy   Customer-intimate organizations aren't interested in one-time transactions. On the contrary, their goal is to forge long-term bonds by providing total solutions to customer needs. These companies don't take a short view of any client relationships. Their aspiration is to build long-lasting unions, during which they can increase their share of the client's business by providing unparalleled levels of service, knowledge, and solutions. The relationship doesn't end when the sale is made—it is frequently just beginning.

In the United States, the department store chain Nordstrom is often cited as an organization that lives and breathes a customer intimacy value proposition. Sales associates are carefully trained to develop a deep knowledge of their customers' needs and provide every possible solution to meet requirements, even those the shopper doesn't know he needs. Not long ago I was conducting a Balanced Scorecard training session for a new client, and during the value proposition discussion mentioned Nordstrom. The word had scarcely left my mouth when a hand sprang enthusiastically from the back of the room. The young woman who raised her hand had worked with Nordstrom prior to joining this organization and confirmed everything I said. In fact, she added to my repertoire by revealing that in her particular store at least, a poster hung in the employees' lounge reading, "If the customer leaves with what they came for, you didn't do your job."

As you've been reading these descriptions have you determined what category of value proposition best represents your own company? Or perhaps, before answering that, I should offer a more basic question: Do you feel your offerings are in fact differentiated in any way from your competition? I'd be surprised if your head isn't nodding in the affirmative on that one; after all, the very basis of strategy is differentiation, and thus all firms must offer some form of differentiated solution in order to succeed. However, perhaps this is a good time to revisit Peter Drucker's admonition to "go and look," discussed previously, because the statistics suggest your customers may not consider you as differentiated as you believe. In one enlightening study, researchers surveyed executives across a wide range of industries and asked how strongly differentiated they felt their product or service was. About 80 percent of executives felt they offered a highly differentiated product. The question was then put to their customers and, in what must be a major blow to any executive's confidence, a scant 8 percent agreed that the company's product was highly differentiated.[16]

WHICH VALUE PROPOSITION IS BEST?

Your customers, voting with their wallets, are the final arbiters of whether your value proposition differentiates you from the crowd, but it's incumbent upon you to do everything you can to ensure it is resonant and reflective of your strategic direction. Choosing (or confirming) a value proposition and reflecting it in your strategy map and Scorecard are among the most important tasks in the entire implementation journey. The choice will be dictated by your current pool of talent, markets you serve, the broader industry dynamics, and a host of other factors. As with every facet of business, there are winners and losers in each of the dimensions outlined earlier, and thus it's impossible to say, with certainty, which is the best path to follow. Interestingly, however, researchers Michael Raynor and Mumtaz Ahmed from Deloitte have adamantly declared that nonprice positions are preferable. The canvas for the study leading to this conclusion was enormous—the 25,000 companies that have traded on U.S. stock exchanges from 1966 to 2010. Using return on assets (ROA), Raynor and Ahmed were able to identify what they termed Miracle Workers, companies that consistently fell in the top 10 percent of ROA for all 25,000 companies. Just 174 companies met their criteria, and the authors suggest, "In most cases outstanding performance is caused by greater value and not by lower price."[17] This is not to suggest that either product leadership or customer intimacy is always a superior position. In fact, the authors of the study cited above correctly note there are perils associated with every strategic position. Again, what matters most is choosing a value proposition and reflecting it in your strategy map and Balanced Scorecard so that it can be analyzed and tested. Before we leave this topic, one last question, something you may have been considering the entire time: Can we have more than one value proposition?

Managing Dual Value Propositions

When it comes to answering the all-important strategic question of "What is our value proposition?," I've always believed any private, public sector, or non-profit organization should choose one of the three possibilities outlined above. The rationale, one shared by many experts, is that focusing on more than one at the same time will lead to contradictory investment choices, misaligned processes, and ultimately produce a fog of confusion over your employees and customers who don't know what the company stands for. But, as we're all well aware, the world of business is changing, and dual value propositions have become well established for some industry-leading organizations.

Changes in the broader economy are often the trigger for exercising a dual value proposition approach. For example, those offering premium products and services can no longer expect a recession-weary public to line up, cash in hand, for their latest wonders. History has demonstrated that many people trade down to lower-priced options in tough times, and increasing numbers will maintain that stance even as economic conditions bounce back. Companies providing high-end offerings must now discover ways to serve the middle- and low-end of the markets or risk being overlooked in favor of competitors who frequently offer a good-enough alternative at a more attractive price point. Conversely, firms relying on low costs to rally purchasers to their doors are finding it more and more difficult to compete with global competitors who are introducing innovative business models and employing new technologies to slash prices and margins ever lower. As the forces of change—among them globalization, lower barriers to entry, new business models, and the growing prominence of emerging markets—continue to gain momentum, adopting a dual strategy may prove to be a necessity.

Beyond its role as a new business imperative, the adoption of a dual strategy can also signal recognition of the duality present in all things—what Chinese philosophers term *yin* and *yang*. This ancient concept suggests that polar or seemingly opposite forces are in fact interconnected and interdependent parts within a greater whole. In the West, we tend to consider the pursuit of dual strategies an exercise in contradiction, and fail to see how the two forces can be reconciled. Not surprisingly, however, Asian companies are more open to the possibilities presented by dual strategies, as the underlying philosophy is embedded in Eastern thought. As changes in the business world continue to shrink our once incomprehensibly large world, it will be important for all companies, regardless of where they find themselves both geographically and philosophically, to welcome this concept. Let's look at two companies that are doing just that.

Singapore Airlines (SIA) has received Conde Nast Traveller's Best Global Airline award for 21 consecutive years. *Travel and Leisure* have named it the Best International Airline for 14 straight years, and for 17 consecutive years it has been heralded as the *Wall Street Journal* Asia's "Most Admired Singapore Company."[18] Everything about this exceptional carrier, launched in 1972 and yet to post an annual loss, shouts differentiation: from the exceptional customer service resulting from an industry-leading four months of training for new hires to the widest seats in business class, SIA offers a five-star experience in every aspect of its operations. What you may not know, however, is that SIA is also a cost leader, boasting a cost per available seat kilometer (a key industry metric) of 4.58 cents, besting that of most European and American budget airlines. SIA balances service excellence and low costs by employing a relatively simple practice: invest heavily in all those things that touch the customer, while employing diligent cost control on everything customers don't see. Often, these forces work in tandem to produce benefits for both customers and the company. For example, SIA operates one of the youngest fleets in the industry, with an average age of 74 months, about half the 160-month average of their competitors. Revenue is enhanced thanks to flyers who appreciate the comfort, amenities, and safety advantage of newer aircraft, but the fleet's relative youth also drives cost advantages as fuel, maintenance, and repair bills are all lower thanks in part to enhanced energy efficiency.

From the rarified air filtering gently through the luxurious cabin of an SIA jet, let's take a trip to your local bus depot. I doubt you'll find any Dom Perignon champagne flowing there, a place often considered the last resort of travelers and, until recently, completely off the radar of business people. Companies like BoltBus, RedCoach, and the venerable Greyhound are trying to change that perception, however. Buses have always been a very price-competitive mode of transportation, earning their firms a well-deserved reputation for cost effectiveness, but now they, too, are crossing the threshold into the arena of dual value propositions. Particularly for short-haul routes like New York to Washington, Orlando to Tampa, and so on, taking the bus is not only the thrifty choice but now affords the rider an experience similar to, or exceeding, that of riding in an airline's first class. On RedCoach, for example, you can stretch out in your leather seat and watch a movie on one of the coach's descending LCD screens, or if you feel like working, lower your lap desk, plug in your computer, and take advantage of free wi-fi. And since the bus never leaves the ground, you can even make a call. Neither the airlines nor Amtrak are shaking in their boots quite yet, but the changes are beginning to take root. As one industry veteran notes: "Now you have sleeker buses and a whole new clientele . . . riding the bus isn't being a second-class citizen. You could take the bus and be proud of it."[19]

In their book, *Built to Last*, authors Collins and Porras implore us to "preserve the core, but stimulate progress."[20] In many ways that sentiment represents the heart of a dual value proposition approach. The companies profiled above have a core that has served them well, in some cases over the course of decades, but they recognize the seismic shifts taking place in the world around us and understand the necessity to adapt in order to maintain their place in an ever-evolving marketplace. It seems that as we continue to stare change in the face the old paradigm of either/or thinking is no longer sufficient. To compete in today's global environment, perhaps it's time to shed the autocratic grip of the *or* and embrace the brilliance of the *and*, as in cost leadership and innovation . . . cost leadership and customer intimacy (see Exhibit 5.5).

Operational Excellence

- Offer best value
- Maximize inventory turns
- Minimize stock-outs
- Reduce customer complaints
- Increase ease of purchase
- Reduce manufacturing defects
- Eliminate service errors
- Grow in targeted segments
- Provide fast and accurate service
- Be easy to do business with

Product Leadership

- Build brand awareness
- Leverage key partnerships
- Increase key product functionality
- Provide the best product in the market
- Develop brand ambassadors

Customer Intimacy

- Increase training on key products offered
- Increase number of solutions per customer
- Grow share of targeted customers' spending
- Ensure all employees have access to customer information
- Utilize analytics to target customer offerings
- Grow number of customer awards received
- Increase average length of customer relationship
- Maximize customer loyalty

EXHIBIT 5.5 Sample Customer Perspective Objectives

Developing Objectives for the Internal Process Perspective

Thus far in our examination of the strategy map we have focused exclusively on the *what* of value creation, that is, what we're hoping to achieve for our targeted customers (as represented in the customer perspective) and what financial rewards await us for successful execution (as they appear in the financial perspective). At this point in the journey we'll shift our efforts from the *what* to the *how*. The question now becomes: How exactly will we fulfill our unique value proposition and exceed customer expectations as outlined in the customer perspective and ultimately achieve the lofty objectives set forth in the financial perspective? The internal process perspective starts us down the road of that discovery.

A consideration of how will often lead to a far broader number of options than the higher level what we discussed in the preceding sections, and that is the primary challenge you face in populating this perspective. A high ratio of how to what is the case in any endeavor. For example, let's say you've decided on Hawaii for this year's family vacation. It's a big investment and of course you want it to be a smashing success, producing a lifetime of cherished memories for the entire family. The what has been settled—it's Hawaii for vacation, but now you must turn your attention to the how of making it the trip of a lifetime, and that opens up a vast expanse of possibilities. When do you go? What airline do you use? From what city do you depart? Which island or islands will you visit? What excursions do you book? Where do you stay—condo or hotel? The inexorable list of questions goes on and on. To ensure your entire clan has a great experience you need to determine which of these how elements are most important to the family's vacation experience and be sure you execute them flawlessly.

The principle is the same when considering the internal process perspective of the strategy map. Given its focus on the how of value creation, and the enormous pool of candidate objectives that question can generate, it typically spawns the greatest number of objectives on the strategy map and correspondingly the largest volume of measures on the Balanced Scorecard. Your significant challenge is in limiting yourself to just those critical processes that truly drive value for your targeted customers and allow you to achieve breakthrough financial results as a result of your unique strategic approach.

Without a doubt this is where I see most strategy maps efforts derailed and where I find the least effective strategic objectives. There are two significant blunders organizations repeatedly commit: The first is failing to make strategic decisions and littering the perspective with an abundance of objectives.

We've already seen that many organizations struggle to make truly strategic decisions; for instance, attempting to serve all customers rather than selecting a core group best suited to their offerings. In the internal process perspective, that inability to make disciplined choices manifests itself through the inclusion of a vast array of sloppy and disconnected objectives which may cover all the corporate bases, but taken as a set don't represent a robust value chain capable of driving customer results. The second error organizations commit in this perspective is composing objectives that are extremely broad and generic. For instance, most conversations on internal operations will eventually turn to the fact that the organization is being victimized by a number of broken processes, and in response someone will boldly declare, "We need an objective to re-engineer all key processes." A chorus of cheers and rounds of backslapping typically ensue. An objective of this sort is nothing but a recipe for disaster. What exactly is a key process? Determining that definition could entail months of vigorous debate. And re-engineering every so-called key process will chew up months, if not years, of precious resources. There is no doubt that every company is plagued by certain processes that simply don't function as well as they should, and those shortcomings are impacting business results. Better to isolate the one or two processes that are erecting very visible barriers to your execution and tackle them than to make a cursory attempt to administer Band-Aids to every potential problem you face.

In the following sections I'll outline two methods for developing relevant and strategic internal process objectives—value chain and clusters.

Value Chain Analysis[21]

Strategy guru Michael Porter introduced the concept of value chains in his highly influential, and still relevant, 1985 book, *Competitive Advantage*.[22] Although the text is quite scholarly, the basic concept of a value chain is simple. Every company in every industry engages in distinct economic functions such as managing the supply chain, operating a sales force, developing new products, and many other distinct processes that Porter terms activities. The specific sequence of activities a company performs to design, produce, sell, deliver, and support its products constitutes its value chain. According to Porter and his many devoted acolytes, in order to achieve competitive advantage a company must be better at performing the same configuration of activities as its rivals or choose to perform a different configuration of activities. He believes that a distinctive value proposition will never translate into meaningful strategy and advantage unless this is the case because otherwise every competitor could

EXHIBIT 5.6   The Generic Value Chain

meet the same customer needs and there would be nothing unique or valuable about the position (see Exhibit 5.6).

The concept is well known and fairly intuitive. However, it is not often used to full advantage, nor is it customarily applied to the Strategy-Mapping process. Value-chain analysis represents a powerful method of decomposing a company into its strategically relevant parts in order to isolate the true value-adding activities. Nowhere is this more important than in the internal process perspective, since core processes serve as the engine to transform intangible assets—such as employee skills and capabilities—into desired customer outcomes and, ultimately, financial rewards.

To utilize this method, begin by plotting the value chain for your industry, laying out the activities a typical player engages in to design, produce, sell, deliver, and support its products. Next, carefully construct your value chain and compare it to the industry's value chain. At this point you've got three vital pieces of information: your previously completed customer perspective (which articulates your target customer, the needs you're serving, and your value proposition), the industry value chain, and your current value chain. Your task is to meticulously examine your current value chain and look for opportunities to distinguish yourself from competitors and drive the value proposition you've laid out in the customer perspective. The unique activities you can isolate and perform, those that differentiate you from competitors, should form the basis of your internal process perspective.

If you cleverly and creatively examine the minutiae of the value chain, you'll find that every industry affords opportunities for differentiation on some dimension. An interesting historical example is supplied by the automotive industry. In the 1920s Ford was the industry leader, but its founder, Henry Ford, refused to offer credit to his customers, believing it was immoral. General Motors had no such conviction, however, and they and other automakers set up consumer finance divisions and began offering customers the opportunity to buy cars on time. By 1930, 75 percent of vehicles were financed, and Ford's once-dominant market share tumbled. GM had discovered a principal point of differentiation in how to sell their cars, one that enabled them to make enormous gains in market share.

Internal Process Clusters

This method of developing objectives for the internal process perspective is provided by Scorecard architects Kaplan and Norton, who identified four clusters of processes which are applicable to virtually any business venture: operations management processes, customer management processes, innovation processes, and regulatory and social processes.[23] A review of each is outlined below.

OPERATIONS MANAGEMENT PROCESSES   The most basic of the four clusters, operations management processes relate to the day-to-day processes necessary to first produce and ultimately deliver a product or service to the market. Of course prior to actually creating a product or service, the materials necessary to bring it to life must be acquired, thus sourcing or purchasing related objectives will frequently find their way on to strategy maps. In addition to sourcing, this cluster of processes may also include the actual production of the product or service, distribution, and risk management. Once again, given the vast number of possible choices for this cluster alone, you must exercise steadfast discipline in focusing on just those processes that allow you to execute your unique strategy.

CUSTOMER MANAGEMENT PROCESSES   Apparently this is the pick-on-Henry-Ford chapter of the book. Of all the quips uttered by the iconoclastic auto baron, it is a virtual certainty he will be best remembered for this famous dictum on customer choice as it related to the Model T: "They can have any color they want as long as it's black." In other words, customers had no choice in the matter. Oh, how times have changed! Thanks to the flood of innovations ushered in during the age of the Internet, the balance of power has swung dramatically from supplier to consumer. Recognizing this undeniable fact of postmodern business life, organizations have begun to pay increasing attention to customer management processes and we would expect to see objectives on your strategy map relating to this critical enabler of success.

A number of subprocesses comprise this cluster, beginning with the acquisition of your target customer group. Acquiring customers is the purview of the marketing function, proactively communicating the company's value proposition in hopes of turning window shoppers into actual paying customers. Proactively is the key adjective in that sentence, as the story of Listerine reveals. You probably didn't know that Listerine was invented in the nineteenth century as a powerful surgical antiseptic. In later incarnations it served as a floor cleaner and a reported cure for gonorrhea. It didn't achieve tremendous success, however, until the 1920s when it was pitched as a solution for chronic halitosis, an arcane medical term for bad breath. The folks at Listerine aggressively marketed the tonic using ads featuring forlorn young men and women, eager for marriage but somewhat repulsed by their mate's rotten breath. Until this campaigning by Listerine, bad breath wasn't considered the debilitating social condition it has since become. In just seven years, the company's revenues rose from $115,000 to more than $8 million.[24]

Before the good people at Listerine had the revelation that halitosis was a condition requiring absolute abolition they would have carefully studied their potential customer base, determined user needs, and targeted their solution accordingly. Understanding customers and customer behavior is a critical process that must be confronted should we hope to reap the rewards of our marketing efforts. Once you've attracted your customers by understanding their requirements and pitching the perfect solution, you shift gears towards the remaining subprocesses in this cluster: retaining clients and deepening your relationship with them.

INNOVATION PROCESSES   The great Austrian economist Joseph Schumpeter, writing in his 1942 book *Capitalism, Socialism, and Democracy*, said:

> The fundamental impulse that sets and keeps the capitalist engine in motion comes from the new consumers, goods, the new methods of production or transportation, the new markets, the new forms of industrial organization that capitalist enterprise creates.[25]

In other words, the driving force of capitalism is, in Schumpeter's view, innovation; whether of new products, services, or business models. With the nature of competition changing so rapidly and dramatically, and gales of creative destruction (another nod to Schumpeter) washing over every industry, even companies focused primarily on either a customer intimacy or operational excellence value proposition cannot neglect the power of innovation.

Outlined next are a number of subprocesses, all of which may generate objectives for your strategy map, residing under the broad umbrella of innovation. The first is identification of opportunities. Creative organizations must constantly be patrolling the shores of their own and other industries, engaging employees, working with lead customers and applying technologies in an attempt to outwit the competition through innovation. Often the most fruitful ideas are taking shape in the corridors and cubicles of your company, as employees ruminate on the challenges and opportunities you face. Recognizing this vast potential, some leading companies have formed affinity groups—associations of employees united by gender, race, ethnicity, or other traits—to create new strategies and products. With appropriate opportunities identified, the next challenge is determining whether you will fund internally, work with joint ventures, or outsource entirely. Regardless of the choice, an objective may be required on your map to ensure this vital link in the innovation chain is progressing as planned. At the heart of the innovation process is our next subprocess, development of the product or service, which may be marked with objectives relating to time, quality, yield, and acceptance. Innovation is frequently compared to a pipeline that is constantly flowing; thus at any given time you may be churning out a number of new products and services, possibly necessitating the inclusion of an objective or objectives relating to the introduction of new products to the market. Our final subprocess sees us actually delivering the product or service, which will often result in objectives regarding distribution channel options and effectiveness.

Given the undeniable power of innovation in stoking sustained advantage, you might assume that the innovator in any industry garners all economic value from new innovations, leaving hungry competitors nipping at their heels for crumbs. Such is not actually the case. Research indicates that in reality, "Nearly 98 percent of the value generated by innovations is captured not by the innovators but by the often overlooked, despised copycats."[26] The history of business abounds with stories of path-breaking innovators who quickly saw their advantage melt away as rivals pounced on, and frequently improved, their breakthroughs. McDonald's, for example, imitated a system pioneered by White Castle, while Visa, MasterCard, and American Express all benefited from the efforts of Diners Club. I'm not suggesting you don't innovate because any novel ideas will inevitably be stolen, with the value quickly evaporating—not at all. This is simply another reminder that in order to sustain your advantage, you must constantly be assessing the unique points of differentiation along your entire value chain, ensuring they remain distinct and keeping you one step ahead of the hungry, capable, and fast-acting pack.

REGULATORY AND SOCIAL PROCESSES   Thus far our discussion of the internal process perspective has maintained a decided focus on what occurs within the four walls of the company. To conclude our look at this perspective, we must recognize that all organizations have important stakeholders and constituents beyond those four walls. Regulated industries must maintain positive relationships with regulators and other governmental officials, and adhere to a number of environmental regulations. Additionally, all organizations must strive to be good corporate citizens in the communities in which they operate. Companies are beginning to realize that this is not only the right thing to do, but it makes good business sense. A study by the Conference Board of Canada found that 80 percent of Canadian managers feel their company's good reputation goes a long way in recruiting and keeping quality employees.

Those organizations required to follow guidelines regarding environmental, health, and safety issues have a wonderful opportunity to use the strategy map and Balanced Scorecard as a tool for moving from strict compliance to leadership. Take for example the case of an electric utility that must adhere to many environmental, health, and safety guidelines enforced by various government agencies. When developing the internal process perspective of their strategy map, these organizations have the opportunity to move beyond simple compliance and establish themselves as leaders in the field. "Be recognized as an environmental leader" may serve as an inspiring objective for all employees, signaling the company's commitment to sustainable business practices.

With increasing frequency and intensity, many companies are using this area of their strategy map to demonstrate allegiance to strong corporate governance practices, and little wonder when the rap sheets of many disgraced CEOs run longer than a politician's list of campaign promises. "Exercise best-in-class governance" is an objective repeated in many strategy maps. As with every other objective appearing on the strategy map, this promise of strict governance must not be cloaked in appealing rhetoric but be backed with specific metrics and initiatives to ensure it becomes a reality in a world demanding improved corporate citizenship.

To prove successful over time, a company both contributes to, and relies heavily on, the well-being of the community in which it operates. While the organization is not solely responsible for the welfare of the surrounding community, it is incumbent upon them, and in their best interests, to monitor community success and ensure they are contributing to the area's ongoing prosperity. Making the community a better place to live, work, and do business has become an important mantra for many corporate executives as global economic conditions remain stubbornly sluggish, prompting civic leaders to expect an assist from business in fostering community development. You can inspire community involvement by making a place for it on your strategy map with objectives such as "Become more involved in our community," or "Encourage community prosperity."

To close the discussion of internal process objectives, let me repeat some advice provided in Chapter 1 regarding cause and effect linkages among the four perspectives of the strategy map. The key linkages you should consider articulating on the Map (and in the Scorecard of measures) are between the internal process and customer perspectives. In many ways, the objectives appearing in the learning and growth perspective, which will be discussed next, are considered the enablers of everything you're attempting to achieve and thus may not warrant one-to-one connections with other sections of the Map. However, the link between processes and customers is key, as it is here we signal two major transitions: from internal (employees, climate, processes) to external (customers) and from intangible (skills and knowledge, etc.) to tangible (customer outcomes and financial rewards). Customer outcomes signal the *what* of strategic execution, and internal processes supply the *how*. Every organization should make an effort to explicitly document this equation, articulating specifically how they expect to transform their unique capabilities and infrastructure into revenue and profit generating results. Exhibit 5.7 shows sample internal process perspective objectives.

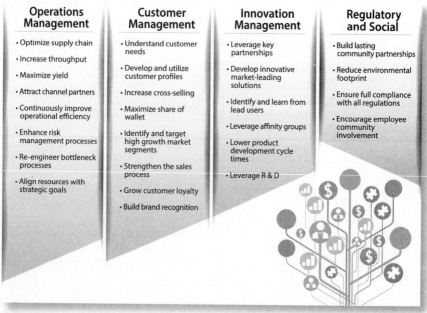

Operations Management	Customer Management	Innovation Management	Regulatory and Social
• Optimize supply chain	• Understand customer needs	• Leverage key partnerships	• Build lasting community partnerships
• Increase throughput	• Develop and utilize customer profiles	• Develop innovative market-leading solutions	• Reduce environmental footprint
• Maximize yield	• Increase cross-selling	• Identify and learn from lead users	• Ensure full compliance with all regulations
• Attract channel partners	• Maximize share of wallet	• Leverage affinity groups	• Encourage employee community involvement
• Continuously improve operational efficiency	• Identify and target high growth market segments	• Lower product development cycle times	
• Enhance risk management processes	• Strengthen the sales process	• Leverage R & D	
• Re-engineer bottleneck processes	• Grow customer loyalty		
• Align resources with strategic goals	• Build brand recognition		

EXHIBIT 5.7 Sample Internal Process Perspective Objectives

Developing Objectives for the Learning and Growth Perspective

In his foreword to *The HR Scorecard*, David Norton wrote,

> The worst grades are reserved for (executives) understanding of strategies for developing human capital. There is little consensus, little creativity, and no real framework for thinking about the subject . . . The asset that is the most important is the least understood, least prone to measurement, and, hence, least susceptible to management.[27]

Research has indicated that upwards of 75 percent of value in today's organization is derived from intangible assets, principally human capital. Norton's remarks were written over a decade ago, but continue to ring true today, as the failure to align human capital and strategy execution continues to plague organizations around the globe.

My experience as a consultant echoes Norton's findings. In conducting strategy mapping sessions with a wide variety of clients, I have observed a troubling pattern. Financial objectives tend to be the simplest to create, as most workshop participants are familiar and comfortable in the economic realm. Enthusiasm also abounds as we discuss customer objectives. As discussed in the sections above, internal process objectives can pose a significant challenge, but the groups remain tenacious and generate active discussion on the points until consensus is reached. Inevitably, learning and growth issues will be the last area of dialog. Perhaps I'm mistaking fatigue for disinterest, but in a disturbingly high number of cases when I introduce this perspective I'll be greeted with, "Oh, HR will take care of those objectives for us," accompanied by a chorus of chuckles. In most cases I know this is a joke, but I'm fairly confident that if the HR representative at the table did offer to relieve the group of their duty to develop learning and growth objectives, he or she would be hoisted on weary shoulders and paraded like some mythical conquering hero.

The majority of organizations, while paying constant lip service to the importance of employees, have yet to make the realization that the value of human capital truly is the distinguishing feature among today's organizations. It's always been that way, regardless of the industry, as this story will show. In *The Confessions of a Rumrunner*, originally published in 1928, author James Barbican weaves a fascinating tale of life as a Prohibition-era rumrunner. For our purposes here, one quote is particularly relevant and revealing of the challenges in running any type of organization: "Life was one constant effort to make smooth running in an organization which I had made theoretically perfect, but which was continually breaking down owing to the failure of the human element."[28] In this section, we'll look at three areas that comprise the objective setting challenge of the learning and growth perspective: information capital, organizational capital, and the nemesis of rumrunners the world over, human capital.

Human Capital: Aligning People with Strategy

The economist John Kenneth Galbraith once noted: "People are the common denominator of progress. No improvement is possible with unimproved people."[29] No improvement, and certainly no strategy execution, is even remotely possible without the right people, armed with the skills and knowledge required to make decisions and allocate resources in alignment with the company's chosen direction. Let's look at some possible objectives relating to human capital.

Recruit the Right People

How important is hiring the right people? Here's a story featuring chocolate magnate Milton Hershey that sheds some light on the question:

> In the mid-1890s Milton Hershey turned to a cousin, William Blair, to manage his caramel company. Blair was a competent but bull-headed man who resisted many of his boss's suggestions. He was sarcastic and had a way of speaking that made Hershey lose his temper. After one particularly heated argument, Blair quit. Shortly thereafter, Hershey traveled to New York, where he had dinner with a sugar salesman one evening. The man ordered a house specialty, a big slab of beef served on an oiled piece of hardwood. With a flourish he demonstrated how a planked steak should be carved. Impressed by the man's sophistication, Hershey hired him on the spot to replace Blair. Unlike Blair, the new fellow was willing to innovate. Unfortunately, a key decision of his to use corn syrup and cut back on the amount of cane sugar in Lancaster caramels, backfired badly. Customers could taste the lesser-quality sweetener and soon the wagons that carried freshly made candy to the railroad depot were coming back fully loaded with caramels returned by unhappy retailers. Hershey lost $60,000, a tidy sum in the 1890s. The man from New York was fired. Blair was rehired. And Hershey came to understand the risk of emotional decisions. At one dinner meeting with his top men, Hershey ordered a planked steak and as he

started to carve, instructed his men to watch closely because "it cost me $60,000 to learn this."[30]

In a world dominated by knowledge, relationships, and networks, it is people that distinguish outstanding companies from also-rans, and, therefore, getting the right people on the bus, as Jim Collins instructs in his blockbuster bestseller *Good to Great*, is imperative for every organization. He notes: "The executives who ignited the transformations from good to great did not first figure out where to drive the bus and then get people to take there. No, they first got the right people on the bus (and the wrong people off the bus) and then figured out where to drive it."[31] I could probably fill a chapter with quotes denoting the unquestionable bond between people and corporate success, but it is self-evident: no organization can succeed without the right people "on the bus" as Collins puts it. This message certainly wasn't lost on Doug Conant, former CEO of the iconic brand Campbell's Soup. Inheriting the reins at a particularly bleak point in the company's history (market value was plummeting rapidly), Conant understood that everything in the company required reimagining and reinvention, but he began with getting the right people on the bus, and just as importantly, getting the wrong people off. Here is how Conant described it:

> We had an incredibly low-trust culture based on what had happened . . . We recognized that we had to change the leadership profile of the company, and we turned over, in the first three years, 300 of the top 350 leaders of the organization—which is to my knowledge unprecedented in the consumer-products industry. Of the 300 people we turned over, 150 people were promoted from within, and 150 were hired from outside: people who were high-character, high-quality.[32]

An objective related to recruitment of strategically aligned employees qualifies as a must-have for strategy map development, but exercise caution in your wording. As General Electric's famous classification scheme of *A*, *B*, and *C* players gained momentum in the mainstream I began to see more and more strategy maps including an objective such as "Recruit and Retain *A*-Level Employees," or "Recruit and Retain the Best and the Brightest." Far from elitist, the authors' intentions are good, but the language inevitably stirs rancor within the rank and file, who scratch their heads and wonder, "Just what does it take to be an *A*-level performer anyway?" Don't be careless with loaded language of this nature. If you plan to use such an objective, ensure you've carefully and clearly documented exactly what you mean by the associated terms.

Close Skill Gaps

Are all jobs created equally? Every person, on every rung of your organizational ladder, undoubtedly possesses unique talents and skills, but do they all contribute equally to your ability to execute strategy? Many organizations, predominantly in the private sector, believe the answer is no. While recognizing the worth of all people in their business, they've come to the conclusion that certain positions within the corporation are more vital in the fight to execute their specific strategy. Kaplan and Norton term these vital players and positions *strategic job families*,[33] and suggest that isolating, analyzing, and closing gaps within them are a critical enabler of strategic success. To determine your strategic job families, begin by examining the objectives in your internal process perspective, and critically review the positions necessary to enable those processes. Ask yourself: Are there any high-leverage positions currently not staffed? Do particular employees, while dedicated to the mission and enthusiastic in their endeavors, lack a number of the necessary skills to perform at the highest level in these roles? Closing skill gaps in the most vital positions throughout your organization will spark significant productivity and effectiveness gains.

When people are matched with the right position, and equipped with the tools they require to carry out their work at peak-performance levels, you're enabling the possibility of *flow* to enter the workforce. Flow is a state characterized by complete immersion in a task, during which it's not uncommon to briefly lose the concept of time, with hours seeming to pass in the span of minutes as you apply all your creative energies to solve the challenge that lays before you. We've all experienced flow moments, whether it's settling in under the hood of an old car we're restoring, creating a photo album of digital memories, or getting lost in a dance routine we've been practicing for weeks. Flow can apply to virtually any endeavor, work included, if the conditions are right. Here is the best description of flow I've ever come across. It comes not from a business book or psychology text, but a novel:

> For the past two hours he's been in a dream of absorption that has dissolved all sense of time, and all awareness of the other parts of his life. Even his awareness of his own existence has vanished. He's been delivered into a pure present, free of the weight of the past or any anxieties about the future . . . This benevolent dissociation seems to require difficulty, prolonged demands on concentration and skills, pressure, problems to be solved, even danger. He feels calm, and spacious, fully qualified to exist. It's a feeling of clarified emptiness, of deep muted joy.[34]

Imagine the power we could unleash if only we could enable the conditions of flow to be ever present in the workplace.

Train for Success

Training is a staple of strategy maps, spanning the entire spectrum of organization types, with virtually every enterprise recognizing the necessity of constantly upgrading skills if they expect to compete in our crowded and ultra-competitive marketplaces. A word of caution is appropriate, however, as you hastily adopt this seemingly obvious objective. Foreshadowing Chapter 6 just a bit, think carefully about the accompanying measure you'll use to gauge your training success. Training is certainly an important component of employee success, but what really drives that success are the results of training, not the simple act of attendance—what is sometimes referred to as the BIC metric: butts in chairs. Therefore, measures of employee training must balance participation with results. Measuring and monitoring those will help you see the whole picture of training. So, before the ink is dry on this objective, look ahead to the next step of measurement, and make an honest assessment of your ability to create a meaningful metric. Incidentally, that advice holds for every objective we're discussing. While you certainly don't want to curtail your ingenuity in any way by second-guessing every chosen objective over the perceived lack of potential measures, you should be cognizant that every objective must be accompanied by a robust measure in order for this system to produce the value you expect.

One area of training I expect to rise dramatically in prominence over the next few years is employee understanding and manipulation of data to make more informed business decisions. This necessity is driven by the rapid growth in business analytics software—tools that sift through millions (or more) of data points in order to reveal customer insights. According to a Conference Executive Board study, currently just 38 percent of employees have the skills to properly derive insight from such data.[35] The report also suggests that analytic skills are concentrated in too few employees. In today's business world, the democratization of data through analytics demands that all employees possess the requisite skills necessary to discern patterns and glean knowledge from the constant flow of information streaming about them.

Engage Your Team

When I was getting started in my business career, a key metric for most organizations was employee satisfaction. Thinking has evolved on this matter and most people now believe that mere satisfaction, which really signifies nothing more than contentment, is not enough to bind someone to their work and propel results. What is required now is engagement, which implies an emotional involvement and commitment to the task at hand necessary to produce results. In a world dominated by knowledge work and the challenging transformation of information to knowledge, our teams must be willing to fully engage in the execution of strategy.

The payoffs associated with engaged employees are numerous and significant. Those who describe themselves as fully engaged are 50 percent more likely to exceed expectations than the least engaged workers. Companies with highly engaged people outperform those with the most disengaged by staggering proportions: 89 percent in customer satisfaction, 54 percent in employee retention, and fourfold in revenue.[36] Engagement is driven by a number of factors, but one that may be overlooked by many (at their peril) is perceived fairness. Strategy, and strategy execution, often require difficult choices that will undoubtedly have a negative impact on some members of your staff. What is most important in communicating these decisions is not the specifics of the decisions themselves, but the justifications and rationale behind them, and the demonstration of fair play throughout the process. If employees understand the *why* of a decision, and see that it was committed in good faith and fairness, they are much more likely to stand behind you and support it themselves. Conversely, poorly-communicated decisions that reek of furtive meetings and an undeniable sense of unfairness will lead to no end of complaints and bitterness. Scientists have determined that living in a situation characterized by unfairness is far more than a nuisance or annoyance, and actually increases people's cortisol (the stress hormone) levels, reduces well-being, and can even negatively impact longevity.[37]

Plan for Succession

According to the Pew Research Center, beginning on January 1, 2011, the oldest members of the Baby Boom generation in the United States celebrated their 65th birthday.[38] They are just the very first trickle of a demographic tsunami that is set to profoundly impact both the composition of the country and the workplace over the coming years. For the next 19 years, 10,000 people a day will celebrate (or not) their 65th birthdays. By 2030, when all members of the Baby Boom generation have reached that age, fully 18 percent of the nation will be at least 65. Fortunately for the Boomers themselves, they are feeling a lot spryer than their age would imply. In fact the typical Boomer reports feeling nine years younger than his or her actual age. Increasingly, this generation of fit and active people are leaving their careers for entirely new challenges, whether exotic travel adventures or giving back in the way of philanthropy. Either way, they and the immense bank of knowledge they possess, are vanishing from corporations around the world.

This demographic meteor leads to just one conclusion: succession planning must be embraced by every organization concerned with capturing the knowledge of long-term workers and passing the torch to the next generation. We all know that balanced diets and more exercise will enhance our health, but do we avail ourselves of tofu and treadmills? Not always, and such is the case with succession planning. Most organizations recognize, at least intellectually, that succession planning should drive leadership development but many fail to take action. Why? Here is what three experts on the subject suggest:

> Many people, from the CEO on down, consider the word "succession" taboo. Planning your exit is like scheduling your own funeral; it evokes fears and emotions long hidden under layers of defense mechanisms and imperceptible habits. Perversely, the desire to avoid this issue is strongest in the most successful CEOs. Their standard operating procedure is to always look for the next mountain to climb, not to step down from the mountain and look for a replacement.[39]

Regardless of the feelings it engenders in tough-as-nails CEOs, the seismic demographic shift taking place in many parts of the world cannot be ignored, and must be acknowledged and acted upon if you hope to retain the most critical currency of modern business—knowledge.

Information Capital: Aligning Information and Technology with Strategy

Given the pervasive influence of technology, virtually every organization should consider an information capital objective when forming their learning and growth perspective. In my experience working with a wide array of organizations, these objectives typically resemble the following: "Improve technology infrastructure," "Leverage technology," "Increase knowledge management and information sharing," and "Gather, share, and use information effectively." The first example relates to the infrastructure component of information capital, ensuring you have the physical tools necessary to deliver information to users. The remaining examples center on the need of gathering stored information, sharing it widely, and having employees harness it in their day-to-day actions. As with human capital, the critical dimension to consider when crafting an information-capital objective is the linkage between technology and strategy. Your individual game plan for corporate success will undoubtedly require the footprint of technology should you hope to outperform your rivals, and thus the choice of objectives should mirror the contribution you require from information technology to execute the strategy.

One emerging area of focus for many companies is making data more usable. In the train for success section, I noted that just 38 percent of employees have the skills to properly derive insight from analytics data. Giving them the benefit of the doubt, perhaps at least a portion of the blame can be placed upon the data itself. Today's knowledge workers require improved data filtering, enhanced visualization techniques, and (again as noted above) more training in order to derive the benefits our troves of data offer.

Organizational Capital—Creating the Climate for Growth and Change

The study of history provides many vivid portraits of men and women toiling against seemingly insurmountable odds and facing what appear to be overwhelming obstacles, only to turn sure defeat into stunning and glorious victory. Military sagas are replete with such tales of heroism and cunning, as is the field of exploration—it seems incomprehensible that early nineteenth-century explorers Lewis and Clark, for example, should lead an expedition into virtually uncharted territory, spanning a vast continent and lasting two years with precious few supplies, to return with a treasure trove of scientific and cultural knowledge and suffer only one casualty. The human spirit is beautifully indomitable and can literally move mountains when inspired by a worthy cause. Within the organizational-capital dimension, we are seeking to draw upon the infinite resources of human strength and capture—as trite and tired as it sounds, "the hearts and minds" of our employees—in an effort to make sustainable growth and change a literal reality. Outlined below are three key elements you may consider when drafting objectives for this section of the strategy map.

Culture

First things first, most would agree that culture is a very difficult term to accurately capture and define. The dictionary definition, using my Merriam-Webster's Collegiate, is: ". . . the set of shared attitudes, values, goals, and practices that characterizes an institution or organization . . ." For a dictionary reference this is pretty straightforward, but I'd recommend peeling another layer from the meaning and putting it even more colloquially. I define culture simply as "The way we do things around here." Every organization in the world, despite many similarities in overall goals (the profit imperative in the private sector for example) has a unique cultural fingerprint that distinguishes and sets it apart. In no two workplaces will you find exactly the same mix of processes, procedures, values, and behaviors. If culture weren't the most touchy-feely of all management topics, the roll call in its class certainly would not take long to conduct.

However soft and fuzzy a topic it is, culture is a vitally important aspect of organizational life and frequently has oversized implications for the bottom line. Take the case of the Boeing 787 Dreamliner.[40] This plane is truly revolutionary, composed largely of carbon-fiber composites that make it significantly lighter and more fuel efficient than its peers, while offering unprecedented comfort and air quality in the cabin. Naturally Boeing was anxious to introduce the jet to the flying public, but in the end its debut was delayed by over three years, and getting it off the ground cost the company billions in overruns. Some observers blame the many calamities befalling the 787 on a clash of cultures stemming from the 1997 merger of Boeing with McDonnell Douglas (MD). Technically Boeing had purchased MD, but many insiders believed "MD in effect acquired Boeing with Boeing's money." MD executives became key players at the new Boeing and brought with them their culture of intense and obsessive cost cutting, which weakened Boeing's historical commitment to, and culture of, new product development. Getting a game-changing plane like the 787 approved in this culture of cost containment was a major challenge, and only took wing when its advocates suggested a development strategy sure to appeal to their cost-conscious colleagues: outsourcing. In the end, some 50 strategic partners controlled vital aspects of the 787's design, engineering, and manufacturing. Boeing ended up building less than 40 percent of the plane. Managing this complex web of suppliers and partners proved a logistical nightmare, and delays became endemic. When all was said and done, instead of saving money from outsourcing, the 787 hemorrhaged cash and went billions over budget.

The Boeing story clearly illustrates the enormous sums of real money that are in play when it comes to managing culture. Further evidence that links culture to the bottom-line is provided by authors Heskett and Kotter. In their book, *Corporate Culture and Performance*, the pair discovered that over a 12-year period, firms with effective cultures achieved stock price growth of 901 percent, compared to just 74 percent for those with ineffective cultures. Over that same span, those with effective cultures saw revenue growth of over 680 percent. while the ineffective group managed only 166 percent gains.[41] In yet another study researchers found that more than 90 percent of companies satisfied with their financial performance believe that culture is as important as strategy for business success.[42] Doug Conant, the former Campbell's Soup CEO whose story of getting "the right people on the bus" I shared earlier in the chapter, made the management changes he did because it was a necessary input to transform the culture. As he put it, "I had to get the culture back on track, because my observation has been, is, and always will be, that you can't have an organization that consistently delivers innovation unless you have a high level of engagement and a high level of trust. People just won't take risks. And we had an incredibly low-trust culture based on what had happened."

What is most important for our purposes is the alignment of culture with strategy. Any misalignment of the two is a volatile cocktail capable of disastrous results, as the story of Encyclopedia Britannica illustrates. Its 32 volumes were considered the ultimate repository of knowledge from art to zoology for much of the firm's venerable history. As the world transitioned from bound books to personal computers in the quest for information, Encyclopedia Britannica was initially well positioned to make the transition. In 1989, they introduced one of the earliest multimedia CD-ROM encyclopedias, Compton's MultiMedia. The culture of the company, however, stood in the way of them maintaining their leadership position. A nationwide force of direct-to-home salespeople, the very force that had made Encyclopedia Britannica a trusted household name, dominated that culture. No one dared to tinker with the traditional sales format on which his or her livelihood depended. The sacredness of the direct sale force business model was the company's Achilles heel. As a result, Encyclopedia Britannica failed to develop a serious strategy for electronic products until it was too late. Annual unit sales collapsed from a high of 117,000 to about 20,000. It took the intervention of an outside investor and the abandonment of the direct-sales approach to save what was left of the company.[43] To avoid such a ruinous fate, your first step should simply entail conducting an informal audit of your culture (using 360 degree feedback and employee surveys) to gauge the amount of alignment between it and your strategy.

Although shaping or manipulating a culture, which can take years of habitual and patterned behavior, is well beyond the scope of this book, I can offer a few concrete steps you can take to help manage and change your culture to ensure it exists in harmony with your strategy.

■ The first is recruiting and selecting people you believe embody the culture you are either attempting to sustain or create. Companies with strong (and perceived by all as positive) cultures, such as Southwest Airlines, are well known for screening applicants primarily based on cultural fit, rather than technical aptitude. Who you choose to carry out your work and liaise with your team is completely within your sphere of control, so take the opportunity to select those individuals who will further your cultural aspirations.

■ Second, you can manage your culture through intense socialization and training initiatives, demonstrating what you expect from employees. The means of accomplishing this are many, varied, and sometimes downright bizarre. As an example of the latter, consider the online brokerage and banking firm E*Trade. During their first meeting at this innovative company, new employees are required to stand on a chair and tell everyone in attendance something embarrassing about themselves. Doing so knocks down a lot of barriers and creates a bond between employees, allowing them to open up and feel comfortable asking questions of co-workers, since appearing to lack a little esoteric corporate information pales in comparison to the loss of face suffered from regaling deep dark secrets.

▪ Finally, culture may be advanced using the formal reward systems of the organization. If you value teamwork, a customer-centric approach and attitude, and innovation, those traits should be tangibly rewarded in an effort to have that culture deeply entrenched.[44]

Before moving on, I'd like to touch on one troubling aspect of many corporate cultures—incivility. Unfortunately, perhaps due to our always-on, must-produce, stress-fueled work environments, rudeness at work is rampant, and growing rapidly. One pair of researchers, polling thousands of workers over the past 14 years, discovered that 98 percent of people experienced uncivil behavior in the workplace at least once a week, up from 25 percent in 1998.[45] Incivility takes many forms—the screaming boss from hell, inconsiderate comments from co-workers, managers who take credit for employees' achievements, teasing and bullying—but they all add up in significant ways. Among workers who have been on the receiving end of incivility: 80 percent lost work time worrying about the incident, 78 percent said their commitment to the organization declined, and 48 percent intentionally decreased their work effort. Think back to our earlier discussion on the importance and benefits of engagement. Incivility instantly eradicates any attempts to boost engagement. As you know, rude behavior isn't confined to boardrooms or break rooms. As customers we've all witnessed unpleasant interactions that, as researchers correctly (and obviously) point out, lead us to generalize about other employees, the organization, and even the brand. The best antidote to incivility is executive modeling of appropriate behavior. Leaders must walk the talk, ask for feedback from colleagues and subordinates on how they actually behave, and be willing to change if necessary.

Recognition and Rewards

I recently re-read Dale Carnegie's classic self-help yarn, *How to Win Friends and Influence People*. There is so much homespun wisdom in that book that, if challenged, I could probably support every notion in this book with a supporting quote from Mr. Carnegie. Here is a particular favorite that fits our discussion of recognition perfectly:

> I once succumbed to the fad of fasting and went for six days and nights without eating. It wasn't difficult. I was less hungry at the end of the sixth day than I was at the end of the second. Yet I know, as you know, people who would think they had committed a crime if they let their families or employees go for six days without food; but they will let them go for six days, and six weeks, and sometimes sixty years without giving them the hearty appreciation they crave almost as much as they crave food.[46]

In case you find that story a little dramatic, consider this nugget from a study of departing employees: 79 percent of those who resign their positions cite perceptions of not being appreciated as a key reason for leaving.[47] Leaders often lament the fact that many variables of business success are out of their control, and sometimes that is the case. Recognition, however, is completely within your direct sphere of control, and it is a muscle that should be exercised in a sincere fashion every single day. One article I read in researching this subject spoke about the importance of recognition and appreciation beginning on an employee's very first day on the job, since, as we all know, first impressions last a long time. I put the article down, and set about conjuring up all of the first days over my working life. Most were pretty typical: I was shuttled around the office at the speed of a blitzing linebacker, introduced to dozens of people, most of whom gave me tight-lipped half smiles and limp handshakes, given a computer that didn't work, taught how to use the phone, and filled out more paperwork than you need to apply for a car loan. But one first day stood out from all the others. At this company, my manager personally guided me through the mundane *administrivia*, made sure I had a companion all day long, went to great lengths to thank me for joining the company, and at the end of the day presented me with a company sweatshirt. It was a small token, but at that moment it capped what I considered to be a near-perfect first day, and I've never forgotten it. Such is the profound value of simple appreciation and recognition.

Alignment

Parents of youngsters participating in soccer leagues frequently and colorfully reflect the problems of misalignment. If you've ever been to one of these matches you know what I'm referring to: a blur of frenzied activity around the ball with not a single player venturing more than a few feet from that maelstrom of action. There is no coordination of activities, just a mad scramble covering a few square yards of the pitch. Of course this is quite amusing if you're watching from the stands with your smartphone catching the moment for posterity, since the stakes are relatively minor. But for organizations, a lack of alignment can prove extremely hazardous to any hope of executing strategy. Employee actions must be aligned with mission, vision, and most importantly, strategy should you wish to fully exploit the advantages of intangible assets such as culture and knowledge. The first step on the road to an aligned organization is ensuring employee understanding of the building blocks of mission, vision, and strategy. Only through understanding will action follow. A simple and effective method to ensure alignment is to review cascaded strategy maps and Balanced Scorecards throughout your organization. While most will rightly contain unique objectives and measures, they should be aligned towards a common strategy, should you hope to have all oars rowing in a winning direction. We'll discuss the notion of alignment and cascading in greater depth in Chapter 8. Exhibit 5.8 shows sample learning and growth perspective objectives.

Human Capital

- Attract employees that match our skill requirements
- Close strategic skill gaps
- Align training with strategy
- Leverage a highly engaged workforce
- Be an employer of choice
- Develop succession plans for key positions
- Retain high quality performers

Information Capital

- Ensure our people have access to the right information at the right time
- Transform information into a competitive advantage
- Use technology to capture, share, and apply information
- Optimize information management through information technology
- Share best practices

Organization Capital

- Foster an environment where people feel valued and can deliver their best
- Build a high-performing, disciplined team
- Clearly communicate expectations, accountabilities, and achievements
- Inspire associates to live the brand

EXHIBIT 5.8   Sample Learning and Growth Perspective Objectives

USING STRATEGIC THEMES IN THE DEVELOPMENT OF A STRATEGY MAP

The concept of strategic themes was introduced in Chapter 3 as a possible method of integrating strategy and the Balanced Scorecard. You'll recall that I described themes as action-oriented statements that serve as broad components of a strategy. Possible examples of strategic themes include: "Excel in operational excellence," "Be customer-focused," and "Innovate constantly."

There are different schools of thought on the use of strategic themes in the development of strategy maps. Some feel the themes represent just that: themes or slogans to guide the creation of objectives in each perspective. Many organizations actually attach a theme to each of the perspectives as a tagline; for example, "Create a workforce that is informed, engaged, and inspired" as the theme for the learning and growth perspective. Most practitioners, however, suggest that three to five themes should be determined before the map is created, then used to demonstrate vertical linkages throughout the map, with each theme containing linked objectives weaving through each of the four perspectives.

Here is my historical perspective on the topic. If you examine the earliest Balanced Scorecard literature, there is no discussion of strategic themes. Scorecard and strategy-mapping pioneers created strategic objectives derived from their unique strategies, and placed them carefully throughout the four perspectives, depicting a strategic narrative or story. Of course, this process is predicated on the assumption that the organization does in fact have a strategy. As argued extensively in Chapter 3, many (if not most) organizations don't have a true strategy—one that clearly indicates a choice of value proposition. Recognizing that limitation, but with a desire to create a strategy map and Balanced Scorecard nonetheless (as these tools became increasingly popular), organizations began developing strategic themes as a shortcut to the strategy process. Once again, as discussed in Chapter 3, since virtually every position on the strategy canvas represents some combination of customer intimacy, innovation, and operational excellence, these became the default themes utilized by most organizations. That leads to many theme-based maps resembling one another and failing to depict true strategic choices and differentiation. By ticking the boxes of each theme the maps become generic, thereby defeating the entire purpose of the exercise. For themes to prove effective they must represent the differentiating strategic elements of the firm—the particular mix of targeted customers, value proposition, value chain, intangibles, and price point.

Author and consultant Sandy Richardson has noted additional concerns associated with the use of strategic themes in strategy-map development:[48]

- **May limit the selection of strategic objectives:** By their very nature, themes act as a constraint, or more simply a box within which you must confine your selections. This of course limits you from accessing the vast universe of potential objectives, some of which may be very appropriate for your particular situation.

- **Hold the potential of creating unnecessary complexity:** The primary function of a strategy map is to clearly communicate what the organization must do well in order to execute its strategy. As Richardson writes, "Strategic themes add a layer of non-actionable information to the strategy map that may actually act as a distraction for stakeholders and employees."[49]

- **Siloed management may result:** Organizations devising their maps by strategic themes will often employ what they term theme teams to both create the objectives and subsequently manage that individual theme. In some respects this is in direct contradiction of the purpose of the map, which is to tell an integrated and cohesive story, fostering cross-functional collaboration to drive execution.

- **Objectives often relate to multiple themes:** Especially in the learning and growth perspective, it is probable (and logical) that the enabling objectives—such as those relating to recruitment, training, use of information, and culture—will impact every objective in the remaining three perspectives. If you choose to include these objectives within each theme, it complicates the management of the objective and adds a layer of confusion that won't be welcomed by most employees.

The choice of whether or not to use themes in the construction of your map will ultimately rest on a number of variables, including the existence of a true strategy, and perhaps most importantly the inclinations of your senior management. If you feel themes represent the best choice for your organization, I would recommend you first create a map with no theme constraints, opening yourself up to the full spectrum of possibilities that lies before you. Then, with those many dimensions of success identified, carefully select from them the objectives that fall naturally into your previously identified three to five strategic themes.

 ## DEVELOPING A SHARED UNDERSTANDING WITH OBJECTIVE STATEMENTS

One of the many reasons I love my job is that I get to witness, on a regular basis, the thrilling sensation that accompanies a true breakthrough. I see these little miracles all the time in strategy-mapping workshops, as passionate debate springing from committed participants leads to the entire team break-ing through intellectual barriers and emerging with a new and valuable insight into their business. Frequently these "aha" moments lead to the creation of a company-specific objective that perfectly captures the spirit of the exercise, and delivers on the Scorecard's promise of business value.

Most of my clients will take a break from a few days to a few weeks between their strategy mapping and measures workshops. Scheduling issues, the call of their day jobs, and the necessity to let the work of the strategy-mapping session sink in all conspire to make these short breaks a practical reality for most orga-nizations. A funny thing tends to happen when they do reconvene to develop the measures for their Scorecard—no matter how inspiring, passionate, and clear the mapping discussion was, when it comes to the specifics behind what we captured on the map, most people draw a blank, including those break-through objectives I noted in the previous paragraph. Sure, broad themes are evident, but the specific nature and tone of each objective is a semantic mystery. That of course, is a big problem. If you can't recall the details of what was behind your reasons for drafting a certain objective, its intent and dimensions, it's very difficult to create an appropriate performance measure. Additionally, if your strategy map in any way resembles the hundreds I've seen over the years it will most likely contain at least a couple, if not a handful, of objectives that border on the vague and nebulous, such as "Enhance productivity." During your animated discussions, the meaning of "Enhance productivity" was undoubt-edly clear to everyone in the room as you enumerated the specific issues and potential solutions that ultimately led to including it on your map. However, the map is meant to serve as a communication tool for your entire organization, and the vast majority of that group didn't have the good fortune to be at the table when you chose the objective and, thus, although its meaning may be plain to you, to them it could mean countless things. Even seemingly straightforward objectives such as "Cut costs" may engender confusion among your workforce as people apply their own filters of perception and experience to the phrase.

Objective Statements Defined

A simple method to avoid situations like this from blocking your progress, and severely testing your sanity, is the crafting of two- to three-sentence narratives for each objective soon after you have completed the strategy map. I refer to these notes as objective statements, and feel they provide several benefits. Their primary function and advantage is to clearly articulate what is meant by each objective appearing on the map; that alone can pay tremendous dividends should your map contain potentially cloudy objectives such as "Enhance productivity," which could be capably gauged by any number of metrics. Curious readers of your strategy map will also be grateful you took the time to pen objective statements, as they serve to supplement what appears on the map, filling in the blanks with crucial and explanatory information about why you chose the specific objectives they see before them. A well-written objective statement should be succinct (you're not writing a novel here; two or three sentences should suffice), clarify with precision what is meant by the objective and why it is important, outline how it links in your chain of cause and effect (if you're employing cause and effect on your map), and finally, briefly outline how it will be accomplished. Here is an example of a well-composed objective statement from a utility company:

> **Innovate to reduce energy cost:** Fuel represents a major percentage of our expenses. Managing this significant expense is the responsibility of everyone in the organization and will require innovative responses to mitigate increasing world energy prices. To achieve this objective we must: minimize fuel acquisition costs, strengthen our hedging, and ensure support functions and services are as streamlined and cost effective as possible.

Creating Objective Statements: Who and When

As important as objective statements are to the overall mapping effort, getting people to take the time to write them can, admittedly, be like pulling teeth—not a fast and painless process. Some organizations will impose a two-week deadline for the submission of all statements. Though the looming deadline poses some urgency, most people will wait until the fourteenth day to craft something, and the results will often reflect a lack of time and attention. The best time to write objective statements is during your mapping workshop, immediately after you've determined the very last objective that will appear on your strategy map. Although it's difficult to muster the additional energy to write objective statements after exerting the intellectual sweat necessary to produce a map, this is the ideal time, since the meaning behind all of the objectives will still be fresh in your mind. As noted above, the longer the interval between creating the map and writing the objective statements, the more difficult the task will become and the less cogent and comprehensive the statements will be. You don't need to channel Shakespeare when compiling these first draft statements. The goal is to simply jot down the key points behind each objective to ensure you captured the essence of why it is being included on the map.

To balance personal biases and perceptions that may emerge from individuals drafting the statements, have small teams of two or three people write them, ensuring what is created reflects the actual discussion of the day and the entire team's collective understanding of each objective. Having said that, recall from Chapter 3 our humorous look at how the U.S. Constitution might have turned out had it been written by committee ("We the people . . . wait, that's not right!"). Have small teams create the first drafts, but the responsibility for locking in the final statements should fall to a very small group (most likely two people) who will ensure consistency in tone, grammar, and structure. Once all statements have been written you can bring them back to the team for final review and approval.

Finalizing the Objective Statements

One of my clients devised an innovative solution to keep objective statements at the forefront of everyone's attention. This organization holds a morning management meeting each day, and my client decided that, until the objective statements were completed, updates would be shared at the meeting. Each day, a small team of two or three was assigned to present at least one objective statement for review with the group. This is a great idea for a couple of reasons:

1. Practically speaking, it ensures that objective statements are crafted in a timely fashion.
2. By following this method, the entire management team can hear and see what is being developed, and discuss it as a team.

The feedback offered helps the writers tighten their statements, while others in attendance learn the best practices of objective-statement writing and can apply them to their endeavors. As noted above, once the drafts were approved, a small team finalized the entire set.

 ## HOW MANY OBJECTIVES ON A STRATEGY MAP?

The French aviator and writer Antoine de Saint-Exupéry once noted, "Perfection is not when there is no more to add, but no more to take away."[50] That sentiment seems rather quaint, or at least iconoclastic, when placed in the context of today's marketplace, which constantly bombards us with new products, new features, new ideas, and always more, more, more. In this era of mass customization, we can have whatever we want, whenever we want it, and most of us want more of what we want, and we'll take that right now thank you very much. As a result, we live in a world drenched in choice and complexity. Want some new apps for your iPhone? As of this writing there are over a million to choose from in the Apple App store. Maybe you're feeling a bit hungry after downloading some new apps. Why not head over to the Cheesecake Factory, where you'll find over 240 selections in the phone-book-size menu? Of course you'll pay for your meal with a credit card, the one whose agreement you never read. And who would? In 1980 the typical credit card contract was about 400 words long. Today it's over 20,000.[51] So, as much as I appreciate the rich buffet of choice all around me, I believe Saint-Exupéry's suggestion of "less being more" is absolutely the case, and that is particularly so with strategy map objectives.

When strategy maps were originally introduced, most companies attempted to depict their execution efforts using no more than 20 objectives spanning the four perspectives. But soon the tempting call of more, more, more proved too powerful to resist, and many strategy maps swelled to more than 30 objectives swimming in a sea of arrows, lines, and assorted geometric shapes. Instead of providing a simple and clear way to describe and articulate strategy to a workforce starving for simplicity, these dizzying charts produced nothing but headache-inducing cases of *MEGO*—my eyes glaze over.

The ballooning number of objectives appearing on first-draft strategy maps is the result of a multitude of factors. One contributing aspect is the atmosphere in mapping sessions, which is typically very positive. This is to be expected since you've convened a team chosen for both their knowledge and enthusi-asm. You're talking about what you do every day, about your organization; and, truthfully, how often do you have the opportunity to spend an entire day analyzing your strategy? It's exciting, liberating, and fun. That upbeat spirit tends to produce more, not less, strategic objectives. I've even witnessed chief executives getting caught up in the frenzy. Prior to one strategy-mapping ses-sion with a client, the CEO stressed to me the importance of keeping the total number of objectives capped at around 10. I agreed that a low number was better for this relatively small organization, and together we vowed to curb any attempts at raising the objective total. But when we got into the session, his tune changed, and changed dramatically. He was the one I couldn't rein in! Suddenly everything seemed critical to the company's success, and before we knew it there were 31 objectives on the burgeoning map.

In my experience as a consultant, working with organizations around the world, I have found that when creating strategy maps there exists an almost over-whelming temptation to cram every conceivable, even remotely strategic objec-tive on the document, as if omitting anything would represent the cardinal sin of strategy execution. The pernicious myth in play here, one most organizations believe without question, is that by simply listing something on the map and creat-ing a corresponding measure it will magically lead to execution, no questions asked.

But real life doesn't work that way, and in fact crowding the map with extraneous objectives violates the number one rule of strategy and strategy execution—focus.

What tends to ensue when you create a bloated strategy map is confusion, which results from attempts to determine, on a day-to-day basis, which objective is most important to focus upon when you're faced with what appears to be an overwhelming array of choices. Choice, paradoxically, seems to paralyze directed action, a fact that has been demonstrated consistently by researchers. For example, in one experiment, shoppers were presented with free samples of six types of jam. Forty percent of passersby approached the table, and 30 percent bought a jar of jam. However, when 24 types of jam were offered, 60 percent of shoppers approached the booth, but only 3 percent bought a jar.[52] Abundant choice overwhelms us and, when applied to strategy mapping and strategy execution, causes us to spread our energy across a multitude of seemingly important priorities and in the end accomplish very little.

A great sculptor, regardless of the medium of choice—wood, clay, stone— begins with an amorphous mass of material. Slowly they chip away, guided by a clear and compelling vision that directs each stroke of the hammer or knife, until from that nebulous form their work of pure art emerges. Creating a strategy map is no different. We must be diligent in constantly focusing on our vision and strategy when crafting this tool of strategy execution. The question to guide us as we sculpt, as Saint-Exupéry astutely notes, is not how much more we can add, but how much we can take away.

Reviewing the Objectives on your Strategy Map

Some may read the advice presented above and breathe a sigh of relief, thinking the pressure of generating a great number of objectives has been removed, and they can focus on the vital few that really matter. Well, in fact, getting to that critical few is very challenging. There is an old story, variously attributed to Mark Twain, Pascale, and others, that goes something like this. Twain (my choice) once wrote a long letter to a friend that he opened by saying, "I tried to write a short letter, but it was too hard so I wrote a long one." Whenever we're forced to exercise true strategic choice, ranking the possibilities and applying preferences, the stakes are raised and the work becomes significantly more challenging. In our case, creating strategy maps from a vast universe of possibilities, we must cut through the clutter, ruthlessly wielding our strategic machetes until we uncover just those objectives that truly document our strategic story. Here are a few techniques to help you review existing objectives and hone your final strategy-map masterpiece.

■ **Ask these questions for each perspective:** Here are some questions to ask when reviewing each perspective of your strategy map:
  ■ Financial: Do our objectives represent an appropriate mix of growth, productivity, and profitability?
  ■ Customer: Do the objectives demonstrate our value proposition and clearly articulate what customers expect?
  ■ Internal process: Have we emphasized the differentiating aspects of our value chain?
  ■ Learning and growth: Have we isolated the key intangibles that will drive process excellence and ensure we achieve our customer and financial objectives?
■ **Sequence the objectives:** While all the objectives you've identified are potentially important, what are the most critical for the next 12 to 18 months (or whatever your strategic horizon)? And what comes after those? Perhaps there is a natural chronological order to the objectives, such as some must be effectively executed before you can proceed to others. Sequencing may help you eliminate objectives that are not immediately necessary for strategy execution.
■ **Look for balance:** The strategy map is an integral part of the overall Balanced Scorecard process, and thus we would expect a roughly equal mix of objectives across the four perspectives of the model. If you're preaching teamwork, quality, and responsiveness to customers, yet your map is overwhelmingly dominated by financial objectives, you're not adhering to the principles of balance. Despite your calls to the contrary, what you'll ultimately communicate in that situation is that the bottom line is all that really matters.
■ **Tell the story:** The objectives appearing on your map should weave together through the perspectives to tell your strategic story. This is accomplished with cause-and-effect linkages among the objectives, demonstrating how they work together to produce strategic results. A compelling story is told when we see how investments in intangibles (learning and growth perspective) yield improvements in key processes, which drive customer-buying decisions, ultimately resulting in improved financial results. Ensure all of the objectives on your map are indeed contributing to your strategic story.
■ **Be realistic:** This pragmatic advice comes directly from a client of mine, the Second Harvest Food Bank in Irvine, California. This nonprofit, which since its inception has provided more than 272 million pounds of donated and surplus food to local charities, recently embarked on a Balanced Scorecard implementation and began with the development of a strategy map. Although the first draft was comprehensive, it was clear that some chiseling was in

order to ensure the final product served its role of clearly and simply communicating strategy and driving execution. Executive Director, Nicole Suydam, explains how they slimmed down the Map: "It was actually a pretty easy process for us to cut a few objectives. We realized that we were being overly optimistic about what we could accomplish and take on, and that a few of our objectives could be combined without losing their value. Since this is a new process for us we want to be careful that we are identifying the things that will bring us the most value and not overwhelm us with data collection later." [53] Second Harvest Food Bank's strategy map is shown in Exhibit 5.9.

■ **Sleep on it:** Working with your colleagues to develop objectives is a challenging task, one that requires full mental engagement. Your prefrontal cortex, like any other energy-hungry body part, pays a price for all of that

Strategy Map FY 2014–2016

Provide our partners with leadership and support to reach people who are food insecure.

- Reduce the Meal Gap
- Build Partner Capacity
- Create Strategic Partnerships

Create a positive and supportive culture committed to living our values and developing our employees and volunteers.

- Develop our Employees
- Engage our Employees
- Maximize Volunteerism
- Maintain a Safe Workplace

Commit to excellence and ensue that our resources are providing the greatest benefit to the community.

- Engage the Community
- Increase Food Donations
- Keep All Food Safe
- Enhance Nutrition Programming
- Provide the Best Service to All

Strengthen our Financial position so we can fund innovative and sustainable solutions to end hunger.

- Expand Fundraising
- Control Expenses
- Pay Off Debt
- Increase Operating Fund Reserve

Mission: To End Hunger in Orange County
Vision: Together we are creating a future in which no one goes hungry. Ever.
Values: Compassion, Integrity, Stewardship, Service Excellence, Diversity

EXHIBIT 5.9   Second Harvest Food Bank (Irvine, CA) Strategy Map

Source: Courtesy of Second Harvest Food Bank, Irvine, CA.

intellectual toil, and by the end of the day you'll most likely be feeling pretty drained. Most of my clients will fight through any fatigue, however, and press on to finalize their map objectives by the end of the workshop. I understand this desire completely. Getting to that final set is a significant accomplishment and puts them one step closer to actually using the Scorecard system. But the end of the day is probably the worst time to make important decisions. As noted above, your brain is tired and thus you're more likely to give in to compromises since you no longer possess the noetic ammunition to mount any kind of defense against your consensus-desiring colleagues. I don't suggest you wait a week before reconvening and finalizing your objectives, but after recharging your mental batteries you'll be in a much better position to critically examine what you've created.

So What Is the Right Number of Objectives?

Sorry to disappoint, but there is no hard-and-fast rule for the right number of objectives. However, as I'm sure you've surmised from the paragraphs above, a useful guideline is less is more. Keep in mind that every objective on the strategy map will spawn an average of one-and-a-half performance measures to accurately capture the intent of the objective. So, for example, 20 objectives on the strategy map would equate to 30 measures for one Scorecard. Multiply that by several cascaded Scorecards throughout your organization and you could quickly ascend to hundreds of measures, resulting in a challenging and burdensome process to manage. To harness the power of the Balanced Scorecard system as both a measurement and communication system, you have to keep the number of objectives on your map to a manageable level. Only you can make the determination of what is manageable, however. That said, I would strongly suggest you cap your objectives between 10 and 15. Doing so ensures a focus on the critical few versus the seduction of the trivial many, and limits the potential number of accompanying performance measures. For the final word, let's end this discussion where it started, with Saint-Exupéry's sage counsel: "Perfection is not when there is more to add, but no more to take away."

NOTES

1. W. Chan Kim and Renee Mauborgne, *Blue Ocean Strategy* (Boston: Harvard Business School Press, 2005), 81–82.
2. Stephen R. Covey, *The 8th Habit* (New York: The Free Press, 2004), 271.

3. Perry Hunt, "Never Underestimate the Power of a Paint Tube," *Smithsonian Magazine* (May 2013).

4. Jennifer S. Mueller, Shimul Melwani, and Jack A. Goncalo, "The Bias Against Creativity: Why People Desire but Reject Creative Ideas," *Psychological Science* 23, no. 1 (2012): 13–17.

5. Robert B. Cialdini, *Influence: The Psychology of Persuasion* (New York: William Morrow, 1993).

6. Accessed at www.zenhabits.net.

7. Michael J. Gelb, *How to Think Like Leonardo da Vinci* (New York: Bantam Dell, 2004).

8. Rita Gunther-McGrath, "How the Growth Outliers Do It," *Harvard Business Review* (January-February 2012): 110–116.

9. Chris Zook and James Allen, *Repeatability: Build Enduring Businesses for a World of Constant Change* (Boston: Harvard Business Review Press, 2012).

10. The McDonald's and Home Depot stories are based on: Robert Simons, "Stress-Test Your Strategy," *Harvard Business Review* (November 2010): 92–100. I have updated some of the numbers (number of restaurants, for example) that appear in the original article.

11. Martin Blumenson, *Patton: The Man Behind the Legend, 1885–1945* (New York: William Morrow, 1985).

12. Roger Martin, "The Innovation Catalysts," *Harvard Business Review* (June 2011).

13. Michael Treacy and Fred Wiersema, *The Discipline of Market Leaders* (Reading, MA: Perseus Books, 1995).

14. Ibid., 63.

15. Daisuke Wakabayashi, "Apple iPhone Sales, Outlook Come Up Short," *Wall Street Journal*, January 27, 2014.

16. Zook and Allen, *Repeatability*.

17. Michael E. Raynor and Mumtaz Ahmed, "Three Rules for Making A Company Truly Great," *Harvard Business Review* (April 2013): 108–117.

18. Statistics accessed at www.staralliance.com/en/about/airlines/singapore_airlines/.

19. Charisse Jones, "BoltBus, RedCoach, other bus lines go for business travelers," *USA Today*, September 21, 2010.

20. James C. Collins and Jerry I. Porras, *Built to Last: Successful Habits of Visionary Companies* (New York: Harper Business, 1994).

21. The value chain background material is drawn primarily from: Joan Magretta, *Understanding Michael Porter: The Essential Guide to Competition and Strategy* (Boston: Harvard Business Review Press, 2012).

22. Michael E. Porter, *Competitive Advantage: Creating and Sustaining Superior Performance* (New York: The Free Press, 1985).

23. Robert S. Kaplan and David P. Norton, *Strategy Maps* (Boston: Harvard Business School Press, 2004), 43.

24. Steven D. Levitt and Stephen J. Dubner, *Freakonomics* (New York: William Morrow, 2005), 91.

25. Quoted in Phil Rosenzweig, *The Halo Effect . . . and the Eight Other Business Delusions That Deceive Managers* (New York: Simon & Schuster, 2007), Kindle edition, location 1801.
26. Odad Shenkar, "Imitation Is More Valuable than Innovation," *Harvard Business Review* (April 2010): 28–29.
27. David P. Norton in Foreword to: Brian E. Becker, Mark A. Huselid, and Dave Ulrich, *The HR Scorecard* (Boston: Harvard Business School Press, 2001).
28. James Barbican, *The Confession of a Rumrunner* (Mystic, CT: Flat Hammock Press, 2007), 126.
29. Quoted in Gerald Nadler and William J. Chandon, *Smart Questions* (San Francisco: Jossey-Bass, 2004), 43.
30. Michael D'Antonio, *Hershey* (New York: Simon & Schuster, 2006), 72–73.
31. Jim Collins, *Good to Great* (New York: Harper Business, 2001).
32. Abram Brown, "How Campbell's Soup Went From Stale to Innovative," *Inc.,* September 14, 2011.
33. Kaplan and Norton, *Strategy Maps.*
34. Ian McEwan, *Saturday* (New York: Random House, 2005), 382.
35. Ken Tysiac, "Employees Need Help to Maximise Analytics Effectiveness, Report Says," *CGMA Magazine,* February 20, 2012, www.cgma.org/magazine/news/pages/20125139.aspx (accessed on April 6, 2012).
36. Rob Goffee and Gareth Jones, "Creating the Best Workplace on Earth", *Harvard Business Review* (May 2013): 98–106.
37. David Rock, *Your Brain at Work* (New York: Harper Collins, 2009), Kindle edition, location 2914.
38. Accessed at www.pewresearch.org/daily-number/baby-boomers-retire/.
39. Jeffrey M. Cohen, Rakesh Khurana, and Laura Reeves, "Growing Talent as if Your Business Depended on It," *Harvard Business Review* (October 2005): 63–70.
40. James Surowiecki, "Requiem for a Dreamliner?" *The New Yorker* (February 4, 2013).
41. John Kotter and James Heskett, *Corporate Culture and Performance* (New York: The Free Press, 1992), 78.
42. Zook and Allen, *Repeatability.*
43. Haig R. Nalbantian, Richard A. Guzzo, Dave Kieffer, and Jay Doherty, *Play to Your Strengths* (New York: McGraw-Hill, 2004).
44. Jennifer A. Chatman and Sandra E. Cha, "Leading by Leveraging Culture," *California Management Review* (Summer 2003).
45. Christine Porath and Christine Pearson, "The Price of Incivility," *Harvard Business Review* (January–February 2013): 114–121.
46. Dale Carnegie, *How to Win Friends and Influence People* (New York: Pocket Books, 1981), 27.
47. Adrian Gostick and Chester Elton, *Managing with Carrots* (Salt Lake City: Gibbs-Smith, 2001), 20.

48. Sandy Richardson, "Do Strategic Themes Add Value in Strategy Mapping?," October 13, 2010. Accessed at author's blog: http://sfo-blog.typepad.com/sfo-blog/2010/10/do-strategic-themes-add-value-in-strategy-mapping.html.
49. Sandy Richardson, *Business Results Revolution* (2013). Self-published.
50. Timothy Ferriss, *The Four-Hour Workweek* (New York: Crown Publishing, 2007), 65.
51. Alan Siegel and Irene Etzkorn, "When Simplicity Is the Solution," *Wall Street Journal*, March 29, 2013.
52. Donald Sull and Kathleen M. Eisenhardt, "Simple Rules for a Complex World," *Harvard Business Review* (September 2012): 68–74.
53. From author e-mail correspondence with Nicole Suydam on August 6, 2013.

6

Create a Balanced Scorecard of Robust Measures, Meaningful Targets, and Strategic Initiatives

 ## WHAT ARE PERFORMANCE MEASURES?

In the last chapter you learned how well-crafted strategic objectives on a strategy map will dramatically improve understanding of a company's strategy. However, simply logging strategic objectives on a map and expecting strategy execution to magically occur reminds me of an old riddle about three frogs on a fence. One of the frogs decides to jump off the fence, so how many are left? The answer is three, because one frog deciding to jump doesn't actually equate to jumping; deliberation isn't the same as action. So it is with the strategy map. Setting out your objectives will not automatically lead to strategy execution. What's needed is a method to assess whether or not you are actually achieving the objectives and advancing towards execution, and that is the province of the performance measure.

I define performance measures as standards used to evaluate and communicate performance against expected results. Unfortunately, like most of the definitions in this book, which are focused on arcane business subjects, this is a fairly dry rendering of performance measures, and certainly doesn't reflect the power they possess. A more colorful, yet completely accurate, description of measures comes from Dubner and Levitt, authors of the quirky economics book, *Freakonomics*. In it they say,

Knowing what to measure and how to measure it makes a complicated world much less so. If you learn how to look at the data in the right way you can explain riddles that otherwise might have seemed impossible. Because there is nothing like the sheer power of numbers to scrub away layers of confusion and contradiction.[1]

What I love most about this quote is the metaphorical scrubbing away of layers of confusion and contradiction, because in business, if we hope to achieve breakthrough results, what we need more than anything else is the clarity that emanates from an accurate picture of the reality we actually face.

Many people believe that measurement has changed the course of history and will continue to do so—paving the way for today's prosperity and tomorrow's breakthroughs. Take for example, the harnessing of steam, an innovation that powered the industrial revolution. Without measurement it may never have occurred. It was the ability to accurately measure the energy output of engines, allowing inventors to determine whether incremental design changes could lead to higher power and less coal consumption, that led to the design and construction of better engines. Looking ahead, Microsoft founder Bill Gates believes measurement holds the key to solving the world's most challenging problems. The billionaire turned philanthropist argues passionately that enhancements in measurement are driving improved outcomes in fields as varied as healthcare in the developing world, to education in the United States.[2]

Joseph M. Juran, a pioneer in the quality movement, once remarked that: "Without a standard there is no logical basis for making a decision or taking action."[3] And make no mistake, regardless of the field of endeavor—health care, education, or the business world—what is required to blaze a trail forward is committed action based on sound judgment. Good and simple performance measures, and the insights they provide for decision making, are the standards that spark progressive deeds and light the path ahead. Let's take a closer look at how you can create robust performance measures to improve your decision making and strategy execution.

 ## CREATING BETTER PERFORMANCE MEASURES

Did you know recent studies suggest that babies can count before they communicate? Researchers at Emory University proved the point with an ingenious experiment. Nine-month-old infants were shown groups of objects on a computer screen, and since babies tend to stare when they see something new, the researchers were able to measure the length of time they looked at the objects to understand how they process information.

Here's how it worked. When the infants were shown images of larger objects that were black with stripes and smaller objects that were white with dots, they then expected the same color-pattern mapping for more-and-less comparisons of number and duration. For instance, if the more numerous objects were white with dots, the babies would stare at the image longer than if the objects were black with stripes. According to the researchers, when the babies look longer, that suggests that they are surprised by the violation of congruency. They appear to expect these different dimensions to correlate in the world.

The findings suggest that humans use information about quantity to organize their experience of the world from the first few months of life.[4]

Talk about being born to measure! But as tempting as it is for me to say something like, measurement is so easy even a baby can do it, that just wouldn't reflect reality, at least as I've experienced it played out in conference rooms around the world. In fact, devising good measures—those that provide real insights—is a decidedly difficult assignment, one that plagues many organizations. On the pages that follow I'll provide numerous tips and techniques to demystify the measurement problem, and ensure that your measures will lead to improved decisions and more focused action.

Avoid Biases in Measure Development

Whether we're consciously aware of them or not, we all harbor certain biases or prejudices that can affect our judgment and actions. Making more informed decisions requires us to uncover these subconscious judgments and bring them into the light of day, where they can be logically assessed. So it is with performance measures; unless you're careful, it's very easy to fall prey to a number of biases that may negatively impact the success of your measurement efforts. The following are some of the key culprits to be on the lookout for.[5]

- **Overconfidence:** Yes or no, do you feel you're a better driver than the average person? Research consistently demonstrates that a majority of people, when polled, say they are a better than average driver. Obviously, it's not statistically possible for most people to be above average but that doesn't stop us from thinking of ourselves that way. Business leaders can also be overconfident in their abilities when it comes to ascertaining the right measure to track a given objective. For example, Stanford researchers observed one fast food chain whose executive team was focused on improving customer satisfaction and profitability. With little in the way of proof to back their claim, they steadfastly clung to the notion that employee turnover was the driver of happy customers, and thus selected it as a key metric and invested substantial sums of money to lower turnover. As the data accumulated, however, executives were shocked to discover that some stores with very high turnover reported both happy customers and increased profitability, while others with low turnover produced anemic results. With time and enhanced analysis, they found that what actually drove satisfaction and profitability was store manager turnover. When you begin selecting measures, it's important to possess the humility to acknowledge that you don't have all the answers, and thus be open to numerous possibilities.

▪ **Availability:** We all have a tendency to assess the cause or probability of an event on the basis of how readily similar examples come to mind—in other words, how available they are. As a result, we're inclined to overestimate the importance of information that we encounter recently, that is frequently found in our environment, or is top of mind for other reasons. This can lead to snap judgments when creating performance measures, causing you to select the first metric that comes to mind simply because it's available, rather than digging deeper for the indicator that truly represents the objective at hand. Financial metrics are prone to this proclivity—EPS, ROI, and other familiar acronyms often spring from the mouths of workshop participants, immediately stifling any potential debate on their actual efficacy.

▪ **Status Quo:** It's always easier to remain on your present course rather than accept the risks that accompany a change in direction. However, this natural tendency of inaction can have dramatic consequences for your Balanced Scorecard, since your metrics must evolve and change to match shifting business realities. Occasionally I'll be contacted by organizations wishing to breathe new life into their Balanced Scorecard system and just a bit of sleuthing on my part usually determines that stale measures are behind the stagnation. As your competitive environment changes, so must your Scorecard metrics. What is effective today may be wildly inappropriate 18 months from now. Take the example of a subscription business like Netflix. At the outset, the acquisition rate of new customers is the most important performance metric. However, as the company matures, its emphasis may shift from adding customers to better managing the ones it has by selling them additional services or reducing churn.

■ **Measuring Against Yourself:**[6] Strategy guru Michael Porter is quick to remind us that what matters most in business is relative, not absolute, performance. If you're creating performance measures that gauge your success in meeting an internal budget target and are achieving beyond your wildest ambitions, yet you're consistently lagging behind your competition, then your measures are not effective. This particular bias is most important to consider when developing financial metrics, a point I'll expand on when discussing measures for each of the four perspectives.

Adopt a Solutions Mind-set

I was fortunate to enjoy most of my college courses, but one that still shines brightly in my memory was organizational behavior. The content was interesting, stimulating, and I'm pleased to report, very much relevant to the career I ultimately chose. I also have fond memories of the professor, a true English gentleman and scholar who had, fortunately for us, somehow found his way to the small Canadian college I attended. He wore old sport jackets with leather patches at the elbows and spoke in a calm and reassuring manner that always made me feel he was a true authority on the subjects he shared with us. One lesson in particular still stands out to me all these years later. In describing corporate cultures he said there was often a tendency, when faced with challenging circumstances for the team to play what he called the "Ain't It Awful" game. In other words, employees would grumble, complain, and whine about the situation, basically engaging in every activity but the problem solving necessary to hoist themselves out of their current predicament.

When it comes to creating performance measures, some organizations have elevated "Ain't It Awful" to professional levels of achievement. They'll arrive at a challenging objective, consider it carefully, and after much deliberation use it as a gateway to launch into a venting session on the million and one problems they face, and ultimately determine the objective can't be measured effectively. I'll talk more about the challenges of measuring "difficult" things a bit later in this section, but for now it's important for you to recognize that perplexing objectives may indeed appear on your map, and the best way to select a measure for them is to avoid the slippery slope of focusing on the problem they represent, and instead adopt a solutions mind-set.

Let's use communication as an example. Many organizations will include an objective relating to improved communication somewhere on their Strategy map, typically in either the Internal Process or Learning and Growth perspectives. This is to be expected, as fluid communication is a vital enabler of the knowledge economy, and I've yet to encounter a company that didn't feel there was room for improvement where communication was concerned. Measuring communication, however, is fraught with difficulties since "good" communication is very much a matter of subjective opinion. That initial challenge alone is often enough to launch workshop participants into long rants about the failure to communicate and the calamities that breakdown leaves in its wake. This is course leads to frustration and occasionally may result in the objective, an important one for most firms, to be dropped from the map. A better approach is to focus on the desired outcome (solution) and forget about the past. If your goal is improved communication, begin with some simple questions to prime a solution, such as: "Describe a time when you witnessed good communication leading to a desired outcome for the company." "What did those involved do differently, that made this communication successful?" "What would it take for all of us to do more of this?"

Beyond the pragmatic benefits of elevating a potentially sour mood in the room, directing your attention to solutions and avoiding problems impacts brain functioning in a number of positive ways.[7] First, by focusing on outcomes you prime your brain to perceive information that is relevant to that outcome, rather than noticing information about the problem. As you scan your environment (and your mind) for solutions, the right hemisphere of the brain is activated, an area helpful for generating insights. Problem-centered attention on the other hand is more likely to create unwanted noise in the brain and inhibit insight generation. Finally, concentrating on solutions creates a "toward" state in the brain as you seek rather than avoid, and this desire to move toward a favorable outcome increases dopamine levels, which is also useful for creating insights.

Embrace Measurement Challenges

With your brain firing on all cylinders thanks to a boost of dopamine, you should be able to easily translate any objective into a meaningful measure, right? Adopting the solutions mind-set discussed above goes a long way toward overcoming difficult measure challenges, but should you encounter objectives that frustrate and confound to the point of near hysteria, try these simple and proven tips:

■ **Ask what it means:** If you've followed my advice thus far, upon completing your strategy map you would have drafted objective statements for each of the strategic objectives appearing on the map. They should, of course, be the starting point for any measure discussion. A well-written objective statement will clearly designate what you mean by the objective at hand and allow you to translate it into a measure that will faithfully gauge success. If, however, certain of your statements are somewhat opaque and leave you wanting more direction, start a discussion of what you mean by the objective. This can be a particularly effective tactic when you reach the often touchy-feely objectives housed in the learning and growth perspective. One example that comes to mine, an objective I've seen a number of times, is "Live a values-based culture." To create a fitting measure this objective requires substantial unpacking, and must be decomposed into specific behaviors that represent its vague meaning. When you consult with employees and ask them to describe examples of when the organization lived by its culture, you'll be in a better position to highlight specific attributes, those you can count in a performance measure.

■ **Visualize behaviors:** Related to the advice above, in addition to carefully dissecting the definition of your objective, it's also helpful to look into the future and visualize what people are doing, how they're behaving as a result of successful fulfillment of the objective. Whatever you see, what they're doing (or not doing) will assist in formulating a measure. A great example of this technique comes from a nonprofit client of mine. This organization, like many budget-conscious nonprofits, relies heavily on volunteer support. In particular they look for senior professionals from other industries to assist in promoting their mission. One of the objectives they created on their strategy map was "Create a culture that attracts and is comfortable to professional-level volunteers." Sounded great until we arrived at the task of attaching a measure to it. The idea of conducting a survey about the culture was lobbed to the group, and received an appropriately lukewarm response. There is certainly nothing wrong with surveys, and it did represent one possible measure, but it would be a very lagging indicator and short on action. To help stimulate the group's thinking, I suggested the visualization technique and asked, "What do you see volunteers doing if you're successful in creating a culture that is comfortable to them?" The group thought about this and ultimately concluded (after lively discussion) that if volunteers feel comfortable in the culture they'll most likely recommend other professionals they know to volunteer. If they're professionals they probably maintain a network, and if they're comfortable in the culture they'll most likely reach out to that network and recommend volunteering. Based on the discussion, the group decided to measure the number of professional volunteer referrals.

■ **Turn your Scorecard into a *CSI* episode:** Virtually all objectives will entail employees acting in a certain way, possibly a new direction, to drive strategy execution. For this exercise, think like the forensic investigators on the television program *CSI* and look for clues in the forms of behaviors you can observe (and somehow count). Also consider whether the objective as it is acted out in the real world leaves any form of tag or trail you can observe and quantify.

■ **Turn to the crowd:** The zeitgeist of modern life is replete with examples of crowd-based decision making. Crowds are utilized to predict movements in the stock market, help companies determine which new products to launch, even decide what films make it to your local cinema. If, despite the best efforts of your Scorecard team, you cannot isolate an appropriate measure for a particularly vexing objective, take it to the crowd. Issue the challenge to your entire employee base, share the difficulty you face, and welcome their unique perspective on the issue. Your staff will appreciate the opportunity to participate in Scorecard development (which drives support for the system), and you'll undoubtedly be delighted by the ingenuity and acumen of your employees.

■ **What does the boss need?** The Balanced Scorecard is a strategy-execution tool, and strategy is the primary domain of your senior executive team. When stuck on a perplexing objective, ask what your executive team needs to know about the objective and what dimensions, aspects, or related behaviors of the objective they need to be regularly discussing in order to gauge progress. Answering those questions may supply clues as to what needs to be measured.

■ **You're not that different:** Some organizations seem to think that, based on the type of work they do, they are somehow unique, not like other businesses, and thus immune to measurement. This is a bias and arrogance you need to check at the door if you hope to execute a differentiating strategy, because measurement is the driving force of execution, and any business can be measured effectively. Take, for example, a film company like Pixar, the name behind blockbusters such as *Finding Nemo*, *Toy Story*, *Cars* and a host of other highly decorated cinematic efforts adored by audiences the world over. Here is how their president, Ed Catmull, describes the company's focus on measurement:

Because we're a creative organization, people tend to assume that much of what we do can't be measured or analyzed. Most of our processes involve activities and deliverables that can be quantified.

We keep track of the rates at which things happen, how often some-thing has to be reworked, whether a piece of work was completely finished or not when it was sent to another department, and so on. Data can show things in a neutral way, which can stimulate discussion and challenge assumptions arising from personal impressions.[8]

With commitment, rigor, and discipline, you can measure anything.

ATTRIBUTES OF EFFECTIVE PERFORMANCE MEASURES

Keeping the advice offered above top of mind will serve you well when you develop the performance measures to gauge strategic success. And while creating good measures can be a taxing exercise, it's likely that at the end of the workshop you'll have more performance measures than you need or want.

Not all performance measures are created equally. Effective metrics provide direction, align employees, ensure accountability, improve decision making, and serve as a basis for resource-allocation decisions. Here are some criteria to consider as you decide upon the measures that will make up your Balanced Scorecard.

Linked to Your Strategy

The Balanced Scorecard was designed to facilitate the description of strategy. It does so by translating your strategy into a set of objectives on the strategy map and measures used to evaluate performance. All measures on the Scorecard should serve as faithful translations of objectives, which in turn, have been translated from your strategy. If you find yourself brainstorming measures that seem important, but not strategic, then perhaps they are better suited to an operational dashboard that may serve as a complement to your Balanced Scorecard.

Quantitative (Most of the Time)

In every article, blog post, newsletter, and book I've written that broaches the subject of performance measures, I've mentioned the importance of ensuring metrics are quantitative in order to avoid subjectivity and reflect objectivity as much as possible. I still feel the vast majority of your measures should be quantitative, something you can count, but as business and the nature of competition changes, there may be a place in your Balanced Scorecard for a few measures of a more subjective variety.

Organizations today must constantly exercise their agility muscles, scanning the environment for changes and acting on signals they pick up from customers, employees, social media commentators, and other key influencers. But how do you know you're open to, receiving, and acting upon the signals swirling about you? Perhaps the best way to measure it would be simply asking the executive team, and maybe others, in the organization, "In the last month do you think we've improved our ability to read and act on signals? Please provide examples for your rationale." Examining the percentage that offers a yes to the statement is innately interesting, but the real value comes in discussing the examples and rationales provided at monthly management meetings.

To generate value from this technique you should pair the subjective measure with a more objective yardstick. For example, let's say you track the percentage of people who believe you've acted on signals in the environment faster in the last month. If that were actually the case, what objective metric might it drive—revenue, profit, more new product development, research and development activity? Of course you may not have a direct one-to-one relationship between the subjective and objective metrics (only statistical analysis conducted over time will demonstrate causation).

The greatest benefit this approach offers is sparking a dialog on what are often ambiguous yet vital dimensions of corporate performance, those that lead to real results. Ironically, since I began this section with a nod to the ongoing relevance of quantitative measures, it's not the numbers that matter, but the discussion that results—the questions raised, assumptions challenged, and so on. Additionally, if you keep talking about these subjective measures they are far more likely to become embedded in the culture of the organization, and that's what you want.

Accessible

Research suggests that upwards of 30 percent of your performance data may be unavailable when you launch a Balanced Scorecard. Many organizations are disappointed to learn this until they realize the missing data represent entirely new ways of monitoring performance that had been neglected in the past. Proclaiming a measure as critical enough to appear on the Scorecard, regardless of initial data availability, signals a strong commitment to focusing on what really matters. While 30 percent is palatable, 70, 80, or 90 percent is not. Never let the best be the enemy of the good. Sounds profound (maybe) but it simply means that a Balanced Scorecard you can use immediately with 70 percent of data available is better than a Scorecard you have to wait a year for because of data availability issues.

Update Frequently

Your primary motivation in launching a Balanced Scorecard was most likely to improve results. Results can only be enhanced through the provision of timely information upon which you can take action. Timely in this context refers to measures that are updated frequently—I recommend monthly or (at the most) quarterly. Semiannual and annual performance measures allow little room for mid-course corrections. By the time you receive your results the actions that led to the performance are long past.

Counterbalance

Recently I worked with a client who was in the process of cascading the Balanced Scorecard throughout their organization; taking that all-important step of using the power of linked Scorecard performance measures to generate alignment from top to bottom. The information technology (IT) department was among the groups developing cascaded metrics, and at one point during the workshop their team lead called me over with a question that had been bothering him.

> **IT Team Member**: We've been told that minimizing expenses is crucial to the organization, and so we've created a cascaded measure of reducing vendor costs. What we're going to do is negotiate with software and hardware vendors and consultants to try and drive down our overall IT costs.
> **Paul**: Sounds good. What's the issue?
> **IT Team Member**: Well, we're concerned that if we insist on lower costs from our vendors that could lead them to cut some corners, and ultimately result in poorer service to our customers here in the company . . . and that's the last thing we want to happen.

It was clear from the look on his face this was a dedicated professional who wanted to do the right thing for the organization, but was concerned that measures on the Balanced Scorecard could actually *harm* his goals by creating some unintended consequences.

He was right to be concerned. It's not uncommon, especially for those who are new to the Scorecard system, to populate their model with measures that have the potential of driving the wrong, or inappropriate, behavior. In this case, if the IT department pursued aggressive targets for vendor-cost reductions, that could very well lead to poorer service, and in turn have a negative impact on other aspects of the organization's strategy-execution efforts; a classic case of a measure producing an unintentional effect.

To overcome this issue, a useful diagnostic test for your Scorecard measures is to critically examine each and ask whether the potential exists for any to drive unintended consequences. If it does, you should add what are often termed *counterbalanced* measures. In the case of my client from the IT department, he knew that reducing costs was important to the bottom line but didn't want those lower costs translating to poorer service for his customers. Therefore, he chose a measure of *customer satisfaction with IT services* to counterbalance vendor costs. Over time he'll monitor the two, looking for correlations that may require his intervention. If, for example, vendor costs do decrease but he also sees a decline in customer satisfaction he can hypothesize the two are correlated and use this information to possibly reconsider targets for vendor cost reduction. Maybe the initial target was too aggressive, leading to a degradation of the services provided to his customers.

This topic reminds of an outstanding quote from Eli Goldratt, author of the popular business novel, *The Goal*. When asked by a client, "What can we do immediately to improve performance in our company?" Goldratt's pragmatic reply was: "Change one key measure that is driving the wrong behavior."[9]

Relevant

The measures appearing on your Scorecard should accurately depict the process or objective you're attempting to evaluate. A good test is whether or not your measured results are actionable. If some aspect of performance failed, you should be able to recognize the significance of the problem and be able to fix it. This issue is demonstrated through the use of performance indices, which many organizations will use on their Scorecards. An index is a combination of several individual measures combined in some way to result in a single, overall indicator of performance. Employee satisfaction may appear on your Scorecard as an index of the weighted-average performance of: turnover, absenteeism, complaints, and survey results. Indices are a great way to quickly depict a number of performance variables in a single indicator, but they have some inherent weaknesses. First of all, they may obscure results and limit action. If turnover at your organization was at an all-time high but was given a low weight in your employee satisfaction index, you may never know there are issues, since the overall index could appear to be on target. If key staff members are among those leaving the firm and you haven't mounted a response, you may soon pay a heavy price in other areas of performance as reflected on the Scorecard. Indices are also frequently difficult for most employees to easily grasp and understand. A logistics index appearing in the internal process perspective may contain valuable information, but be baffling to those outside of the supply-chain side of the organization.

Measures, Not Strategic Initiatives

It's not uncommon for Scorecard developers to include at least a measure or two to the effect, "Complete project X by September 30." This reflects an initiative— an action taken to assure success on the measure—not a measure itself. Should they be fortunate enough to complete the project, does the measure simply vanish from the Scorecard? In this case, the Scorecard creators should ask, "What happens on September 30? How are we better off as an organization? How are prospects improved for our customers or clients?" In other words, "Why are we embarking on this initiative?" Answering these questions may lead to the development of a more appropriate performance measure. If, however, the initiative is vital to the organization's strategy, you may include a variant of it on the Scorecard by tracking milestone completions on the path to completing the initiative. Once the project is finished, you can transition to a measure that reflects why the organization invested in the initiative.

Mix of Lag and Lead Indicators

Writing in his book, *Leadership*, former New York City mayor Rudy Giuliani recounted an interesting story of how Department of Corrections personnel were able to use performance measures to head off any potential riots in their facilities.[10] Using their performance-measurement system, the department tracked commissary sales in its jails. They determined that if sales of cigarettes and candy suddenly increased, a riot might be in the planning stages. Inmates realized that they would be confined to their cells immediately after any kind of uprising, and therefore stocked up on supplies. A spike in candy and cigarette sales in this case was a *leading* indicator of the number of prison riots (*lag* indicator). Knowing this relationship existed allowed prison officials to take action, averting potentially dangerous confrontations.

The anecdote above is a great example of using both lag and lead indicators to portray a richer picture of strategic priorities. Lagging indicators, the number of prison riots in our story above, are measures that track past events.

They trail behind reality and offer accurate, but historical views of the facts. Leading indicators, on the other hand, are measures you feel hold predictive power and have the ability to drive or lead the longer-term lagging indicators. In the prison example above, corrections officers used the measure of commissary sales as predictive of future riots. The Balanced Scorecard should contain a mix of lag and lead indicators of performance. If you track nothing but lag indicators, historical representations of performance, you know little about the *how* of your operation. Conversely, a preoccupation with leading indicators will not reveal whether improvements are leading to improved processes and customer results.

Here is another novel, but entirely relevant and modern, application of leading indicators in the television advertising industry.[11] Historically the popularity of TV shows has been measured by simply counting viewers, with the venerable Nielsen ratings constituting the industry measurement standard. Advertisers with the means would naturally gravitate towards the programs with the highest number of viewers.

However, in today's buoyant market, advertisers looking to seize value have turned to new metrics in order to evaluate which programs are actually the most popular with viewers. One key metric, which we could easily categorize as a leading indicator, is social media buzz attached to a program. Sophisticated tracking devices allow advertisers to count mentions on Facebook, Twitter, and other social media venues, providing a more sophisticated assessment of a program's current popularity and future potential. The findings are often enlightening in an industry where billions of dollars are in play each year. For example, at one point the ultra-popular *Glee* was ranked number 55 by number of viewers, but when the social media activity the show generates was taken into account, it rocketed to number 2. Ad buyers recognize that mentions of programs on Facebook and Twitter increasingly spur people to watch them. In other words, social media buzz is a leading indicator of future viewers. This information is vital to advertisers who naturally wish to ensure their products and messages are associated with the most relevant and popular programs.

Depending on the nature of the metric itself, one of the most oft-cited challenges associated with leading measures is the difficulty of collecting data. For example, a residential construction company plagued with accidents knew their very existence depended on improving safety conditions and reducing accidents. They chose the logical lagging measure of number of lost time accidents, but were unsure as to the best leading indicator to track. Many opinions were sought, voices heard, and discussions held until finally it was determined that the best leading indicator—the truest driver of accidents—was compliance with safety standards. The company identified a number of safety standards, such as wearing hard hats, gloves, boots, eyewear, and using scaffolds and roof braces, they believed strongly influenced the number of accidents. The challenge was in collecting the data. Whereas accidents were simple to track at the end of a period, measuring compliance with safety standards would require physical observation on the part of construction supervisors, who already faced a never-ending stream of distractions. While initially reluctant, the supervisors recognized the peril of not following through with the collection effort and soon got into the habit of recording compliance statistics. Within a year of identifying and measuring this leading indicator the company achieved the best safety record in their 30-year history.[12] Gathering data for lead measures will almost always be more difficult than for lags, but that sacrifice in time and effort is the price you must pay to drive strategic performance forward.

I'll warn you, some people on your Scorecard team may suggest every measure is in effect lagging because, by their very nature, all metrics are collected at the end of some period, and thus historical in nature. It's very easy to get off track and engage in a semantic discussion, but in the end it boils down to a simple principle. When selecting measures ask, "What drives this measure?" Whenever you choose one measure and can hypothesize a relationship with a related metric you feel drives the performance of the first measure, you've determined a lag and lead relationship (see Exhibit 6.1).

Last But Not Least . . . Keep Them Simple

I want to end this section by sharing with you what I feel is the most important attribute any performance measure can possess: simplicity. When I use the word simplicity I'm implying both simplicity in the design of the measure and ease of understanding by your entire employee population.

During Scorecard consulting engagements, one of the greatest battles I see my clients waging is the quest to create a perfect measure for every objective on their strategy map. Never satisfied with the results of extensive brainstorming and endless debate among their colleagues, many continue to strive for that one holy grail of a measure that will bring perfect clarity and insight to their pursuit of strategy execution. For some the level of frustration eventually reaches a boiling point, inevitably expressed with some form of the sentence, "You just can't measure what we do!" which, as we discussed earlier, is of course completely false.

	Lag Measures	Lead Measures
Definition	Measures focusing on results at the end of a time period. Normally characterizing historical performance	Measures that "drive" or lead to the performance of lag measures. Normally measure intermediate processes and activities
Examples	• Revenue • Employee satisfaction	• Time spent with customers • Absenteeism
Advantages	Normally easy to identify and capture	Predictive in nature, and allow the organization to make adjustments based on results
Issues	Historical in nature and do not reflect current activities. Lack predictive power	May prove difficult to identify and capture. Often new measures with no history at the organization

The Balanced Scorecard should contain a mix of lag and lead measures of performance.

EXHIBIT 6.1 Lag and Lead Performance Measures

I'm all for tenacity, drive, and commitment to finding measures that illuminate the truth and reduce uncertainty, but after close to two decades in the measurement trenches it has become clear that so-called perfect measures don't really exist. But that certainly doesn't mean you should abandon your efforts and leave your quest for execution to chance because what you're attempting to measure is difficult to quantify in a precise fashion. On the contrary, as Jim Collins reminds us, what matters is not finding the perfect measure, but setting upon a consistent and intelligent method of assessing your results, and then tracking your trajectory with rigor.[13] Let's examine the stories of two organizations that did just that and, as you'll discover, these aren't exactly the type of organizations that can simply count widgets. If they can isolate the simple measures that drive success, you can too.

When Tom Morris assumed control of the Cleveland Symphony Orchestra in 1987, he asked board members what they expected of him during his tenure. Their response: Make an already great orchestra even greater, defined by artistic excellence. There is no simple metric you can pick up off the shelf to correspond directly with artistic excellence, but that didn't stop Morris and his team from following Collins' advice and brainstorming a number of consistent and intelligent metrics they could use to serve as proxies for excellence. In the end they counted the number of standing ovations they received, number of pieces played to perfection, invitations to prestigious festivals, and ticket sales in other venues outside of Cleveland. Morris and his colleagues realized early on that finding an exact measurement of "artistic excellence" would prove as difficult as performing Brahms' Double Concerto with one hand tied behind their backs, so they settled on simple things they could count, discuss, and learn from.

From a stately concert hall we now move to a sold-out stadium of screaming fans and one legendary rock band's measurement treasure.[14] When Van Halen ruled the rock universe back in the early 1980s, their shows were a legendary mix of over-the-top showmanship and, for the time, dazzling technology. To accomplish the technology component of the equation, the band was accompanied on the road by nine 18-wheelers full of gear. Because of the complexity of their shows, Van Halen relied on an extremely detailed contract with venues to ensure nothing was left to chance. David Lee Roth, the band's lead singer, said it was like a version of the Chinese Yellow Pages. This is how a typical article in the contract would read: "There will be 15 amperage voltage sockets at 20-foot spaces, evenly, providing 10 amperes." Imagine hundreds of such technical specifications spanning untold pages and you can bet the typical concert promoter's head was spinning in confusion. The band knew it was a distinct possibility the entire contract wouldn't be read, and therefore, problems could result at the show. To ensure that didn't happen Van Halen buried a special clause in the middle of the contract, called Article 126. It read, "There will be no brown M&Ms in the backstage area, upon pain of forfeiture of the show, with full compensation." So when Roth arrived at a new venue, he'd walk backstage and glance at the M&M bowl. If he saw brown M&Ms he'd demand a line check of the entire production. "Guaranteed you're going to arrive at a technical error," he said. "They didn't read the contract. Sometimes it would threaten to just destroy the whole show." Roth didn't have the time, or the inclination one would speculate, to spend hours checking the amperage of every socket. He needed a quick and easy way to assess whether or not the stage-hands were focused on the specifics of the contract, and the brown M&M clause did the trick every time. And so an extremely simple metric, "Number of brown M&Ms," served as a proxy for a process that was crucial to concert success.

"The number of standing ovations received" and "Number of brown M&Ms" are not perfect indicators, but what measure is? School test scores are flawed, customer service data is often unconvincing, even medical tests can prove mistaken. What matters is not striving for perfection in measurement, but tracking a small number of simple items, discussing them frequently, ana-lyzing them with rigor to learn from what they're telling you, and tracking your progress towards your mission.

To help you make the hard choices among competing measure alter-natives, I've developed a worksheet for ranking your metrics. List your measures under the appropriate perspective, and award a score to in rela-tion to each criterion. Consider rating each out of a possible 10 points (see Exhibit 6.2).

Balanced Scorecard—**Measure Selection Worksheet**

Perspective	Linkage to Strategy	Quantitative	Accessible	Frequency of Updating	Counter-Balanced	Relevance	Measure, not strategic initiative	Simplicity	Comments
Financial									
Measure 1									
Measure 2...									
Customer									
Measure 1									
Measure 2...									
Internal Process									
Measure 1									
Measure 2...									
Learning and Growth									
Measure 1									
Measure 2...									

EXHIBIT 6.2 Worksheet to Select Balanced Scorecard Measures

MEASURES FOR EACH OF THE FOUR PERSPECTIVES

Good news for those of you thinking this book doesn't contain nearly enough pictures. In this section you'll find exhibits (okay, not really pictures, but the best I can do) that list a number of possible measures for each of the four perspectives (see Exhibits 6.3, 6.4, 6.5, and 6.6). I am including a few paragraphs on the financial perspective because, as you'll read, most companies default to the same list of metrics, and I believe there is much room for improvement in this perspective that represents the end in mind of our strategic journeys.

As you review the inventory of possible metrics for each perspective, keep in mind that no universal set of right or wrong performance measures exists in practice; they will prove beneficial only in the context of your specific objectives and strategy. So feel free to peruse the lists, and if you see measures that could serve as faithful translations of your strategic objectives, by all means include them on your Balanced Scorecard. However, it's important to remember that the final slate of measures must represent your unique strategic situation.

• Earnings per share	• Return on invested capital
• Total assets	• Value added per employee
• Total assets/employee	• Compound growth rate
• Profits/% of total assets	• Dividends
• Return on net assets	• Market value
• Return on total assets	• Share price
• Revenues/total assets	• Shareholder mix
• Gross margin	• Shareholder loyalty
• Net income	• Cash flow
• Profit as a % of sales	• Total costs
• Profit per employee	• Credit rating
• Revenue	• Debt
• Revenue from new products	• Debt to equity
• Revenue per employee	• Times interest earned
• Return on equity (ROE)	• Days sales in receivables
• Return on capital employed (ROCE)	• Accounts receivable turnover
• Return on investment (ROI)	• Days in payables
• Economic value added (EVA)	• Days in inventory
• Market value added (MVA)	• Inventory turnover ratio

EXHIBIT 6.3 Sample Financial Perspective Measures

• Likehood to recommend	• Customer visits to the company
• Customer satisfaction	• Hours spent with customers
• Customer loyalty	• Marketing cost as a percentage of sales
• Market share	• Number of ads placed
• Customer complaints	• Number of proposals made
• Complaints resolved on first contact	• Brand recognition
• Return rates	• Response rate
• Response time per customer request	• Number of trade shows attended
• Direct price	• Sales volume
• Price relative to competition	• Share of target customer spending
• Total cost to customer	• Sales per channel
• Average duration of customer relationship	• Average customer size
• Customers lost	• Customers/employees
• Customer retention	• Customer service expense per customer
• Customer acquisition rates	• Customer profitability
• Percent of revenue from new customers	• Frequency (number of sales transactions)
• Number of customers	• Percentage of customers who act as
• Annual sales per customer	references
• Win rate (sales closed/sales contacts)	

EXHIBIT 6.4   A Sample of Customer Measures

• Average cost per transaction	• Cycle time improvement
• On-time delivery	• Continuous improvement
• Average lead time	• Warranty claims
• Inventory turnover	• Lead user identification
• Environmental emissions	• Products and services in the pipeline
• Research and development expense	• Internal rate of return on new projects
• Community involvement	• Waste reduction
• Patents pending	• Space utilization
• Average age of patents	• Frequency of returned purchases
• Ratio of new products to total offerings	• Downtime
• Stock-outs	• Planning accuracy
• Labor utilization rates	• Time to market of new products/services
• Response time to customer requests	• New products introduced
• Defect percentage	• Number of positive media stories
• Rework	• Social media hits
• Customer database availability	• Reputation index
• Market segmentation	• Number of risks identified
• Number of customer profiles created	• Key process cycle time
• Breakeven time	

EXHIBIT 6.5   Possible Internal Process Measures

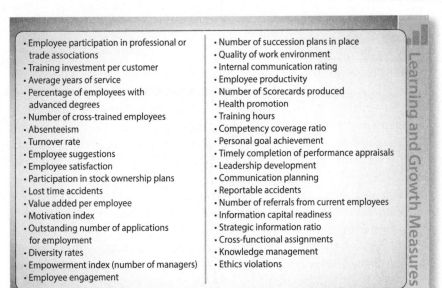

- Employee participation in professional or trade associations
- Training investment per customer
- Average years of service
- Percentage of employees with advanced degrees
- Number of cross-trained employees
- Absenteeism
- Turnover rate
- Employee suggestions
- Employee satisfaction
- Participation in stock ownership plans
- Lost time accidents
- Value added per employee
- Motivation index
- Outstanding number of applications for employment
- Diversity rates
- Empowerment index (number of managers)
- Employee engagement

- Number of succession plans in place
- Quality of work environment
- Internal communication rating
- Employee productivity
- Number of Scorecards produced
- Health promotion
- Training hours
- Competency coverage ratio
- Personal goal achievement
- Timely completion of performance appraisals
- Leadership development
- Communication planning
- Reportable accidents
- Number of referrals from current employees
- Information capital readiness
- Strategic information ratio
- Cross-functional assignments
- Knowledge management
- Ethics violations

Learning and Growth Measures

EXHIBIT 6.6   A Sample of Learning and Growth Measures

Fortifying the Financial Perspective

In most writing on the Balanced Scorecard, including mine, you will find substantially less ink devoted to the financial perspective than to the customer, internal process, and learning and growth perspectives. This is certainly not a surprise to people familiar with the Scorecard model, as it was created with the goal of supplementing lagging financial measures of performance with the drivers of future financial success. Anyone who has worked in the field of business has undoubtedly been exposed to the standard toolkit of financial metrics, but what drives financial success is often a mysterious black box of many possibilities. Thanks to the Scorecard system, with its inclusion of nonfinancial perspectives of performance, firms are now in a much better position to solve the value-creation mystery and discover what does in fact drive future financial results.

Over the years I've reviewed countless Scorecards and can say unequivocally that the financial perspective is home to the most commonly used, least differentiated set of measures, none of which will be unfamiliar to you: revenue, growth, profitability, return on sales, and so on. As noted above, this is to be expected, as the financial perspective is home to the lagging measures that detail how success in the other perspectives impacts the bottom line. While financial yardsticks of performance are typically the most widely known and available, most organizations underutilize this perspective of performance to convey their true economic success.

Most companies operating in a competitive environment consider results from the financial perspective to represent the ultimate arbiter of absolute success. The key word in that last sentence is *absolute*. The measures they employ provide an outstanding view of the company's *absolute* performance, meaning the actual dollars in sales they've generated, exact percentage of growth, precise ratio of profits to sales, and so on. What they don't tell us, however, is how well the firm has performed relative to its competition.

Michael Porter reminds us repeatedly that "Competitive advantage is a relative concept,"[15] meaning that results must be stacked up against those of other companies operating in the same industry who face a similar competitive environment. Without this comparison, absolute performance is meaningless. If your company achieved sales growth of 10 percent last year, that might be cause for cheers and backslapping all around until you learn that your key competitors all surpassed 20 percent. Knowing that, you quickly realize how much economic value you've left on the table.

What we're ultimately attempting to capture in the financial perspective is a verdict on the company's success in achieving competitive advantage over its rivals. Since most companies track only their absolute performance on financial yardsticks, they're unable to gauge their success when judged against peers. I would argue that virtually all financial metrics must be compared to industry averages or other key benchmarks in order to prove effective in judging competitive success. So, rather than raw sales growth, you would calculate sales growth percentage versus the industry average. Instead of return on equity, it's return on equity versus the industry average. Perhaps the most important metric in this perspective will be return on invested capital (ROIC). This fundamental measure examines a company's profits versus all the funds (both operating expenses and capital) it has invested to generate those profits. Returning to Porter, he cogently argues this is the only metric that reflects the true economic purpose of every profit-seeking enterprise: to produce goods or services whose value exceeds the sum of the costs of all the inputs, thereby ensuring resources have been used effectively. And once again, to ensure efficacy, ROIC should be compared to others in your industry.

We must never lose sight of the fact that for-profit businesses are attempting to achieve competitive advantage that leads to superior profitability. All industries have defined profit pools, and therefore it's vital that when assessing financial results that we do so in the context of performance versus rivals. Only then does a firm possess a true and meaningful picture of the competitive advantage it does or does not enjoy.

 RECORDING YOUR MEASURES: CREATING A PERFORMANCE MEASURE DATA DICTIONARY

Once you've settled on a set of performance measures, the next step is to catalog the specific characteristics of each in a data dictionary. My dictionary's definition of the word *dictionary* is a "book that lists . . . the topics of a subject." That is precisely what you're crafting in this step of the process—a document that provides all users with a detailed examination of your Balanced Scorecard measures, including a thorough list of characteristics. Creating the measure-data dictionary isn't necessarily a fun or glamorous task, but it is an important one. When you present your Balanced Scorecard to senior managers and employees alike, they will undoubtedly quiz you on the background of each and every measure. "Why did you choose this measure?" "Is it strategically significant?" "How do you calculate the measure?" "Who is responsible for results?" These and numerous other queries will greet your attempts to share your Scorecard with colleagues. The data dictionary provides the background you need to quickly defend your measure choices and answer any questions your audience may offer. Additionally, chronicling your measures in the data dictionary provides your team with one last opportunity to ensure a common understanding of measure details.

Exhibit 6.7 provides a template you can use to create your own measure dictionary. There are four sections of the template that must be completed. In the first section, shown at the top, you provide essential background material on the measure. The second lists specific measure characteristics. Calculation and data specifications are outlined in the third component of the dictionary. Finally, in the bottom section, space is provided to outline performance information relating to the measure. Let's examine each of these sections.

Measure Background

At a glance, readers should be able to determine what this measure is all about, and why it's important for the organization to track.

- **Perspective:** Displays the perspective under which the measure falls.
- **Measure Number/Name:** All performance measures should be provided a number and name. The number is important should you later choose an automated reporting system. Many will require completely unique names

Perspective: Customer	**Measure Number/Name:** C01/Customer Satisfaction	**Owner:** E. Crawford
Strategy: Expand program offerings.	**Objective:** Serve customers with passion and integrity.	

Description: Customer Satisfaction measures the percentage of surveyed customers stating they are satisfied with our current service offerings. Satisfaction is judged using a number of criteria, including: access to services, timeliness, and overall quality. We feel that only by ensuring current customers are satisfied will we be able to expand our offerings, and grow revenue.

Lag/Lead: Lag	**Frequency:** Quarterly	**Unit Type:** Percentage	**Polarity:** High values are good.

Formula: Number of quarterly survey respondents feel satisfied with current access, timeliness, and quality of our services divided by the total number of surveys received.

Data Source: Data for this measure is provided by our survey company, "SST." Each quarter they perform a random survey of our customers and provide the results electronically to us. Data is contained in the form of MS Excel spreadsheets (CUST SURVEY.xls, lines 14 and 15). Data is available the 10th business day following the end of each quarter.

Data Quality: High—received automatically from third party vendor	**Data Collector:** K. Tobin

Baseline: Our most recent data received from SST indicates a Customer Satisfaction percentage of 59%.	**Target:** Q1 2001: 65% • Q2 2001: 68% Q3 2001: 72% • Q4 2001: 75%

Target Rationale: Achieving customer satisfaction is critical to our strategy of service expansion. The quarterly increases we're targeting are higher than in past years but reflect our increased focus on satisfaction.	**Initiatives:** 1. Transportation services for targeted customers 2. Customer management software program implementation 3. Customer Service Training

EXHIBIT 6.7   Balanced Scorecard Data Dictionary

for each measure, and since you may track the same measures at various locations or departments, a specific identifier should be supplied. The measure name should be brief, but descriptive. Again, if you purchase software for your reporting needs, it may limit the number of characters you can use in the name field.

■ **Owner:** Not only does the Balanced Scorecard transmit your strategy for success to the entire organization, it also simultaneously creates a climate of accountability for results. Central to the idea of accountability is the establishment of owners for each and every measure. Simply put, the owner is the individual responsible for results. Should the indicator's performance begin to decline, it's the owner we look to for answers and a plan to bring results back in line with expectations.

- **Strategy:** Displays the specific strategy you believe the measure will positively influence. This box is customarily used should you have employ strategic themes, which we discussed in Chapter 5.
- **Objective:** Every measure was created as a translation of a specific objective. Use this space to identify the relevant objective.
- **Description:** After reading the measure name, most people will immediately jump to the measure description, and it is therefore possibly the most important piece of information on the entire template. Your challenge is to draft a description that concisely and accurately captures the essence of the measure so that anyone reading it will be able to quickly grasp why the measure is critical to the organization. In our example, we rapidly learn that customer satisfaction is based on a percentage, what that percentage is derived from (survey questions), and why we believe the measure will help us achieve our strategy of expanding program offerings.

Measure Characteristics

This section captures the basic aspects of the measure you'll require when you begin reporting results.

- **Lag/Lead:** Outline whether the measure is a core outcome indicator or a performance driver. Remember that your Scorecard represents a hypothesis of your strategy implementation. When you begin analyzing your results over, time you'll want to test the relationships you believe exist between your lag and lead measures.
- **Frequency:** How often do you plan to report performance on this measure? Most organizations have measures that report performance on a daily, weekly, monthly, quarterly, semi-annual, or annual basis. However, I have seen unique timeframes such as school-year for one government agency. Attempt to limit the number of semi-annual and annual measures you use on your Scorecard. A measure that is only updated once a year is of limited value when you use the Scorecard as a management tool to make adjustments based on performance results.
- **Unit Type:** This characteristic identifies how the measure will be expressed. Commonly used unit types include numbers, dollars, and percentages.
- **Polarity:** When assessing the performance of a measure you need to know whether high values reflect good or bad performance. In most cases, this is very straightforward. We all know that lower costs and increased employee satisfaction are good, while a high value for complaints reflects

performance that requires improvement. However, in some cases the polarity issue can prove quite challenging. Take the example of a public health organization. If they choose to measure caseload of social workers, will high values be good or bad? A high number of cases per social worker may suggest great efficiency and effectiveness on the part of the individual workers. Conversely, it could mean the social workers are juggling far too many clients and providing mediocre service in an attempt to inflate their caseload numbers. In such cases you may want to institute a dual-polarity measure. For example, a maximum of 25 cases per social worker may be considered good, but anything over 25 would be a cause for concern, and necessitate action.

Calculation and Data Specifications

Information contained in this section of the dictionary may be the most important, yet pose the greatest difficulty to gather. To begin reporting your measures, precise formulas are necessary, and sources of data must be clearly identified.

- **Formula:** In the formula box you provide the specific elements of the calculation for the performance measure.
- **Data Source:** Every measure must be derived from something—an existing management report, third party, vendor-supplied information, customer databases, the general ledger, and so on. In this section you should rigorously attempt to supply as much detailed information as possible. If the information is sourced from a current report, what is the report titled, and on what line number does the specific information reside? Also, when can you access the data? This information is important to your Scorecard reporting cycle, since you'll be relying on the schedules of others when producing your Scorecard. The more information you provide here, the easier it will be to begin actually producing Balanced Scorecard reports with real data. However, if you provide vague data sources, or no information at all, you will find it exceedingly difficult to report on the measure later. A warning—spend the time you need to thoroughly complete this section. I have seen a number of Scorecards proceed swiftly through the development stage only to stall at the moment of reporting because the actual data could not be identified or easily collected.
- **Data Quality:** Use this area of the template to comment on the condition of the data you expect to use when reporting Scorecard results. If the data

is produced automatically from a source system and can be easily accessed, it can be considered high. If, however, you rely on an analyst's Microsoft Word document that is, in turn, based on some other colleague's Access database numbers that emanate from an old legacy system, then you may consider the quality low. Assessing data quality is important for a couple of reasons. Pragmatically, you need to know which performance measures may present an issue when you begin reporting your results. Knowing in advance what to expect will help you develop strategies to ensure the data you need is produced in a timely and accurate fashion. Also, data-quality issues may also help direct resource questions at your organization. If the information is truly critical to strategic success, but current data quality is low, perhaps the organization should invest in systems to mine the data more effectively.

- **Data Collector:** In the first section of the template you identified the owner of the measure as that individual who is accountable for results. Often this is not the person you would expect to provide the actual performance data. In our example, E. Crawford is accountable for the performance of the measure, but K. Tobin serves as the actual data contact.

Performance Information

In the final section of the template you note your current level of performance, suggest targets for the future, and outline specific initiatives you'll use to achieve those targets.

- **Baseline:** Users of the Balanced Scorecard will be very interested in the current level of performance for all measures. For those owning the challenge of developing targets the baseline is critical in their work.
- **Target:** You may be saying, "At this point in the process we haven't set targets, so what do we do?" Fortunately, some of your measures may already have targets. For example, perhaps you've currently stated an expectation to cut costs by 15 percent next year. Whenever targets exist, use them now. For those measures that don't currently have targets, you can leave this section blank and complete it once the targets have been finalized. If you do have at least some targets, list them based on the frequency of the measure. In this example, I've shown quarterly customer satisfaction targets. Some organizations may find it difficult to establish monthly or quarterly targets and instead opt for an annual number, but track performance toward that end on a monthly or quarterly basis.

■ **Target Rationale:** As above, this will only apply to those measures that currently have a performance target. The rationale provides users with background on how you arrived at the particular target(s). Did it result from an executive planning retreat? Does it represent an incremental improvement based on historical results? Was it based on a mandate? For people to galvanize around the achievement of a target they need to know how it was developed, and that while it may represent a stretch, it isn't merely wishful thinking on the part of an over-zealous senior management team.

■ **Initiatives:** At any given time most organizations will have dozens of initiatives or projects swirling about. Often, only those closest to the project know anything about it, hence any possible synergies between initiatives are never realized. The Scorecard provides you with a wonderful opportunity to evaluate your initiatives in the context of strategic significance. If an initiative or project cannot be linked to the successful accomplishment of your strategy you have to ask yourself why it is being funded and pursued. Use this section of the template to map current or anticipated initiatives to specific performance measures. As with targets, at this point in the process you may not have settled upon your final portfolio of strategic initiatives. If that is the case, you can leave this section blank and complete it once you have determined your final roster of initiatives.

As with the objective statements discussed in the last chapter, it's important to complete data dictionaries soon after selecting your Balanced Scorecard measures. Many organizations will use the process to screen potential measures, employing the fields provided to assess the probable efficacy of each measure, and determine if it is possible to capture the data necessary to report it.

Since the data dictionary template is quite comprehensive, completing one for each candidate measure may prove to be a time-consuming task. Therefore, I recommend filling out a minitemplate at the conclusion of your measures workshop as a very first-draft, first-cut examination of the measures. Rather than a comprehensive list of fields as presented in Exhibit 6.7, this document will contain just the essential information necessary to make a preliminary judgment on the potential usefulness of the metric, and the likelihood of it advancing to the next stage of dictionary completion. Possible fields for the minitemplate include:

■ Whether we currently track the measure
■ Frequency of reporting

- Potential owner
- Preliminary formula, and so on

How Many Measures on a Balanced Scorecard?

When Sam Liang was president of medical device manufacturer Medrad, Inc., one of his core priorities was managing by metrics. Despite the fact that Medrad is a substantial company, with more than 2,000 employees and revenue in excess of $500 million, Liang recognized the genius of keeping things simple when it comes to using performance measures. In his words:

> You have to keep it simple. Some companies will come up with 40 different metrics and what's interesting to me is when you're a small company you say you have to be focused. When you're a large company, the biggest mistake I think large companies can make is, "Hey, because we're a big company, have more money, have more resources, we can do more things." You actually find in large company settings you have to focus even more, because think about the inertia (you must overcome) to get a whole organization of people to go in a certain direction. My advice is to keep it very simple. You can adjust metrics year to year, but from a business perspective I would keep it simple.[16]

I agree with Liang's advice, and whether your company is small or large, my bias is towards fewer performance measures, under 20 whenever possible. There is a lot of noise in modern organizations, and a good Balanced Scorecard should rise above the ruckus, providing you with a view of the real drivers of success in your organization. Limiting your measures to the vital few means making the commitment to monitor strategic measures and place less relevance on operational indicators. Concentrating on the strategic doesn't mean the operational necessarily vanish. My car monitors speed, fuel, temperature and a few other critical variables, but that doesn't mean I'm not concerned about what happens under the hood. I just don't need to be monitoring those myriad activities unless something occurs out of a normal range. Your organization is the same, as leaders you have an obligation to focus on the strategic, the core drivers of performance. Examining performance measures related to activities three levels below you is an inefficient use of your time and the organization's resources. If there are metrics you feel are important, but not strategic, then consider the use of an operational dashboard to house and monitor them. But for the most part, concentrate on maximizing your time, abilities, and effectiveness by choosing to monitor only those few variables that truly correspond to success.

One final piece of advice on the number of measures: There is an opportunity cost associated with a large crop of metrics and that cost holds your most precious resources: time and attention. Modern companies are virtual whirlwinds, simultaneously twirling vortexes of chaos, exhilaration, and never-ending challenges. As noted above, whether a small firm or multinational corporation, what's most vital in combating the whirlwind, and staying one step ahead of global competitors, is focus. The more metrics you employ, the greater the diffusion of your attention and focus on what truly matters to your company. Although it's difficult, isolating the true measures of success and tracking them with rigor and discipline is the key to effective strategy execution.

 TARGETS: THE GOALS THAT BRING MEASURES TO LIFE

What Are Performance Targets? Why Are They Important to the Balanced Scorecard?

Poet, painter, and novelist Kahlil Gibran once noted, "To understand the heart and mind of a person, look not at what he has already achieved, but at what he aspires to do."[17] We all have aspirations, which range from the grand—writing the great American novel—to the practical—painting the back fence before the first snowfall. Targets bring our aspirations to life and give us something to shoot for in the quest for improvement. The young writer may set a target of writing 10 pages per day, while the suburban homeowner may vow to paint the fence over two weekends in November. Both actions will improve overall results in their specific situations.

In the context of a Balanced Scorecard, targets represent the desired result of a performance measure. By comparing actual performance results against a predetermined target, we receive information that is imbued with value and meaning. For example, our company's on-time delivery rate of 65 percent takes on a lot more relevance when we learn the industry standard is 80 percent and our chief competitors all have percentages hovering in the high 70s. Armed with this knowledge we see that our rate requires improvement if we are to compete effectively in the marketplace. We might now set an aggressive target of 85 percent on-time delivery for the coming year. As performance data accumulates, it is now endowed with meaning in the context of the target, and we can evaluate trends and make decisions regarding how to guarantee we meet or exceed that target.

Targets are powerful communication tools, informing the entire organization of the expected level of performance required to achieve success. As a result, they typically drive a focus on continuous improvement, as the organization strives to constantly better its performance. Finally, assigning ownership for results to an individual responsible for achieving the target fosters accountability, which is a prized commodity in most organizations.

Types of Performance Targets

If we define a target as the "desired result of a performance measure," there is the strong connotation of an orientation toward the future. Targets represent our goals for some period that has yet to elapse. They may be established by month, quarter, half year, year, or multiple years. In this section we'll examine three types of targets, each corresponding to different time frames (see Exhibit 6.8).

Long-Term Targets: Big Hairy Audacious Goals (BHAGs)

In Chapter 3, I shared with you a portion of President John F. Kennedy's inspirational May 25th, 1961, proclamation: "I believe that this nation should commit itself to achieving the goal, before this decade is out, of landing a man on the moon and returning him safely to the earth." That lunar ambition represents the very essence of a Big Hairy Audacious Goal, or BHAG. The unlikely acronym, so often at the lips of senior executives with galactic-sized ambitions, was coined by *Built to Last* authors Jim Collins and Jerry Porras to represent the

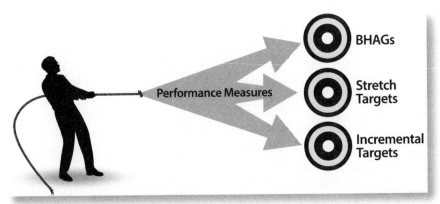

EXHIBIT 6.8   Three Types of Targets

seemingly outrageous goals established by organizations, serving as powerful mechanisms to stimulate progress.

BHAGs are intended to tear an organization loose from business-as-usual thinking and prompt the innovation and creativity necessary to climb to new and unprecedented positions. They are typically 10 to 30 years in duration, the time frame synchronizing with the level of difficulty associated with reaching the finish line. Private sector firms have embraced the idea of BHAGs for some time, but the idea is catching on in the public and nonprofit arenas as well. For example, in Canada, the federal government announced a wide range of long-term targets aligned with closing the gap in the quality of life between First Nations Canadians and the rest of the population. Among the goals to which they've held themselves accountable are: reducing infant mortality, youth suicide, childhood obesity, and diabetes by 50 percent in 10 years and closing the educational gap so that by 2016 the high school graduation rate for aboriginal students will equal that of other Canadian students.[18]

Midrange Targets: Stretch Goals

Targets established in the three- to five- (or occasionally longer) year period are often assigned the term *stretch*. Their purpose is to keep the organization focused on a midrange goal that is in alignment with their vision and mission, the achievement of which will bring them closer to their BHAG. As with BHAGs, the achievement of stretch targets will often require the organization to abandon the status quo and alter the way they do business in order to meet the dramatic challenge represented by the lofty target.

By their very nature, BHAGs may appear wild in their proportions, with the stratospheric goal meant to stimulate entirely new ways of thinking and operating. Stretch targets must be a bit more down to earth in order to captivate and motivate; the caveat with any stretch target is that it contain some semblance of realism. A target that simply reflects the wishful thinking of an overzealous management team is certain to be greeted with tremendous skepticism by employees, and could actually prove debilitating to performance. Before establishing a stretch target you hope will transform your organization consider the following.

- Ensure reaching the target is truly critical to your success.
- Determine whether you possess the skills within your organization to help you reach the target.
- Gauge the organization's willingness to accept a challenge of this magnitude. A workforce lacking the necessary motivation to beat the target will probably result in a Sisyphean endeavor.

One of the best pieces of self-help advice I have ever received was this: "Whatever you focus on expands." Think about that for a moment, recalling times in your life when you had a single-minded determination to achieve something, or better yet, start living it today, focusing intently, and sending positive energy towards what you want in your life. The principle is similar within organizations. The goals we set are reflective of our energy and our focus. Business guru Michael Hammer suggests, "Your reach should exceed your grasp. If you set modest goals, you'll never do anything but perform modestly."[19] As we all know, in this age of hypercompetition, modest performance is a sure ticket to being steamrolled by our competitors.

I noted above that stretch targets must be somewhat realistic or else you risk alienating your team. That said—don't shy away from a worthy stretch because you're afraid it's not achievable. By their very essence, stretch targets are about moving—at first uncomfortably—to a new and unfamiliar position. As I write this, I've recently begun practicing yoga. My initial attempts at many of the poses were painful, as my body contorted to positions it was unaccustomed to (probably painful for others to watch, too), but I've remained committed, and with each session I can feel my body moving with less hesitation into hitherto unthinkable positions. Each time I practice I remind myself that if I can't twist myself into a position, or hold it for more than a few seconds, I'm not failing, I'm simply generating results from which to learn. It's the same with businesses—should you fall a bit short on a stretch target you're not failing, you're simply generating results you can learn from to improve your performance in the future.

Short Term: Incremental Targets

Most organizations will develop annual performance targets for their performance measures. In keeping with the theme of cause and effect discussed throughout the book, the achievement of annual performance targets will help lead to the accomplishment of long-term stretch targets, and ultimately, BHAGs. Whenever possible, it is desirable to decompose annual targets into increments corresponding to your Scorecard reporting frequency. For example, you may have a customer satisfaction target of 90 percent for the year. If you survey your customers more than once a year, break the target down. Perhaps you'll be shooting for 75 percent in the first quarter, 80 in the second, 85 in the third, and finally 90 at year-end. Rather than waiting until the end of the year to take action on the results, you can now make customer satisfaction a regular and routine part of your decision-making process.

DO YOU NEED ALL THREE TYPES OF TARGETS?

Based on the discussion in the previous sections, we see that the three types of targets can link together and positively shape an organization's future. BHAGs set the desired long-term future, maybe decades in the making; stretch targets provide the midrange systems designed to propel us towards the BHAGs; and finally, incremental targets supply feedback on the attainment of stretch goals. Sounds great, but in practice just devising incremental targets can pose a significant test to organizations not fortunate enough to be conversant in the art, who are starting with a slate composed of several entirely new measures for which no performance baseline even exists.

Creating BHAGs for every measure on your Balanced Scorecard, and expecting to achieve them, is about as realistic as me expecting this book to be featured in Oprah's book club. It would be virtually impossible to manage BHAGs for every metric, and almost certainly lead to a diffusion of priorities throughout the organization. One galvanizing BHAG is probably more than enough for most organizations. Stretch targets, on the other hand, may be applied in liberal quantities to your Scorecard effort. They require loosening the grip on the status quo, and their achievement will yield a crop of substantial results. And of course, incremental targets should accompany every Scorecard measure.

Setting targets is a delicate balancing act: become overly optimistic and you'll find a workforce bathed in skepticism and confusion. Plunge to the opposite of the target pool, however, by settling for LHMGs—Little Hairless Mediocre Goals[20]—and you miss a golden opportunity to motivate and align your team around a shared goal.

Setting Performance Targets

Over the past three decades, Edwin Locke and Gary Latham have produced compelling research demonstrating that difficult, specific goals and targets lead to improved task performance. Why have performance targets proven to be so effective? Maybe there is more at work here than just the motivational power of a goal. Actually, social scientists have long argued that we humans will always align with our commitments.[21] As a result, when we make public commitments, such as those in a written performance target, we tend to stick with them. Recall the classic 1955 experiment we reviewed in Chapter 2 that supports this assertion, where students were asked to estimate the lengths of lines on a screen. Some students were asked to write down their estimates, sign them, and turn them over to the researcher. Others were asked to write them down on an erasable slate, then erase the slate immediately. A third group was instructed to keep their decisions to themselves. The researchers then presented all three groups with evidence that their initial choices may have been wrong. By a wide margin, the group most reluctant to shift from their original choices were those who had signed and handed them to the researcher. Those who made a public commitment were the most hesitant to move away from that pledge. This underscores the importance of having written performance targets as part of your Balanced Scorecard. Their achievement may just be human nature.

Before selecting targets, however, it's important to establish baselines of performance for your performance measures. Knowing where you currently stand will help determine the rate and trajectory of improvement required. Only then can you create relevant and meaningful targets.

Even with current baselines of performance documented, many organizations encounter serious difficulty developing targets for their measures. In certain cases, managers appear hesitant to commit themselves to an actual target they will be judged against and bound to honor. With coaching, positive feedback, and the passage of time, this reluctance may be overcome. Often, however, it is not managerial apathy that precludes the development of targets, but simply a case of the measure being brand new with no baseline to work from, or a lack of potential sources of target information, that hold people back. Here are a number of places you may find information that will help you create targets for your particular measures.

- **Benchmarking:** Examining best-in-class organizations and attempting to emulate their results is effective—to a point. It's very important to try and achieve the level of success as star performers in your industry and, particularly with financial measures, you must ensure your targets will elevate you above your competition. However, benchmarking must be conducted with caution. First of all, most organizations will simply focus on one element of operations when conducting a benchmarking study— perhaps innovation processes, month-end closing processes, or marketing. The problem with this approach is that the best-in-class organization you're studying probably has a number of different activities it combines to drive a unique mix of value for customers (the essence of strategy as espoused by Michael Porter). Copying just one element of this formula may lead to isolated improvements in that area but fail to bring about breakthrough performance. Additionally, the organizations you review may have different customers, processes, and resources. Perhaps they allocate significant human and financial resources to the process under the microscope, and that's what accounts for their success.

■ **Trends and baselines:** If past data for the measure exists, you can use it to create a trend line or baseline projection into the future. Examining past data and trends will allow you to choose a target representing a meaningful challenge, while staying within the ballpark of reality.

■ **Industry averages:** There are a number of credible agencies that monitor the performance of virtually all industries. J.D. Power and Associates comes to mind when thinking of the automobile industry. Your organization is most likely affiliated with some industry or trade association that may have valuable information regarding performance across your industry on selected metrics. Be careful to ensure any data you use is consistent with your methodology for measurement. Many organizations follow vastly different methods of calculating even the most common performance measures.

■ **Employees:** Never forget that those closest to the action are frequently in the best position to provide insight on what represents a meaningful target. Involving employees in the process not only makes great sense based on the knowledge they possess, but not approaching them could lead to alienation and lack of buy-in, which in turn may translate to decreased attention on the chosen target.

■ **Feedback from customers and other stakeholders:** Expectations from these important groups may yield information you can use when establishing performance targets. Customers may have explicit or implicit standards to which they expect all vendors to adhere. Involving stakeholders in the target-setting process also demonstrates your commitment to working with everyone involved with your enterprise to produce mutually beneficial results. Don't miss this opportunity to engage your customers in a dialog about what constitutes great performance in their minds.

■ **Executive interviews:** When you interviewed executives earlier in the process (Step four in the development phase) they may have shared required levels of performance to achieve success. Similarly, your executive workshops, conducted throughout the process of developing a Scorecard, will likely yield potential Scorecard targets.

■ **Internal/external assessments:** If you've recently gone through any kind of strategic planning process, you've undoubtedly conducted an assessment of strengths, weaknesses, opportunities, and threats (SWOT). Information from these assessments will help you determine appropriate targets to maximize opportunities and minimize threats.

I hope one of the themes to emerge from this book is the power of story. The virtues of storytelling have been extolled at several junctures already—sharing your strategic story (through cause and effect modeling) and creating objectives on your strategy map that must weave together, are just a couple of instances. Although targets will almost certainly be quantitative in nature, the opportunity still exists to enlist the strength and inspiration of a well-told story when contemplating targets.[22] As you assemble targets for each measure try imagining a narrative to accompany the successful accomplishment of that target. Rather than greeting your team with this stale edict: "Our target for customer engagement in the fourth quarter is 87 percent," regale them with a tale of what your world will look like when you've achieved the target. What it will feel like, what it will look like, how customers will act, and how they'll share their experiences with the world. When both creating and sharing your targets, try embracing the vivid qualities of sight, sound, movement, and color to break from the cold world of numbers to the warmth and comfort of story.

STRATEGIC INITIATIVES: PROJECTS THAT DRIVE BREAKTHROUGH PERFORMANCE

We've covered a lot of ground in these past two chapters. We examined the steps necessary to develop a strategy map of performance objectives, translated those objectives into performance measures, and, most recently, considered the role of performance targets. A final step remains in the development of our Balanced Scorecard, one that will translate our targets into reality and drive success on our measures and objectives: initiative setting.

Initiatives are the specific, finite-duration projects you will engage in to help ensure you meet or exceed your performance targets. An initiative could be anything from building a customer service portal on your website to launching a career-development program for employees to redesigning your financial management system. While the nature of initiatives will vary tremendously, the common thread that should run through all is a linkage to strategic objectives, measures, and targets.

Most organizations do not suffer from a lack of initiatives. In fact, many will be bursting at the seams with initiatives, since they frequently begin their performance management efforts with initiative development. The logic works this way: We'll engage in this initiative in order to better meet our customers' needs, and then we'll develop goals and objectives to track our progress. I believe this approach is fundamentally flawed. The stake in the ground provided by mission and the aspiration of vision should always begin your performance management efforts. Strategy follows, outlining the broad priorities necessary for success. Next up are performance objectives and measures that tell us what we must excel at in order to execute the strategy, and how we'll gauge our progress. Targets supply a star to shoot for, and finally, initiatives are put in place that will help us achieve our targets. Following this logic path will lead to the design and implementation of a manageable number of initiatives directly aligned with your strategy, which is vital since, by some estimates, upwards of 50 percent of initiatives are not aligned with organizational strategy.[23]

Ensuring Strategic Initiatives Support Your Strategy

A careful analysis of your current crop of initiatives may reveal the seemingly contradictory finding that you simultaneously have too many and too few. You may have any number of initiatives vying for scarce human and financial resources that have literally no effect on the ability to implement your strategy. Concurrently, your Balanced Scorecard may identify entirely new performance objectives and measures that are not represented by a single initiative.

Therefore, a useful exercise to undertake upon completing your Scorecard is the mapping of current organizational initiatives to your strategy map objectives. Any initiative that cannot demonstrate a clear linkage to an objective should be considered a strong candidate for removal. This is often easier said than done, as many projects are backed by senior executives who have stationed the very significant power of their office behind the project and may remain committed to it despite evidence of its ineffectiveness or irrelevance. In this case, you'll rely on the data to tell the story. If certain projects are not moving the performance needle on associated key metrics of success (and experience suggests about 20 to 30 percent have this trait), they must be abandoned so that resources may be reallocated. While some may consider quitting anathema to any aspect of corporate life, in reality it should be seen for what it is: liberating. Think back once again to the quote I shared from Saint-Exupéry in Chapter 5: "Perfection is not when there is no more to add, but no more to take away." This sage advice should be kept top of mind throughout the Balanced Scorecard process.

If you're searching for a quick economic payoff to justify your investment in the Balanced Scorecard, this step could be exactly what you're looking for. Consider the potential drain of organizational resources an ineffective initiative represents. Naturally, financial resources have been committed that would be better served elsewhere. Additionally, staff time and attention have been diverted from truly strategic endeavors in the pursuit of activities that produce no value. Using the crystal clear focus provided by the strategy map, you can put your current initiatives under the microscope and separate those that contribute real value from those that merely drain all-too-scarce human and financial resources.

The first step in mapping initiatives to objectives involves seeking out each and every initiative currently being sponsored within the organization. Since all initiatives entail the allocation of financial resources, your finance team may be able to provide you with a list of current projects. Next, you should create a grid similar to that displayed in Exhibit 6.9. Strategy map objectives are listed on the left side of the document, while initiatives will be outlined across the top. Your considerable challenge is to critically examine each initiative in light of all strategy-map objectives. To conduct such an analysis in a

Perspective	Objectives	Benchmarking	Maintenance Overhaul	Frequent Purchase Program	ISO 9002	IT Tools & Training	360 Feedback	Global Communication	Partner Program	Just in Time Manufacturing	Decision Training	Facility Modernization	New Pricing Programs
Financial	Grow Revenue												●
	Increase Asset Utilization	●									●		
Customer	Increase Partnering								●				
	Build Loyalty					●							
	Grow Market Share					●							
Internal Process	Develop Customer Information						●						
	Reduce Downtime		●	●									
Learning and Growth	Develop Core Competencies									●			
	Increase Empowerment							●				●	

EXHIBIT 6.9 Mapping Initiatives to Objectives

meaningful fashion requires that you perform a good deal of due diligence on each of the initiatives. Read background on the project, speak with the sponsor, and review financial information to ensure you have a solid understanding of the project's true essence. For those initiatives that support strategy map objectives, put a check in the corresponding box of the grid. Any initiatives that do not meet your criteria of being strategic in nature should be carefully reviewed, possibly reduced in scope, or even discontinued.

Eliminating initiatives that don't contribute to your strategy frees up valuable resources within the organization. These resources, both human and financial, can now be directed towards drafting new initiatives that do in fact propel you toward your goals.

Creating New Strategic Initiatives

Eliminating nonstrategic initiatives that produce little value is a rewarding exercise, and while the goal in this process is compiling a relatively small portfolio of strategic initiatives (usually under 10), an analysis of the mapping exercise above may reveal that entirely new strategic initiatives are necessary to drive the execution of vital objectives, measures, and targets. A common question is: Do we need an initiative for each objective on the map? The answer is a resounding no. Again, strategic initiatives entail the allocation of money, staff time, and perhaps most importantly, management attention. Therefore, smaller is preferable. New strategic initiatives are typically only required for vital objectives with associated measures that show a large gap between current and targeted performance. For example, let's say you're investing in a customer intimacy strategy in order to create long-term relationships with your customers. "Share of customer spend" is your chosen metric and the baseline of current performance is 20 percent. If your target level of performance is 40 percent the delta is substantial and a strategic initiative may be required to help bridge the considerable gap.

Should you require new initiatives to fill the void created by new performance objectives or measures, develop them on a solid foundation. Ensure there are:

- An executive willing to sponsor the initiative
- Clearly defined plans and project scope
- A legitimate budget
- The commitment of resources necessary to successfully complete the initiative

Perhaps most important is simply tracking your strategic initiatives to ensure they're delivering the strategic benefits promised by zealous sponsors. This seems like common sense, but a survey by global consulting firm McKinsey discovered that barely over 50 percent of organizations actively track their strategic initiatives.[24]

To help you crisply document any new initiatives you are considering, Exhibit 6.10 provides a template outlining the attributes and fields you should consider.

You'll be amazed at how imaginative your team can be when it comes to creating new initiatives. Take the case of the Boston Lyric Opera (BLO), whose story is well entrenched in Balanced Scorecard lore.[25] When creating their Balanced Scorecard, employees at this performing arts company rose to the

Strategic Initiative Overview Template

Date: _____

This template is intended as an enterprise-wide tool to enable the Executive to quantify, assess, and prioritize proposed strategic initiatives based on their impact on strategic objectives.
Please limit input and commentary to the space provided and use minimum 10 pt. font.

Line of Business/Business Unit: _____

Strategic Initiative Name: _____

Executive Owner: _____   Initiative Leader: _____

Anticipated Start Date: _____   Anticipated End Date: _____

Initiative Description/Scope:

Strategic impact

Describe Strategic Impact: Strategic Impact (H, M, L)

Financial:		
Customer:		
Internal Process:		
Employee Learning & Growth		

Resource Allocation Requirements

Capital & Operating Budget ($000)	2002	2003	2004	2005
Capital Spending Profile	$0	$0	$0	$0
Operating Budget Spending	$0	$0	$0	$0

Economic Fit	
NPV: Net Present Value	
IRR%: Internal Rate of Return	
Payback Period	

Investment Summary ($000)	2002	2003	2004	2005
Revenue (incremental)	$0	$0	$0	$0
Revenue (retained)	$0	$0	$0	$0
Expense Savings	$0	$0	$0	$0

Net FTE Impact (+/- FTEs)			

EXHIBIT 6.10   Strategic Initiative Template

Strategic Initiative Overview Template - *Continued*

Key Dependencies

Key Risks to Successful Implementation and Mitigation Activities

Describe Internal Impact (employees/processes) of this Initiative

Describe External Impact (customers/suppliers/shareholders) of this Initiative

Milestones, Deliverables, and Corresponding Due Dates

Key Milestone	Deliverables	Due Date

Key Initiative Resources *(Top 5 Involvement)*

Name	Time Allocation (%)	Explanation of Time Allocation

EXHIBIT 6.10   *(Continued)*

call and suggested a number of inventive approaches to achieving targets. The most successful initiative to emerge was the production of "Carmen on the Common." To meet the strategy-map objective of increasing community support, the BLO staged two free outdoor performances of the classic opera before appreciative audiences of more than 130,000 people. What better way to increase community support than to bring opera to the public? For many who took advantage of this unique opportunity, it was their first exposure to opera but most assuredly will not be their last. Only a creative approach resulting from the discussion of initiatives could lead to such a breakthrough.

Prioritizing among Strategic Initiatives

Now that you've created a number of potential strategic initiatives, you must rank them in order to make resource-allocation decisions (assuming you don't have unlimited financial and human resources) and decide upon the final portfolio. The key is basing your decision on a common set of criteria that will determine the most appropriate initiatives given your unique priorities.

Obviously, the initiative's impact on driving strategy is the chief concern, but you can't ignore investment fundamentals like cost, resources, and projected time to complete. Essentially, every initiative should have a valid business case to support its claim as being necessary to achieve your strategy. Once you've drafted business cases for each of the initiatives, you can use a template similar to that shown in Exhibit 6.11 to assist in making the prioritization decision. Each criterion you choose is assigned a weight, depending on its importance within your organization. The assignments are subjective, but strategic importance should always carry the greatest weight in the decision. Next, each initiative must be scored on the specific criteria listed in the chart. You may use ratings of between 0 and 10 or, if you prefer a wider scale, use 0 to 100. I use 0 to 10 in my example. Before assigning points to each, you must develop an appropriate scale. For example, a net present value of greater than $2 million may translate to 10 points. NPV of $1.75 million yields 9 points, and so on. Involving more than one executive on a full-time basis may translate to a score of 2 points in the resource requirements section, since their involvement could impose a heavy burden on the organization. Develop scales that work for you; however, to ensure mathematical integrity, a high value should always represent preferred performance. Those initiatives generating the highest scores should be approved and provided budgets to ensure their timely completion. Notice in our example, initiative 1 generates a higher total score than initiative 2, despite the latter's impressive scores on five of the six criteria. The reason for the discrepancy is the critical variable of strategic linkage. Initiative 1 demonstrates a strong linkage to strategy, while 2 is missing that connection.

Exhibit 6.12 provides an alternate approach to rationalizing strategic initiatives, using a 1–3–5 scale for ranking purposes.

Criteria	Weight	Description	Initiatives							
			1		**2**		**3**		**4**	
			POINTS	SCORE	POINTS	SCORE	POINTS	SCORE	POINTS	SCORE
Linkage to Strategy	45%	Ability of the initiative to positively impact a strategic objective.	7	3.2	1	.45				
Net Present Value	15%	Present value of initiative benefits discounted five years.	5	.75	10	1.5				
Total Cost	10%	Total dollar cost including labor and materials.	5	.50	10	1.0				
Resource Requirements *(key personnel)*	10%	Key personnel needed for the initiative including time requirements.	8	.80	10	1.0				
Time to Complete	10%	Total anticipated time to complete the initiative.	8	.80	10	1.0				
Dependencies	10%	Impact of other initiatives on the successful outcomes anticipated with this initiative.	3	.30	10	1.0				
				6.35		5.95				

EXHIBIT 6.11 Prioritizing Balanced Scorecard Initiatives

The Rewards Are Worth the Effort!

Developing and prioritizing initiatives to support your Balanced Scorecard can be one of the most difficult aspects of the implementation. Making these decisions can affect long-standing relationships between different functional areas and result in negative perceptions of organizational power wielding. However, this important task can also provide you with the first of many opportunities to show the economic value of the Balanced Scorecard by distinguishing those initiatives that legitimately lead to the fulfillment of your strategy from those that merely soak up precious resources. Aligning initiatives with strategy also greatly facilitates the use of the Balanced Scorecard as a strategic-management system by providing a method of linking the budgeting process with strategy and strategic planning. Finally, clarifying and prioritizing is another opportunity to utilize the Scorecard as a means to increase accountability. Every

		1–3–5 Scale		
Criteria	**Weight**	**Result of 1**	**Result of 3**	**Result of 5**
Linkage to Strategy	45%	The initiative has a negative or no impact on the objective.	The initiative has a slightly positive impact on the objective.	The initiative has a definite positive impact on the objective.
Total Cost	20%	The initiative has significant cost implications.	The initiative has a moderate cost component.	The initiative has little or no cost implications.
Resources *(key personnel)*	15%	The initiative will require significant resources.	The initiative will require moderate resources.	The initiative will require very few resources.
Time to Complete	10%	The initiative will require a lot of time to complete (>1 year).	The initiative will require some time to complete (<1 year).	The initiative will require very little time to complete (<6 months).
Mandated	10%	This initiative is not mandated.		This initiative is mandated.

EXHIBIT 6.12 Prioritizing Balanced Scorecard Initiatives Using a 1–3–5 Scale

initiative will have an executive sponsor who feels passionate about the project and strongly believes it will yield tremendous results. Using the Balanced Scorecard to validate your investments allows you to confirm or deny those beliefs on the part of your senior team.

Many organizations have harnessed the value of aligning initiatives with strategy by using the Balanced Scorecard to great advantage. Scorecard architects Kaplan and Norton cite the case of Wells Fargo's online banking division. Through consolidation and delegating operational initiatives, they were able to reduce the number of initiatives actively supervised by executives from more than 600 down to about a dozen.[26] Beyond the economic value generated from such a dramatic abatement, think about the concurrent leap in focus, and the benefits it brings. Executive attention, once pulled in hundreds of scattered directions, can now converge upon that select portfolio of strategic initiatives that deliver true strategic value.

NOTES

1. Steven D. Levitt and Stephen J. Dubner, *Freakonomics* (New York: William Morrow, 2005), 14.
2. Bill Gates, "My Plan to Fix The World's Biggest Problems," *Wall Street Journal*, January 26, 2013.
3. Quoted in Ed Barrows and Andy Neely, *Managing Performance in Turbulent Times; Analytics and Insight* (Hoboken, NJ: John Wiley & Sons, 2012), Kindle edition, location 1999–2001.
4. Study information accessed June 15, 2010, at www.futurity.org.
5. The first three biases are based on Michael J. Mauboussin, "The True Measures of Success," *Harvard Business Review* (October 2012): 4656.
6. Andrew Likierman, "The Five Traps of Performance Measurement," *Harvard Business Review* (October 2009): 96–101.
7. David Rock, *Your Brain at Work* (New York: Harper Collins, 2009), Kindle edition, location 3415.
8. Ed Catmull, "How Pixar Fosters Collective Creativity," *Harvard Business Review* (September 2008): 64–72.
9. Dean R. Spitzer, *Transforming Performance Measurement* (New York: AMACOM, 2007), 15.
10. Rudolph W. Giuliani, *Leadership* (New York: Hyperion, 2002), 87.
11. Emily Steele, "New Tools for Picking Hits," *Wall Street Journal*, May 23, 2011.
12. Chris McChesney, Sean Covey, and Jim Huling, *The Four Disciplines of Execution: Achieving Your Wildly Important Goals* (New York: Free Press, 2012) Kindle edition, location 1348.
13. Jim Collins, *Good to Great and the Social Sectors: A Monograph to Accompany Good to Great* (New York: HarperCollins, 2005), 7–8.
14. Chip Heath and Dan Heath, "The Telltale Brown M&M," *Fast Company*, March 2010, 36–37.
15. Joan Magretta, *Understanding Michael Porter* (Boston: Harvard Business Review Press, 2012).
16. Gregory Jones, "Sam Liang Never Stops Improving Medrad, Inc." Accessed on August 2, 2011, at www.sbnonline.com/2011/08/sam-liang-never-stops-improving-medrad-inc/?full=1.
17. Gibran, Kahlil. *Sand and Foam*. Knopf, 2008.
18. Beth Duff-Brown, "Canada Pledges $4.3B for native people," Associated Press release reported in *North County Times*, November 26, 2005.
19. Ellen M. Heffes, "Measure Like You Mean It: Q & A with Michael Hammer," www2.financialexecutives.org/magazine/articles/3-4-2002_BP_measure.cfm.
20. Peters, *Re-Imagine* (London: Dorling Kindersley Limited, 2003), 199.

21. Robert B. Cialdini, "Harnessing the Science of Persuasion," *Harvard Business Review* (October 2001): 72–79

22. This section was inspired by: Stacey Barr, "Setting Sensible Targets for your KPIs." Accessed at http://kpilibrary.com/topics/setting-sensible-targets-for-your-kpis.

23. Jeroen De Flander, *Strategy Execution Heroes* (Brussels, Belgium: The Performance Factory, 2010), 146.

24. Ed Barrows and Andy Neely, *Managing Performance in Turbulent Times; Analytics and Insight* (Hoboken, NJ: John Wiley & Sons, Inc., 2012). Kindle edition, location 1698–1702.

25. Robert S. Kaplan, "The Balanced Scorecard and Nonprofit Organizations," *Balanced Scorecard Report* (November–December, 2002): 1–4.

26. Robert S. Kaplan and David P. Norton, *The Execution Premium* (Boston: Harvard Business School Press, 2008), 107.

CHAPTER SEVEN

Hold Strategy Execution Meetings So Good, People Actually Want to Attend

 FROM THEORY TO PRACTICE

A client once shared an acronym I had never heard before: SPOTS. Any guesses? It stands for strategic plan on the shelf. The term is indicative of organizations that go to great and painstaking lengths to develop a strategy, only to have it sit on a shelf or be used to prop up a projector during presentations—fairly ignominious results for the much vaunted strategic plan! The last thing you want is a BSCOTS. Okay, it's not as catchy as SPOTS, but you get the picture.

Developing performance objectives on a strategy map and translating them into measures, targets, and supporting initiatives on a Scorecard, is a challenging task. However, people also find it exhilarating and thought provoking. With the frenetic pace of most organizations, there is precious little time reserved for contemplating high-level strategy and how it will be executed. Creating a Balanced Scorecard system provides that opportunity, that mental fresh air, to reveal a new perspective on your organization. Beneficial and thought provoking yes, but it's still largely an academic exercise. Not until you begin reporting your Balanced Scorecard results does the tool transform from a cognitive simulation into a real business solution.

Every organization will launch the Balanced Scorecard for individual reasons; however, improving results and enhancing accountability are frequently cited. These Scorecard traits are not realized until you begin reporting your results. Only then will you see the true power of the Balanced Scorecard, the ability to drive alignment from top to bottom, to improve communication, and to learn about your business through strategic conversations arising from an analysis of reported results. The nexus of strategic learning is the strategy execution review meeting, and in this chapter I'll share tools and techniques to ensure your management meetings fully engage participants and spark conversations that drive true strategic learning. But to begin, let's take a look at how meetings actually play out in most organizations.

Not So Breaking News: Meetings Are Flawed!

I know the following dramatization bears absolutely no resemblance to what takes place at your company, so just for a chuckle at how the other half ambles aimlessly through their days, please follow along as I outline the first 20 minutes or so of a typical meeting at many organizations. The meeting is scheduled to start promptly at 9:00 a.m.

8:55: Room is completely empty, no lights on.

9:00: The first of five invited participants arrives (feeling early), turns on the lights and sits as far from the head of the table as possible.

9:05: Two more attendees shuffle in—looking confused, wondering if there actually is a meeting today—and when assured there is, take their seats.

9:07: Amid chatter about last night's baseball game, calls are placed to the extensions of the tardy, and the technically savvy of the group begin fiddling with the ancient laptop and Prius-sized overhead projector in the room.

9:08: One of the missing—the meeting organizer as it turns out—arrives with stacks of papers in both arms, apologizing profusely, blaming his belated appearance on a call he had to take. No one really notices, however, because all eyes are riveted on the nonfunctioning projector.

9:10: A volunteer is dispatched to round up Phil, the last missing person. Chatter subsides, and the first pangs of tension: "Why am I here, I have so much work to do today?" begin to announce themselves to those present. The projector is suspiciously quiet. One person contorts their body painfully to ensure the projector cord is reaching the receptacle under the table. It is.

9:12: General murmuring begins anew, accompanied by griping about the lack of food: "If you have a 9:00 meeting you could at least have coffee." No sign of the intrepid searcher or Phil.

9:15: Volunteer returns, apparently Phil got called into another meeting (more important being the subtext) at the last minute and won't be coming. On the plus side, the projector and laptop have been reunited successfully, with the appearance of the Windows logo on the screen signaling once again man's prominence over machine.

9:16: Heads swivel until the person who arranged the meeting calls it to order.

9:17: The first of 44 PowerPoint slides is beamed across the room, but no agenda for the meeting is shared.

9:19: Yawns are concealed, pens are toyed with, and legs shuffle as the group settles in.

Cynical? You're right, I'm way off base. Actually, the complaints about the food start a lot sooner. Sadly, this tale is a faithful representation of many such gatherings I've had the displeasure to attend over the years. Of course I'm not alone in criticizing what passes for meetings in most organizations; sessions during which, by one tally, 80 percent of the time is spent on items creating less than 20 percent of the organization's value.[1] *USA Today* once conducted a poll and found that over 25 percent of those asked would prefer to visit the dentist, read the phone book, or mop their kitchen floor than attend a meeting at their company.[2] See Exhibit 7.1.

There is actually an historical precedent for nonproductive meetings that stretches all the way back to the early days of the United States senate. Listen to this impressive account of the day's activities in the hallowed chamber, recorded by Senator William Maclay on April 3, 1790:

> Went to the Hall. The minutes were read. A message was received from the President of the United States. A report was handed to the Chair. We looked and laughed at each other for half an hour, and adjourned.[3]

Maybe Nietzsche had it right when he said: "Madness is the exception in individuals but the rule in groups."[4]

Why do we suffer from such ineffective meetings, wasted opportunities of near-epic proportions? Author and management consultant Patrick Lencioni has suggested that most meetings suffer from two near-fatal flaws: they lack conflict and contextual structure.[5] Let's begin with the paucity of conflict. Unless your organization is a member of the tiniest of minorities, you can

EXHIBIT 7.1 What People Would Rather Do Than Go to a Company Meeting

probably relate to Lencioni's call to arms. In most management gatherings, the rules of etiquette dictate that only the politest of questions be asked, if any are raised at all, to which vanilla answers of shallow substance are provided in response, and the group moves along, smiling, realizing they are one step closer to the door. The tough questions, the ones that could lead to actual insights, are stifled, the result of participants fearing the wrath of their colleagues should they violate the norms guiding such civilized sessions. Well, it's time to remove the cheap gold plating of silence from meetings, and glaze the process with meaningful queries, bold statements, and heated debate. Lencioni, in his provocatively titled book, *Death by Meeting*, suggests that meeting participants should be jolted within the first 10 minutes of a session with topics edgy enough to uncover relevant ideological conflict. Small-group research has consistently demonstrated that diversity of opinion is the single best guarantee the group will garner any benefits from a face-to-face discussion. The open confrontation with a dissenting view forces those holding the majority opinion to interrogate their own views more closely, and this can often lead to revelations that spring the entire group forward.[6]

Lou Gerstner, the architect of IBM's turnaround throughout the 1990s, understood the principle of conflict and applied it liberally during his days at the helm of the corporate giant. He tells the story of an early strategy meeting, convened just after he assumed the role of CEO in 1993. At the appointed time his managers began parading in to the room, each followed by legions of binder-touting assistants, and took their assigned space at the large conference room table. When the meeting got into full swing, or perhaps full crawl, Gerstner was bitterly disappointed by the rote slides being presented and the lack of meaningful discussion and debate he knew was necessary to tease out real learning. In what he called the "click heard round the world," he finally jumped from his chair and pulled the plug on the overhead projector, insisting on real dialog and discussion from his team. It set a powerful precedent and laid out his expectations in no uncertain terms.[7]

As for Lencioni's second proposed flaw of meetings—the lack of contextual structure—that's just a nice way of saying most management get-togethers serve up a steaming pot of meeting stew. Lacking a formal agenda to guide the proceedings, the roll call of discussion topics often include such disparate points as operational reviews, the annual picnic, and hotly contested parking spaces. The organization's strategy suffers as this pot of urgent, yet hardly important, topics boils over; strategy receives a paltry three hours of coverage each month, according to researchers.[8]

Executing a strategy requires a near ceaseless assault on the data coming into the organization: what is it telling us, what does it mean for our people, our processes? Are course corrections required? How should we conduct this strategy audit? The answer: Use the Balanced Scorecard to drive the agenda of your management meetings. Doing so sends a resonant signal that strategy will now be the core topic discussed at these sessions, with all background noise aggressively tuned out. In the sections below I outline a new management meeting, one with strategy squarely in the crosshairs, which uses the Balanced Scorecard to generate candid and progressive discussions of results.

Not to be dramatic, but the longer I work with the Balanced Scorecard, and the more exposure I gain to all types of organizations from every corner of the globe, the more I'm convinced that reengineering your meeting process to harness the focusing power of the Balanced Scorecard is perhaps the single most important change your organization can make to generate improved results.

First Things First: This Is a Strategy Execution Review Meeting

There is no shortage of meetings at most companies: Daily stand-up meetings, weekly executive conferences, monthly operations reviews, quarterly business unit reviews, semi-annual strategy conferences, all-hands meetings—the list goes on and on. Whether all are necessary is a question only you can answer, although most people are inclined to believe we have far too many meetings and that the ones we conduct are of dubious value.

The meeting I'll be dissecting on the pages that follow is strictly confined to a review of strategy execution using your Balanced Scorecard. No deep dives on operational bottlenecks in this session; the focus is centered exclusively on gauging your effectiveness in executing strategy by examining in detail the objectives, measures, targets, and strategic initiatives comprising your Balanced Scorecard.

We'll begin by considering what must occur before the meeting commences, the foundational elements necessary to ensure your time in session is well spent. From there we'll transition to the meeting itself, examining options for reviewing results, setting the right tone in the meeting, fighting the apathy that may occasionally creep in, and a number of other subjects. If your company has no history with strategy-execution meetings it's important to temper expectations for the initial sessions. I'll share what you can expect as you pore over your Scorecard results. Finally, we'll look at what must be done after the meeting to keep accountability and interest high.

 ## BEFORE THE MEETING

Super Bowl–winning quarterback Russell Wilson of the Seattle Seahawks has been asked many times what is necessary for success in the ultra-intense National Football League, where every player is constantly searching for the slightest edge over competitors. Wilson's reply: "Separation is in the preparation."[9] In other words, success on the gridiron is dictated by an unrelenting commitment to preparation off the field, the work that goes on behind the scenes before the team is charging on to the field in front of 70,000 screaming fans. So, whether it's winning in the NFL or scoring a metaphorical touchdown by conducting a truly effective meeting, success in both is predicated upon disciplined preparation. Outlined below are a number of items to consider before you hold your first strategy execution review meeting.

Schedule the Meetings in Advance

Just before the Christmas holidays, Professor Peter Gollwitzer asked his students to assist in a study on how they planned to spend their Christmas vacation. To receive credit for participation, the students had to write and submit the report within 48 hours. In reality, Gollwitzer wasn't concerned with the students' holiday activities, but instead was very curious about how people dealt with goals when there were a lot of distractions. And for most people, scurrying from party to party, buying last-minute gifts, or simply catching up with family, Christmas is a time of near-constant distraction, thus a perfect setting for such a study.

One group of students received no special instructions other than to write and submit the report within 48 hours of arriving at home. The second group, however, was provided with additional guidelines. They were given an extra questionnaire on which they had to record exactly when and where they were going to write the report within the 48 hours. When the results were tabulated the findings were dramatic: only 33 percent of those students simply asked to write and return the report actually did so, while a whopping 75 percent of the second group, those asked to also note when and where they would do it, completed the assignment.[10] Hundreds of subsequent studies have replicated Gollwitzer's findings, proving that in order to effect real change, it must be translated from lofty ambitions to specific behaviors that spell out in detail when and where activities will take place.

Despite the substantial work you've completed in creating your strategy map of objectives and Scorecard of measures, targets, and strategic initiatives, unless you begin to actually use the tool, your investment amounts to little more than a stimulating intellectual exercise. Generating value from a Balanced Scorecard system requires analyzing results, discussing them thoughtfully, and making informed decisions as a result. Getting from the creation of the system to the utility it promises requires specific behaviors in the form of people actually making the time and effort to show up at the appointed time for meetings. Therefore, just like our Christmas activity–journaling students above, once you create your Scorecard system, the first priority must be to schedule strategy execution review meetings and ensure every participant notes the time and place in their calendar and commits to attending.

As with much of the advice contained in these pages, scheduling meetings in advance may appear to be common sense. Unfortunately, however, I've seen my share of Scorecard implementations fail not because of a fundamental flaw in the system or its unique construction for specific companies, but simply because the organization failed to hold regularly scheduled meetings to discuss results. In the experiment noted above, Professor Gollwitzer chose Christmas because he was well aware of the myriad distractions his students would face once they began their break. In reality, every day is like Christmas at most modern companies, where the tornado of urgent activities never stops spinning and the attention of even the most disciplined among us is constantly stretched to the edges. Clear the path for your team and make it easy to employ the Scorecard by documenting exactly where and when you'll be discussing results.

Regarding how often you should hold the review sessions, I suggest monthly. Some organizations will declare that quarterly reviews are more appropriate, but I believe that is a mistake. Circumstances change so rapidly that you simply cannot afford to let as many as 90 days pass without holding a rigorous review of the results you hope will propel you toward strategy execution. Customer requirements may be subtly shifting, the political landscape may be altered, and the economic environment in which you operate may be undergoing seismic shifts. Ignoring the warning signs, not to mention the opportunities, in front of you is done entirely at your peril.

Choose Your Facilitator

Practitioners are mixed on this point; some tap their Office of Strategy Management (OSM) leader to guide the review session, and others rotate the assignment among the senior management team. Both options have merit. Using the OSM leader ensures the meeting will be led by a guiding hand well-schooled in the mechanics of the Balanced Scorecard, its principles, and its functions, thereby helping the group avoid digressing into the weeds of the organization's operations and missing the big picture being portrayed by Scorecard results.

Having a member of your senior management team conduct the session can also prove beneficial since one of your aims in pursuing the Balanced Scorecard is to drive ownership and accountability for strategy execution throughout the highest ranks of your organization chart. An additional benefit of employing this option is it challenges the senior manager facilitator to step out of his or her usual silo and think broadly about organizational success, engaging them in dialog with other business-unit leaders and brainstorming creative solutions to cross-functional challenges.

Determine Who Will Attend

The obvious choice here is your senior executive team, those individuals responsible for both the crafting and effective execution of your strategy. Beyond your senior leadership, I've read and heard others advocate that when filling the seats for strategy execution review meetings you throw away the organizational chart, and invite people based purely on the criteria of who can meaningfully contribute to the dialog. Follow this seemingly sound and politically correct advice and your meeting will be populated not only by senior executives but, possibly, by those holding lower ranks who have an intimate knowledge of Scorecard results as well.

My populist inclinations cause me to cheer this sentiment. However, the pragmatist dwelling deep within is skeptical. Here's what can happen. You tell a midlevel manager that due to their outstanding erudition on a Scorecard measure, they'll be presenting the results to the executive team at an upcoming meeting. Once the initial shock passes, the chosen employee develops a narrative, rehearses it until he or she can deliver it with the clarity and conviction of a stumping politician, and then waits for the big day to arrive. At the appointed time they are shuttled into the room—normally they have to wait outside until the exact moment they are to deliver their findings. The first few moments go very well, and why shouldn't they—the speech has been honed to a fine edge thanks to countless sessions in front of a bathroom mirror. About a minute in however, a chink appears, as the perceived enormity of the situation—delivering a presentation to a group of faces they normally see gracing the pages of the annual report—produces a vice in their stomach that won't let go. Their mouth dries, pulse quickens, and then . . . the . . . words . . . just . . . won't . . . come . . . out.

An overactive imagination is not the source of the woeful story above. I've seen it play out many times. In fact, I can still recall witnessing such a meltdown many years ago. It was very early in my career, and a colleague and I had been invited to a senior team session to deliver updates. I was the first person to speak, an enormous boon, because the nervous germ had virtually no time to penetrate my wafer-thin defenses. I just got up there, did my thing, and retreated swiftly to a waiting chair at the back of the room. My friend wasn't as fortunate. His talk was scheduled for the very end of the session, leaving ample time for the projector in his mind to flash every doomsday outcome imaginable. It happened no more than a minute or two into his scheduled 10 minutes. He went completely blank. Actually, not completely blank, as he was muttering something incoherent, trying desperately to find his way back to the track of pure thoughts he'd delivered a thousand times in his head. I could have jumped in, tossed him a softball question that would surely have righted his mental ship, but I, like everyone else in the room, sat transfixed. It was like driving past a car accident—you know you shouldn't, but you just have to crane your neck and take a look.

You may read this and believe you can mitigate the disastrous results chronicled above by inviting lower-level members of your team but not burdening them with an assigned role. Instead, they can be called upon to add color commentary and expert analysis based on their close proximity to the inner workings of the objectives and measures. Once again, my experience suggests this is not the case. Too often, invited guests will sit quietly, and despite their deep repository of knowledge, they may feel intimidated and not willing to take a risk at what they perceive as such a high-level gathering. Thus, feel free to invite managers with a point of view who can contribute, and perhaps call on them with questions of clarification, but, at its core, strategy execution is the responsibility of the senior management team and they must actively engage in and ultimately own this process.

Share Materials in Advance

Few things frustrate me more after weeks of hard work and preparation than to arrive at a client location and find that the materials I sent well in advance were not copied or distributed as promised. Productive discussions are rendered practically impossible when the participants don't possess the raw materials necessary to contribute meaningfully to the dialog.

So it is with strategy execution review meetings. Sharing materials prior to the session is an absolute must to derive the benefits these meetings are capable of delivering. Snappy and clever spontaneous dialog is delivered effortlessly in movies and on television, but in the real world your participants will need help to frame the discussions you hope will lead to creative tension and breakthrough discoveries. That assistance comes in the form of materials delivered approximately one week in advance of the meeting, including your strategy map, Balanced Scorecard measure results, commentaries on performance, and updates on key strategic initiatives. When distributing meeting materials, challenge executives to immediately assign a time in their calendars when they will review the documents and prepare for the upcoming meeting.

 ## IN THE MEETING

Since the meeting was scheduled well in advance, everyone is here and they're eager to participate thanks to the materials you sent for review. The facilitator steps to the front of the room and it's time to get started. Let's look at the elements necessary to make this meeting a win for everyone (see Exhibit 7.2).

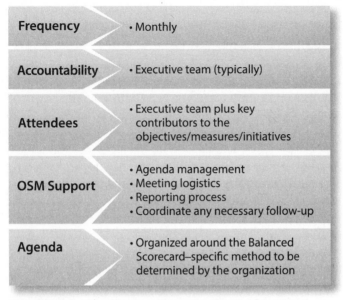

Frequency	• Monthly
Accountability	• Executive team (typically)
Attendees	• Executive team plus key contributors to the objectives/measures/initiatives
OSM Support	• Agenda management • Meeting logistics • Reporting process • Coordinate any necessary follow-up
Agenda	• Organized around the Balanced Scorecard–specific method to be determined by the organization

EXHIBIT 7.2   The Strategy Execution Review Meeting

Reviewing Scorecard Results—Options Abound

At its core, the meeting is designed to review results from your Balanced Scorecard system. There are a variety of options from which to choose when considering how you will actually review those outcomes. Let's consider some of the more popular alternatives:

■ **Worst to first:** In this method, designed to take advantage of the time-tested power of peer pressure, the owner whose measure results are poorest is the first to present to the group. New York City, General Electric, and Siemens use this technique. All note the focus placed on poor performers to improve their performance lest they open the show each and every month.

■ **The strategic story:** If your strategy map and Scorecard have made good use of cause and effect linkages—weaving a powerful strategic story through the four perspectives of the model—you may choose to use these causal paths as your roadmap to review performance. You might begin with the financial perspective and work through the chain evident in the other perspectives, all the while challenging the hypotheses suggested by the linkages you created when developing the map and measures.

- **No stone unturned:** This process features the sequential review of all four perspectives, beginning with the financial and dutifully scanning performance on each objective and measure through the learning and growth perspective.
- **Exception based:** Those employing this approach look first to measures operating significantly out of a predetermined range of acceptable performance and take a deeper dive to the inner workings of the metric in an attempt to ferret out the root causes of the aberration and get things back on track. It is similar to the worst-to-first method without the associated psychological pressure.
- **Three questions:** In the next section I'll elaborate on the power of good questions, but for now, here are three simple questions you can use to unlock better discussions:
  - What happened?
  - Why did it happen?
  - What are we going to do about it?
- **Quick wins:** Early in your implementation, it's often beneficial to begin the Scorecard review by discussing a measure result that provides insights into a customer issue or any pressing problem. At this point in your Scorecard evolution you're attempting to solidify buy-in and support for the tool, and by focusing on measures that supply insights, you can persuade skeptical onlookers that the Scorecard provides tangible benefits. Similarly, one client began their initial review meetings with what they called a Good News component, during which they discussed measures that had exceeded their target values for the period and thus warranted a celebration from the team.

As with most things Balanced Scorecard, there is no one right way or absolute method for running your review meetings. In fact, the modus operandi of the session runs a distant second to the actual conversation produced by the investigation itself. Regardless of the tack you use to steer the ship, what really matters is the discussion spawned along the way. The primary task of the facilitator is to use the results simply as a spark lighting a flame of intense discussion during which conventional views are challenged, assumptions exposed, and hypotheses about the strategy tested. Allow yourself some room for experimentation as you structure your meetings with the Balanced Scorecard as the agenda, and make alterations and improvements as you find a style that suits your culture and meets your unique needs.

Focus on Questions as Much as Answers

Quotes from two men, living and writing in different centuries, perfectly capture the spirit of this section. First is the eighteenth-century French philosopher Voltaire, who noted, "A man is judged by his questions, rather than his answers." Writing nearly two full centuries later, the father of management thinking Peter Drucker argues, "The most serious mistakes are not being made as a result of wrong answers. The truly dangerous thing is asking the wrong questions."[11] Ironic as it may first appear, to meet the challenges we face today, it's not a rapidly flowing stream of answers emanating from voluble and zealous managers who drive insights but, rather, the formation of carefully crafted questions that lead to a deeper understanding of all facets of the situation. Only when we carefully examine our circumstances through challenging questions can we expect to produce real insights.

Most people I work with understand this notion intellectually, and enthusiastically agree with the premise, but when it comes time to put it into practice in review meetings, the answer first, ask questions later instinct rushes to the fore. Not surprising really, since managers and executives rise through corporate ranks primarily on their ability to provide answers, often extemporaneously, on how to circumvent each and every obstacle appearing on the company's path. Not knowing the answer and knowing it quickly can be perceived as a lack of knowledge and can easily derail the progress of an up and coming executive.[12]

The leaders I've worked with over the past two decades whom I would deem most effective are humble and honest enough to recognize they don't have all the answers, and quick to frame the challenges they face in the form of thought-provoking questions designed to stimulate the entire group's thinking. These visionaries seem to know instinctively how to frame questions in a fashion that unearths hidden views and assumptions, bringing them to the foreground where they can be unmasked and critically examined. The CEO of a utility company I worked with several years ago provides a great example of how asking better questions can yield breakthroughs. This gentleman was relatively new to the position and had joined the company after a long stint in the financial industry. In every workshop I conducted, whenever the group would reach some sort of impasse, frustrated at the inability to overcome a seemingly insurmountable issue, he would ask a series of questions designed to expose the team's assumptions and deeply held views on the subject. With the facts (as the team saw them) clearly expounded and written in black and white on a flip chart, the team was able to verify what it knew to be true and what was open to interpretation. His series of humble inquiries eventually led the group to consider entirely new options that only hours ago might have been so intellectually buried they never would have seen the light of day.

As tempting as it may be to fire off answers for every problem the company faces, it's usually evident that most problems are immune to simple solutions upon deeper reflection. When reviewing Scorecard results during your strategy execution meetings, always start with questions before proceeding to possible answers. The deeper you burrow into a challenge or issue, the more elements of it you expose. With the problem peeled back, its dimensions standing in bold relief, you're much more likely to then generate strategic insights.

This section began with quotes, so let's end with one as well. Albert Einstein was once asked about his inspiring genius. The iconic scientist paused, then earnestly replied: "I have no special talents, I am only passionately curious."[13] This is what we should all strive for in life as well as business: a hunger to uncover the truth, to move beyond the shiny veneer of simple answers, and penetrate deeper until we reach the core essence of any challenge.

Set a Tone of Continuous Learning

The make or break variable of a successful meeting is the tone or overall atmosphere that pervades the session. Your challenge, and it's a considerable one, is to infuse the room with a spirit of open and honest debate, challenging everything in your quest to unlock the truth and move further down the path of strategy execution. That path to truth and strategic enlightenment can quickly transform into a painful road, however, should you choose to push the envelope of inquiry and enter the territory of blame.

To experience the cleansing fresh air of open dialog and debate that leads to breakthroughs, your people need to feel psychologically safe; able to unearth sacred cows and previously taboo subjects without fear of sanctions, be they rendered in the form of stinging criticism, telling silence, or informal reprimands levied back in the workplace. An interviewer once asked former Dell Computer CEO Kevin Rollins what would happen to a Dell manager whose product or sales region falls off track and starts losing money. Without missing a beat Rollins replied smugly, "They'd become a pariah."[14] Dell has tumbled from its perch atop the computer mountaintop, recently announcing they would be delisting their shares and become a private company. Where that road will lead I don't know. What I do know is that a culture characterizing underperformers as pariahs is most likely never going to reap the benefits of true strategic learning. The Rollins quote was drawn from an article titled, "Execution Without Excuses." At the risk of never being hired by those who subscribe to this no-holds-barred, Wild West school of management—I think it stinks! You can intimidate people into performing for a while, and short-term results will surely follow as the career of Chainsaw Al Dunlop, the corporate turnaround specialist best known for his ruthless methods of downsizing, will attest.

With every criticism and each belittling remark, long-term damage is sewn into the culture and a toxin of fear and mistrust is spread throughout the organization that will one day manifest itself as an organizational cancer ready to exact its revenge. As a footnote, Rollins' approach didn't work very well at Dell. He oversaw one of the largest layoffs in Dell history (8,000 people) that destroyed morale, while Dell's stock price declined 9 percent during his tenure. His decisions and, ironically, failure to execute led to his dismissal in 2007. No need to shed tears for Mr. Rollins, however; he was paid $48.5 million in cash related to expired stock options upon his departure.

Contrast the punitive environment at Dell with the more nurturing mood at data storage firm Adaptec. During his tenure as the firm's CEO, John Adler drove the company's valuation from $100 million to over $5 billion because he had a very healthy attitude about business goals and financial results. For him, results were not a punitive weapon but a useful diagnostic and learning tool. When the firm, at one point, missed a quarterly goal, he and his management team calmly analyzed all the factors contributing to the shortfall. They discovered that, as a result of an unusual quality-control issue, the company had been unable to make some end of quarter shipments. Instead of reacting emotionally and assigning blame, Adler asked rigorous questions of the senior management team, which was able to uncover the root cause of the problem. He then communicated this information broadly to ensure organizational learning.[15]

In the Dell example, it's clear that failure was not an option for managers during that juncture, but of course they were not alone. For most of the history of modern business, failure was seen as, well, the ultimate failure. Fortunately that view is changing as enlightened leaders are warming to the idea that success and failure really aren't polar opposites, and, in fact, you often need to endure the latter to enjoy the former. Failure can provide lessons that will never surface from success, spur creativity, and help you avoid potential destruction, as the story of Ford attests. When Alan Mulally took over Ford in 2006 one of his first acts was to demand that executives admit their failures. He asked managers to color code their performance reports—a spectrum that ranged from green for good to red for trouble. Early in his tenure, when meeting with executives, he was astonished to be awash in a sea of green, even though Ford had lost several billion dollars the previous year. The company's recovery began when the stigma of failure was removed, and his team confronted the brutal circumstances facing them.[16]

Learning, and not the assignment of blame, must always be the primary objective of the strategy execution review meeting, should you hope to create a culture in which continuous learning about the strategy is truly seen as everyone's job.

Listen More

I previously shared advice on listening more effectively in Chapter 4, in the discussion of Balanced Scorecard workshops. The counsel applies equally well here, as cognitive breakthroughs and strategic insights are much more likely to emerge from a thoughtful consideration of your colleagues' points of view. However, when I sit in on client meetings it sometimes occurs to me that everyone around the table is just waiting, very impatiently, for a chance to speak. When that time comes, based on the new direction in which they spin the conversation, it's quite obvious they didn't really hear a word the previous speaker uttered, and are simply intent on getting their point across. After four of five people have voiced their opinions the room seems to be swirling in confusion and contradiction, with no one really cognizant of what anyone else has said.

Productive dialog is dependent upon active listening, and the stakes in your execution review meeting are too high to dismiss this in favor of barking out any unrelated comment with no regard to what others have shared. As Benjamin Franklin once noted: "Gain knowledge by use of the ear, rather than the tongue". Try this simple rule of thumb at your next meeting: before providing your own opinion, share what you believe you heard others say and don't progress until you can express it to their satisfaction.

Gaze Out, Not In

Picture this: In one home lives a child being raised by nonworking parents on welfare, neither of whom completed high school. In a second home resides a child whose parents are both college graduates, own their own home, and hold professional occupations. Which child is destined to have the higher IQ? Seems glaringly obvious, doesn't it? The child with well-educated, professional parents who possess the means necessary to provide for their offspring will be given every opportunity to succeed, and thus find herself at a distinct advantage. Interestingly, however, studies have shown that when it comes to a child's success, the biggest differentiator is not money or education, but language. It turns out that kids with professional parents hear 30 million more words in their first three years than kids of poor parents. That river of words pays off; the greater the number of words children hear from their parents or caregivers before they are three, the higher their IQ and the better they perform in school.[17] It's not simply the volume of words, either, but the kind of words. In the first three years, professionals' kids hear about 500,000 words of encouragement and 80,000 words of discouragement. It's the opposite in poor households: 80,000 of encouragement, and 200,000 of discouragement.

Language matters a great deal, whether we're examining the IQ of children or assessing the success of corporations. In one study on the use of language in a corporate setting, researchers looked at a sample of meetings, counting the utterances and classifying them as internal or external. The teams in the best performing organizations had external focus in more than 70 percent of their comments, whereas the worst performing teams were the reverse.[18] This is an important statistic to keep in mind as you begin discussing performance results from your Balanced Scorecard. In Chapter 6 I mentioned that some teams like to play the "Ain't It Awful" game, grumbling and whining about their sorry predicament and avoiding real action. When reviewing Scorecard results it's easy to turn the dialog inward, bemoaning the internal roadblocks that have been erected (be they certain people, policies, or procedures) in your quest, while avoiding the discussion that really matters—what those impediments mean for your customers, and how they may affect your financial returns.

The Balanced Scorecard has four perspectives of performance, two are externally focused (customer and to a lesser extent, financial), and two are primarily, but not exclusively, focused on internal aspects of the organization (internal process and learning and growth). Your study of the customer and financial perspectives will lead naturally to external evaluations, but you may wonder how an internal focus can be avoided, at least part of the time, when reviewing the internal and learning and growth perspectives. Naturally you'll want to thoroughly examine both the internal and learning and growth perspectives, and consider the ramifications on your internal operations, but my suggestion is to ensure that when reviewing both you additionally commit to determining how performance in those perspectives impacts customer outcomes, and ultimately, financial success.

Fight Apathy!

One of the most dispiriting moments for any meeting facilitator is that moment, often late in the day, when after much discussion and debate, and just as you're on the verge of making an important decision someone says, "It doesn't matter to me, I'll go along with whatever the group decides." With that, like the air rushing from a balloon, the energy in the room is gone in an instant. If you don't act quickly and decisively, the indifference virus that was unleashed by a single person will infect the entire team in a matter of seconds, putting the success of your meeting, and perhaps your personal stake in that success, in jeopardy.

Should the apathy bug make an unscheduled visit at your strategy execution review meeting, here are some ways to combat it:

- **Recognize it:** Apathy doesn't materialize suddenly; the symptoms often appear well in advance, and you can easily recognize them most of the time: lack of discussion on key points, body language suggesting indifference and a lack of concern (such as crossed arms), and people leaving the room frequently. If you see any of these behaviors, reorient the team by asking simple questions, such as: "Is everyone with me?" "Does this make sense?" You might even consider asking whether there is an issue with the process you've put in place. Perhaps that is inhibiting the group's creativity.
- **Get to the root:** People will sometimes check out of a discussion because of a perceived slight, or because they feel they're not being understood. If you sense this is the issue, draw the person out, have them articulate their thoughts, and attempt to have others restate the opinion to their satisfaction. This way they'll know colleagues understand their point of view and will be more inclined to vigorously defend it.
- **Shake things up:** Civility is vital in any meeting; the last thing you want are personal attacks that can leave permanent emotional scars on the entire team. However, as previously discussed, it is possible to create an environment in which people feel safe to challenge entrenched views and pursue vigorous debate in a spirit of honest exchange. Such healthy debate should be encouraged. Doing so puts you in good company; while researching his bestselling book, *Good to Great*,[19] author Jim Collins discovered that many of the companies making the ascent frequently engaged in passionate and heated discussions, all in a spirit of inquiry and learning.
- **Stick to the agenda:** This is my most pragmatic piece of advice, but one that must never be overlooked. If you allow rambling, off-topic monologues to persist unchecked, you're sure to engender apathy in all those held

captive by a loquacious colleague. Walk over to the person, and respectfully interject by saying something like, "How does (what they're saying) relate to the point we're currently discussing? Can you make that link for us?" Then draw the entire group back to the agenda topic at hand and encourage others to share their points of view.

■ **Raise the stakes:** To ensure the sustained interest of an audience, filmmakers often attempt to raise the stakes of the situations in which the characters find themselves. For example, instead of simply having two men stranded on the ocean in a lifeboat, the film will put a slow leak in the dingy, show a storm developing on the horizon, and introduce the fact that one of the men was having an affair with the other's wife. Now you've got some stakes! You probably won't be able to (nor would you want to) create such drama in a review meeting, but you can introduce the corporate equivalent by reminding the group of the importance of the task at hand, reorienting them to their ultimate purpose, and denoting the necessity of their unique contribution.

AFTER THE MEETING

The primary action required after the meeting is to ensure accountability for follow-up items. On the subject of accountability, and making the most of time spent in meetings, authors Bossidy and Charan are crystal-clear in their book *Execution*: "Never finish a meeting without clarifying what the follow-through will be, who will do it, when and how they will do it, what resources they will use, and how and when the next review will take place and with whom."[20] Ideas are the currency of the knowledge economy, and during these strategy execution review sessions ideas and associated actions will flow freely. But, as we all know, ideas are only as good as their execution, and they require follow through to reach fruition. Always compile a list of action items flagged during the meeting and ensure updates are provided at the next gathering.

What to Expect from Your Strategy Execution Review Meetings

We laugh about it later, but there have been moments when sitting at client review meetings that I know everyone around the table is thinking, "We spent all that time building a Balanced Scorecard to get to this?" I have no psychic abilities, so how am I able to ascertain this acerbic level of subconscious chatter? Body language that silently screams frustration is one thing, but it's usually the stinging glares of contempt from every person in the room that really give them away. There is no way to sugarcoat this news: your initial strategy execution review meetings are very likely to be painful as you grope in the strategic darkness attempting to make sense of the data coming from your Balanced Scorecard.

For most organizations, everything about these meetings is new and disturbingly unfamiliar: the Balanced Scorecard system itself is new; many of the objectives, measures, and initiatives are new, and the method of reviewing results is new. And, as we all know, new is confusing, intimidating, and difficult. When immersed in such challenging times it's imperative that you adopt what psychologists term a growth mind-set, recognizing (and believing) that while you may get metaphorically knocked down initially, with time and practice you'll get better, and in the end you'll succeed. Recall from earlier in the chapter the anecdotes relating to the importance of failure, and how failure is almost always a necessary prerequisite of ultimate success. So it is with your strategy execution review meetings; by accepting and slogging through the initial meetings with a commitment to constant learning, you will ascend step by step, until a day comes when it simply clicks—everyone around the table feels the energy, and the discussion and insights you generate prove you're on the right track. What is most important to move along the meeting-quality spectrum is to have the willpower to get through the initial difficult sessions, knowing that a better future is in store. That last part is vital—believing that things will improve in the future. Researchers have found that the mere promise that practice would improve performance on a difficult task helped people push past willpower exhaustion.[21] Therefore, ensure you're constantly reminding yourself that with rigor and discipline the meetings will continue to improve until you settle into a comfortable rhythm.

Value from these meetings is derived in waves. If you're like most of the organizations I've studied and worked with, the first benefit, typically achieved after a small number of sessions, is enhanced support for the Scorecard and better meetings. After just a couple of meetings, one of my clients described it this way: "The good news is we sense a critical mass of support and excitement among key people. I don't think there's any going back. Just the improved meetings have huge dividends you can feel even if you can't yet measure." Once the flywheel of momentum begins spinning, you'll feel the rhythm of the events improving in unison, and it isn't long before the Scorecard numbers that at first seemed puzzling and incoherent become the starting point for stimulating discussions that lead to the second and far more important wave of value—competitive knowledge and strategic insights. Exhibit 7.3 provides a pictorial representation of the meeting trajectory you can expect.

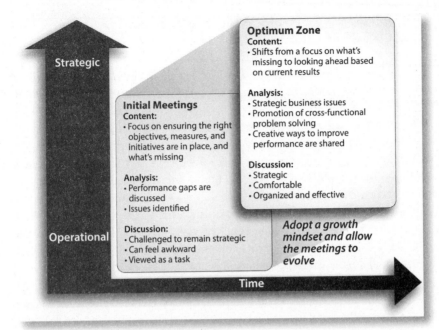

EXHIBIT 7.3 The Evolution of Strategy Execution Review Meetings

Concluding Thoughts on Strategy Execution Review Meetings

In many regards, my assessment of meetings in this chapter has been quite cynical. I don't think we need to call in a psychologist; it's probably all a thinly veiled attempt to mask my frustration with what could be the most beneficial activity managers engage in each and every day.

We've all spent countless hours in meeting rooms during the course of our careers, and unless there is a drastic change in the way we conduct business, we are destined to spend many more in the years to come. As a leader in your organization—and you don't need to be the CEO for this to apply—I urge you to follow the advice offered in this chapter. From the seemingly benign task of scheduling your meetings in advance all the way to the pinnacle of embracing a spirit of inquiry and learning as you struggle through your initial sessions, seize the opportunity and transform the meeting experience today. You, your organization and, dare I say, the world, will all be better for it.

REPORTING RESULTS WITH BALANCED SCORECARD SOFTWARE

Not long after the city of New Orleans was devastated by Hurricane Katrina, people whose lives had been drastically upended began searching for any shred of normalcy, any event that would help them shed the effects of the tragedy, even if only for a few hours. The quest led some people to high school football, the Friday night tradition that borders on religion in many parts of the United States. So putting aside their troubles for a while, disheveled citizens packed stadium stands in anticipation of a closely contested game between two heated rivals. Excitement was in the air as the ball was kicked off and the game began. Soon after, however, something was missing. There were no cheers, no wild clapping, no screaming at referees over missed calls. In fact, no one seemed to be paying attention to the game at all. It turns out that the scoreboard had blown down during the storm and had yet to be replaced. As a result, no one in the crowd knew what down it was, how much time was left, or what the score was. There was a game going on, but nobody in the stands seemed to know that.[22] Whether it's football or the Balanced Scorecard, we need to know whether we're winning or losing, and a visually compelling tool goes a long way towards assisting us with this most basic tenet of human nature.

When I began working with the Balanced Scorecard, reports generated on an Excel spreadsheet and illustrated with some clip art added a stylistic flourish that was considered avant-garde and often yielded expressions of awe from Scorecard reviewers. Whenever I mention that, I feel as though I'm recounting one of those stories you might hear from your grandfather: "When I was your age we walked eight miles to school in the snow . . . uphill both ways." We weren't suffering in our technology deprived state, but in retrospect we could have achieved much more from the Scorecard had we been able to avail ourselves of the many benefits present in even the most modest of Scorecard software systems available today.

As the Balanced Scorecard evolved from a pure measurement system to a strategic management system, to a powerful communication tool with the advent of strategy maps, the paper-based reports used by early adopters were hard pressed to keep up with progress in the field. Organizations were cascading the Scorecard from top to bottom, linking it to budgeting and, in many cases, compensation as well. The reporting, analysis, and communication requirements represented by these advances required new tools. Software providers were swift in their response, and soon developed a number of sophisticated programs capable of everything from simple reporting to strategy mapping and scenario planning.

Automating your Balanced Scorecard provides a number of benefits. The advanced analytics and decision support provided by even the simplest Scorecard software allow organizations to perform intricate evaluations of performance and critically examine the relationships among their performance measures. Automation also supports true organization-wide deployment of the tool. Cascading the Scorecard across the enterprise (having lower-level groups develop their own Scorecards) can often lead to the development of dozens of Scorecards if not more. Without the use of an automated solution, managing the process and ensuring alignment can prove difficult. Communication and feedback may also be dramatically improved with software. Commentaries used to elaborate on a specific measure's performance may spawn a company-wide discussion and lead to creative breakthroughs based on collaborative problem solving made possible only through the wide dissemination of Scorecard results. Information sharing and knowledge are also enhanced by the software's ability to provide relevant links to interested users. A hyperlinked measure may be just the beginning in the user's journey to a variety of knowledge enhancing sites including the mission statement, the latest comments from a valued customer, or the results of a much anticipated benchmarking study.

 ## CRITERIA FOR SELECTING SOFTWARE

Selection of the right software for your organization is a crucial decision. Not only are you shopping for a system to report your Scorecard results and provide a platform for future evolution of the tool, but you must ensure whatever you buy will suit the needs of your workforce and be accepted as a useful tool. Software selection is typically a process of five sequential steps:[23]

1. **Form a software team:** Just as you used a team to develop your strategy map and Scorecard, so too will you rely on a number of people to make the crucial software decision. Include your executive sponsor, the Office of Strategy Management, a representative of your information technology (IT) group, and an individual representative of the typical Scorecard user. The team should begin their work by reviewing the current landscape of Scorecard software, and speak to end users regarding their requirements for this tool. Remember that different users will demand specific functionality. Executives may simply be interested in one-page summary reports; while analysts may focus on data input, retrieval,

and complex reporting. The team should also develop a software project plan outlining key dates and milestones on the path to the software decision.

2. **Develop a short list of candidates:** You'll find dozens of potential vendors ready and willing to supply you with Scorecard software. Use the criteria listed in subsequent sections to help you determine three or four finalists.

3. **Submit a Request for Proposal (RFP):** Compile your needs and specifications into a document for distribution to your finalists. Each organization you contact should provide you with a written summary detailing how their product stacks up to your requirements.

4. **Arrange demonstrations:** Invite software candidates to conduct a demonstration of their product at your facility. To ensure the demonstration is relevant to your needs, send a copy of your strategy map and measures to the vendor in advance, and have them base the demonstration on your data.

5. **Create a summary report and make your selection:** Determine which functionality and specifications are most vital to you, and rank each product against them. The software program that most closely matches your requirements should be selected.

Exhibit 7.4 displays a screen shot from Corporater, a leading Balanced Scorecard software provider.

Design Issues: Configuration of the Software

In this section, we'll examine a number of the Scorecard software setup and design elements.

- **Setup wizards:** Your software solution should provide easy to use and understand wizards to guide new users through the initial setup process.
- **Time to implement:** Software programs for the Balanced Scorecard run the gamut from simple reporting tools to sophisticated enterprise-wide management solutions. Therefore, major differences exist in the time and resources necessary to implement the system. You must determine what your thresholds are in terms of timing and resource requirements necessary to have the system up and running. Carefully consider the resource requirements you have, and are willing to dedicate to, the Scorecard software.

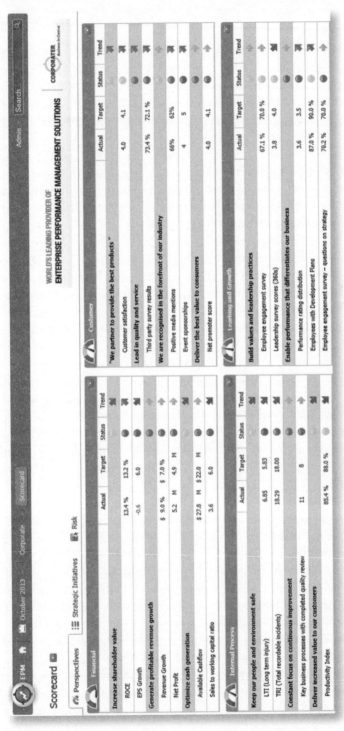

EXHIBIT 7.4 Screen Shot of Corporater Balanced Scorecard Software

Source: Courtesy of Corporater.

- **Various Scorecard designs:** This book focuses exclusively on the methodology of the Balanced Scorecard. However, you may at some point wish to track other popular measurement alternatives such as the Baldrige award criteria, total quality management (TQM) metrics, or any number of different methodologies. The software should be flexible enough to permit various performance management techniques.

- **User interface/display:** Most Balanced Scorecard software will feature a predominant display metaphor. It may use gauges similar to those you'd see in an automobile dashboard, boxes that are reminiscent of organizational charts, or color-coded dials. Some of these simply look better (i.e., more realistic and legitimate) than others. That may sound insignificant, but remember: you're counting on your workforce to use this software faithfully, and if they find the instrumentation unrealistic or unattractive that could significantly impact their initial reaction and ongoing commitment.

- **Number of measures:** In all likelihood you will use the Scorecard software for tracking performance measures from around your entire organization. Ensure your software is equipped with the flexibility to handle a significant volume of measures.

- **Objectives, measures, targets, and initiatives:** As the backbone of the Scorecard system, you should be able to easily enter all of the above elements in the software. The software should also allow you to specify cause-and-effect relationships among the objectives and measures.

- **Strategy maps:** Capturing the strategy map with compelling and easy-to-understand graphics is critical should you hope to benefit from the information sharing and collective learning to be derived from the Balanced Scorecard.

- **Multiple locations:** The software should accommodate the addition of performance measures from a variety of locations.

- **Descriptions and definitions:** Simply entering names and numbers into the software is not sufficient for communication and eventual analysis. Every field in which you enter information must be capable of accepting textual descriptions. Upon launching the software, the first thing most users will do when looking at a specific performance indicator is to examine its description and definition.

- **Assignment of owners:** The Scorecard can only be used to enhance accountability if your software permits each performance indicator to be assigned a specific owner. Since you may also have another individual acting as the owner's assistant and yet another as data enterer, it is beneficial if the software provides the ability to identify these functions, as well.

- **Various unit types:** Your performance indicators are likely to come in all shapes, sizes, and descriptors, from raw numbers to percentages to dollars. The tool you choose must permit all types of measures.

- **Appropriate timing:** Your performance measures are sure to have different time increments. Expenses may be tracked monthly, while customer satisfaction is monitored quarterly. The software should accommodate varied reporting frequencies.

- **Relative weights:** All measures on the Balanced Scorecard are important links in the description of your strategy. However, most organizations will place greater emphasis on certain indicators. For example, with public and nonprofit organizations, customer indicators are of vital importance and may warrant a higher weight. A good Scorecard tool should permit you to weight the measures according to their relative importance.

- **Aggregate disparate elements:** Your program should be able to combine performance measures with different unit types. This can best be accomplished with the use of weighting (see the preceding element). Measures are accorded a weight that drives the aggregation of results regardless of the specific unit type of each indicator.

- **Multiple comparatives:** Most organizations will track performance relative to a predefined target; for example, the financial budget. However, it may be useful to examine performance relative to peer performance, in light of last year's performance, or compared to a best-in-class benchmarking number. Look for the software to allow a number of comparatives.

- **Graphic status indicators:** With a glance, users should be able to ascertain the performance of measures from a status indicator. Many programs will take advantage of our familiarity with red (stop), yellow (caution), and green (go) metaphors. Fortunately, they usually offer greater color ranges.

- **Dual polarity:** For the software to produce a color indicating measure performance, it must recognize whether high values for actual results represent good or bad performance. Up to a certain point results might be considered good, but beyond a certain threshold they may be a cause for concern. For example, it may be perfectly appropriate for a call center representative to answer 12 to 15 calls an hour, but responding to 30 may indicate the representative is rushing through the calls and sacrificing quality for the sake of expediency. The software solution should be able to flag such issues of dual polarity.

- **Cascading Scorecards:** Users should be able to review Balanced Scorecards from across the organization in one program. Ensure your software allows you to display aligned Scorecards emanating from throughout the organization.

- **Personal preferences:** The information age has heralded a time of mass customization. And so it should be with your Balanced Scorecard software. Users should be able to easily customize the system to open with a page displaying indicators of importance to them. Having relevant information immediately available will greatly facilitate the program's use and, as noted in the opening of this section, the easier it is for people to know whether they're winning or losing, the better.
- **Intuitive menus:** Menus should be logical, easy to understand, and relatively simple to navigate.
- **Helpful help screens:** Some help screens seem to hinder users' efforts as often as helping them. Check the help screens to ensure they offer relevant, easy-to-follow information.
- **Levels of detail:** Your software should allow users to quickly and easily switch from a summary view of performance to a detailed view comprising a single indicator. Navigating from data tables to summary reports and back to individual measures should all be easily accommodated. The user community will demand this functionality as they begin actively using the tool to analyze performance results.

Reporting and Analysis

Any software solution you consider must contain robust and flexible reporting and analysis tools. In this section we'll explore a number of reporting and analysis factors to be considered during your selection process.

- **Drill-down capabilities:** A crucial item. The tool must allow users to drill-down on measures to increasingly lower levels of detail. Drill-down might also be considered in the context of strategy maps, which should be easily navigable at the click of a mouse.
- **Statistical analysis:** Your software should include the ability to perform statistical analysis on the performance measures on your Balanced Scorecard. Additionally, the statistics should be multidimensional in nature, combining disparate performance elements to display a total picture of actual results. Simply viewing bar charts is not analysis. Users require the opportunity of slicing and dicing the data to fit their analysis and decision-making needs.
- **Alerts:** You will want to be notified automatically when a critical measure is not performing within acceptable ranges. Alerts must be built into the system to provide this notification.

▪ **Commentaries:** Whether a measure is performing at, above, or below targeted expectations, users (especially management) need to quickly determine the root cause of the performance and be aware of the associated steps necessary for sustaining or improving results. Commentary fields are essential to any Scorecard software program and most, if not all, will include them.

▪ **Flexible report options:** "What kind of reports does it have?" is invariably one of the first questions you'll hear when discussing Scorecard software with your user community. We're a report-based culture, so this shouldn't come as a surprise. What may in fact come as a surprise is the wide range of report capabilities featured in today's Scorecard software entries. Test this requirement closely because some are much better than others. An especially important area to examine is print options. We purchase software to reduce our dependency on paper but as we all know it doesn't necessarily work that way. Ensure the software will print the information clearly and concisely.

▪ **Automatic consolidation:** You may wish to see your data presented as a sum, average, or year to date amount. The system should possess the flexibility to provide this choice.

▪ **Flagging of missing data:** At the outset of their implementation, most organizations will be missing at least a portion of the data for Balanced Scorecard measures. This often results from the fact that the Scorecard development process has illuminated entirely new measures never before contemplated. The software program should alert users to those measures that are missing data, whether it is for a single period, or the measure has never been populated.

▪ **Forecasting and what-if analysis:** Robust programs will possess the capability of using current results to forecast future performance. It's also very useful to have the ability to plug in different values in various measures and examine the effect on related indicators. This what-if analysis provides another opportunity to critically examine the assumptions made when constructing the strategy map.

▪ **Linked documents:** Users should have the ability to put measure results into a larger context by accessing important documents and links. Media reports, executive videos, social media links, discussion forums, and a variety of other potential links can serve to strengthen the bond between actual results and the larger context of organizational objectives.

▪ **Automatic e-mail:** To harness the power of the Balanced Scorecard as a communication tool, users must be able to launch an e-mail application and send messages regarding specific performance results. Discussion forums or threads may develop as interested users add their perspective on results and provide insights for improvements.

Technical Considerations

In this section, we'll examine the technical dimensions of both hardware and software to ensure the tool you select is right for your technical environment.

- **Compatibility:** Any software you consider must be able to exist in your current technical environment.
- **Integration with existing systems:** Data for your Balanced Scorecard will most likely reside in a number of places. Your software should be able to extract data from these systems automatically, thereby minimizing manual data entry. Users who appear reluctant to use the Scorecard software will often point to redundant data entry as a key detraction of the system. Therefore, a big win is delivered should you have the ability to automatically extricate information with no effort on the part of users.
- **Acceptance of various data forms:** In addition to internal sources of data you may collect performance information from third-party providers.
- **Data export:** Getting information out is as important as getting it in. The data contained in the Balanced Scorecard may serve as the source for other management reports to boards, regulators, or the general public. A robust data export tool is an important component of any Scorecard software.
- **Web publishing:** Users should have the option of accessing and saving Scorecard information using a standard browser. Publishing to both an internal intranet and the Internet is preferable.
- **Trigger external applications:** Users will require the capability of launching desktop programs from within the Balanced Scorecard software.
- **Cut and paste to applications:** Related to the preceding element, users may wish to include a graph or chart in another application. Many programs provide functionality that enable users to simply copy and paste with ease.
- **Application service provider (ASP) option:** An application service provider (ASP) is a company that offers organizations access to applications and related services over the Internet that would otherwise have to be located in their own computers. As information technology outsourcing grows in prominence, so too does the role of application service providers.
- **Scalability:** This term describes the ability of an application to function well and take advantage of changes in size or volume in order to meet a user need. Rescaling can encompass a change in the product itself or the movement to a new operating system. Your software should be scalable

to meet the future demands you may place on it as your user community and sophistication grow.

Maintenance and Security

Ensuring appropriate access rights and ongoing maintenance are also important criteria in your software decision. Here are a few elements to consider:

- **System administrator access:** Your software should allow for individuals to be designated as system administrators. Depending on security (see the third and fourth entries in this list) a number of these users may have access to the entire system.
- **Ease of modification:** Altering your views of performance should be facilitated easily with little advanced technical knowledge required.
- **Control of access to the system:** My proclivities are toward open-book management with complete sharing of information across the organization. Organizations practicing this form of management give it glowing reviews for the innovation and creativity it sparks among employees. The Scorecard facilitates the open sharing of information through the development of a high-level organizational Scorecard and a series of cascading Scorecards that allow all employees to describe their contribution to overall results. However, not all organizations share this view and many will wish to limit access to the system. Therefore, a software program should allow you to limit access to information by user, and develop user groups to simplify the measure publishing process.
- **Control of changes, data, and commentary entry:** Related to the preceding, not all users will necessarily be required to make changes, enter data, or provide result commentaries. Only system administrators should have the power to change measures, and only assigned users will have access to entering data and commentaries.

Evaluating the Vendor

With the large and growing number of players in this market, you'll be presented with a wide array of software choices from both industry veterans and upstarts attempting to disrupt the status quo. Either way, performing a little due diligence on the vendor is always a good idea.

- **Pricing:** As with any investment of this magnitude, pricing is a critical component of the overall decision. To make an informed decision, remember to include all dimensions of the total cost to purchase and maintain the software. This includes the per-user license fees, any maintenance fees, costs related to new releases, training costs, as well as salaries and benefits of system administrators.

- **Viability of the vendor:** Is this provider in for the long term or will any vicissitudes of the economy spell their demise? Since they're in the business of providing Scorecard software, you would expect them to steer their own course using the Balanced Scorecard. Ask them to review their Scorecard results with you. For reasons of confidentiality they may have to disguise some of the actual numbers but you should still glean valuable information on the organization's future prospects.

- **References and experience:** By examining the profiles of past clients you can determine the breadth and depth of experience the vendor has accumulated. While no two implementations are identical, it will be reassuring to know the software company has completed an installation in your industry. References are especially important. When discussing the vendor with other organizations that have been through the process, quiz them on the vendor's technical skills, consulting and training competence, and ability to complete the work on time and on budget.

- **Long-term service:** You'll inevitably experience bumps in the road as you implement your new reporting software. Bugs hidden deep in the program will be detected, patches will be required, and thus a lifeline to the vendor is crucial. How much support are they willing to offer, and at what cost? Do you have a dedicated representative for your organization or are you at the mercy of their call center? These are just a couple of questions to ask. And never forget that software companies owe a lot to us, the users. New functions and features are very often the product of intense lobbying on behalf of function-starved users who sometimes end up knowing more about the product than the vendor. So don't be shy with your requests.

Exhibit 7.5 displays an easy-to-use template that will assist you in ranking various software choices. This example includes only the configuration and design elements, but you can expand it to include all aspects of the decision. In this example, the configuration and design items have been weighted at 50 percent of the total decision. Specific elements comprising the category are listed in the first column, and the competing vendors are shown in the third, fourth, and fifth columns. Each vendor is accorded a score out of a possible 10 points demonstrating how well it satisfies each element of the decision. For example, vendors 1 and 3 each have easy-to-use setup wizards and are awarded

Criteria	Weight	Vendor 1	2	3
Configuration and Design	50%			
Setup wizards		10	9	10
Time to implement		9	10	10
User interface/display		8	8	10
Various Scorecard designs		8	9	10
Number of measures		9	9	10
Strategies, objectives, measures, targets, initiatives, and cause and effect		8	7	10
Strategy maps		8	7	10
Multiple locations		8	5	10
Cascading Scorecards		7	8	10
Descriptions and definitions		5	9	10
Assignment of owners		10	10	10
Various unit types		6	10	10
Varied reporting frequencies		6	10	10
Relative weights		10	8	10
Aggregate disparate elements		9	7	10
Multiple comparatives		10	10	10
Graphic status indicators		6	9	10
Dual polarity		5	10	10
Personal preferences		5	10	10
Helpful help screens		9	8	10
Levels of detail		7	8	10
Total		163	181	210
Total Points		38.80	43.10	50.00

EXHIBIT 7.5   Ranking the Software Alternatives

10 points. On many elements of the analysis, subjectivity is sure to make its way into the decision. All vendors may offer the option of graphically displaying your strategy map, for example. Your point decision will then be based on the ease of importing the Strategy Map, graphical appearance, and so on. Once all evaluations have been made, the points are totaled for each vendor. In this

example, vendor 3 has scored perfect 10s on all points and therefore receives the full 50 points available.

Developing Your Own Balanced Scorecard Reporting System

Investing in a technological solution to report your Scorecard results is neither a guarantee nor a prerequisite of success. Long before software companies sensed the burgeoning Scorecard opportunity, many early adopters were blazing their own trail with paper-based reports created on desktop computers. The success of the Balanced Scorecard today is due in large part to the efforts and tenacity of these pioneers who quickly grasped, and gained, the Scorecard benefits of alignment, accountability, and strategy execution with nary a thought to graphic user interfaces or data import functions.

Necessity is the mother of invention, and when it comes to building in-house Scorecard applications, creativity can surge. I've witnessed everything from humble paper reports with a few graphs and charts, to large white boards custom-designed to hold Scorecard data, to relatively sophisticated intranet applications. The chief executive of one client of mine, known for his creativity and often quirky solutions, devised a unique approach to the reporting challenge. He created a three-sided board, about 6 feet tall, complete with wheels for ease of transport. Each month results were posted on the board: corporate-measure updates on one side, key strategic initiatives on a second side, and, probably the most viewed of the three, the monthly incentive-compensation calculator on the third side. The wheels turned out to be the greatest innovation, however, transforming the device from a wacky conversation piece to a roaming meeting agenda. The CEO insisted his managers roll the board into conference rooms when conducting meetings, and use the posted results to stimulate discussions on corporate and business unit progress. When not roaming the hallways, the board was posted in common areas such as the company's foyer—where it caused more than one unsuspecting visitor to cast a quizzical double take—and the cafeteria where, coffee stains notwithstanding, the board served as grist for many a lunchtime conversation. The total cost of this investment was minimal but the payback in the form of enthusiasm and frank discussion has been substantial.

Your choice of reporting formats will depend on a number of variables, including the resources you're willing to expend, available expertise to craft the reports, and the preferences of your senior managers. Here are a couple of key considerations to keep in mind before developing any in-house reporting tool.

◼ **Before producing the first manual Balanced Scorecard report, create a mock-up with dummy results:** Circulate it to the executive group for their approval. This is important, since senior leaders may have different style preferences and wishes. By creating a mock-up, the team has the opportunity to incorporate executive feedback into the process and design a reporting tool that satisfies all.

◼ **Be cognizant of the data collection issues that may accompany your in-house solution:** Virtually all software solutions will provide bridges from the system to various data sources spread throughout your organization. Should you build your own system, however, manual data entry is a distinct possibility. Perhaps the least favorable association for the Balanced Scorecard is with the word redundancy. If those charged with the task of loading Scorecard data feel it is a task being duplicated in other areas, resistance, if not downright anarchy, will surely follow. Manual data entry also introduces typing errors to the performance data. Unreliable data is a huge Scorecard momentum killer.

Style, cultural resonance, and creative flair are important elements when creating your Scorecard-reporting solution, but what matters most is, as noted in the opening of this section, a visually compelling tool that quickly lets people know whether you are winning or losing your strategy execution battle.

 ## NOTES

1. Michael C. Mankins, "Stop Wasting Valuable Time," *Harvard Business Review* (September, 2004): 58–65.
2. Julia Neyman and Julie Snider, "USA Today Snapshots," *USA Today*, November 14, 2004.
3. John F. Kennedy, *Profiles in Courage*, new ed. (New York: Harper Collins, 2003), 27.
4. James Surowiecki, *The Wisdom of Crowds* (New York: Doubleday, 2004), xv.
5. Patrick Lencioni, *Death by Meeting* (San Francisco: Jossey-Bass, 2004), 228.
6. Surowiecki, *The Wisdom of Crowds*, 183–184.
7. Michael Beer and Russell A. Eisenstat, "How to Have an Honest Conversation About Your Business Strategy," *Harvard Business Review* (February 2004): 82–89.
8. Mankins, "Stop Wasting Valuable Time."
9. CoachUp.com. "The Separation Is in The Preparation" – 5 Steps to Be Successful Like Seattle Seahawks Quarterback Russell Wilson." Available at blog. coachup.com/2014/01/29/the-separation-is-in-thepreparation-5-steps-to-be-successful-like-seattle-seahawks-quarterback-russell-wilson/.

10. Jeroen De Flander, "The Execution Shortcut" (Brussels: The Performance Factory, 2013), 136.
11. Robert Simons, "Stress Test Your Strategy," *Harvard Business Review* (November 2010).
12. Ed Barrows and Andy Neely, *Managing Performance in Turbulent Times; Analytics and Insight* (Hoboken, NJ: John Wiley & Sons, Inc., 2012), Kindle edition, location 3491–3499.
13. Walter Isaacson, *Einstein* (New York: Simon & Schuster, 2007), 548.
14. Thomas A. Stewart and Louise O'Brien, "Execution Without Excuses," *Harvard Business Review* (March 2005): 102–111.
15. John Hamm, "The Five Messages Leaders Must Manage," *Harvard Business Review* (May 2006): 114–123.
16. Joseph Schumpeter, "Fail Often, Fail Well," *The Economist*, April 16, 2011.
17. Tina Rosenberg, "The Power of Talking to Your Baby," *New York Times Opinionator*, April 10, 2013.
18. Chris Zook and James Allen, *Repeatability: Build Enduring Businesses for a World of Constant Change* (Boston: Harvard Business Review Press, 2012).
19. Jim Collins, *Good to Great* (New York: Harper Business, 2001).
20. Larry Bossidy and Ram Charan, *Execution* (New York: Crown Business, 2002), 128.
21. Kelly McGonigal, *The Willpower Instinct: How Self-Control Works, Why It Matters, and What You Can Do To Get More of It* (New York: Avery, 2011), Kindle edition, location 1137.
22. Chris McChesney, Sean Covey, and Jim Huling, *The Four Disciplines of Execution: Achieving Your Wildly Important* (New York: Free Press, 2012), Kindle edition, location 1442.
23. Christoper Palazzolo and Kent Smack, "The Four Steps to BSC Software Selection," *Balanced Scorecard Report* (November–December, 2002): 15–16.

CHAPTER EIGHT

Let Everyone Demonstrate Their Contribution by Cascading the Balanced Scorecard

THERE IS A CHARMING STORY, perhaps apocryphal, about former President Lyndon B. Johnson touring Cape Canaveral during the space race to the moon. During his visit, the President came across a man mopping the floor, and asked him, "What's your position here?" The gentleman looked up from his pail and proudly replied, "I'm helping to send a man to the moon, Mr. President." Such is the power of alignment, when every person, regardless of role or rank, possesses a clear line of sight between their job and the organization's loftiest goals.

You may not be sending a man to the moon, or maybe you are. Whatever you're working towards requires the total commitment and alignment of all your people. This chapter discusses how the Balanced Scorecard framework can be used to drive organizational alignment from top to bottom through the process of cascading. We'll explore what the concept is all about, why it's critical to both employees and the organization, and examine techniques you can use to develop aligned Scorecards at your company.

WHAT IS CASCADING?

In a poll conducted by Harris Interactive of 23,000 U.S. residents employed full time, only 37 percent said they have a clear understanding of what their organization is trying to achieve and why. The same study discovered that only 9 percent believe their work teams had clear, measurable goals.[1] Another report, performed by consulting firm Watson Wyatt, obtained similar results, with just under half (49 percent) of employees saying they understand the steps their companies are taking to reach new business goals. In reviewing the data, one researcher said: "There is tremendous positive impact to the bottom line when employees see strong connections between company goals and their jobs. Many employees aren't seeing that connection."[2] It's clear that organizations benefit greatly when employees see the connection between what they do everyday and how those actions affect overall goals.

Cascading the Balanced Scorecard is a method designed to bridge the considerable learning gap that exists in most organizations. Specifically, cascading refers to the process of developing Balanced Scorecards at lower levels (anything and everything below the corporate level) of your organization. When I use the phrase Balanced Scorecard in this context, I am referring to the overall process. Some organizations will cascade both strategy maps of objectives and Balanced Scorecards of measures from top to bottom, while others will choose to create just one high-level strategy map, and cascade measures only. We'll return to that issue later in the chapter.

Cascaded Scorecards align with your highest-level Balanced Scorecard by identifying the objectives and measures lower-level groups will track in order to gauge their contribution to overall success. Some objectives and measures will be used throughout the organization, and appear on every Scorecard. Employee engagement is a good example. However, in many respects the real value of cascaded Scorecards is evident from the unique objectives and measures lower-level groups engineer to signal their specific contribution to overall strategy implementation. When I introduced this concept to one client, a participant half-jokingly commented, "So you're not talking about the stuff I use to clean my dishes?" No, we're not talking about Cascade dishwasher detergent here, but the cascading process will clean away something far more important—the misunderstanding and confusion existing between employee and organizational goals.

Every organization today must make continuous learning a core competency in order to survive the unprecedented changes we face. Cascading facilitates learning by fostering a two-way flow of information up and down the organizational hierarchy. As Scorecards are created at lower levels of the organization, employees of every function and rank are given the opportunity to demonstrate how their actions can lead to improved results for everyone. Simultaneously, as results are analyzed across the firm, leaders benefit from the ability to view results that span their organization. Analysis is no longer limited to a few high-level indicators that must serve as abstractions for an entire company; instead, cascaded Scorecards provide real-time data for decision making, resource allocation, and most importantly, strategic learning (see Exhibit 8.1).

In his book on Olympic rowing, *The Amateurs*, David Halberstam writes:

> When most oarsmen talked about their perfect moments in a boat, they referred not so much to winning a race but to the feel of the boat, all eight oars in the water together, the synchronization almost perfect. In moments like that, the boat seemed to lift right out of the water. Oarsmen called that the moment of swing. When a boat has swing, its motion seems almost effortless.[3]

EXHIBIT 8.1 Knowledge and Information Flow Two Ways When Cascading the Balanced Scorecard

I can't imagine a better description of the graceful power that can be achieved when people work together towards a common goal. Cascading holds the promise to bring that same feeling of effortless motion to your organization.

Not only does the cascading process align employee actions with strategy, it is consistently cited as a key factor in the success of Balanced Scorecard programs. In fact, Kaplan and Norton have discovered that the greatest gap between Balanced Scorecard Hall of Fame organizations (those achieving breakthrough results with the system) and all others occurs in aligning the organization to the strategy: "This demonstrates that effective organizational alignment, while difficult to achieve, has probably the biggest payoff of any management practice."[4] This is not surprising when you consider that through alignment you harness the greatest resource known to business: the minds and hearts of your employees. Successful Scorecard implementers know that those on the front line must embrace and use this tool if it is to reach the level of effectiveness it's capable of achieving. Cascading the Scorecard allows you to reach your entire organization and supply them with the means of answering the critical question, "How do I add value and make a meaningful contribution to our success?" The answer lies in the objectives and measures embedded in Balanced Scorecards throughout your organization.

 ## THE SEARCH FOR MEANING

Man's Search for Meaning is among the most powerful and gripping books I have ever read; the Austrian psychiatrist Victor Frankl describes his experiences as he clung to life in a Nazi concentration camp. He had lost everything, and yet it was his discovery that a greater purpose can allow us to rise above even the bleakest of circumstances that led to his psychological emancipation from the Nazis. He used the experience in the development of logotherapy, which focuses on the meaning of human existence as well as man's search for such a meaning.[5]

Does a search for meaning end upon entering the workplace? Does the first ring from the phone on our desk erase any existential cravings? The answer is an unequivocal no. Now, more than ever, people hold expectations beyond a paycheck from their jobs; they demand a higher purpose. The organization's guiding mission and vision compel today's employees who are asking, "Why is my organization important to society, how does it contribute something of value?" A lack of alignment between personal objectives and broad organizational goals obscures any hope of discovering true meaning through our work. Cascading the Balanced Scorecard restores the pledge of organizations to help all employees find meaning in their chosen professions. The creation of objectives and measures that forge a direct link to high-level goals provides all employees with the opportunity to demonstrate that what they're doing is indeed critical to success.

 ## THE CASCADING PROCESS

One very successful corporation that grasps the importance of alignment is Honda Motors. This recognition most likely stems from their founder Soichiro Honda, who described the Sacred Obligations of Senior Leadership this way:

1. Craft a vision: What we will be
2. Create goals: What four or five things must we do to get there
3. Alignment: Translate the work of each person into alignment with the goals

He's really describing the process of cascading performance measures very well. First, we craft the vision that will guide the organization. Next, we develop key performance measures we can track, and finally we translate the work of each person into alignment with the goals. Mr. Honda didn't go on to say how to create alignment, but we now know the best way to do that is through cascading performance objectives and measures. In this section we'll examine how you can successfully align employee objectives and measures throughout the organization.

Develop Implementation Principles

Stop for a moment to reflect upon how far you will have traveled to get to this point in your Balanced Scorecard implementation. It began as an idea: perhaps someone read an article, attended a seminar, or learned of the Scorecard from a colleague. You then undertook the challenging tasks of forming your team, gathering materials, reviewing your mission, vision, and strategy, and finally developing objectives on a strategy map and measures on your Scorecard. It would be an understatement to suggest that you learned a thing or two about the Balanced Scorecard, and its implementation at your organization, along the way. Before you begin your cascading efforts, pause for a moment to reflect on and catalog those key insights.

The Balanced Scorecard system you created is a true team effort. Your cross-functional team contributed the knowledge that exists in every far corner of your company to craft a strategy map and Scorecard that clearly articulates your strategic story. However, the cascading process may represent more of a diffused effort going forward. Your team members may now be tasked with the responsibility of leading the development of cascaded Scorecards within their work group or business unit. Consistent implementation practices across the organization are an absolute must should you hope to gain the benefits offered by true strategic alignment. To ensure your cascading efforts are consistent and aligned, consider convening your Balanced Scorecard team, Office of Strategy Management (OSM), and any other individuals who will have a hand in leading the development of cascaded Scorecards. A one-day session where you review the lessons you've learned along the way and specifically document the principles you expect to employ going forward will go a long way towards ensuring that your Scorecards paint a consistent picture. Outlined below are several key elements to consider when developing your cascading plan.

Cascading Strategy Maps and Balanced Scorecards, or Just Scorecards

The initial question to answer is: Will you cascade both strategy maps and Scorecards, or simply Scorecards? My database of clients is split on this, although if pressed to do the math, I would estimate a slight majority cascade both elements of the framework. My recommendation is to cascade both, since a strategy map provides a powerful communication tool that can be employed in any unit, department, or group to signify the key elements of success, with the accompanying measures providing the link to accountability for results. Most practitioners agree with the value of communication but argue that creating maps throughout the enterprise is an unnecessary step that can lead to paralysis by analysis—too many maps, spawning an abundance of unique measures, that unleash a heavy administrative burden to manage.

Balanced Scorecard Perspectives

Will all groups be required to use the four perspectives of the Balanced Scorecard: financial, customer, internal process, and learning and growth? This assumes you used the standard roster. If not, the question still applies—will you require all groups to adopt the perspectives you've chosen at the highest level of the organization? Or, will individual groups have the liberty to develop their own perspectives, and perspective names? Personalizing the map and

Balanced Scorecard may produce benefits in the form of enhanced buy-in and local understanding, but dissimilar terms scattered throughout the organization may lead to confusion. Most clients of mine prefer that all Scorecards use the perspective names adopted at the highest level of the company.

Number of Objectives and Measures

Will you impose a limit on the number of objectives and measures any group may have as part of their Balanced Scorecard? Keep in mind that as you begin cascading the Scorecard you could quickly generate dozens, if not hundreds, of performance measures throughout the organization. My advice is to avoid choosing one single number and instead focus on a not-to-exceed total of objectives and measures.

Use of Corporate Objectives and Measures

Corporate in this case refers to your highest-level strategy map and Scorecard. When developing their maps and Scorecards, will groups be required to use certain corporate objectives and measures, or have carte blanche in developing unique indicators that tell their story? Some organizations will ask groups to use the same objectives and measures (whenever possible) as those used at the highest level. The goal is to encourage uniformity and consistency throughout the organization. A possible disadvantage of this approach is limiting the creativity of groups as they determine how they can best influence high-level objectives and measures. As a compromise, organizations will sometimes impose a limited number of required objectives and measures on all groups, while also including shared objectives among interdependent groups and, of course, allowing unique additions as well.

ENSURE UNDERSTANDING OF YOUR HIGHEST-LEVEL STRATEGY MAP AND SCORECARD BEFORE CASCADING

You may have hesitated to write objective statements as described in Chapter 5, or bristled at the thought of completing the data dictionaries presented in Chapter 6, but you're about to receive the payback for those arduous tasks. They are just a couple of the tools you can use to ensure everyone involved in the cascading process has a detailed understanding of your highest-level strategy map and Balanced Scorecard.

Your corporate-level map and Scorecard represent the starting point for your cascading journey. They contain the objectives and measures that weave through the four perspectives, informing everyone of your strategic story. For those individuals shouldering the responsibility of leading cascading efforts, in-depth knowledge of the strategy map and Scorecard is vital. Imagine someone leading a cascading session in a low-level department and beginning the workshop with a comment like this, "Okay, we say here on the strategy map we're going to delight the customer. I don't really know what that means. What do you think?" Not exactly the stuff oratorical legends are made of. Contrast that with someone who possesses a deep understanding of high-level objectives and measures. He or she is in a position to offer something of this nature: "Delight the customer is our first customer objective. This is critical to our strategy of expanding into new services since current clients are our best source of referral information. We'll measure it using quarterly surveys consisting of five questions . . . " Context has been established, which will allow for thought-provoking and beneficial conversations about the objective.

Understanding your strategy map and Scorecard is achieved mainly through communication and education, which is accomplished by utilizing:

- Your intranet
- Presentations from the OSM and Scorecard team members
- The strategy map
- The Scorecard
- Brochures
- Newsletters
- Town hall meetings

Influence Is the Key to Cascading

The goal of cascading is to allow all groups within your organization the opportunity to demonstrate how their actions contribute to overall success. In describing this process, I assume you are cascading the highest-level strategy map to all levels of your organization. In other words, low-level groups will have the opportunity to develop their own strategy maps that offer their aligned objectives. Given this assumption, their next step would be the creation of measures for each of the objectives appearing on their strategy map. Let's use Exhibit 8.2 to review this concept. To fit the page, the exhibit has been truncated, with each perspective displaying objectives (the domain of the strategy map) along with measures, targets, and initiatives (found in a Balanced Scorecard).

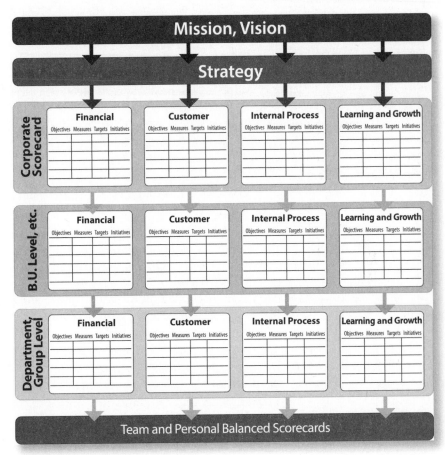

EXHIBIT 8.2 The Cascading Process

It all begins with your highest-level strategy map, what most would refer to as the corporate-level or organization-wide map. The objectives appearing on this strategy map represent what you consider to be the critical variables driving your success. Therefore, every map subsequently created, at all levels of the organization, should link back to this document.

The first level of cascading occurs as business units (as described in Exhibit 8.2; your terminology may differ) examine the high-level strategy map and ask, "Which of these objectives can we influence?" The answers to that question will form the basis for their own strategy map. Chances are, they won't be able to exert an impact on each and every objective appearing on the high-level map. After all, organizations build value by combining the disparate skills of all employees within every function. Therefore, each group should rightly focus on the objectives over which they may exert an influence. However, if a group is unable to demonstrate a link to any objectives, you would have to seriously consider what value they are adding to the whole. The business unit may choose to use the language shown in the high-level strategy map or create objectives that more accurately reflect the true essence of how they add value to the organization.

Once the business unit develops its own strategy map, one that aligns with the highest-level map, and demonstrates how the unit influences success, their job transitions to the development of performance measures for each objective. Once again, they should return to the top and determine if measures used on the highest-level Balanced Scorecard are applicable to their operations. Some objectives and measures, often in the financial and learning and growth objectives, will flow freely from top to bottom in an organization. For example, it's quite common to see an objective such as "Enhance employee engagement" appear in the learning and growth perspective of the top-level strategy map, with the corresponding measure of "Employee engagement score" materializing on the Balanced Scorecard. Every group within the organization could adopt this objective and measure with no change to the wording of either.

Once business units have developed strategy maps and Balanced Scorecards, the groups below them are ready to take part in the process. Individual departments will now review the strategy map and Scorecard of the business unit to which they report and determine which of the objectives they can influence. Their map is formed by making that determination. With a strategy map formed, they develop performance measures to gauge their success. Once again, they may use similarly termed objectives and measures, or develop unique names for their elements.

Let's look at an example of cascading using a fictional city government organization. Exhibit 8.3 provides excerpts from strategy maps and Scorecards at three levels of this organization, which will demonstrate the principles of cascading just discussed.

Within the customer perspective of their strategy map, the city has chosen an objective of providing safe, convenient transportation. To gauge their effectiveness on this objective they will measure the increase in average ridership of public transportation. A 10 percent increase for the year is the target at which they'll aim.

The Department of Transportation is one of several business units within the city. When developing its own strategy map, organizers began by closely inspecting the city's map to determine which of the objectives they could influence. As is the case with all city business units, the Department

Map and Scorecard Excerpt:
Local City Government

Perspective	Objective	Measure	Target
Customer	Provide safe, convenient transportation	Increase in average ridership of public transportation	10%

Map and Scorecard Excerpt:
Department of Transportation

Perspective	Objective	Measure	Target
Customer	Provide safe, convenient transportation	Percentage of fleet available	90%

Map and Scorecard Excerpt:
Operations Group

Perspective	Objective	Measure	Target
Customer	Provide safe, convenient transportation	Percentage of vehicle repairs completed within 24 hours	75%

EXHIBIT 8.3   Cascading the Balanced Scorecard

of Transportation is anxious to show how their important work links to the city's overall goals. When reviewing the city's customer perspective, they see the objective of providing safe, convenient transportation and feel they have a strong impact on this objective. They, too, have a goal of providing safe and convenient transportation so they carry the objective forward to their own strategy map with no change in the wording. However, the measure of increased ridership is not considered appropriate for them. It's a critical indicator, but they would like to develop a measure that indicates how *they influence* ridership. The team concludes that by ensuring the city's entire public transportation fleet is available every day they can help the city increase ridership. Hence, they measure the percentage of the fleet that is available.

There are several groups comprising the Department of Transportation, one of which is the Operations Department. Among their many responsibilities is ensuring the city's fleet of vehicles is serviced efficiently. When developing their strategy map they begin by reviewing the map of the business unit to which they report, the Department of Transportation. Upon review they see the objective of providing safe and convenient transportation. They feel they can have an impact on this objective, and thus choose it for their own customer perspective; they also adopt the language used in the objective with no change necessary. They ask themselves how they might influence the measure of fleet availability and realize that if they're able to complete vehicle repairs in a timely fashion, the department will have more vehicles at its disposal, and the public will have more riding options. They strive to complete at least 75 percent of vehicle repairs within 24 hours.

Although each of the three strategy maps profiled in this example share a common objective, the measure chosen for the Scorecard at each level is representative of what is necessary for the group to contribute to overall success. Those linked objectives and performance measures are the key to ensuring alignment throughout the city. Employees in the operations department are now able to conclusively demonstrate how their activities link back to a key goal for the city. Likewise, city officials can rest assured that operations personnel are focused on the necessary elements to drive value for the city's citizens.

Support Group Balanced Scorecards

Support groups such as human resources, finance, and information technology (IT) often feel like the Rodney Dangerfield of the organization: They get no respect! And, in fact, some reading this may feel I'm contributing to that predicament by using the moniker support group. No disrespect intended, we're all well aware that corporate resource groups, shared service, support groups— whatever term you choose—provide valuable offerings, without which actual service delivery to customers would be compromised severely. However, there exists among many firms a temptation to label these groups as pure overhead and diminish their valuable roles.

The Balanced Scorecard can change all that. Support groups should have the same opportunity as any other department to illustrate their contributions, and the Scorecard provides the forum. Typically, units that have the responsibility for providing services to the entire organization will look to the high-level organizational strategy map and Scorecard when developing their own objectives and measures. Their quest is to examine the objectives on the corporate strategy map and contemplate how the group plays a role in their success.

In addition to demonstrating alignment with the highest-level strategy map and Balanced Scorecard, support-unit maps and Scorecards typically display a number of common themes across the perspectives.[6] Within the financial perspective, we would expect the group to report on both the efficiency and effectiveness of their operations. The customer perspective of a support group outlines how the group will add value to *their* customers—other departments and the organization as a whole—and customarily includes objectives centering on customer knowledge and solution delivery. Internally, support groups must focus on forging partnerships and working collaboratively with other departments, operating at the upper bands of high efficiency, and innovating to produce the solutions their customers demand. Finally, within the learning and growth perspective the group will turn the spotlight inward, ensuring their team possesses the skills they require, the information necessary to deliver on internal and customer objectives, and a supportive work environment.

Unlike their colleagues working with external customers and other stakeholders of the organization, support-group employees are often shielded from much of the direct service provision taking place. Cascading the Scorecard to these units lifts the strategy veil and provides a much-needed line of sight between support work and the mission of the organization.

Personal Balanced Scorecards

In a survey conducted by Salary.com of 2,000 employees and 330 human resource (HR) professionals, the researchers found a glaring, but probably not entirely surprising, contradiction: 66 percent of HR professionals believed their company's performance reviews were effective, while only 39 percent of employees echoed that view.[7] It seems as though the annual performance appraisal process is one fraught with issues for both management and employees alike. Companies will expend significant energy in promoting a formal appraisal process, issuing memos, providing templates with information on the competencies and behaviors they desire to see, and training employees on how to develop an effective plan. However, there is often little follow up beyond this initial splash of activity. Former General Electric (GE) CEO turned corporate curmudgeon Jack Welch blames it on the paper chase, suggesting, "If your evaluation system involves more than two pages of paperwork per person, something is wrong!"[8] One of Welch's apostles at GE, Larry Bossidy, who has been a very successful CEO in his own right, agrees with the succinct approach to performance reviews advocated by his former boss. He suggests a simple one-page form listing what the employee does well, what he can improve upon, and how they can work together to fill any gaps.[9]

When I discuss the performance-appraisal process with new clients I'm often greeted with rolling eyes and shaking heads. Even for those organizations that do follow up on the appraisal process and hold review sessions with employees, they are invariably behind schedule. Amazing how this critical activity involving the most precious of resources tends to get pushed to the back burner. But when we critically examine the process at most organizations, there is little wonder why this sorry state of affairs exists. Very often the performance ratings are completely subjective and based purely on a manager's or supervisor's limited view of employee performance. This does little to engender trust on the part of employees and instead creates suspicion of the process. Throughout the performance period there is infrequent feedback to employees, and even when feedback is offered it typically concerns outcomes and results, not behaviors. But the most egregious omission of the process is the lack of alignment between personal and organizational goals. Employees have little or no idea how success on their performance review will positively impact the company's success.

Cascading the Balanced Scorecard to the individual employee level can mitigate, if not entirely eliminate, many of the issues we find with the normal performance-appraisal process. Here are some of the many benefits to be derived from having employees develop their own personal Balanced Scorecards.

- **Build Awareness of the Balanced Scorecard:** Develop Scorecards at the individual level to provide another opportunity to share with all employees the principles and techniques inherent in the Balanced Scorecard system.
- **Generate Commitment to the Scorecard:** There is little doubt that increased involvement in virtually any activity will tend to increase commitment to that cause. So it goes with the Balanced Scorecard. Have employees learn about the Scorecard and develop their own series of linked objectives and measures to boost support from this critical audience.
- **Increase Comprehension of Aligned Scorecards:** In order to develop their individual Scorecards, employees must first understand the objectives and measures appearing in all cascaded Scorecards from the high-level organizational Scorecard to the business unit Scorecard to their team or department's Scorecard. Thus cascading supplies an outstanding training opportunity.

- **Offer a Clear Line of Sight from Employee Goals to Organizational Strategy:** Develop personal Balanced Scorecards that align to team or department Scorecards so every employee can demonstrate how their specific actions are making a difference and leading to improved overall results.
- **Builds Support for the Goal-Setting Process:** Use the Balanced Scorecard to breathe new life into often tired and irrelevant employee goal-setting processes.

The format you follow for personal Balanced Scorecards is limited only by your imagination. Exhibit 8.4 provides one possible version of a template your employees can utilize to develop personal Balanced Scorecards. This template is based on the cascading efforts of an electric utility organization. The document merges two key areas: cascaded Scorecards and personal development plans. To maximize educational and practical value, the

Personal Balanced Scorecard

Name: Department: Date Covered:

Mission: Provide low-cost energy to help our communities prosper
Vision: Be the #1 energy supplier by 2020
Strategy: Utilize state of the art technology and human capital principles to drive profitable growth

Perspective	Corporate Scorecard Measures	Business Unit Measures	Department Measures
$ **Financial**	F1—Return on Equity	F1—Service Agreement Costs	F1—Administrative Spending F2—Capital Spending F3—Miscellaneous Revenue
Customer	C1—Customer Loyalty Rating C2—Sales Volume	C1—Customer Loyalty Rating C2—Outage Performance Index	C1—Customer Loyalty Rating C2—Meeting Commitments C3—Meter Reading C4—Call Center Performance C5—Reliability Index
Internal Process	I1—Environmental Performance I2—Number of New Products and Services	I1—Environmental Performance I2—Service Quality	I1—System Maintenance I2—Service Quality
Learning and Growth	E1—Safety Rating E2—Employee Commitment Rating	E1—Number of Accidents E2—Employee Commitment Rating	E1—Number of Personal Accidents E2—Number of Vehicle Accidents E3—Employee Commitment Rating

EXHIBIT 8.4 Personal Balanced Scorecard Template

Department Manager - Personal Balanced Scorecard

Perspective	Objective	Measure	Weight	Threshold	Midpoint	Stretch	Related PDP Goals
Customer 25%	Increase Customer Loyalty	Presentations to local trade groups	40%	10	15	20	• Develop five new professional contacts this year.
	Ensure Outage Reliability	Plant visits	60%	20	30	50	• Join 2 trade associations.
Learning and Growth 25%	Promote Safety	Departmental injuries	60%	2	1	0	• Attend safety training course.
	Develop Skill Sets	% Employees completing business education	15%	80%	90%	100%	• Complete facilitator training.
	Develop Skill Sets	Complete personal development plan	10%	—	—	—	• Complete PDP by mid-year.
	Enhance Employee Commitment	Departmental commitment rating	15%	75	80	85	• Support employee volunteer efforts.
Internal Process 25%	Provide Meter Reading & Meter changes	% on time readings	50%	90%	95%	100%	
	Enhance System Maintenance	Conduct plant audits	50%	25	40	45	
Financial 25%	Minimize Administrative Spending	Local costs	55%	Budget	Budget less 1%	Budget less 2%	• Complete 2 courses in finance.
	Grow Revenue	Increase departmental miscellaneous revenue	45%	5% increase	10% increase	25% increase	• Lead departmental brainstorming sessions on revenue enhancement.

EXHIBIT 8.4 (Continued)

document is split into two pages. Page one serves the important purpose of outlining the mission, vision, and strategy, and establishing a line of sight for the employee. The remainder of the page illustrates the cascading Scorecards relevant to that individual. Summarized versions of the organizational, business unit, and departmental Balanced Scorecards are provided. Displaying this individualized cascading demonstrates the path that has led to this point and greatly facilitates the completion of the personal Balanced Scorecard on page two.

While we might consider page one a learning opportunity, page two has a more specific purpose—allowing the individual employee to define the specific objectives and measures he will pursue to help his department reach its objectives and outline the action steps he'll take to achieve success. The first step for the individual is to develop the objectives, measures and targets that comprise his individual Scorecard. By displaying all linked Scorecards on page one, with discussion and coaching the development of personal goals should flow quite smoothly. Next, the employee may begin to construct a personal development plan (PDP) based on the goals established on their Scorecard. This document may or may not replace the need for a formal PDP, but it will certainly facilitate the development of that document by identifying the key areas of focus for the individual.

This section focused almost exclusively on the benefits employees can derive from developing personal Balanced Scorecards—knowledge of the Scorecard system, understanding of organizational objectives and measures, and alignment with overall goals. However, senior managers also have much to gain from this process. Cascading to this level allows managers to gain a high level of visibility into the specific actions contributing to, or detracting from, overall organizational results. Take the case of one travel agency I worked with. Senior managers at this organization monitor a productivity index that tracks the number of tickets issued per hour by individual agents. The measure appears on the corporate Balanced Scorecard but is also cascaded down to the individual agent level. When actual results began to lag expectations, senior managers looked to their cascading Balanced Scorecards for an answer. Examining regional performance (the first level of cascading) on the productivity index provided little information, since most areas were generating similar results. However, when managers examined specific site Scorecards they found some very interesting deviations that were driving the high-level corporate outcome. It turns out that agents who catered to professional service firms (attorneys, accountants, consultants) were producing consistently lower results than other groups. When questioned, they noted that clients from these firms were frequently changing plans, which made it difficult to actually issue a ticket. Without the questions spawned by the Balanced Scorecard, senior management could have made the faulty and dangerous assumption that these sites were simply poor performers and taken inappropriate action. Armed with the knowledge gleaned from cascaded Balanced Scorecards, managers were able to adjust the targets to more accurately reflect the nature of clients served by different sites.

Checking the Alignment of Cascaded Balanced Scorecards

We all know the many dangers inherent in making assumptions. The point was driven home for me in a razor-sharp way by a junior high school teacher who made his way to the blackboard one day and wrote a sentence that has remained with me to this day, I'm sure you've heard of it: "When you assume, you make an a** out of you and me." I can't remember if he actually spelled it out or not. Cascading the Balanced Scorecard is no different. The act of developing Scorecards up and down the organizational hierarchy can prove to be an exciting and liberating effort, but you must be sure there is true alignment existing from top to bottom. Assuming alignment where none exists could lead to unrealistic targets, missing measures, departments inadvertently working against one another, misallocated resources, and a whole lot of confused people.

As each level of cascading is completed, pause to review the Scorecards just created to validate the presence of alignment. Each chain of Scorecards should be evaluated to ensure the objectives and measures flow in a demonstrable pattern leading towards the objectives and measures embodied in the highest-level Scorecard. Upon conclusion of the critique, your OSM should meet with developers at lower levels and discuss any modifications that would improve the quality of their Scorecards. Exhibit 8.5 provides some additional things to look for when reviewing cascaded strategy maps and Scorecards.

Linkage to Related Maps and Scorecards:
Don't forget the key principle here is cascading—driving the Scorecard process to lower levels in the organization. Each strategy map and Balanced Scorecard should contain objectives and measures that influence the next group in the chain.

Linkage to Strategy:
The Balanced Scorecard is a tool for translating strategy. The objectives and measures appearing on cascaded maps and Scorecards should demonstrate a linkage to the organization's overarching strategy, and their achievement should signal progress towards the mission.

Appropriate Targets:
Target setting can be a difficult exercise requiring significant professional judgment. Ensure cascaded targets will lead to the fulfillment of higher-level targets throughout the chain.

Coverage of Key Objectives:
The chief tenet of cascading is that of influence. What can we do at our level to influence the next Scorecard in the chain? Not every group will influence every high-level objective and measure, but across the organization, the complete population of highest-level objectives and measures should receive adequate coverage.

Adherence to Cascading Principles:
Ensure cascaded maps and measures conform to the principles you developed; for example, consistent use of perspective names and number of objectives and measures permitted.

EXHIBIT 8.5   What to Look for When Reviewing Cascaded Strategy Maps and Scorecards

Making Cascading Work

The processes outlined above for creating Scorecards at all levels represent the textbook approach, and you'll be rewarded if you follow the guidance of focusing on how you can influence higher-level Scorecards. However, some organizations will experience challenges when cascading. The most common (and troubling) phrase I hear from those struggling to build cascaded Scorecards is: "Well, I guess we could measure _____" Whenever I hear that I know the group is trying to fit a square peg into a round hole, and missing the spirit of the exercise. What do I mean by fitting a square peg into a round hole? Chances are the group feels they must influence every objective on the corporate strategy map (or the map residing above them in the chain) and thus try to create measures that force fit with corporate objectives, causing them to suggest metrics that really don't matter or are irrelevant to them on a day-to-day basis. Additionally, the four perspectives themselves represent another problem for some people when they cascade. The perspectives can be viewed as limiting and artificial borders, constraining the group's thinking on what really matters for their success.

To help overcome these challenges and ensure the objectives and measures created are in fact valuable to those who will be steering their ship by them, consider preceding any cascading session with these questions:

- **What is your business unit/department/team's mission?** Whether it's written down or not, every group has a core purpose. Articulating it before cascading helps create necessary context for the task by allowing the group to achieve consensus on their purpose, which they can use as a stake in the ground when developing cascading objectives and measures.
- **How do you support the organization's mission and strategy?** In broad strokes, how does the group contribute to the company's success? This question will yield mostly process-related responses, but that's okay, as they can serve as the drivers of objectives and measures in the remaining perspectives.
- **What do you feel are the most important things you need to measure to gauge your group's success?** This question is designed to have participants think freely about what is necessary to succeed without the constraints or limits some may perceive the four perspectives representing. Later, when engaged in the actual cascading exercise, the measures generated here can be slotted in to the four perspectives, as well as additional

measures created to ensure the group's entire strategic story has been captured.

■ **What are the greatest strengths we can leverage in contributing to the organization's success?**[10] Related to the previous question, this one challenges your team to conjure up what they're best at to ensure those qualities are represented on their Scorecard.

■ **What weaknesses must we overcome in contributing to the organization's success?** The mirror of the question above, here the team is forced to consider what is holding them back in an effort to create measures that will gauge their ability to close performance gaps.

Even the most fit among us wouldn't simply hop off the sofa, grab their shoes, and hit the trail for a 10-mile run without first stretching—warming up the muscles and preparing the body for the work that lies ahead. Think of the questions above as the cascading equivalent to warming up and stretching. Answering them will ensure your groups are mentally loose, limber, and prepared to passionately document their unique contribution.

Really Making It Work

As with virtually every other aspect of the Balanced Scorecard system, for cascading to reach its potential you must have the support and assistance of senior leaders who recognize the importance of the exercise and are willing to lend a hand when necessary. Your senior executives must truly understand the Balanced Scorecard, how it works, and, perhaps most importantly, how they want to use it within the organization. The leader or leaders must know the organization's strategy extremely well and also have in-depth knowledge on the Scorecard objectives and measures—why they were chosen and why they're critical to strategy execution success.

The ideal cascading approach would see senior leaders (not the entire leadership team, just one or two representatives) engage in tandem with your OSM to work one-on-one with the leaders of each group for which a cascading Scorecard will be developed. Take the time and effort to first explain what they expect from the cascading and then work sequentially through the map and measures, critically examining each and every objective and measure, determining how the group will influence it. This could take at least half a day and most likely a whole day for each group, and thus represents a significant investment of executive time. It could entail weeks of executive time and effort to complete all the groups you wish to cascade. However, if your goal is true alignment, that's the level of commitment necessary.

Executives and OSM representatives must roll up their sleeves in these sessions and ensure each and every measure will prove useful to the group. For example, as measures are debated, they will have to insist that projects (strategic initiatives) will not be accepted in place of measures (as is frequently the case in cascading sessions), sloppy measure writing (with no numbers of any kind, for example) will not be tolerated, and measure frequencies greater than quarterly will be rejected. The leaders must say, when necessary, "This is what you are going to measure, and why." You want the team's buy-in and support, of course, but at the end of the day the organization needs to benefit from this exercise and for that to happen senior leaders must ensure that what should be measured is in fact being monitored. Next, conscientious leaders will insist that the groups or departments have regular meetings during which Scorecard measures are reviewed. Most likely the executives themselves will need to attend the first few to make certain the conversation is focused and strategic.

In the end it all boils down to executive commitment to the program. If they believe in it and want it to succeed, they need to be present and give it the attention it requires. Otherwise it's very likely that you'll achieve suboptimal results.

A Final Thought on Cascading

Of those items within your control, cascading may be the single most important ingredient of a successful Balanced Scorecard implementation. You can't control the level of executive sponsorship you receive, or predict any crisis that may derail your efforts. You can, however, make the decision to drive the power of the Balanced Scorecard system to all levels of your organization.

Developing a high-level strategy map and Scorecard is a great start, but how many people are really involved in the effort? Involvement is the key to ownership. If you want your employees to take true ownership of your collective success, let them carve out a share for themselves. Allow them to create a language of success with themselves at the center. Everyone wins as interest, alignment, accountability, knowledge, and results are all enhanced in the process.

 NOTES

1. Stephen R. Covey, *The 8th Habit* (New York: The Free Press, 2004), 2.
2. Stephen Taub, "Dazed and Confused," *CFO*, September 11, 2002.

3. Quoted in James Surowiecki, *The Wisdom of Crowds* (New York: Doubleday, 2004), 176.

4. David P. Norton and Randall H. Russell, "Best Practices in Managing the Execution of Strategy," *Balanced Scorecard Report*, (July–August 2004): 3.

5. Victor E. Frankl, *Man's Search for Meaning* (Boston: Beacon Press, 1992).

6. Robert S. Kaplan and David P. Norton, *Alignment* (Boston: Harvard Business School Press, 2006), 139.

7. Yasmin Ghahremani, "How'm I Doing?," *CFO*, February 2007, 21.

8. Jack Welch with Suzy Welch, *Winning* (New York: Harper Business, 2005), 104.

9. Larry Bossidy, "What Your Leader Expects of You," *Harvard Business Review* (April 2007): 58–65.

10. The final two questions are adapted from Chris McChesney, Sean Covey, and Jim Huling, *The Four Disciplines of Execution: Achieving Your Wildly Important Goals* (New York: Free Press, 2012), Kindle edition, location 2303.

CHAPTER NINE

Integrating Change Management Techniques to Drive Balanced Scorecard Success

T'S NO SECRET THAT CHANGE is difficult for many of us. In fact, studies suggest the number of people who voluntarily disengage from addictive or obsessive-compulsive behavior, even when their very lives are on the line, is shockingly low, at around 1 in 10.[1] Embracing even simple changes that could make our lives easier or more convenient has also been consistently resisted throughout time. Take the case of the telephone. When first introduced, many people avoided it because they felt it was almost supernatural. At that time hearing voices when nobody was present was a defining characteristic of insanity, and few people fathomed how it was possible that electricity could convey a human voice. Such was the fear that the *Providence Press* said, "It is difficult to really resist the notion that the powers of darkness are not in league with it."[2]

The challenge of change is amplified in the corporate world because we're dealing with the collective behavior of large groups of individuals, and any change efforts must take place while the company is actively operating, sort of like repairing a ship at sea. But adapt we must, should we hope to remain competitive in a world in which constant change and upheaval are the new status quo.

Throughout the book I've provided the latest tools and procedures to assist you in crafting a powerful strategy-execution system. The guidance has included a number of change-management recommendations. In this chapter I'm going to summarize the change tips (their original location in the book will be referenced) and add a few original ideas, because I believe utilizing change techniques represents the key to a successful Balanced Scorecard implementation. When I examine my roster of clients and differentiate those achieving breakthrough results from those who have struggled with the system, it is glaringly apparent that the difference always comes down to change. Organizations with the most robust Scorecard systems have harnessed change techniques throughout the development process to ensure the final product represents their best collective thinking and enjoys a foundation of buy-in and support. Upon completion of the initial model, those utilizing the tool to full advantage recognize and embrace the fact that Scorecard use must be accompanied by thoughtful change-management principles, which smooth the transition from the creation of a management system to its ongoing use. I encourage you to include the principles listed below (and others you may encounter yourself) in your Balanced Scorecard development.

 ## PREPARING FOR SCORECARD SUCCESS

Send Yourself a Postcard from the Future

Even your most ardent Scorecard supporters, those who understand the tool intellectually, and recognize the potential it promises, will most likely wonder exactly why you've chosen to implement it within your organization at this specific time. People are overwhelmed, and although the Scorecard can transform your strategy-execution efforts, most employees will initially sigh, wondering why you must add on yet another burdensome task. You must carefully answer the why question using both rational and emotional appeals. In Chapter 2 I suggested you send yourself a destination postcard that clearly and convincingly outlines why the Scorecard is necessary at this time in your history and how it will help you craft a more desirable future for the entire organization.

Start with a Provocative Action

There's a place for speeches, posters, and assorted Scorecard-emblazoned swag when setting on the path to building your Balanced Scorecard, but to really kick start your effort, and win your share of people's ever-dwindling attention, you need to shelve the rhetoric and start with an emotion-inducing, provocative action.

This approach worked for sixteenth-century Spanish explorer Hernan Cortes. Facing the increasing possibility of a mutinous crew, he didn't attempt to hold their loyalty with a fiery speech. Instead he took the very provocative step of scuttling his ships, effectively stranding his crew in Mexico. Here is another somewhat less dramatic, but no less effective, example of someone who recognized when it comes to igniting a spark of change, actions trump words every time. The CEO of a mid-sized company was disappointed because his people weren't taking advantage of 401(k) matching opportunities, when in fact he knew they could all use the money. He calculated how much they'd left on the table to be close to $10,000. In a provocative display to jolt them from their inertia, he stuffed $10,000 in a bag, brought it into a meeting, and dumped the cold hard cash on a table. The powerful sight of all the money they'd neglected put his staff on a quick path to action. In Chapter 2, you'll find more information on, and examples of, organizations that embraced the notion of showing rather than telling in order to ignite a dramatic change.

Shrink the Change to Overcome Skepticism

Several years ago a good friend of mine relocated from the west to the east coast of Canada. Rather than fly to his new home, he decided to drive the nearly 5,000 kilometers that separated the two locations. By his account, the first portion of the drive, across the endless straight line that cut through the Prairie Provinces, was by far the most difficult. "I thought it would never end," he told me later. So it is at the beginning of any long journey of change; the finish line seems to be another galaxy away from the starting point, and it's difficult to engender the energy to sustain the journey. In Chapter 2, we discussed the importance of shrinking the change. When you embark upon your Scorecard implementation, it's vital to show employees that you're not as far from the destination as it may appear. In the case of the Scorecard, you may have a newly minted strategy and a base of current-performance measures, perhaps even a culture accustomed to making evidence-based decisions. Anything that demonstrates a head start will provide much needed fuel to propel you towards your ultimate destination.

Executives Must Put on a SCARF

This acronym was introduced in Chapter 2. It stands for status, certainty, autonomy, relatedness, and fairness. Each of these areas must be considered by executives should they hope to win the support of change-weary employees.[3] Here is a recap of each element of the acronym.

- **Status:** It's vital for executives to be cognizant of the fact that status differences may impact the effectiveness of their communications. Rather than issuing stuffy decrees, executives must acknowledge the challenges facing the company and appeal to the entire workforce in overcoming them.
- **Certainty:** Remind people of the desired future you're working towards by frequently referencing your mission, vision, and strategy.
- **Autonomy:** Involve employees in the process (through Scorecard town hall meetings, cascading, and other means) to enhance understanding and support of the system.
- **Relatedness:** As with status, effective leaders understand they must enlist the entire company to execute strategy. Revealing humility and acknowledging the fact that it takes the unified efforts of every individual will create a powerful sense of relatedness among your team.
- **Fairness:** Keep your promises and be sure to demonstrate transparency throughout the implementation process.

Create an Office of Strategy Management to Shepherd the Scorecard

In my opinion, those who are unable to exploit the benefits of the Balanced Scorecard often suffer from the delusion that it is similar to a piece of software—you open it up and it works, simple as that. However, as I've explained throughout the book, the Scorecard represents a system that must be nurtured on an ongoing basis and ultimately ingrained in your culture should you hope to reap its many benefits. No single person, not even the CEO, is capable of leading that charge on a day in and day out basis. The Office of Strategy Management marshals the resources and drives the Scorecard's linkage to multiple value-creating management processes. For more on the OSM concept, revisit the section in Chapter 2.

Communicate Constantly

Change efforts suffer for a number of reasons, but one pervasive issue is a lack of communication. When moving in a new direction your team requires information to help make sense of the changing landscape that lies before them. During the change it's vital that people understand the progress you've made and why sustaining the momentum to reach the ultimate target is so important. Creating a communication plan for your Balanced Scorecard implementation is a simple but powerful step to overcome inertia, win hearts and minds, and shape the road ahead. See Chapter 2 to learn how you can build a communication plan for your Scorecard implementation.

Critically Examine the Existence of Common Change Blockers

Before committing to the sizable challenge of building a Balanced Scorecard that will serve as your exclusive strategy-execution device, conduct a review of your organization to root out any common change blockers such as complacency, immobilization, anger, and pessimism. I've seen all of these play out to varying degrees in Scorecard engagements and have witnessed their pernicious effects. Ensure you're prepared to combat each one. See Chapter 2 for more on this topic.

 ## WHEN BUILDING THE BALANCED SCORECARD

Clear the Path for Your Team

The construction of a Balanced Scorecard is very much a team effort, and to get the most from your group you must make it as easy as possible for them to fully engage in the process. Researchers describe this phenomenon as *clearing the path* by, as the moniker implies, removing any obstacles that may prevent individuals from participating intently in the process. Quite frequently, clearing the path amounts to simply being clear about what is going to take place during the process, when, how, and why. In your Scorecard implementation you can clear the path by making it easy for participants to complete homework assignments through detailed instructions, and, once in the workshops, perhaps providing easy to use templates for objective and measure development. See Chapter 4 to learn more.

Use the Power of Story

In Chapter 4, I suggested you open your Scorecard workshops with a story that is both amusing and informative, one that will entertain your attendees and cleverly outline the importance of their collective task. This should not, however, be the only time you draw upon the merits of a good story to win the support of your team. Throughout the implementation, at every stage in both development and use, look for opportunities to unite and bind your employees to the Scorecard through entertaining yarns that simultaneously inspire and educate.

Prime Participants for Success

As we learned in Chapter 4, priming describes the concept of providing a stimulus that influences near-term future thoughts and actions, even though the priming word may not appear to be connected to the future action. For example, in one study subjects were primed with words related to the stereotype of elderly people (Florida, forgetful, wrinkle). The priming words did not explicitly mention speed or slowness, however, those who were primed with the words walked more slowly when exiting the testing booth than those who were primed with neutral words. As noted in that section, priming can be used to great effect with participants in your Scorecard workshops by introducing words and concepts that link to the creation of innovative and relevant Scorecard objectives, measures, targets, and initiatives.

Avoid Multitasking

In today's always-on, wired world we're constantly bombarded with potential distractions, and they exact a substantial toll on our productivity. In one study, the researchers found that office distractions gobble up an average 2.1 hours of each employee's day. Another study found that workers spend an average of just 11 minutes on a project before being distracted. After an interruption, it takes them 25 minutes to return to the original task, if they do at all.[4] Distractions are particularly damaging when we're engaged in new activities for which our neural pathways are still relatively weak. That is exactly the case when building a Balanced Scorecard. Despite the fact that you've assembled your best and brightest, for most the notions of strategy maps and Scorecards will be new and simply mastering the vocabulary and putting disparate thoughts into context will be a big enough challenge, without simultaneously responding to texts from problem-stricken subordinates. To counteract the deleterious impact of multitasking (they can only be counteracted and mitigated, not eliminated) I recommend the use of full attention required (FAR) moments. Learn more about these topics in Chapter 4.

Be Open to Creative Ideas

Of all the research I encountered when writing this book, the material suggesting we have an innate bias to reject creative ideas, even when creativity is an espoused goal, was perhaps the most counterintuitive and surprising. As I first noted in Chapter 5, you must be ever vigilant for the appearance of this bias as you create your strategy map and Balanced Scorecard, since new and innovative objectives and measures will ultimately drive the execution of your strategy. Warn your workshop participants of this proclivity and challenge them to remain open to any and all ideas offered during the workshops.

Avoid Biases in Measure Development

In Chapter 6, I outlined four common biases in measure development:

1. **Overconfidence:** Feeling certain that a specific measure is best without the benefit of quantitative evidence
2. **Availability:** Settling for the most recently available and familiar metrics
3. **Status quo:** Using irrelevant metrics
4. **Measuring against yourself:** Focusing on absolute rather than relative performance

It's very interesting to note that two of these biases (availability and status quo) appear to confirm the existence of the bias noted in the previous section— our tendency to eschew creative ideas. Your challenge when creating measures (as well as objectives, targets, and initiatives) is to be fully present and mindful, and draw these biases into your consciousness where they can be rationally assessed and, hopefully, mitigated.

 ## USING THE BALANCED SCORECARD

Schedule Strategy Execution Review Meetings in Advance

This advice is consistent with the recommendations relating to clearing the path presented earlier. Unless Scorecard results are actively monitored, analyzed, and discussed, the entire implementation amounts to little more than an academic exercise. It's absolutely paramount to regularly convene your team, roll up your sleeves, and dig into the data offered by the Scorecard. To ensure these meetings occur, put them on everyone's calendar months in advance and make them sacrosanct. Making any type of change stick in an organization is dependent on establishing habits and routines, ingraining the new behaviors as second nature. Your strategy execution review meetings must become an entrenched habit should you expect to derive any payback from your Balanced Scorecard investment. Learn more about this topic in Chapter 7.

Follow Through, and Follow Up, on Action Items from Strategy Execution Review Meetings

Holding regular meetings is an enormous step in the right direction, but if you fail to enforce accountability for follow up on actions outlined in the meeting, many of the benefits will evaporate. Another discipline you must cultivate is to ensure all topics nominated for additional study or actions are indeed acted upon, with status reported at future sessions. See Chapter 7 for more information.

Live by the Balanced Scorecard

Real change starts at the level of individual behaviors, but that's a difficult place to begin because the gravitational pull of inertia and the temptation of clinging to the status quo are powerful forces in most organizations. When forced with difficult choices you need your people to go to the strategy map (and Scorecard) and declare, "This is where I need to focus." The objectives and measures should be considered nonnegotiable pacts with employees. Should you deviate from your chosen objectives and measures, the integrity and effectiveness of the Scorecard will quickly be called into question. For example, placing an objective of teamwork on your strategy map but later hoarding information or rewarding individual effort will destroy the tool's credibility while concurrently breeding skepticism and doubt.

Bake the Balanced Scorecard into the Organization's Culture

In *The Heart of Change*, authors Kotter and Cohen recognize the imperative of culture change in effecting lasting change when they say:

> In the best cases, change leaders throughout organizations make changes stick by nurturing a new culture. A new culture—group norms of behavior and shared values—develops through consistency of successful action over a sufficient period of time.[5]

The Balanced Scorecard's success will ultimately be measured by its inclusion as part of the fabric of the organization, its transition from a one-time project to "the way we do things around here." From day one of your implementation you must begin sewing the Scorecard into that cultural fabric by cascading it throughout the organization, linking it to key processes, and, most importantly, using it to evaluate the execution of your strategy.

Be Resilient

Creating a Balanced Scorecard that will prove transformative to your organization is no easy task. Challenges are lurking in every shadow and simply keeping up with the vortex of normal operations while you construct your system will amply test your fortitude. However, years of experience on the front lines of this movement have convinced me that the rewards substantially outweigh the effort. What is required along the way is a good dose of resilience when times get tough. To help you with that task, I'll conclude this section with a story about resilience I'm certain you'll find very uplifting and inspiring.[6]

Back in the 1970s, as the World Trade Center gleamed triumphantly over New York City, a Callery Pear tree was placed in a planter near Building 5. Each spring its delicate white blossoms breathed life into a surrounding world of concrete. After the attacks of September 11, 2001, the tree, like all those around it, disappeared beneath the remains of the fallen towers. Amazingly, a few weeks later a cleanup worker discovered the tree smashed and pinned between blocks of concrete. Its condition was dire: decapitated, trunk charred black, roots broken, with just one branch clinging to life. Parks Department personnel felt the tree was unsalvageable but cleanup workers convinced them to give it a chance at survival. Reluctantly, city workers dispatched the tree, barely 8 feet tall at the time, to a Parks Department nursery in the Bronx. Workers there were no more sanguine about its prospects, but committed to do everything possible to save the tree. Remarkably, once the dead, burned tissue had been cut away and its trimmed roots placed in rich soil, the tree, now affectionately known as Survivor, began to improve, eventually making a full recovery.

Unfortunately, however, more turmoil awaited Survivor. In the spring of 2010 a terrible storm with winds gusting at over 100 miles per hour hit the area, and Survivor was ripped from the ground, roots completely exposed. Once the storm passed, nursery workers again rallied to Survivor's aid, packing it in compost and mulch and gently spraying water upon it to minimize the shock. It wasn't easy, but again the tree proved its mettle and survived the best that nature could throw at it. Ron Vega, now the director of design for the 9/11 Memorial site, was a cleanup worker in 2001, and when he learned that Survivor was still alive he immediately decided to incorporate the tree into the memorial design. Today, you'll find Survivor standing nearly 30 feet tall near the footprint of the South Tower, an enduring symbol of hope, resilience, and renewal.

 ## BALANCED SCORECARD IMPLEMENTATION CHECKLISTS

Modern change management is composed of a sometimes quizzical amalgam of psychology, neuroscience, and management, all scholarly disciplines with long and storied histories. But for those of us who rely heavily on good old common sense and simple methods of managing change, it's encouraging to witness the venerable and humble checklist enjoy a recent surge in popularity and prominence. The modest tool has been employed with great success in health care, aviation, and many other fields, allowing users to ensure they remain on track and adhere to key principles and guidelines necessary for success. In that spirit, I'd like to close the book by providing some checklists you should keep close at hand when creating your Balanced Scorecard. See Exhibits 9.1 through 9.6.

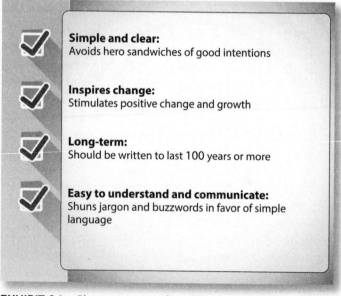

Simple and clear:
Avoids hero sandwiches of good intentions

Inspires change:
Stimulates positive change and growth

Long-term:
Should be written to last 100 years or more

Easy to understand and communicate:
Shuns jargon and buzzwords in favor of simple language

EXHIBIT 9.1   Characteristics of an Effective Mission Statement

Quantified and time bound:
Must be a concrete representation of the desired future

Concise:
Grabs attention with succinct yet powerful language

Appeals to all stakeholders:
All those with a stake in the company's success should be represented

Consistent with the mission:
Vision further translates the mission

Verifiable:
Avoids subjectivity

Feasible:
Challenging but grounded in reality

Inspirational:
Stirs the passions of every employee

EXHIBIT 9.2 Characteristics of an Effective Vision Statement

Before the workshop:

- Plan carefully.
- Determine where to hold it.
- Choose the right day.
- Determine who will attend.
- Assign pre-work to participants.

During the workshop:

- Use the power of story to get off to a good beginning.
- Review the agenda and all activities in detail.
- Be prepared for the "Why are we here" question.
- Prime participants for success.
- Choose your facilitation method.
- Deal with distractions.
- Be present; listen more.
- Avoid rabbit holes.

EXHIBIT 9.3 Conducting Engaging and Successful Workshops

Start with a verb:
Desired action of the objective should be clear.

Determine what's holding you back:
Objectives should help you overcome critical strategic challenges.

Be open to creative ideas:
Avoid the status quo and welcome all ideas.

Benchmark with caution:
Ensure all objectives reflect your unique strategic situation.

Critically examine expert advice:
Look for a fit with your circumstances.

Make the difficult choices:
Fewer objectives is preferable.

EXHIBIT 9.4 Creating Powerful Strategy Map Objectives

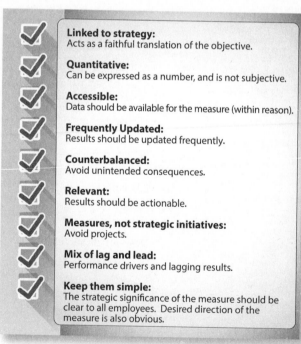

Linked to strategy:
Acts as a faithful translation of the objective.

Quantitative:
Can be expressed as a number, and is not subjective.

Accessible:
Data should be available for the measure (within reason).

Frequently Updated:
Results should be updated frequently.

Counterbalanced:
Avoid unintended consequences.

Relevant:
Results should be actionable.

Measures, not strategic initiatives:
Avoid projects.

Mix of lag and lead:
Performance drivers and lagging results.

Keep them simple:
The strategic significance of the measure should be clear to all employees. Desired direction of the measure is also obvious.

EXHIBIT 9.5 Characteristics of Effective Measures

Before the meeting:	During the meeting:	After the meeting:
• Schedule them in advance	• Determine how to review results (worst to first, strategic story, no stone unturned, exception-based, three questions, quick wins)	• Follow through and follow up on all actions
• Choose your facilitator	• Focus on questions as much as answers	
• Determine who will attend	• Set a tone of continuous learning	
• Share materials in advance	• Listen more	
	• Gaze out, not in	
	• Fight apathy	

EXHIBIT 9.6 Conducting Engaging and Valuable Strategy Execution Review Meetings

---

 NOTES

1. Jeffrey Schwartz, Pablo Gaito, and Doug Lennick, "That's the Way We (Used to) Do Things Around Here," *Strategy + Business* 62 (Spring 2011).
2. Charlotte Gray, *Reluctant Genius: Alexander Graham Bell and the Passion for Invention* (New York: Arcade 2006), 159.
3. David Rock, *Your Brain at Work* (New York: Harper Collins, 2009), Kindle edition, location 3757.
4. Ibid., location 874.
5. John P. Kotter and Dan S. Cohen, *The Heart of Change: Real-Life Stories of How People Change Their Organizations* (Boston: Harvard Business School Press, 2012).
6. Jane Goodall, "The Roots of a Naturalist," *Smithsonian* (March 2013): 75–84.

About the Author

PAUL R. NIVEN is a management consultant, author, and noted speaker on the subjects of Balanced Scorecard, strategy, and strategy execution. He has developed successful Balanced Scorecard systems as both a practitioner and consultant for organizations large and small around the globe. His clients include Fortune 500 companies, public sector agencies of all levels, and non-profit organizations. Paul's previous books include: *Roadmaps and Revelations* (a management fable on strategic planning), *Balanced Scorecard Step by Step* (now translated into more than 15 languages), *Balanced Scorecard Step by Step for Government and Nonprofit Agencies*, and *Balanced Scorecard Diagnostics*. He may be reached through his Web site at www.senalosa.com.

Index